CONTESTING

KNOWLEDGE

Museums and Indigenous Perspectives

Edited by Susan Sleeper-Smith

University of Nebraska Press | Lincoln and London

Acknowledgments for the previous publication of material included herein appear at the end of the respective chapters, which constitute an extension of the copyright page.

Publication of this volume was assisted by a grant from Michigan State University.

Library of Congress Cataloging-in-Publication Data
Contesting knowledge : museums and indigenous perspectives / edited by Susan Sleeper-Smith.
p. cm.
Includes bibliographical references and index.
ISBN 978-0-8032-1948-9 (pbk. : alk. paper)
1. Ethnological museums and collections. 2. Indians — Museums.
3. Indian museum curators — Attitudes. 4. Museums — Acquisitions — Moral and ethical aspects.
5. Museum exhibits — Moral and ethical aspects. 6. Museums — Collection management. 7. Racism in museum exhibits. 8. Indians in popular culture.
9. Indigenous peoples in popular culture. I. Sleeper-Smith, Susan.
GN35.C64 2009
305.80074 — dc22
2009002209

Set in Minion Pro by Kim Essman.
Designed by A. Shahan.

To President Lou Anna K. Simon, whose
enduring support of American Indian Studies
has created an inclusive, caring environment
for Michigan State University students
and faculty. And to the CIC (Committee on
Institutional Cooperation) Liberal Arts and
Letters Deans for their generous support
in funding the CIC–American Indian Studies
Consortium. Thank you.

Contents

Illustrations

CONTESTING **KNOWLEDGE**

Contesting Knowledge

Museums and Indigenous Perspectives

SUSAN SLEEPER-SMITH

At the time of European encounter, the first residents of the Americas were divided into at least 2,000 cultures. The original inhabitants of the Western Hemisphere did not conceive of themselves as one or even several nations. Most people knew very little about distant communities—awareness was often circumscribed by kin and trade networks. Consequently, because Indigenous peoples did not possess a collective vision of themselves, the idea of the *Indian* or *Indians* emerged as a white image or stereotype. Indians became a single entity for the purposes of description and analysis.

Simultaneously, by categorizing all Indigenous people as Indians, the newcomers downplayed the differences between Indigenous peoples, leading to a centuries-long confusion and a melding of fundamentally incorrect ways of understanding human societies. When Columbus applied the term *Indian* to people in the Caribbean, its use became embedded in narratives of encounter and has continued to the present day. Even early eyewitness accounts that described a specific tribe or community were generalized and often evolved as descriptive of all Indians. Present-day people who use the word *Indian* have little idea of the diversity of cultures and of tribal communities that this term encompasses.

Global expansion created new notions about human nature and embedded knowledge: about the types of societies that met across this stage of encounter in a wealth of objects that were collected from "foreign" cultures and transported to Europe. Many objects were received through the traditional exchange of goods; and, like written narratives, these objects were displayed as a way of telling stories about Indians. Museums, like literary texts, were also purposefully constructed to tell stories about

1

Western, rather than Indigenous, society. When the objects collected for "cabinets of curiosity" were moved from the private to the public sphere, they visually reinforced the stereotypes associated with Indians. Notions about the "primitive" nature of Indian society influenced what was collected and how it was displayed. Most frequently, Indigenous peoples were described in terms of deficiencies. Consequently, Indians were measured against the ideals of Western society; and whether describing beliefs, values, or institutions, they were measured against the institutions that Western society most cherished about themselves at the time.

The public museum became a meeting ground for official and formal versions of the past. Because history was constructed through objects, curators created the interpretative context for each object. Objects that were placed in museums were initially decontextualized and made to tell an evolutionary narrative about the progress of Western societies and the primitiveness of Indigenous communities. Museums functioned as powerful rhetorical devices that created dominant and often pathological allegiances to a cultural ideal. In the first section of this volume, Ray Silverman shows how these essays explore stereotypes about Indigenous people who shaped the early period of contact. In both Brazil and South Africa, violence was perpetuated against Native peoples and "just wars" were rationalized as a means of imposing a "civilized" order on Indigenous space. For instance, the inscription of "primitive" behaviors, which described Indigenous people as cannibals, raises important issues about how public exhibition space functioned. In displays of human beings as objects, we see how Africans were not silenced even when they allowed themselves to be exhibited. As Zine Magubane tells us,

> Those denied the opportunity to express themselves verbally used their bodies, facial expressions, and other nonverbal forms of communication to show that they were sentient beings who knew how humiliating their circumstance was and who wished to live differently. Those who mastered the language and mores of English society were more direct. They challenged the supremacy of English culture and values. They demonstrated their awareness of the shortcomings of English society. And they, like their silenced brethren, insisted on the necessity of independence and self-determination. Others chose the path of si-

lence—showing their displeasure through a deliberate refusal to engage. And still others, like Ota Benga, chose death.

In the Western exhibition of colonized people, the Indigenous voice could not be silenced. Initially, there were no Indigenous museums that described the horrors associated with colonization. As Jacki Rand points out, in the second section of this volume, it was only in the mid-twentieth century that Indigenous people were invited to share power with museum professionals. Museums that sought Indigenous consultation encouraged Native people to make a case for their own humanity and to educate others about ties to ancestral lands. The founding of the National Museum of the American Indian made an attempt to speak directly to the problematized space of public museums and to the troubled relationship between Native and non-Native people. While the National Museum of the American Indian (NMAI) aspires to a mutually interactive voice that incorporates the museum's professional staff and Native collaborators, the viability of that partnership has often been problematic. The central location of the museum on the mall has transformed the Indian into a prominent public figure, but often the incorporation of multiple storylines into one narrative has constrained the multiplicity of those voices that create those narratives.

In section three, Brenda Child describes the dramatic contrast between the National Museum of the American Indian and the movement toward the creation of tribal museums. Tribal museums represent one of the most effective ways of serving diverse communities. Each Indigenous nation possesses a distinct historical tradition, and it is the tribal museum that embodies Indigenous perspectives and serves the more varied needs of individual communities. Tribal museums function as preservation projects that teach traditional narratives and lifeways and, above all, serve the needs of the individual communities. Educating the broader public remains part of the tribal museum project, although it is no longer at the heart of these newer museums.

The last section of this volume is devoted to exploring how tribal museums have changed since the early days of the 1960s and 1970s. As the beneficiaries of enhanced public awareness and changing educational priorities, they have increasingly functioned as both museums and centers of community life. All of these museums are remarkable because in their diversity they testify to the ongoing revitalization of Native life.

Many of the changes that are apparent in the museums across North America are also evident across the global landscape. The demand to create alternative narratives and to give force to formerly colonized peoples parallels the same issues that have evolved in Indian Country. Indigenous museums founded within communities remind us that colonized landscapes were once the homelands of these oppressed peoples. While museums may have emerged as part of the original colonial project, they have been put to new purposes. Their reinvention parallels the changes that are taking place in Indian Country. Whether it is South Africa or all of Africa, Mexico and Brazil or all of South America, Indigenous people are using museums to emerge from invisibility and to deconstruct the colonization narrative from the viewpoint of the oppressed. At the heart of these projects is a multiplicity of voices, a variety of narratives, and the use of museums as tools of revitalization. While techniques vary, the ability to construct meaningful narratives, defined by a variety of perspectives, has led to a global surge in the number of tribal museums.

These chapters were presented as papers on September 24, 2007, at the Newberry Library as part of the CIC/Newberry Library American Indian Studies Fall Symposium entitled Indigenous Past and Present: First Annual Symposium, Contesting Knowledge: Museums and Indigenous Perspectives. The symposium was organized and supported by the CIC–American Indian Studies Consortium. The CIC–AIS Consortium faculty are drawn from the Big Ten universities and the University of Chicago, and they share an interest in American Indian Studies. This pool of CIC faculty relies on the consortium to foster faculty research and to share in the training of graduate students. CIC faculty teach workshops, seminars, and encourage networking across the graduate student body through the annual spring graduate conference. Additional information about the CIC–AIS Consortium is located on their website: http://www.msu.edu/~cicaisc.

This symposium has been supported by the CIC–Liberal Arts and Sciences Deans and their support has generously been supplemented by the administration of the Michigan State University campus. Our sincere thanks to Dean Karen Klomparens, the dean of Graduate Studies; Paulette Granberry Russell, the director and senior advisor to the president for diversity; Kim Wilcox, the provost of Michigan State University; Doug Estry, office of the associate provost for undergraduate education; and Ian Gray, vice president for research and development.

1

Ethnography and the Cultural Practices of Museums

The Legacy of Ethnography

RAY SILVERMAN

The four essays included in this section address a range of subjects associated with museums and heritage; they each in one way or another consider how Indigenous peoples have been represented in a variety of cultural and historical settings — in the archive, in the "ethnographic theater," and in the museum. The essays offer a variety of historical and institutional contexts for (re)presenting Indigenous culture, and as a group they raise a number of questions that foreground issues germane to virtually all papers delivered at the symposium. As such, they help frame our critical discourse concerning the role of the museum in (re)presenting Indigenous pasts and presents.

The thread that binds these four seemingly disparate essays together is how ethnography has influenced European modes of representing the people whom they colonized. Ethnography has provided the "scientific" justification for much of the colonial project in the Americas and in Africa. The strategy emerged two hundred years ago and persists to this day — it is a mode of thinking that has proven difficult to shake off and continues to influence how Indigenous peoples are represented in museums and related cultural institutions.

Hal Langfur's essay focuses not on museums but on the archive. He critically examines how the accounts of early nineteenth-century European naturalists and other travelers who encountered Brazil's Indigenous peoples, specifically the Botocudo, were used to construct a very specific image of these peoples as "quintessential primitives." In these accounts, emphasis was placed on references to cannibalism, as perhaps the most poignant evidence of Botocudo savagery. Langfur argues that this method of writing and reading ethnography not only served to rationalize the colonial project in Brazil but also provided the foundation for how Brazil's

Indigenous peoples would be represented in the nation's first museums, archives, and historical societies.

Although Langfur focuses primarily on written accounts, one might suspect that the artifacts that these nineteenth-century ethnographers collected reinforced popular European perceptions of Native Americans as primitive and savage.

The situation in nineteenth-century Brazil is not unlike colonial encounters in other parts of the world. Contemporary travel accounts of Europeans visiting North America, Africa, and the Pacific Islands are replete with such imagery. This "data" fueled various European ideologies, including social Darwinism, and offered the justification to subjugate and reform the "primitive." Indeed, this mode of representation was central to the civilizing mission of Europe well into the twentieth century.

Zine Magubane's essay examines another dimension of this phenomenon: the theatrical display of Africans in Europe and the United States in the nineteenth and early twentieth centuries. The essay focuses on the ethnographic showcase — theatrical performances involving individuals who were brought, supposedly of their own free will, from Africa to Europe and the United States, where they were exhibited as exotic ethnographic specimens. These performances were, in effect, "human zoos." Other venues for exhibiting Africans in this manner included world's fairs and expositions. These displays were predicated on the popular understanding of the "science" of ethnology but, as Magubane points out, went far beyond science and education, often assuming the character of a commercial freak show staged for the amusement of the masses. Once again, such exhibits can be seen as a manifestation of the colonial project. Magubane observes, "the popularity of ethnographic showcases and the progress of the British Empire were always closely linked."

In addition to describing the nature of human exhibits, Magubane begins to examine evidence that counters the prevalent understanding that those who appeared in these "theatrical" settings were passive, acquiescent individuals. Here, the careful reading of the archive reveals that individuals such as Saartjie Baartman (South Africa) and Ota Benga (Congo), in fact, were not complacent victims but confronted and resisted the "handlers" who exploited them. This is a line of inquiry that deserves a great deal more attention.

Evidence that this mode of representation still persists appears in the presentation of Africans in zoos in Europe and North America. Still exoticized as people who live close to nature, as they always have, Africans living in "villages" are now integrated with displays of African animals in zoos around the world. Once again, "ethnographic authenticity" is invoked as the rationale for developing such exhibits, thus reinforcing long-held, distorted stereotypes of Africans. However, such practices do not go unnoticed. Recent events at zoos in Augsberg in Germany and Seattle in the United States have sparked local debates concerning the propriety of such representations.

The critique of another mode of ethnography is the subject of Ann McMullen's essay, in which she reexamines the work of George Gustav Heye, the man whose collection of 700,000 artifacts serves as the core collection (85 percent) of the National Museum of the American Indian (NMAI). The essay does not deal much with the representation of Native American culture but focuses on how Heye himself has been represented in and by museums. The custom in the NMAI has been to treat his memory with considerable ambivalence. He is often dismissed as "just a crazy white man" with an indiscriminate penchant for acquiring Indian artifacts. McMullen engages the archive in an attempt to set Heye in a more objective light, to understand the man's motivations for building his huge collection, and to place his collecting methods in a historical context.

The primary rationale for Heye's collecting activities was the "salvaging" of traditions that were perceived as disappearing—a strategy championed by anthropologists of his day such as Franz Boas. But what exactly was salvaged? McMullen relates how Heye sent his agents into the field to purchase objects, often with little attention paid to properly documenting the provenance or cultural context of the objects. What then is the National Museum of the American Indian going to do with all this material? At present, the museum's curators are using objects primarily as props to tell stories about the Americas and their Indigenous peoples, past and present. Do the objects themselves have any stories to tell? In some cases cultural memory still exists pertaining to the meaning these objects had when they were first collected, but this is more the exception than the rule. Their value today lies primarily in the conversations that occur around the objects, and the new meanings that are ascribed to them. Everything Heye collected that now serves as the tangible core of the NMAI presents something of a paradox. How will it be used? What meaning do all these things hold for societies, such as those of Native Americans, that for the most part do share the same values with Euro-American society concerning the preservation of material objects but that also place greater value in preserving the intangible traditions with which the objects are associated? The situation in which the NMAI currently finds itself raises an interesting question, one that faces many museums that are attempting to (re)present local Indigenous tradition. Is the concept of the object-centered museum an appropriate model for representing Native American culture and history?

A related issue that is raised tangentially in McMullen's essay is a theme that appears in several of the essays presented in this volume. This concerns the NMAI's struggle to deliver on the expectations that it set for itself. McMullen cites a report that she authored herself in 2006, which states that the NMAI strives to become an "international center that represents the *totality* [my emphasis] of Native experiences," apparently for all Native peoples of the Western Hemisphere. How does a museum accomplish this, especially as a government-supported *national* institution, a national museum representing hundreds of nations?

This is not a problem unique to the NMAI. At the African International Council of Museums (AFRICOM) meeting, held in Cape Town, South Africa, in October 2006, a major topic of conversation concerned decolonizing the museum. One response to the issue that is particularly poignant came from the director of the National Museums of Kenya, Dr. Idle Omar Farah. He suggests that not until African museums are economically independent — that is, they do not have to rely on support from Europe — will they be able to shake off colonial or neocolonial agendas that still drive a good deal of what goes on in African museums. As part of the Smithsonian, can the NMAI be decolonized?

The fourth essay, written by Ciraj Rassool, directly confronts this issue by arguing that, despite having moved into a postcolonial era, museums still struggle with how formerly colonized peoples are represented. This is because museums continue to employ exhibit strategies grounded in colonial legacies, specifically those associated with ethnology and ethnography. Rassool's discussion, situated in postapartheid South Africa, reveals that the identity and community politics lying at the heart of heritage debates are shared among Indigenous peoples around the world. A diorama displaying Khoisan life installed at Iziko, the National Museum of South Africa, has been the source of considerable debate for decades—still unresolved, it raises many of the same issues concerning Native American dioramas installed in natural history museums in the United States. Similarly, there is a good deal of resonance here in the United States with challenges that Iziko faces pertaining to if and how it should represent Indigenous culture. Their struggle is not unlike that currently experienced in our large metropolitan museums that represent Native American peoples. The same holds true for issues concerning the repatriation of human remains.

Rassool presents the work of the District Six Museum in Cape Town as an example of an institution that has made considerable progress in redressing the injustices of the apartheid era and approaching "issues of community, restitution, and social healing in ways that give a non-racial and anti-racist character to its museum methods."[1] The success of the District Six Museum reveals that it is in local community-centered museums—not national museums—that the most innovative and exciting work is being undertaken. New modes of representation are being created that offer a means for confronting history and establishing a place for the individual and community in today's national and global societies.

Another dimension of the District Six Museum that is worth noting is that it represents a very successful partnership between a community and the academy. Ciraj Rassool has played an active role in the District Six community, specifically in the work of its museum. He has brought his knowledge of social and political theory to the museum and, in turn, has learned from the expertise of the various community members who have been involved in museum-related activities. This partnership is a testimony to the value of public scholarship—a model worth emulating.

Rassool's essay demonstrates the degree to which the challenges of representation of Indigenous, formerly disenfranchised, peoples are shared between North American and South African culture workers. It also makes apparent the potential benefits of comparative and collaborative work relating to the representation of people and culture in museums.

Notes

1. Ciraj Rassool, "Abstract of Paper for the First Annual Symposium: Contesting Knowledge; Museums and Indigenous Perspectives," paper presented at the Newberry Library, Chicago, September 24, 2007.

1

Elite Ethnography and Cultural Eradication

*Confronting the Cannibal in
Early Nineteenth-Century Brazil*

HAL LANGFUR

When Prince Regent João declared war against the Indigenous inhabitants of Brazil's eastern forests in 1808, cannibalism served as the principal basis for deeming the military action legal and just. From the onset of Portugal's colonization of the Atlantic coastline between Salvador da Bahia and Rio de Janeiro in the sixteenth century, native peoples who inhabited the inland mountains and river valleys were targeted for violent conquest on the same moral grounds. The coastal Tupi-speaking peoples were similarly condemned for consuming their enemies, but they did so for ritual purposes only. Their conduct could be altered, many church and secular authorities thought, through conversion to Christianity and hard work in the burgeoning sugar-plantation economy. The inland speakers of Gê-based languages, by contrast, ate people for basic sustenance, colonists believed. Known variously as the Tapuia, the Aimoré, and by the mid-eighteenth century the Botocudo, these Indians were considered exceptionally savage. As a rule, plans for the colonization of the territory occupied by these highly mobile hunters and gatherers focused on their flight or eradication. The climactic violent confrontation between settlers and the various ethnic groups of the eastern forests escalated well before the declaration of a "just war" in 1808. After prospectors in the 1690s discovered gold and, later, diamonds farther inland in the region that became the captaincy of Minas Gerais, the Portuguese Crown placed the coastal forests off-limits. By banning exploration and settlement, the Crown sought to defend the mining district from potential outside in-

1. The eastern sertão of Brazil, Minas Gerais, ca. 1800. (All boundary lines are approximations and were disputed.) Map by Susan Long.

truders and to stanch the flow of untaxed contraband through the forests to smugglers waiting along the coast. During the second half of the eighteenth century, as many of the most accessible mineral washings waned, occupants of the mining district began to challenge this prohibition with increasing insistence, often supported by captaincy authorities. As they searched for alternative sources of gold or simply for more land for farming and ranching, they had new reasons to eye the coastal forests to the east. Known in Minas Gerais as the eastern sertão (backlands), these forests became the site of intense conflict between colonists and the Botocudo, the Puri, the Pataxó, and other groups. If these purported cannibals had once served royal interests by discouraging access to the forested no-man's-land, their continued dominance by the final decades of the colonial era seemed intolerable. The 1808 military mobilization signaled the Crown's adoption of a policy of violent conquest that had long since emerged at the captaincy level.[1]

Charges of cannibalism tended to proliferate at such moments of great antagonism. This correlation alone reminds us to exercise extreme caution in accepting such accusations at face value. Present-day scholars who fret over this problem, which extends far beyond Brazil to innumerable colonial battlegrounds where Indigenous peoples stood accused of heinous crimes, are far from the first to do so.[2] In the immediate aftermath of the 1808 war, a cadre of European naturalists descended on the eastern forests to study this region and its natives, who were then, for the first time, accessible to scientific or at least quasi-scientific investigation. These early ethnologists took particular interest in verifying the practice of cannibalism. As might be expected, they came to no consensus, either with respect to its pervasiveness or its objective characteristics.

My intention in this chapter is not to revisit this debate but to explore a related issue: how authorities, both civil and scientific, both Brazilian and foreign, responded when they had no doubt that the Indians they sought to eliminate, pacify, or study ate other humans. The chapter explores the case of an obscure frontier official who thought cannibalism could be countered with fishhooks and glass beads, followed by the counterexample of his superiors who opted for war. Discussion then turns to a European ethnographer, probably more directly involved in the conflict than any other, who found the state's response to cannibalism as appalling as the practice itself. His position prompted a radical proposal that state officials learn to think and act more like the man-eaters they sought to subjugate.

The divergent approaches of these individuals to what they considered to be quintessential savagery suggest a simple proposition: the transformation of tangible interethnic conflict into abstract ethnographic knowledge involved a process that was more complicated and contradictory than we perhaps suspect. Before we can conclude that we know what elite characterizations of native cultures meant, confident that we understand elite intentions, we have a great deal more work to do in the archives. Only by exploring the relationships between Indigenous practice, personal ambition, official intent, and scientific findings will we improve our understanding of the production of knowledge eventually enshrined in institutions charged with presenting Indigenous cultures in the public sphere.

In the Atlantic Forest

The first encounter with cannibals that I wish to examine involves a midlevel frontier official who was based in northeastern Minas Gerais. At the beginning of the nineteenth century, José Pereira Freire de Moura headed the small Indian *aldeia* (village) of Tocoiós, located along the upper Jequitinhonha River in a region then covered by the Atlantic forest.[3] At the time, Tocoiós lay at the outer reaches of settlement in Minas Gerais. To the east, beyond the village, the Jequitinhonha River plunged into the forest, descending through rugged, mountainous terrain and spilling into the Atlantic Ocean north of Porto Seguro, not far from the site where Pedro Álvares Cabral first anchored off the Brazilian coast in 1500. Gold had been discovered in the area no later than the 1720s by *bandeirantes* (backwoodsmen) from São Paulo. Colonization of the surrounding forests stalled, however, in part because of resistance from the region's seminomadic Indigenous peoples. Settlers moved in with greater impetus in the early nineteenth century, fanning out from the declining central mining district, attracted to the area by the spread of cotton cultivation.[4]

As administrator of the nascent aldeia, Moura became preoccupied by a series of encounters with an elusive group of highly mobile Indians, which he identified as a band of Botocudo. These encounters occurred as soldiers worked to secure the river valley for further colonization and for the transport of goods between the mining district and the coast. Moura was convinced that the natives contacted were Botocudo principally because of their reported cannibalism, along with other characteristics including the wooden ornaments they wore in their ears and lower lips, their language, their rudimentary dwellings, and their itinerant hunting and foraging. In a report issued on these contacts in 1809, he noted that Botocudo cannibalism went hand in hand with a proclivity for violence and irrationality. He recalled one confrontation between fifty Botocudo warriors and more than 200 armed colonists. The Indians had "fought until they had used up all of their arrows." All of them died in battle except one, "who grabbed hold of the trunk of a tree to avoid being killed. He refused all food for three days and in the end beat his head against the tree trunk so many times that he died."

Evidence of cannibalism among these forest dwellers was recent and verifiable. According to Moura, in an incident that occurred around the turn of the century, a band of Botocudo had devised a cruel plot to devour three runaway black slaves. The Indians convinced the fugitives to follow them to a spot along the banks of the Jequitinhonha River, where they promised gold could be found in abundance. There they killed two of the three blacks. The third escaped to Tocoiós and described the murders. His tale was investigated with horrific results. When a group of colonists pursued the Indians, they discovered the vestiges of a cannibal feast. The remains of the victims consisted of "heaps of bones . . . scorched by a fire and thoroughly gnawed." The crime remained fresh in the memory of local settlers: as evidence of the Indians' savagery, their pursuers had brought back the skull of one of the victims and placed it in the settlement's cemetery, where it stood as a daily reminder of native atrocities.

Beginning in 1804, Moura provided instructions to a series of expeditions that were aimed at coaxing these Indians peacefully into settled society. The first of these expeditions descended the Jequitinhonha River under the leadership of a corporal named Manoel Rodrigues Prates.[5] On an island that was deemed suitable for the planned encounter, the corporal erected a tent and set up a portable forge. With steel and iron that had been carried to the site, his troops fabricated machetes and fishhooks. When they finally sighted the Botocudo along the far bank of the river, they approached them with the help of an Indian translator who had been brought to the area from the Doce River basin to the south. They invited the reputed cannibals to join them on the island in order to receive the manufactured tools. At first the Indians proved to be wary. A member of their band, described as black skinned, unlike the others, warned them to suspect a ruse. They would be captured and killed, just as members of his family had once been murdered by whites. After some delay, lured by assurances from the troops, the others ignored the warning and crossed to the island on canoes.

Corporal Prates then urged the Botocudo to return upriver some twenty leagues (about 130 kilometers) to Tocoiós. They consented, reaching the aldeia ahead of the troops. As head of the settlement, Moura welcomed them with "all due kindness and friendship," distributing more gifts. Over the course of the next two years, the Indians returned for further visits. Then, mysteriously, they disappeared. Prates led forest patrols every year for three consecutive years in an attempt to contact the Indians, but they were not to be found. Moura suspected that they were purposefully avoiding contact, because fresh signs of their presence in the forest were always evident. They likely remained hidden as a response to the increasing mobilization for the declared war that was then underway.

Moura had personal reasons for his accommodating approach to the Indians of the Jequitinhonha River valley, reasons which involved three generations of his family. He was orchestrating a plan that stood little chance of success without the cooperation of the Botocudo, a plan that first emerged when he discovered an undated document among the papers of his deceased father. The document described a route down the Jequitinhonha River and then overland through the dense forests to a place described as Lagoa Dourada, the Golden Lagoon. Like an account of El Dorado or a map of buried treasure, imbued with the same potential to inspire dreams of undiscovered riches, the document was a signed, first person description of an expedition manned by bandeirantes from São Paulo. These men had wandered through the region, probably more than a century before, and uncovered evidence of ample gold deposits, which they had not had the time or wherewithal to unearth. Moura wished to retrace their steps, but increasing age and infirmity prevented him from doing so. He next sought to mount an expedition, to be led by one of his sons, in search of the Golden Lagoon.[6]

This quest would entail descending the Jequitinhonha River in canoes to a point where waterfalls made it impassable. The troops would then march overland, making contact with various fractured ethnic groups known to be living in the area. Moura described these groups as the "remains of nations . . . fleeing their total destruction" in raids launched by Botocudo from the Doce River basin to the south, the most violent theater of the war. Moura remained convinced of the merits of attracting the Botocudo rather than attacking them, despite their famed hostility, not the least because the stakes were so high for him personally. The region he was attempting to explore, he wrote, "always was the one most exposed to invasions by the Botocudo." Although he had managed to win the friendship of some, they could easily launch a "treasonous" attack if they sensed weakness or became dissatisfied. "In this case," he explained, "I and my family will be the first ones sacrificed."[7]

To ensure the success of his plan, Moura sought permission from the highest authorities in Brazil. He sent a second son to Rio de Janeiro, carrying a letter addressed to the venerable count of Linhares, Rodrigo de Souza Coutinho, the royal minister of war. He explained that his increasing knowledge of the unsettled forests, a consequence of his efforts to interact with the natives, had convinced him that "great wealth" could be found if the expedition he proposed were allowed to follow the old itinerary. For this reason, he asked the war minister to appeal to the monarch himself. In Rio de Janeiro Moura's son would purchase powder, shot, iron, and other supplies for the expedition, including a stock of *quinquilharias* (trifles), the term customarily used to describe gifts that were considered by settlers to be of little value—mirrors, beads, ribbons, for example—but useful for appeasing wary natives. The expedition could be resupplied from the coast if necessary, since Moura gauged that the old route would place the explorers closer to the sea than to the settled interior of Minas Gerais. In addition to financial support, Moura sought a series of orders from the prince regent, requiring both the governor of Minas Gerais, Pedro Maria Xavier Ataíde e Melo (1803–1810), and other officials to cooperate.[8]

The text of Moura's letter made it clear that he had been stymied by the standard chain of command, ascending through local military officers to the governor. Moura sought to circumvent those he suspected of foiling his attempt to locate the site. For starters, royal backing would allow him to round up recruits, by force if necessary, and press them into service. His efforts would bear fruit, he wrote the war minister, only "if Your Excellency would be kind enough to lend your authority in order to remove the obstacles that might impede me." With such support, he predicted his mission would be of "great utility" to the Crown's vassals and its treasury.[9]

The existing evidence suggests that an expedition of substantial size eventually did set out from the distant frontier outpost where Moura dreamed of untapped gold. Another note he drafted listed more than three dozen men whom he designated as participants, some of them being identified as "prisoners." He had asked the district military commander to place these individuals under his command. An unsigned document, also apparently written by Moura, contains orders that had been issued to his son, detailing instructions for leading a *bandeira*, or wilderness expedition. The orders indicated that the men were expected to spend six months or more in the forest. They also stipulated that the expedition must "never attack the Indians without previous provocation from them." Their "good treatment" was to be guaranteed by the distribution of machetes, fishhooks, knives, and trinkets. The Botocudo were even to be invited to join the expedition, if possible. The document makes reference to a separate order issued by the prince regent to purchase supplies. The evidence, if incomplete, suggests that Moura succeeded in his effort to sway the Crown to accommodate his attempt to placate cannibals rather than kill them.[10]

Given the main currents of state Indigenous policy at the time, this was no small achievement. Elsewhere in the eastern forests, the monarch carried on with his declared war, a paradox that serves to emphasize the issue that most concerns me here: accusations of cannibalism and savagery could be used by colonists and the state for a full range of purposes, including those that were diametrically opposed. It is important to recognize the extent to which this frontier official's approach was distinctive, which is not to say unique since there were always others who favored cultural accommodation. Given his immediate and gruesome experience of cannibalism, Moura could have been impelled to judge the Indians to be irredeemable, candidates for enslavement or extermination in accordance with prevailing Crown and captaincy policies. This was not the case. Convinced that he was negotiating with man-eaters, Moura proceeded to attempt to woo them into the village that he administered. He thought it was no great leap of faith to insist that with patience and persistence such natives could be gradually assimilated. While labeling Indians as cannibals may have always served the colonial project, Moura's approach demonstrates that more specific objectives differed according to individual colonists, including officials committed, as he was, to loyal service to the Crown. That Moura, who lived closer than most to the source of wartime fear and conflict, could react with equanimity to what he deemed to be irrefutable proof of Botocudo cannibalism should caution us against assuming that we automatically know the implications of the impulse to represent Indians as devourers of human flesh.

At the Centers of Power

During the years in which Moura labored at Tocoiós, Indian resistance to conquest intensified to match a growing state commitment to colonization. Writing to the governor of Minas Gerais in 1807, Diogo Ribeiro de Vasconcelos, a Portuguese-born member of the local elite who occupied numerous high government posts, called for the river valleys and forests to the east of the mining district to be opened to navigation and definitively settled. Recognizing that barriers both "moral and physical" stood in the way, Vasconcelos nevertheless urged the captaincy governor to move aggressively. "Incalculable are the advantages in terms of exports and imports that can come to the captaincy by way of navigation" of the rivers linking Minas Gerais to the coast, he argued. "Apart from commerce, we would equally obtain the vast riches that cover those lands." Unfortunately, travel through the area remained blocked by the "hostilities of cannibals," which could be countered once and for all only with "sufficient military force."[11]

The influence of men like Vasconcelos, a resident of Vila Rica, the captaincy capital, helps explain why Moura's pursuit of patient interactions with the Botocudo met with opposition from his superiors. Vasconcelos was well aware of Moura's efforts. Before Moura decided to appeal directly to the Crown, Vasconcelos took note of his search for the place where "the Paulistas of long ago discovered the gold mines of the Golden Lagoon." He even referred to Moura as an able administrator of the aldeia at Tocoiós. The two men, however, could not have differed more sharply when it came to basic strategy concerning the region's independent Indigenous peoples. Where Moura favored nonviolent interaction based on the premise of cultural malleability, Vasconcelos pressed for military conquest, being convinced of the Indians' rigid savagery.[12]

All peaceful methods were doomed, Vasconcelos argued. "Barbarous men are not persuaded to abandon their customs with iron utensils and glass beads, with bagatelles." The practice of establishing state-run Indian villages would ultimately fail to lure natives out of the forests. The Botocudo were "devourers of animals of their same species, insensible to the voices of reason and humanity that invite them to participate in society." They should be "hunted down and run through with knives, until such evils subject the remainder of them to their obligations." Force would "effect what through kindness we have been unable to achieve," Vasconcelos concluded. "Force is appropriate for men incapable of education and principled action."[13]

Vasconcelos wrote these heated passages on the eve of the war's declaration. He did so from frustrated resignation, which he construed to be the consequence of the refusal of the eastern Indians to accept the compassionate terms of colonial authority. A self-appointed captaincy historian, he fixed on force as the only viable solution after poring over the official records at his disposal. His research turned up royal orders that were "worthy of the pious and enlightened sovereigns that imposed them." A string of governors had done their utmost to achieve peaceful relations with the natives. Even Vasconcelos's contemporary, the belligerent governor Melo, had done what he could to apply "kindness in reducing the savages to the church and state." All such attempts to "settle the Indians in aldeias and civilize them" had amounted to nothing. "There is no hand powerful enough, no eloquence capable of persuading them to abandon their ways and the dense woods in which they are born," Vasconcelos lamented. "The cannibal Botocudo does not allow for the conventions of peace and friendship." The only rational response to such savagery, he reasoned, was violence.[14]

Such arguments contributed to a hardening of Indigenous policy leading up to the declaration of war. The war signaled the final abandonment of the Crown's longstanding commitment to maintaining the eastern forest as a forbidden, unsettled zone occupied by hostile Indians. This earlier policy, which had eroded over the previous decades, was part of the reason that Indians had remained so dominant in the region, even though it lay just inland from the Atlantic coast. Opting for war, the Crown bowed to the pressures of an increasing number of miners, farmers, ranchers, and captaincy officials. In the face of dwindling gold production, they had forged an incompatible local policy of opening the territory to exploration and settlement.[15]

The extent and success of Indian resistance to this encroachment provided whatever further justification Prince Regent João needed to recast royal Indigenous policy. By his formulation, it had been Indian aggression alone that forced the declaration of war. Forgotten were decades of provocative actions by authorities and soldiers as they searched for more gold and diamonds, circumventing royal restrictions. Ignored, too, was the slow but persistent advance of settlers as they continued to push eastward from the mining district into the coastal forests. The prince regent had accepted the view that once-desirable native opposition to the presence of colonists could no longer be sanctioned.

He declared war against the Botocudo on May 13, 1808, just three months after arriving in Rio de Janeiro from Lisbon, where he had been cast into exile by Napoleon's advancing armies. An uncompromising military offensive then seemed the only answer to the outcry of those who had labored unsuccessfully to settle the eastern forests. From the monarch's new perspective and geographic position in the colonial capital, these lands stretched northward over a great distance, separating Rio de Janeiro from the two other most important centers of colonial settlement in Minas Gerais and Bahia.

Now it became the monarch's turn to represent the native cultures of this territory, making meaning and policy out of accusations decrying their cannibalism. Addressing his war declaration to Governor Melo, the monarch wrote that his determination to act derived from "grave complaints" that had reached the throne about native atrocities. He condemned the "invasions that the cannibal Botocudos [were] practicing daily," especially along the banks of the Doce River and its tributaries. The Indians had managed to "devastate all of the fazendas located in those areas . . . [and] forced many landowners to abandon them at great loss to themselves and to my royal Crown." To achieve their ends, they dared to perpetrate "the most horrible and atrocious scenes of the most barbarous cannibalism." They "assassinated" settlers and "tame Indians" alike. The Indians opened wounds in their victims and drank their blood. They dismembered them and consumed their "sad remains." Echoing Vasconcelos's report of the previous year, the monarch maintained that such conduct demonstrated, once and for all, "the uselessness of all human efforts" to civilize the Botocudo, to settle them in villages, and to persuade them "to take pleasure in the permanent advantages of a peaceful and gentle society." As a consequence, he then declared the end of what he termed his "defensive" policy. He replaced it with one of "just" and "offensive war," a war that would "have no end," until settlers returned to their habitations and the Indians submitted to the rule of law.[16]

To prosecute the war, the governor was to deploy six detachments of foot soldiers, each responsible for a particular sector of those lands "infested" by the Botocudo. Selecting soldiers who were fit for such "hard and rugged" duty, the commanders of these detachments would form "diverse bandeiras." These wilderness patrols would "constantly, every year during the dry season, enter into the forests," until they had effected the "total reduction of [this] . . . cruel cannibal race." Armed Indians who were captured in these actions would be considered prisoners of war and subject to a ten-year period of enslavement. Although the decree singled out the Botocudo, the governor was to understand that it pertained to the "reduction and civilization . . . of other Indian races," as well.[17]

The wholesale destruction of surviving native cultures in this forested refuge zone spread rapidly through eastern Minas Gerais, inland Espírito Santo, and southern Bahia. One European naturalist, who was traveling in the area in the immediate aftermath of the worst violence, described the results with unconcealed shock. He observed that "no truce was granted the Botocudo, who proceeded to be exterminated wherever they were encountered, without regard to age or sex." The war, he wrote, "was maintained with the greatest perseverance and cruelty, since it was firmly believed that [the Botocudo] killed and devoured any enemy that fell into their hands." Another observer estimated the number of troops who were permanently deployed in the eastern sertão at 400 in 1810, although 2,000 were reported to have been mustered for one of the war's largest expeditions.[18]

These developments attest to the limits, during the years immediately following wartime mobilization, of Moura's contemporaneous vision of gradual Indian assimilation. The prince regent had opened his 1808 declaration by describing acts of almost unimaginable brutality. In particular, it was cannibalism that made the war legal beyond contention. It was cannibalism, denounced in the interest of military conquest, that outweighed evidence presented by men like Moura who believed the eastern Indians could be incorporated by other means. As was perennially the case with such accusations by the state, the monarch had little direct evidence to support his charge that the Botocudo practiced routine anthropophagy. Only after the declaration was issued did the war minister order the governor of Minas Gerais to send to the royal court, under strict security, one Botocudo male and one female "of the same species" to satisfy the monarch's "curiosity to see this cannibal race."[19] In the past, authorities had used the fear of cannibalism to discourage illicit activity by colonists in the eastern sertão. The prince regent's action marked the end of that era, which had been decades in coming, as changing events transformed perceived Indian savagery from an asset into an outrage in the minds of those who set policy for the region. Cannibalism came to play its more customary role in colonial conquest as a representation of radical alterity, a threat to the social order that must be eliminated.[20]

A Scientist's View

By 1831, when the war on the Botocudo and other groups officially ended, the military phase of conquest had already given way to less organized and, importantly, less expensive methods. Eloquent diatribes condemning the use of military force—including those put forth by José Bonifácio de Andrada e Silva, who was the leading statesman of independence-era politics, and Baron Wilhelm Ludwig von Eschwege, who was a prominent German scientist active in Minas Gerais—had helped secure the Crown's sympathy, if not the approval of all settlers and captaincy officials. Bonifácio famously proposed a more tolerant approach to Brazil's Indigenous peoples, focusing on the revitalization of an Indian village system that improved upon colonial precedents. Eschwege argued that the offensive war policy served only to deepen the Indians' hatred of colonists, while encouraging the migration of settlers away from established urban centers where their labor was sorely needed. Given that Eschwege carried out his investigations at the request of the monarch and claimed to have personally witnessed acts of cannibalism, it is his position that provides telling final evidence concerning the ways in which authorities struggled over how to interpret cultural practices that they deemed to be savage.[21]

Trained primarily as a geologist, mineralogist, and mining engineer, Eschwege was not the most expert of the European naturalists who contributed to an important body of early nineteenth-century literature on the seminomads of eastern Brazil.[22] Although he resided longer than most in Brazil—between 1809 and 1821, primarily in Minas Gerais—more sophisticated studies were made by others, especially by Prince Maximilian of Wied-Neuwied, another German naturalist who traveled there between 1815 and 1817, and by Auguste de Saint-Hilaire, a French botanist who did so between 1817 and 1822.[23] If we are to gauge the influence of such experts in representing Indigenous cultures, however, their shortcomings as ethnologists are as important as their strengths. For instance, in a journal entry written in 1816, Eschwege made notes about the smell of the human subjects he had met in Brazil, observing that "the ammoniac sweat of the black man is hardly repugnant compared to the repulsive, sweetish odor of the Indian." In another, he maintained, "there is no human uglier than an old, nude Botocudo woman, saliva running endlessly down her lower lip" as a result of the deformation caused by her wooden lip plug.[24] Similar examples of pseudoscientific excess and ethnocentric conceit are to be found in the works of all of these writers.

After examining much of the data they collected and comparing it to local archival sources, I am convinced that allegations of routine cannibalism among the eastern Indians reveal far more about the colonial imagination than about native conduct.[25] It will likely never be known exactly to what extent, or even definitively whether, the Botocudo, the Puri, and other groups in the eastern forests engaged in this practice. Some ethnologists accused settlers and officials of exaggerating this claim; others gathered evidence to support it. Among the first group, the skeptical Saint-

Hilaire speculated that many denunciations stemmed from "the ancient hatred of the Portuguese for the Botocudo, hatred that one supposes has been the origin of more than one calumny." Traveling in northeastern Minas Gerais, he heard more than one story deploring the discovery of human remains. Among these stories was the version Moura had recounted in Tocoiós, with certain details altered, about the gnawed bones of runaway slaves. Saint-Hilaire found such evidence inconclusive. Colonists could invent tales about any pile of bones; certain Botocudo, moreover, had a vested interest in perpetuating settlers' worst nightmares.[26]

Maximilian reached perhaps the most evenhanded conclusion, based on the greatest amount of information. Regarding the Botocudo and Puri, he wrote that "it is difficult to believe, as some affirm, that they eat human flesh as a matter of preference." He pointed out that against such a conclusion stood the evidence that they kept alive at least some of the prisoners they captured. "There is no doubt, however, that out of revenge they devour the flesh of their enemies killed in battle."[27] The German prince offered additional details: "The Portuguese . . . universally assert that the Puris feast on the flesh of the enemies they have killed, and there really seems to be some truth in this assertion . . . but they would never confess it to us. When we questioned them on the subject, they answered that the Botocudos only had this custom. [An English traveler] relates that the Indians at Canta Gallo ate birds without plucking them. I never saw a savage do this; they even carefully take out the entrails, and probably had a mind to amuse the English traveller by shewing [sic] him some extraordinary trick."[28]

Such "tricks" likely figured into reports on eating humans. As had always been the case, the question of cannibalism proved to be a particularly effective means of articulating the irreconcilable differences between colonists and Indians when the former resorted to violence. To the extent that anthropophagy occurred, the practice probably also served the natives when they sought to underscore such difference for their own purposes. Considering the allegations by the Puri about Botocudo conduct, this seems to have held true not only between the Indians and the Portuguese but also between separate Indigenous groups that were at odds with one another. Furthermore, some intriguing evidence, including Maximilian's assessment of Puri motives in the presence of the British observer and Saint-Hilaire's skeptical comments, suggests that if and when the eastern Indians did practice cannibalism they were seeking to give form to and thus exploit obvious European phantasms as opposed to engaging in a culturally intact, precontact practice.[29]

A final passage by Maximilian complicates the matter still further:

> That the Puris do in fact sometimes eat the bodies of their slaughtered enemies is attested by various witnesses in this part of the country. Father João, at [the Indian village of] St. Fidelis, assured us that he had once on a journey to the river Itapemirim found in the forest the body of a negro, who had been killed by the Puris, without arms and legs, and round which a number of carrion vultures had assembled. We have observed above that the Puris would never confess to us that they eat human flesh; but after the authentic testimonies that have been adduced, their own denial cannot have much weight.[30]

The anecdote clarifies that any ability to authenticate cannibalistic conduct depends on accounts in which experts assessing the facts at the time rejected the reliability of the Indians themselves as authorities on their own cultural practices.

The problem of obtaining reliable information is no less apparent in Eschwege's writings, despite the fact that, over the course of several months, he traveled a significant distance into Botocudo territory, navigating portions of the Doce River. His reputation for scientific zeal notwithstanding, he could not suppress fundamental misgivings about the character of his native subjects. His travels in Botocudo territory came close to the height of the violence following the 1808 declaration of war. He reached Minas Gerais in 1811, being charged with a range of official duties by the Crown, including devising a plan for enhancing navigation on the Doce River, authoring a new map of the captaincy, "establishing friendly relations with the anthropophagous Botocudo," as he put it, "and presenting uniform plans to civilize them."[31] Like many other European naturalists, Eschwege denounced the colonists' abuses of the Botocudo; but his writings leave little doubt about the preconceptions he brought to the challenge of forging such relations.

Resorting to information drawn from a Jesuit text that was written more than half a century earlier and using the name for the Botocudo current during an earlier era, he wrote the following about the Aimoré Indians: These Indians "have always caused great harm" to the Portuguese, he related. They lived in "inhospitable regions, where they constitute a terrifying nation." In the remote forests, they had forgotten their original language and devised another to replace it, one that all other natives found incomprehensible. They were "indomitable and savage," feared even by other Indians as "ferocious animals." In one instance reminiscent of the story Moura had recounted, a number of Botocudo had been taken prisoner. Behaving like "savage animals in captivity," they refused all food and died. Eschwege further cited the Jesuit text in explaining that the Botocudo lived "at war with all of the tribes that they encounter," roaming the forests in groups of several dozen bowmen, preferring ambushes to open battles, attacking boldly when their enemies seemed weak, and fleeing when they seemed valiant.[32]

On the subject of cannibalism, Eschwege returned to firsthand experience, speaking of exposing himself to the "great danger of . . . being devoured by the Botocudo." Although he escaped this fate, it was not without seeing "abominable scenes and robust men reduced to slices of roasted meat." With evident repugnance, he claimed that he had once seen this "horrible food, freshly captured . . . constituted of hands, arms, and legs, barely scorched and not roasted."[33] As such, the usually meticulous Eschwege gathered evidence to support the charge that the eastern Indians ate their enemies; yet these descriptions bore the characteristics not of an eyewitness account but of the repetition of generic images of anthropophagi that were employed by some Europeans and debunked by others, since colonization began in the sixteenth century.[34]

Despite his grim view of the Indians, Eschwege insisted that violent conquest was not the best response. Particularly in unpublished policy prescriptions that were sent directly to officials who were charged with prosecuting the war, he softened his stance considerably, at times contradicting the more lurid descriptions intended for his European readers. He argued that, apart from their cannibalism, the Botocudo were not as fierce as they were held to be and that the military effort should be aimed not at conquest but at winning their friendship. They could be civilized despite the dominant view to the contrary, a view to which his harsher published observations surely contributed. In his correspondence with Brazilian authorities, by contrast, he placed the current military mobilization in the context of a long history of "fanaticism, ignorance, and cruelty" wrought by the conquerors of the Americas. "To civilize with a sword in hand is a contradiction," he wrote. "The Indian has his customs; he has his religion, whatever it may be, and it is very natural that he defends it with his life, as long as he is not persuaded to do the contrary." What was required was time—time to convince the Botocudo that mutual trust was possible, that opposing and sharply different peoples could find common ground. They should be left to live in peace, allowed to practice their own customs. Gradually introducing certain luxuries among them would produce needs that would lead them to civilization, even if such luxuries were also capable of turning the civilized into barbarians. "Civilization will increase with necessities to the point that there will be no other remedy except to subject oneself voluntarily to our laws." In a striking rhetorical flourish, he went even further: progress toward a solution depended on first convincing the natives that "we ourselves are Botocudos and cannibals."[35] One can hardly conceive of a statement more prophetic of a later cultural relativism.

Eschwege proceeded to criticize the royal declaration of war against individuals who continued to live "in the state of innocence." He thought the policy of attempting to conquer a territory as vast as the eastern forests with a few hundred soldiers was absurd. Even more ridiculous was the idea of populating this region with civilized inhabitants when much of the rest of Minas Gerais had insufficient population. The effort would only spread the current settler population even more thinly over the captaincy, making it more difficult to govern and less productive, contributing to "the ruin" of the entire region, he warned. To the present point, the war had amounted to a few divisions of soldiers penetrating twenty or thirty leagues into the forests, killing a dozen or so Botocudo, and returning to their barracks. The policy had served only to exacerbate the Indians' hostility. Meanwhile, the deployed divisions, as few and as distant from one another as they were, provided nothing but a false sense of security to frontier settlers. He argued for a defensive position vis-à-vis the Botocudo and a halt to new settlement in the area, until troops had more success in opening roads and improving navigation.[36]

When Eschwege wrote this condemnation of countering cannibals with military might, the conquest of the frontier remained far from complete, as his assessment attested. Violence between soldiers, settlers, and Indians persisted into the 1820s and well beyond. In some areas settlers still fearing Botocudo aggression had failed to push more than two leagues (thirteen kilometers) into the forests from the coast, even though maps of the region then pictured what one cartographer had labeled as the new "line of forts to repel the Indians." Subsequent maps drafted as late as the 1860s still characterized extensive swaths of the Eastern Sertão as "unsettled lands" and "little-known forests inhabited by indigenes." By the 1880s the great bulk of the estimated remaining twelve to 14,000 Botocudo were described by a contemporary anthropologist as "still in the savage state, forming the most numerous and one of the fiercest wild tribes in East Brazil" and still practicing cannibalism. The Botocudo remained in control of substantial territory, especially to the north of the Doce River, until the early twentieth century.[37]

If cannibalism had once provoked a declaration of war, it ultimately outlasted the state's will to prosecute that war. Nearly a decade after independence came in 1822, the government unceremoniously revoked the declaration in 1831, although the official military offensive had largely ended by 1811, corresponding with the criticism issued by Eschwege and others. Milder legislation governing the treatment of the region's Indians had been adopted by 1823.[38] The formation of dozens of hastily established state-controlled aldeias, like the one Moura supervised at Tocoiós, provided one measure of the disruption that was caused by the war to the Botocudo, whose population in the region extending from eastern Minas Gerais to the coast was estimated at 20,000 individuals during this period. These villages brought together natives who had been forced out of the forests. In exchange for food, shelter, consumer goods, and protection from armed assault, the Indians submitted to the village regime, which included religious conversion and sedentary agricultural labor. Between 1800 and 1850 in the area bounded by the Doce and Pardo rivers, seventy-three of these villages were formed and ultimately placed under the centralized administration of the French émigré Guido Tomás Marlière, another forceful critic of the military approach and a colleague of

Eschwege. Many of these villages would later evolve into townships that survive to this day.[39]

These village Indians served as the primary native sources for the conclusions drawn by the European naturalists about the nature of the Indigenous cultures of the Atlantic forests. With rare exceptions, in other words, these Indians were no longer independent masters of their own lives; rather, they were splintered, subjugated groups living in close proximity to settler society. Colonized and detribalized Indians have generated a fascinating literature of their own, crucial for revising misleading preconceptions that permeate the scholarly literature about so-called pure or uncontacted Indians and their allegedly degraded brethren in European-controlled missions, villages, and towns.[40] The point here is not to dismiss as worthy subjects the Indians who provided nineteenth-century ethnologists with information but simply to emphasize that their experience should not be mistaken for those who either earlier or concurrently led autonomous lives.

This issue also helps place in proper perspective the work of the European naturalists, who have long provided essential source material for historians of Brazil.[41] Shaping what came to be known and remembered about the natives of Brazil's coastal forests, these authors gathered ethnographic data of uneven quality, based on firsthand encounters, existing written sources, and, in some cases, mere hearsay. Although their accounts generally evinced more interest in Indigenous cultures than documents that were drafted by colonists, they remained highly biased when not overtly racist, crafted to appeal to an emerging European scientific community as well as to a growing popular audience with an appetite for vicarious foreign adventure. In the transatlantic representation of Brazilian Indians as quintessential primitives, these authors succeeded admirably. By midcentury, in no less iconic a work than *Madame Bovary*, for instance, Gustave Flaubert could mention the Botocudo in passing, assuming readers would recognize the reference. At one point in that novel, the pharmacist Monsieur Homais, disturbed by his wife's unconventional methods in raising their children, chastises her with the query, "Do you intend to make Caribs or Botocudos out of them?"[42] I know of no scholar who has tied this passage to Eschwege, although his writings were cited by other prominent European intellectuals such as Goethe and Marx.[43]

Flaubert certainly had access to texts by any number of other naturalists active in nineteenth-century Brazil, including those of his countryman Saint-Hilaire. While these travelers may have afforded Brazil's Indians a degree of renown, their quasi-scientific texts had clear limits when measured as a source of reliable ethnographic evidence.

Published in the form of travel journals and scientific treatises, these accounts profoundly influenced how Brazilian elites thought about the surviving Indigenous inhabitants of the new nation they aspired to lead as it achieved independence from Portugal. Their findings, observations, and opinions permeated discussions on the founding of the primary institutions that were responsible for accumulating, codifying, and promulgating knowledge concerning Indians. The most important of these were the Royal Museum (soon to be called the National Museum or Museu Nacional) and the Brazilian Historical and Geographic Institute (Instituto Histórico e Geográfico Brasileiro). Both were founded during the early nineteenth century in Rio de Janeiro. The first was founded in 1818 by the author of the war declaration, who had by then ascended to the throne as King João VI; the second, twenty years later under the regency, which was then ruling the nation. The European naturalists gathered artifacts and specimens that swelled the museum's initial holdings, including a particularly valuable collection of gems and minerals contributed by Eschwege. They submitted correspondence and other esteemed reports to the institute. One text, drafted by the Bavarian naturalist Karl Friedrich Philipp von Martius, won an essay contest sponsored by Emperor Pedro II, the grandson of João VI, on how best to write the history of Brazil.[44]

It is beyond the scope of this essay to investigate in greater detail the sway that was held by individual ethnographers over the institutionalization of Brazil's Indigenous past and present. My more modest objective is to identify some of the primary currents contributing to this process as it unfolded during the first half of the nineteenth century, directly in the aftermath of the war waged against the eastern Indians. However persuasive the European experts may have been, their expertise was only part of a larger context in which the colonial and, later, national state moved forward with efforts to incorporate, by force when necessary, major regions that were still controlled by native peoples. Alongside the contribution of the emergent scientific community, the openly hostile position of key members of the Luso-Brazilian elite who were instrumental in this institutionalization process, including the king himself, must equally be considered.

The evidence assembled here also demonstrates that the expert ethnographers were only the most widely known as opposed to the best-informed observers of native peoples. On the remote frontier, as director of the Tocoiós aldeia, José Moura had argued that the exchange of provisions could lure hunter-gatherers into settled society without resorting to violence. His vision of peaceful accommodation, driven by personal as much as moral considerations, had not prevailed for the critical period immediately following the declaration of war, except in the most limited of forms. It is perhaps fitting that, as far as the sources reveal, he never found his Golden Lagoon. Only after several years of state-sponsored aggression did the Crown finally begin to search for an alternative policy as it faced the financial strain on the royal treasury that had been caused by the war. The notion of fostering material exchange with natives who were condemned as cannibals resurfaced in the writings of Baron von Eschwege, among other European naturalists, this time corresponding with the state's search for solutions other than its frustrated attempt at military conquest.

By way of conclusion, in order to underline the contrasting ways in which observers of Indigenous cultures and the state reacted to the radical alterity of the Atlantic forest dwellers, I want to return for a moment to Moura's encounters with the Botocudo of the Jequitinhonha River valley. Several times during 1809, the year following the declaration of war, small groups of a dozen or so natives again made contact with troops in the forest and with Moura back in his settlement. They were always treated hospitably, Moura reported, but he could not keep up with their desire for metal tools. The Indians told him that they planned to return in greater numbers, that they would bring their children in order to receive more fishhooks and other gifts, and that they found the aldeia an agreeable dwelling place, particularly since food was more readily accessible there than in the forest. This exchange concluded with a startling revelation: the Botocudo told Moura that "without doubt" they would settle permanently at the aldeia if it were possible to convince their wives, who they said "were very wild and feared they would be killed and eaten."[45]

Was there a firm basis for this fear? Would the Botocudo be consumed—not just metaphorically—if they entered settled society? Since their ancestors first came into contact with the Portuguese along Brazil's Atlantic coastline in the sixteenth century, for a span of what now amounted to three centuries, the Botocudo had witnessed almost every imaginable act of violence. They had been the victims of various official and unofficial military assaults that were designated as "just wars." They had been murdered and enslaved. They had watched from the woods as Portuguese soldiers cut off the ears of their fallen clansmen as proof of victory in battle. They had seen their women and children marched off to white settlements in a longstanding slave trade that was expanding at precisely the time that Moura was active on the Jequitinhonha River. When these kinfolk disappeared, there was ample reason to suspect the worst, especially if Botocudo practices with their own captives matched the hideous reports that circulated in the region.[46]

Apart from the question of verifiable cannibalism is the apparently incontestable truth that fears of Portuguese cruelty elicited a full range of responses among the native forest dwellers.[47] Among these responses, if the statement Moura recorded is to be believed, some Botocudo were struggling with a dilemma not unlike that of their colonial antagonists. They were striving, that is, to convince wary members of their cohort that the enemies they had encountered in the forest, while volatile and untrustworthy, could best be dealt with as other human beings, despite the dread of being killed, dismembered, and potentially consumed. They were attempting to interpret a radically different culture, which in the heat of conflict they only imperfectly understood. One wonders how they might have represented this culture in ethnographies, museums, and historical societies of their own.

Notes

Abbreviations used in the endnotes are as follows: Arquivo Histórico do Exército, Rio de Janeiro (AHEx); Biblioteca Nacional, Rio de Janeiro (BNRJ); Seção de Manuscritos (SM); Documentos Biográficos (DB); Library of Congress, Washington DC (LC); Geography and Map Division (GMD); *Revista do Arquivo Público Mineiro*

(*RAPM*). I wish to thank Susan Sleeper-Smith for the opportunity to participate in the Newberry Library Symposium, at which this chapter was first presented.

1. Hal Langfur, *The Forbidden Lands: Colonial Identity, Frontier Violence, and the Persistence of Brazil's Eastern Indians, 1750–1830* (Stanford CA: Stanford University Press, 2006), esp. chap. 1. Other recent contributions to the history of Brazil's eastern Indians during this period include B. J. Barickman, "'Tame Indians,' 'Wild Heathens,' and Settlers in Southern Bahia in the Late Eighteenth and Early Nineteenth Centuries," *Americas* 51, no. 3 (1995): 326–27; Judy Bieber, "The Aldeia System Reborn: Botocudo Communities on the Espírito Santo–Minas Gerais Frontier, 1808–1845" (paper presented at the Latin American Studies Association Conference, Chicago IL, September 24–26, 1998); Judy Bieber, "Shifting Frontiers: The Role of Subsistence, Disease, and Environment in Shaping Indigenous Definitions of Frontiers in Minas Gerais, 1808–1850," (paper presented at the American Historical Association Conference, San Francisco CA, January 2002); Maria Hilda Baquiero Paraíso, "O Tempo da dor e do Trabalho: A Conquista dos Territórios Indígenas nos Sertões do Leste," (PhD diss., Universidade de São Paulo, 1998); and Maria Leônia Chaves de Resende, "Gentios brasílicos: Índios coloniais em Minas Gerais setecentista," (PhD diss., Universidade de Campinas, 2003).

2. The extent to which cannibalism in Brazil, the early modern Americas, and the non-Western world in general constituted a reality or a myth that was propagated to justify conquest and enslavement continues to divide anthropologists. Notable contributions to this debate include W. Arens, *The Man-Eating Myth: Anthropology and Anthropophagy* (New York: Oxford University Press, 1979); Frank Lestringant, *Cannibals: The Discovery and Representation of the Cannibal from Columbus to Jules Verne*, trans. Rosemary Morris (Berkeley: University of California Press, 1997); Francis Barker, Peter Hulme, and Margaret Iversen, eds., *Cannibalism and the Colonial World* (Cambridge: Cambridge University Press, 1998); Laurence R. Goldman, ed., *The Anthropology of Cannibalism* (Westport CT: Bergin and Garvey, 1999). See also Beth A. Conklin, *Consuming Grief: Compassionate Cannibalism in an Amazonian Society* (Austin: University of Texas Press, 2001); Barbara Ganson, *The Guaraní under Spanish Rule in the Río de la Plata* (Stanford CA: Stanford University Press, 2003), 22–23; Alida C. Metcalf, *Go-Betweens and the Colonization of Brazil, 1500–1600* (Austin: University of Texas Press, 2005); Neil L. Whitehead, *Dark Shamans: Kanaimà and the Poetics of Violent Death* (Durham NC: Duke University Press, 2002), 191–95, 236–43; H. E. Martel, "Hans Staden's Captive Soul: Identity, Imperialism, and Rumors of Cannibalism in Sixteenth-Century Brazil," *Journal of World History* 17, no. 1 (2006): 61–69.

3. Except where otherwise indicated, the following account is recorded in José Pereira Freire de Moura, "Notícia e Observaçoens Sobre os Índios Botocudos que Frequentão as Margens do Rio Jequitinhonha, e se Chamao Ambarés, ou Aymorés," Tocoiós, December 1809, and is reprinted in *RAPM* 2, no. 1 (1897): 28–31.

4. Raimundo José da Cunha Matos, *Corografia Histórica da Província de Minas Gerais (1837)* (São Paulo: Editóra Itatiaia, 1981), 1:194, 2:168; Auguste de Saint-Hilaire, *Viagem pelas Províncias do Rio de Janeiro e Minas Gerais*, trans. Vivaldi Moreira (Belo Horizonte, Brasil: Editóra Itatiaia, 1975), 284n428.

5. José Pereira Freire de Moura identifies this corporal by name, Moura to the War Minister, Tocoiós, January 5, 1810, reprinted in RAPM 2, no. 1 (1897): 32.

6. Moura to War Minister, RAPM: 31–34; José de Sousa Caldas, "Copia do Roteiro para se Procurar a Lagoa Dourada," n.d., reprinted in RAPM 2, no. 1 (1897): 34. The Lagoa Dourada described in these sources should not to be confused with the municipal district bearing the same name in southern Minas Gerais, near the city of São João del-Rei.

7. Moura to War Minister, RAPM: 31–34. Moura identified the refugee groups in the forests as the "Camanachos, Capoches, Pantimes, e Maquary." I suspect he meant the Kumanaxó, Kopoxó, Panhame, and possibly the Makoni. See Langfur, *Forbidden Lands*, 24.

8. Moura to War Minister, RAPM: 31–34.

9. Moura to War Minister, RAPM: 31–34.

10. José Pereira Freire de Moura, "Lista dos Homens q. Pedi de Auxilio ao Com.te do Districto de S. Domingos," reprinted in RAPM 2, no. 1 (1897): 35–36; José Pereira Freire de Moura, "Instruçoens q. se Darão ao Chefe da Bandeira q. for Procurar a Lagôa-Dourada," reprinted in RAPM 2, no. 1 (1897): 35–36.

11. Diogo Pereira Ribeiro de Vasconcelos, *Breve Descrição Geográfica, Física e Política da Capitania de Minas Gerais* (1807; repr., Belo Horizonte, Brasil: Fundação João Pinheiro, 1994), 144–50, 156–57.

12. Vasconcelos, *Breve Descrição Geográfica*, 144–50, 156–57.

13. Vasconcelos, *Breve Descrição Geográfica*, 144–50, 156–57.

14. Vasconcelos, *Breve Descrição Geográfica*, 144–50, 156–57.

15. Langfur, *Forbidden Lands*, chap. 1.

16. "Carta Régia [royal edict] ao Governador e Capitão General da Capitania de Minas Gerais Sobre a Guerra aos Indios Botecudos," May 13, 1808, in *Legislação Indigenista no Século XIX: Uma Compilação (1808–1889)*, ed. Manuela Carneiro da Cunha (São Paulo: Universidade de São Paulo, 1992), 57–60.

17. "Carta Régia," in Cunha, *Legislação Indigenista*, 57–60.

18. Maximilian, Prinz von Wied, *Viagem ao Brasil*, trans. Edgar Süssekind de Mendonça and Flávio Poppe de Figueiredo (Belo Horizonte: Editóra Itatiaia, 1989), 153; Wilhelm Ludwig von Eschwege, "Copia de Huma Carta Feita pelo Sargento Mor Eschwege (Acerca dos Botocudos e das Divisões da Conquista) com Notas pelo Deputado da Junta Militar, Matheus Herculano Monteiro," n.p., 1811, Document 66, codex 8, 1, 8, SM, BNRJ. On the largest expedition, see X. Chabert, *An Historical Account of the Manners and Customs of the Savage Inhabitants of Brazil; Together with a Sketch of the Life of the Botocudo Chieftain and Family* (Exeter,

UK: R. Cullum, 1823). On the war more generally, see John Hemming, *Amazon Frontier: The Defeat of the Brazilian Indians* (Cambridge MA: Harvard University Press, 1987), 92–3, 99–100; Maria Hilda Baquiero Paraíso, "Os Botocudos e sua Trajetória Histórica," in *História dos índios no Brasil*, ed. Manuela Carneiro da Cunha (São Paulo: Companhia das Letras, 1992), 417–23; Barickman, "'Tame Indians,'" 359–65.

19. War Minister to the Governor, Rio de Janeiro, August 4, 1808, codex I-1, 1, 34, fol. 23v, Livros da Capitania, Minas Gerais, 1808–1811, AHEx.

20. See Langfur, *Forbidden Lands*, chap. 8; Beatriz Perrone-Moisés, "Índios Livres e Índios Escravos: Os Princípios da Legislação Indigenista do Período Colonial (Séculos XVI a XVIII)," in Carneiro da Cunha, *História dos índios no Brasil*, 115–32; Jill Lepore, *The Name of War: King Philip's War and the Origins of American Identity* (New York: Knopf, 1998), 106–13.

21. Eschwege, "Copia de Huma Carta Feita pelo Sargento Mor Eschwege"; José Bonifácio de Andrada e Silva, "Apontamentos para a Civilização dos Índios Bravos do Ímpério do Brasil," in *O Pensamento Vivo de José Bonifácio* (1823: repr., São Paulo: Livraria Martins, 1961), 78–107. See also Manuela Carneiro da Cunha, "Pensar os Índios: Apontamentos Sobre José Bonifácio," in *Antropologia do Brasil: Mito, História, Etnicidade* (São Paulo: Brasiliense / EDUSP, 1986), 165–73; Cunha, prologue to *Legislação Indigenista*, 1–34; and David Treece, *Exiles, Allies, Rebels: Brazil's Indianist Movement, Indigenist Politics, and the Imperial Nation-State* (Westport CT: Greenwood Press, 2000), 81–82.

22. The most relevant published discussions by Eschwege of Brazil's eastern Indians appear in Wilhelm Ludwig von Eschwege, *Brasil, Novo Mundo*, trans. Domício de Figueiredo Murta, Coleção Mineiriana, Série Clássicos (Belo Horizonte, Brasil: Fundação João Pinheiro, 1996); Wilhelm Ludwig von Eschwege, *Pluto Brasiliensis*, trans. Domício de Figueiredo Murta, 2 vols. (Belo Horizonte, Brasil: Editóra Itatiaia, 1979); Wilhelm Ludwig von Eschwege, *Jornal do Brasil, 1811–1817, ou Relatos Diversos do Brasil, Coletados Durante Expedições Científicas* (Belo Horizonte, Brasil: Fundação João Pinheiro, 2002). For two recent biographical sketches, see Friedrich E. Renger, "Eschwege, o Brasilianista," in Eschwege, *Jornal do Brasil, 1811–1817*, 11–17; and Douglas C. Libby, "Eschwege e os Primeiros Anos no Brazil," in Eschwege, *Jornal do Brasil, 1811–1817*, 19–24. See also Waldemar de Almeida Barbosa, *Barão de Eschwege* (Belo Horizonte, Brasil: Casa de Eschwege, 1977).

23. In addition to Eschwege's texts, the most relevant works by European naturalists on Brazil's eastern Indians include Maximilian, *Viagem ao Brasil*; Saint-Hilaire, *Viagem pelas Províncias*; and Auguste de Saint-Hilaire, *Viagem ao Espírito Santo e Rio Doce*, trans. Milton Amado (Belo Horizonte, Brasil: Editóra Itatiaia, 1974). Hemming provides brief biographies and a helpful chronology of these and other explorers, naturalists, and adventurers in *Amazon Frontier*, 483–511.

24. Eschwege, *Brasil, Novo Mundo*, 69; Eschwege, *Jornal do Brasil, 1811–1817*, 81.

25. I develop this argument at some length in Langfur, *Forbidden Lands*, chap. 7.

26. Saint-Hilaire, *Viagem pelas Províncias*, 217, 254.

27. Maximilian, *Viagem ao Brasil*, 126–27, 153, 313–15.

28. Maximilian, Prinz von Wied, *Travels in Brazil in the Years 1815, 1816, 1817* (London: Henry Colburn, 1820), 119.

29. Hal Langfur, "The Forbidden Lands: Frontier Settlers, Slaves, and Indians in Minas Gerais, Brazil, 1760–1830," (PhD diss., University of Texas, 1999), 304–5; John M. Monteiro, "Entre o Etnocídio e a Etnogênese: Identidades Indígenas Coloniais," (paper presented at the Latin American Studies Association Conference, Dallas, Texas, March 27–29, 2003); Whitehead, *Dark Shamans*, esp. 242. For a discussion concerning practices of violence more generally, see Hal Langfur, "Moved by Terror: Frontier Violence as Cultural Exchange in Late-Colonial Brazil," *Ethnohistory* 52, no. 2 (2005): 255–89.

30. Maximilian, *Travels in Brazil*, 138.

31. Eschwege, *Pluto Brasiliensis*, 1:42.

32. Eschwege, *Brasil, Novo Mundo*, 238–40. On the longstanding debate over whether the Aimoré and Botocudo were different names for the same ethnic group, see Langfur, *Forbidden Lands*, 313n16.

33. Eschwege, *Pluto Brasiliensis*, 1:43; Eschwege, *Brasil, Novo Mundo*, 240n61. In an earlier text, in contrast, Eschwege wrote that his knowledge of Botocudo cannibalism was derived not from his own experience but from interviews with an eyewitness. See Eschwege, *Jornal do Brasil, 1811–1817*, 81.

34. Comparable images, for example, appear on sixteenth-century maps of Brazil in the figures of Indians roasting human body parts on spits. In his famous account of life among the coastal Tupinambá in the 1550s, Jean de Léry noted the error of such portrayals of native cannibalism, which he corrected from personal experience, detailing instead a process of boiling, butchering, and then roasting not on spits but on a *boucan*, or a "big wooden grill." See, for example, the figures drawn by Diego Gutiérrez on the map *Americae sive Quartae Orbis Partis Nova et Exactissima Descritio*, Antwerp, 1562, Lessing J. Rosenwald Collection, GMC, LC. Jean de Léry, *History of a Voyage to the Land of Brazil*, trans. Janet Whatley (Berkeley: University of California Press, 1990), 79, 125–27.

35. Eschwege, "Copia de Huma Carta Feita pelo Sargento Mor Eschwege."

36. Eschwege, "Copia de Huma Carta Feita pelo Sargento Mor Eschwege."

37. Carlos Cezar Burlamaqui, "Esboço do Estado Atual das Comarcas de Porto Seguro e Ilheus," July 5, 1820, I-28, 29, 11, SM, BNRJ, Rio de Janeiro; A. H. Keane, "On the Botocudos," *Journal of the Anthropological Institute of Great Britain and Ireland* 13 (1884): 205, 207; Paraíso, "Os Botocudos," 418–23; Hemming, *Amazon Frontier*, chap. 18; Izabel Missagia de Mattos, "'Civilização' e 'Revolta': Os Botocudos e a Catequese na Província de Minas," (PhD diss., Universidade de Campinas,

2002); Angelo Alves Carrara, *Estruturas Agrárias e Capitalismo; Ocupação do Solo e Transformação do Trabalho na Zona da Mata Central de Minas Gerais (Séculos XVIII e XIX)* (Mariana, Brasil: Editóra Universidade Federal de Ovro Preto, 1999), 15; Paraíso, "O Tempo da dor." The noted maps include John Luccock, *A Map of the Table Land of Brazil*, London, 1820, reprinted in John Luccock, *Notes on Rio de Janeiro and the Southern Parts of Brazil; Taken During a Residence of Ten Years in That Country, from 1808 to 1818* (London: Samuel Leigh, 1820), frontispiece; Carlos Krauss, "Mappa Geral das Colonias S. Leopoldina, S. Izabel, e Rio Novo na Provincia do Espirito Santo," Rio de Janeiro, 1866, GMD, LC; and Carlos Krauss, "Mappa Geral da Provincia do Espirito-Santo relativo as Colonias e Vias de Communicação," Rio de Janeiro, 1866, GMD, LC. As their legends and notations indicate, Krauss's maps were designed to lure European immigrants to settle Brazil's eastern forests.

38. Hemming, *Amazon Frontier*, 365–84; Paraíso, "Os Botocudos," 417–23; Barickman, "'Tame Indians,'" 359–65; Bieber, "The Aldeia System Reborn." Legislation enacted in 1823 and 1824 created Indian directories and ordered directors to employ peaceful means to settle Indians into villages along the Doce River in Minas Gerais and Espírito Santo. See "Decisão 22," February 20, 1823; "Decisão 85," May 24, 1823; and "Decreto 31," January 28, 1824, in Cunha, *Legislação Indigenista*, 111–14, 137.

39. Bieber, "The Aldeia System Reborn"; Paraíso, "Os Botocudos," 418; Paraíso, "O Tempo da dor." The population estimate is from Guido Tomás Marlière, "Direção Geral dos Índios de Minas Gerais," RAPM 12 (1907): 530; Oiliam José, *Marlière, O Civilizador* (Belo Horizonte, Brasil: Editóra Itatiaia, 1958). Eschwege recounts his 1814 visit with Marlière at the São João Batista presidio in his *Jornal do Brasil, 1811–1817*, esp. 67–128.

40. See, for example, Muriel Nazzari, "Vanishing Indians: The Social Construction of Race in Colonial São Paulo," *Americas* 57, no. 4 (2001): 497–524; Resende, "Gentios brasílicos"; Barbara A. Sommer, "Negotiated Settlements: Native Amazonians and Portuguese Policy in Pará, Brazil, 1758–1798" (PhD diss., University of New Mexico, 2000); Maria Regina Celestino de Almeida, *Metamorfoses Indígenas: Cultura e Identidade nos Aldeamentos Indígenas do Rio de Janeiro* (Rio de Janeiro: Arquivo Nacional, 2002); Stuart B. Schwartz and Frank Salomon, "New Peoples and New Kinds of People: Adaptation, Readjustment, and Ethnogenesis in South American Indigenous Societies (Colonial Era)," in *The Cambridge History of the Native Peoples of the Americas*, ed. Stuart B. Schwartz and Frank Salomon (Cambridge: Cambridge University Press, 1999), vol. 3, pt. 2, 443–501; Serge Gruzinski, *The Mestizo Mind: The Intellectual Dynamics of Colonization and Globalization* (New York: Routledge, 2002); Monteiro, "Entre o Etnocídio e a Etnogênese."

41. For the most prominent example of scholarship relying on travelers' accounts as

a basis for Brazilian Indigenous history, see Hemming, *Amazon Frontier*. Chapters 5 and 18 of that work focus on the Botocudo and other groups of Brazil's central Atlantic coast. On nineteenth-century travel accounts with specific attention to women as both writers and subjects, see June E. Hahner, ed., *Women through Women's Eyes: Latin American Women in Nineteenth-Century Travel Accounts* (Wilmington DE: Scholarly Resources, 1998), xi–xxvi. See also Paulo Berger, *Bibliografia do Rio de Janeiro de Viajantes e Autores Estrangeiros, 1531–1900*, 2d ed. (Rio de Janeiro: SEEC, 1980); Regina Horta Duarte, "Facing the Forest: European Travellers Crossing the Mucuri River Valley, Brazil, in the Nineteenth Century," *Environment and History* 10 (2004): 31–58; Karen Macknow Lisboa, *A Nova Atlântica de Spix e Martius: Natureza e Civilização no Viagem pelo Brasil (1817–1820)* (São Paulo: Hucitec, 1997); Mary Louise Pratt, *Imperial Eyes: Travel Writing and Transculturation* (London: Routledge, 1992).

42. Gustave Flaubert, *Madame Bovary*, trans. Mildred Marmur (New York: Signet Classics, New American Library, 1964), 125.

43. João Antônio de Paula, "Eschwege, o Mundo e o Novo Mundo" in Eschwege, *Brasil, Novo Mundo*, 17–20.

44. On Eschwege's contribution to the National Museum, see Mário Guimarães Ferri, preface to *Pluto Brasiliensis*, by Eschwege; and Eschwege, *Jornal do Brasil, 1811–1817*, 393. On the historical and intellectual origins of the museum, see Jens Andermann, "Empires of Nature," *Nepantla: Views from South* 4, no. 2 (2003): 283–315; Maria Margaret Lopes, "O Local Musealizado em Nacional: Aspectos da Cultura das Ciências Naturais no Século XIX, no Brasil," in *Ciências, Civilização e Império no Trópicos*, ed. Ald Heizer and Antonio Augusto Passos Videira (Rio de Janeiro: Access, 2001), 77–96; Maria Margaret Lopes, "The Museums and the Construction of Natural Sciences in Brazil in the 19th Century," in *Cultures and Institutions of Natural History: Essays in the History and Philosophy of Science*, ed. Michael T. Ghiselin and Alan E. Leviton (San Francisco: California Academy of Sciences, 2000); and Maria Margaret Lopes and Irina Podgorny, "The Shaping of Latin American Museums of Natural History, 1850–1990," *Osiris*, 2nd ser., 15 (2000): 108–18. On European contributions to and influences on the Brazilian Historical and Geographic Institute, including its scholarly journal, the most important in nineteenth-century Brazil, see Rollie E. Poppino, "A Century of the *Revista do Instituto Histórico e Geográfico Brasileiro*," *The Hispanic American Historical Review* 33, no. 2 (1953): 307–23, esp. 313–14. For Martius's winning essay, see Karl Friedrich Philipp von Martius, "Como se Deve Escrever a História do Brasil," *Revista do Instituto Histórico e Geográfico Brasileiro* 6, no. 24 (1845): 381–403. See also Heloisa M. Bertol Domingues, "Viagens Científicas: Descobrimento e Colonização no Brasil no Século XIX," in Heizer and Videira, *Ciências, Civilização e Império no Trópicos*, 55–75; M. L. S. Guimarães, "História e Natureza em

von Martius: Esquadrinhando o Brasil para Construir a Nação," *História, Ciências, Saúde: Manguinhos* 7, no. 2 (2000): 389–410.

45. Moura, "Notícia e Observaçoens Sobre os Índios Botocudos," RAPM: 28–31.

46. On violence perpetrated against the Botocudo, see Langfur, *Forbidden Lands*, esp. chap. 7. On the trade in Botocudo slaves along the Jequitinhonha River, see Saint-Hilaire, *Viagem pelas Províncias*, 250. Botocudo perceptions of European fears may have been honed by their own. When one of Brazil's finest ethnologists interviewed a handful of surviving Botocudo regarding their origin myths and religious belief in the mid-twentieth century, he learned that the Botocudo, too, dreaded being consumed, not only by wild animals but also by cannibals. Curt Nimuendajú, "Social Organization and Beliefs of the Botocudo of Eastern Brazil," *Southwestern Journal of Anthropology* 2 (1946): 93–115, esp. 115.

47. For extensive evidence that some Botocudo successfully navigated an amicable or at least sustainable entrance into colonial society, see Langfur, *Forbidden Lands*, chap. 6. See also Resende, "Gentios brasílicos."

2

Ethnographic Showcases as Sites of Knowledge Production and Indigenous Resistance

ZINE MAGUBANE

The Ethnographic Exhibit Unveiled
The Intersection of Show Business and Racial Science

In May of 1853 the *Athenaeum*, a popular British magazine, carried an item in the weekly gossip column about the popularity of human exhibitions (also known as ethnographic showcases). The article noted that "a man may travel a great deal without seeing so many varieties of the human race as are constantly to be seen in London."[1] Ethnographic showcases were the equivalent of human zoos wherein Indigenous people were exhibited for the amusement of the English viewing public and for the profitability of show owners and exhibitors as well as to satisfy the evidentiary needs of ethnographers and anthropologists. This paper will discuss the role that ethnographic showcases played in the production, dissemination, and ordering of knowledge about Africa and Africans. Although ethnographic showcases played a key role in staging Africa and Africans in ways that supported the aims of colonialism, the Africans who were exhibited did not allow themselves to be silenced. By reading between the lines of the historical record, it is possible to retrieve and reconstruct African voices and opinions—about European society, Europeans, colonialism, and conquest. Ethnographic showcases were immensely popular in England during the nineteenth century. As displays, they were "living nineteenth century versions of the early twentieth century museum diorama."[2] The showcases provided a unique degree of excitement and titillation because they featured racial "others" in states of near or complete undress performing the intimate rituals surrounding everything from weddings to warfare. The ability to gawk and gaze, without restraint, was something large numbers of the English viewing public found irresistible. The following description of an ethnographic showcase, "The Zulu Kaffirs at the St. George's Gallery, Knightsbridge,"[3] which appeared in the *Illustrated London News* of May 28, 1853, gives some of the flavor of what these shows were like:

> This brand of wild but interesting savages are taking such high rank among the metropolitan exhibitions of the present season, and represent so faithfully the manners, habits, and costume of their tribe, that we give an Illustration of a scene in their performances. A number of huts, such as they occupy, are placed upon the stage with an African landscape in the background; and, one by one, the savages make their appearance, engaged in the pursuits of their everyday life. After a supper of meal, of which the Kaffirs partake with their large wooden spoons, an extraordinary song and dance are performed, in which each performer moves about on his haunches, grunting and snorting the while like a pair of asthmatic bellows. . . . The scene illustrative of the preliminaries of marriage and the bridal festivities might leave one in doubt which was the bridegroom, did not that interesting savage announce his enviable situation by screams of ecstasy which convulse the audience. . . . The exhibition is illustrated by some excellent panoramic scenery, painted by Marshall, from sketches made in Kaffirland. The various scenes in the entertainment are explained by an intelligent young lecturer.[4]

South Africa was a particularly rich source of human subjects for ethnological exhibits. Indeed, a stroll through what the *Illustrated London News* of June 12, 1847, called, "the ark of zoological wonders—Egyptian Hall, Piccadilly," yielded a view of, "extraordinary Bushpeople brought from South Africa."[5] Visitors to Cosmorama, Regent Street, could see "a very interesting exhibition of three natives of Southern and Eastern Africa."[6] The sight of "Bushmen in their trees" and "the preliminaries of Kaffir marriage and bridal festivities" entertained visitors to the St. George's Gallery in Knightsbridge. The latter came courtesy of a Mr. A. T. Caldecott, who returned from Natal with twelve Zulus in tow.[7]

The popularity and availability of Africans from South Africa stemmed in large part from the frontier wars that the British were waging against African people in their quest for imperial dominance. The so-called Kaffir Wars of 1835, 1847, 1851, and 1879, for example, were waged by the British with the sole objective of reducing the Xhosa people to impotence through systematic invasion and confiscation of their lands and cattle. The English were of the mind that "the only really effective way to reduce the Xhosa to complete dependence was to burn his huts and kraals, to drive off his cattle, to destroy his corn and other food, in short, to devastate his country."[8]

Ethnographic showcases both benefited from and were of benefit to the task of imperial warfare. Exhibitors benefited from these wars because captives were often forced to become performers in these humiliating human zoos. The *Illustrated London News*, for example, encouraged readers to attend "a very interesting exhibition of three natives of Southern and Eastern Africa." The paper described one member of the exhibition, Bourzaquai, as being, "a fine athletic fellow, twenty-five years of age, of middle stature, with a copper-coloured skin, heightened in places with red clay. . . . The Kaffir wields his light and sharp assegai, or lance, with great dexterity. His prowess was often proved against the British in the late war."[9] Likewise, the paper's May 1853 edition reported that one of the "Zulu Kaffirs" exhibited at St. George's Gallery, Knightsbridge, was a chief, Maxos, who was formerly "a soldier in one of King Panda's regiments. He is the son of a Zulu chief, under Chaka and Dingaan, who was slain. . . . Maxos has also been in battle, and has been wounded several times: an assegai wound above the left eye, and one in the back, are still to be seen."[10]

Ethnologists, phrenologists, craniometrists, and anthropologists, on the other hand, benefited from having living specimens to examine and upon whom to base their theories. The *Phrenological Journal*, for example, carried a report about an exhibit during the Christmas holidays featuring "six busts of the male Ojibbeway's [sic] and the half breed interpreter, who were recently in Manchester, exhibited in all the finery they love so much and with their faces painted red and green as in life. . . . Near these is a collection of national types of heads, including . . . Eskimo, Kaffir, Negro, & etc."[11] Likewise, the *Illustrated London News* of June 12, 1847, reported on "The Bosjemans at the Egyptian Hall, Piccadilly." The newspaper noted that "ethnological characteristics of the Bosjemans, literally 'Bushmen' the public have been made acquainted with through the writings of Lichtenstein, Burchell, Campbell, Thompson, Pringle, and other intelligent travelers in Africa." The journal went on to observe, "the present Exhibition is important, especially in illustration of Ethnology, which is every year advancing in popularity."[12] The following year, the journal of the Academy of Natural Sciences of Philadelphia announced that Dr. Samuel Morton, an American physician who collected skulls from around the world in order to compare the cranial capacities of different races, had "offered some observations of the Bushman Hottentot boy, now in this city, and who was brought here under the kind and paternal auspices of Capt. Chase, United States Consul at the Cape of Good Hope." The report went on to describe the bodily proportions, skin color, facial features, and hair texture of the young man, noting that "the mental and moral questions connected with the history of the youth, possess an extreme interest, but can only be correctly judged after more extended inquiries."[13]

Ethnology and phrenology were gaining so much popularity because of their importance in justifying conquest by making it appear that civilization and subjugation were two sides of the same coin. As the article on the Egyptian Hall exhibit went on to explain, "The Bosjemans are a branch of the Hottentot race, which separated from the rest long before the establishment of the Europeans in Southern Africa, and took to a wandering life in the northern and more inland parts of the country. They are now beginning to be surrounded by civilization; and, consequently, they must either become civilized themselves or become extinct."[14] An article in the May 18, 1847, *Times of London* on the same exhibition noted that the Africans were "in appearance little above the monkey tribe and scarcely better than mere brutes of the field . . . mere animals in propensity and worse than animals in appearance." Ethnology was one arm of imperial racial "science" that sought to assign, rank, and evaluate physical characteristics. Thus, all descriptions of imperial exhibits included detailed descriptions of the hair texture, skin color, and skull size of the captured. These descriptions were always done with the intent of ascertaining how far the exhibited deviated from the European "norm" and thus how low they ranked in civilization. Thus, the description of the aforementioned exhibit of the so-called Bushmen concluded by noting, "Altogether this is an exhibition of unusual interest and value. The first effect, on entering the room, may be repulsive; but, the attentive visitor soon overcomes this feeling, and sees in the benighted beings before him a fine subject for scientific investigation, as well as a scene for popular gratification, and rational curiosity."[15] The author went on to specifically reference the "racial logic" that underwrote the exhibition by contrasting the superiority of the white exhibitor and the Africans he exhibited: "It was strange, too, in looking through one of the windows of the room into the busy street, to reflect that by a single turn of the head might be witnessed the two extremes of humanity—the lowest and highest of the race—the wandering savage, and the silken baron of civilization. The portrait of the background of the sketch, we should add, is that of the gentleman under whose care the Bosjemans have been brought from the native country to form one of our metropolitan sights."[16]

Ethnographic showcases not only encouraged viewers to revel in their racial superiority; they also invited ordinary English people to imagine themselves as colonial overlords. The periodical *Household Words*, for example, ran an article that encouraged prospective immigrants to the cape to visit an ethnographic exhibition as a way of imagining running a farm or large estate in the Cape Colony with dozens of African laborers at their command.

> Just go and look at the wagon exhibited by Cumming in his South African Exhibition at Hyde Park Corner! Imagine such a machine, with twelve or fourteen oxen attached to it by a long rope of plaited hide (called a treck-tow) attached to the pole, and to which are fastened the yokes of the oxen. Then a fancy little Hottentot lad, very much like one of the Bushmen lately exhibited in London (but, perhaps, hardly so handsome) leading the two front oxen by a strip of hide fastened to their horns (called a reim) and a full grown Hottentot seated on the driving seat, in the front of the wagon, with an enormous whip in his hands. . . . Your Hottentots soon collect fuel, the wagon is drawn up close by a mimosa or some other bush, a fire is lighted, the kettle set up to boil, the coffee prepared, the steaks cooked in a frying pan, and perhaps some hot cakes made of meal baked for you.[17]

Thus, the popularity of ethnographic showcases and the progress of the British Empire were always closely linked. Ethnographic exhibitions, alongside travel and evangelical texts, were key means whereby images of empire became a part of the English people's everyday reality.[18] According to Veit Erlmann, ethnographic showcases incited a sort of "spectatorial lust," through which "empire and unreality [came to] constitute each other in ways rooted in the deepest layers of modern consciousness."[19]

The Production of Reality Effects in the Ethnographic Showcase

A cursory glance through advertisements for ethnographic exhibitions demonstrates the degree to which these showcases produced meanings in the public sphere that, although they claimed to convey the real, were far more concerned with repressing the real in favor of the pursuit of verisimilitude. The *Illustrated London News*, for example, reported, "the Zulus must be naturally good actors; for a performance more natural and less like acting is seldom if ever seen upon any stage."[20] Earlier, in an article on the Bushmen at Egyptian Hall, the *Illustrated London News* noted that one particular member of the exhibition "would make a capital melodramatic actor."[21]

The extent to which exhibitors manipulated reality in order to put on an entertaining show led missionary David Livingstone to complain that "the Bushmen specimens brought to Europe have been selected, like costermongers' dogs, on account of their extreme ugliness; consequently English ideas of the whole tribe are formed in the same way as if the ugliest specimens of the English were exhibited in Africa as characteristic of the entire British nation."[22] It was precisely the privileging of verisimilitude that made many evangelicals (who prided themselves on the authenticity of the representations of Africans) see these showcases as inimical to their aims, despite the fact that the entertainment industry relied upon, and oftentimes praised, their work.

Lectures from evangelical itinerants like Robert Moffatt and David Livingstone drew extremely large crowds of supporters, particularly from the middle classes, who eagerly assembled at mission halls and public theaters to be entertained by tales of adventure from Calcutta to the cape coast. For example, upon his return from South Africa, missionary Robert Moffat was so in demand that he "was hurried from town to town with scant opportunity for a moments rest."[23] When David Livingstone toured England in 1857, there was an "anxiety on the part of all classes to see and hear him."[24] When missionaries returned with African or Asian converts, they were even more enthusiastically received. In 1837, missionaries John Philip and John Read toured England accompanied by John Tzatzoe and Andreas Stoffles, two "native Christians" from South Africa. "On one occasion the two Africans were invited to spend an evening with the students at Highbury College—vivid recollections of which remain in many minds."[25]

Although ethnographic showcases afforded people of all classes a glimpse at what the *Illustrated London News* called "savages engaged in the pursuits of their everyday life," class politics provided a set of rules about "looking."[26] For the most part, the wealthy were the privileged subjects who took part in this new synthesis of knowledge and power. The extent to which the upper classes—dowagers, belles, and gentlemen—were the privileged viewing subjects is aptly demonstrated in the following satiric poem, entitled "Thoughts on the Savage Lions of London," which appeared in *Punch* magazine.

> Kaffirs from Borioboola, or somewhere—
>   There are delighting the civilized world Belles from
> Belgravia in afternoons come there;
>   Thither the fairest of May-fair are whirl'd.
> Dowagers craving for something exciting,
>   Gentlemen blasé with Fashion's dull round,
> Those who find novelty always delighting,
>   With those dear Kaffirs may daily be found.[27]

The poem can be seen as simultaneously explaining popular attitudes toward these exhibitions and providing a guide for the attitude the well-heeled should adopt. The opening line of the poem immediately establishes the propriety of adopting an attitude of studied indifference to the particulars of what one is viewing. However, the extensive press coverage of the Kaffir Wars in South Africa, the existence of numerous ethnographic exhibitions such as the one described, and the frequent public lectures by returned missionaries made it highly unlikely that the average person — particularly if they were wealthy and well educated — would *not* know where the so-called Kaffirs hailed from. The poem underscores that, ultimately; the particulars of where these black bodies came from and how they happened to end up in England is unimportant. They could have been from South Africa, West Africa, or even the fictitious Borioboola — what really matters is that they have been brought to Europe, incorporated into its theatrical machinery, and rendered up as objects to be viewed with "delight" by the "civilized world."

Paradoxically, this studied attitude of indifference to particularity — especially the particularity of individual African lives — had, as its concomitant, a cultural obsession with ethnographic detail, which produced the effect of direct and immediate experience with Africa. As Strother explains, the exhibitors self-consciously sought to "solicit the attendance of the well-educated, those familiar with travelogues," as part of their publicity strategy.[28] Indeed, even a cursory glance through the publicity literature of the time demonstrates the degree to which ethnographic showcases were intimately linked to the travel and evangelical writings explored in the previous chapter. An exhibition of five "Bushmen" at Exeter Hall, for example, was accompanied by a lecture from Robert Knox, an army surgeon who spent five years on the South African frontier, that was advertised as being particularly addressed to those interested in "the Kaffir war, in the great question of race, and the probable extinction of the Aboriginal races, the progress of the Anglo-African empire, and the all-important questions of Christian mission and human civilization in that quarter of the globe."[29]

Subjects and Objects in the Ethnographic Showcase

How do we account for this curious paradox whereby the viewing subjects were expected to be familiar with ethnographic detail yet adopt a studied attitude of indifference about particularity? It turns out that this paradox actually can tell us quite a lot about what Mitchell terms "a method of order and truth essential to the peculiar nature of the modern world."[30] The ways in which ethnographic showcases ordered and presented the other demanded the viewing subject adopt certain attitudes — both to the world and to him or herself. First, that they be "curious" about the world in a very particular way — in such a way as to "contemplate" Africa and

Africans, even as they turned away, to immerse oneself and yet still stand apart. "The curiosity of the observing subject was something demanded by a diversity of mechanisms for rendering things up as its object."[31] This mode of addressing objects in the world inculcated a particular way of viewing the world and the individual's relationship to it. "Ordinary people were beginning to live as tourists or anthropologists, addressing the object world as the endless representation of some further meaning or reality."[32] Thus, the world itself came to be "conceived and grasped as though it was an exhibition."[33]

Ethnographic showcases were a means of engineering the real, whereby everything came to be organized, like in an exhibition, to recall some larger meaning beyond it. This attitude toward the world, in turn, engendered a particular conception of and about reality. As Mitchell explains, reality came to take on a "citationary nature" whereby what is represented is, "not a real place, but a set of references, a congeries of characteristics, that seems to have its origin in a quotation, or a fragment of a text, or a citation from someone's work . . . or some bit of previous imagining or an amalgam of all these . . . it is the chain of references that produces the effect of the place."[34] The world, like the exhibit, came to be nothing more than a collection of objects that recalled a meaning beyond reality. In other words, the "characteristic cognitive move of the modern subject" was to transfer onto objects "the principles of one's relation to [them]" and to conceive of them as "totally intended for cognition alone."[35]

The Exhibited Speak Back
The Contradictions of the Cash Nexus

The men who ran the ethnological exhibits faced a curious paradox. The express purpose of their exhibits was to depict Africans as perpetual primitives who were doomed to remain mired in their own barbarism absent the benevolence of British explorers and missionaries. The showmen were traffickers in human difference; the more graphic and shocking the difference, the more profitable the show. However, they wanted exhibits to appear as not purely exploitative. As early as 1810, at the time of the exhibition of Saartjie Baartman, the "Hottentot Venus," exhibitors had come under legal and moral scrutiny. The African Association for Promoting the Discovery of the Interior of Africa sued Baartman's captor and exhibitor, Henrik Cezar, on her behalf. As Zachary Macauley stated in the affidavit filed on her behalf, his purpose was to determine "whether [Baartman] was made a public spectacle with her own free will and consent or whether she was compelled to exhibit herself."[36] Those who were opposed to her exhibition debated less about whether her confinement represented a moral blight than whether she was owned by someone else, and hence subject to forced exhibition, or if she belonged to herself, and was thus acting freely. The *Report of the King's Bench* reported, "the decency of the exhibition was not brought into question; it appearing that the woman had proper clothing adapted to the occasion."[37] Rather, the case turned on whether "she had been clandestinely inveigled from the Cape of Good Hope, without the knowledge of the British Governor, (who extends his peculiar protection in nature of a guardian over the Hottentot nation under his government, by reason of their general imbecile state) and that she was brought to this country and since kept in custody and exhibited here against her consent."[38] The debate over the abolition of slavery provided the critical backdrop to the court case as the *London Morning Chronicle* of October 12, 1810, reported: "The air of the British Constitution is too pure to permit slavery in the very heart of the metropolis, for I am sure you will easily discriminate between those beings who are sufficiently degraded to show themselves for their own immediate profit where they act from their own free will and this poor slave."

Thus, the proprietors of ethnographic showcases were always quick to stress that the exhibited individuals were doing so of their own accord, that all transactions had the blessing and consent of the colonial authorities, and that the terms were favorable for all. For example, the exhibit at Egyptian Hall was described in these positive terms: "The curious creatures at the Egyptian Hall are grouped upon a raised stage at one end of the large room; with a flat scene, set vegetation, handing wood and etc. from the country of the Bushmen, cleverly painted and arranged by Mr. Johnstone. . . . The mother sat nursing her bantling; and the other men sat smoking at the opposite corner. . . . The mother occasionally left her child to receive money from the spectators, and kissed with fervour the donor's hand. The man, too, gratefully received a cigar, but did not leave off smoking his hemp-seed to enjoy the higher flavoured luxury."[39] The May 28, 1853, edition of the *Illustrated London News* reported this:

These Kaffirs (twelve in number) have been brought from Natal by Mr. A. T. Caldecott, who, for this purpose, memorialized the colonial authorities at Natal for permission to ship the natives; which application was complied with, on Mr. Caldecott having entered into a recognizance, himself in the sum of £500, and two sureties in £250 each, that such natives were willing to accompany him to England and would be properly treated on the voyage, duly reported and, if required, produced to the Secretary of State for the Colonies, and finally brought back to Durban. And the natives were further, previous to their embarking, taken before the diplomatic agent to testify their full and voluntary concurrence.[40]

Three years earlier, the September 14, 1850, edition of the paper had taken care to assure readers that the "Kaffir man," "Amaponda woman," and "Zoolu [sic] chief" who were being exhibited at Cosmorama, Regent Street, had been "brought to this country by Mr. Cawood, subject to a bargain made with them before leaving the Cape, with the consent of Sir Harry Smith, the Governor, and their chief. The agreement is for two years. Their behavior, since their arrival, has been unexceptional; they seem pleased with the change, and enjoy English living, giving preference to mutton as food."[41]

The lopsided nature of these "agreements" did not escape the notice of the editors of the satirical magazine, *Punch*, which ran a story called "An Affair with the (Knightsbridge) Caffres" in its October 8, 1853, edition. The story takes a wry look at what might happen if the exhibited took it upon themselves to strike out on their own as showmen, absent the "help" of European agents or intermediaries.

We thought we had heard enough of the rows with the Caffres at the Cape; but there have lately been some Caffres cutting the oddest capers at Hyde Park corner. It seems that a noble Caffre chieftain had entered into an agreement for himself and a few of his tribe to howl, leap, brandish tomahawks, and indulge in other outlandish freaks, coming under the head of native customs for a year and a half, during which period the howlings, tomahawkings, &c., are to be the exclusive property of an individual who has speculated on the appetite of the British public for yells and wild antics. . . . The Chief was seized with a generous desire to make a gratuitous exhibition of himself and, accordingly, NKULOOCOLLO — as the chief calls himself — took a turn in the Park on Thursday with four of his fellow countrymen.

The proprietor of the yells and native dances, fearful that the gilt would be taken of the gingerbread complexions of the Caffres if their faces were made familiar to the public in Hyde Park, sent a policeman to take the chief into custody. NKULOOCOLLO, however, who seems to take the thing coolly as well as cavalierly — or Caffrely — refused to walk in, but stood outside the door, rendering it hopeless than anybody would pay a half crown to "walk up," when the chief was to be seen "alive, alive" for nothing at the threshold. The proprietor endeavoured to push the chief inside, but the chief gave a counter-push. There seemed to be a probability of a war-whoop being got up at the expense, rather than for the benefit of the enterprising individual who engaged the whoopers. . . . Upon this the chief was taken into custody and charged with an assault. . . . The complaint, was, however, most properly told by the Magistrate that the Caffres cannot, by law, be restrained from going wherever they please. . . . If a Caffre chooses to take a walk in the park, or anywhere else, he has a perfect right to do so, if he does not break the law by tomahawking the public or any other "native" eccentricity.[42]

The point of the ethnographic exhibit was to reinforce the idea that "geographic distance across space [can be] figured as a historical difference across time," and, further, that "imperial progress across the space of empire is . . . a journey backward in time to an anachronistic moment of prehistory."[43] The Africans exhibited at Cosmorama, Regent Street, for example, were described thus: "In common with most Africans, they have no notion of time, cannot tell their own age, or fix a date for any recent event in their lives."[44]

However, the seamlessness of this narrative was continually interrupted by the exigencies of exhibiting, which required that Africans be recognized as what Johannes Fabian calls "coevals." Fabian uses the term "denial of coevalness" to describe the difficulties that arise when anthropologists must use evidence gleaned from "native informants" to make legitimate their claims that Indigenous people inhabit not only a different geographic space, but also a different temporal zone.

> As a discipline of practices of making and representing knowledge, anthropology is marked by a contradiction. Anthropology has its foundation in ethnographic research, inquiries which even hard nosed practitioners . . . carry out with communicative interaction. The sharing of time that such interaction requires demands that ethnographers recognize the people whom they study as their coevals. However, and this is where the contradiction arises—when the same ethnographers represent their knowledge in teaching and writing they do this in terms of a discourse that consistently places those who are talked about in a time other than that of the one who talks. I call the effect of such strategies the 'denial of coevalness'.[45]

Thus, the same article that described the exhibited Africans as having no sense of time also admitted, "the Kaffir, Bourzaquai, is quickest of apprehension and has already picked up some words of English."[46] Georges Cuvier, the same scientist who described Saartjie Baartman as looking and acting like a monkey, also had to admit in the *Discours sur les Revolutions du Globe* that "she spoke tolerably good Dutch, which she learned at the Cape . . . also knew a little English . . . [and] was beginning to say a few words of French."[47]

The Contradictions of Coevalness

The tensions introduced into European narratives by the contradictions of coevalness thus provide a space for us to retrieve and reconstruct African voices and opinions—about European society, European religion, colonialism, and conquest that differed markedly from the narratives presented by the English. For example, one thing that becomes immediately apparent in these descriptions is the degree to which the purveyors of the shows, despite their repeated assurances that the Africans in their midst were happy and content, were continually confronted with evidence of their captives' dissatisfaction. The article about the "Bosjemans at the Egyptian Hall, Piccadilly," for example, after describing the exhibited as "grateful," went on to observe, "During our visit, the party went through a variety of performances illustrative of their customs in their native country. Their whoops were sometimes startling. They seemed more than once to consider the attentions of a spectator as an affront, and were only stayed by their attendant from resentment."[48] Three decades earlier, the affidavits filed in the Saartjie Baartman case likewise indicated that there were "apparent indications of reluctance on her part during her exhibition."[49] The affidavit of Mr. McCartney, the Secretary of the African Association, which sued her captors on her behalf, reported that Baartman "frequently heaved deep sighs, seemed anxious and uneasy, and grew sullen when she was ordered to play some rude instrument of music."[50]

Ota Benga along with a troupe of his fellow Batwa from the Congo were put on display at the 1904 St. Louis World's Fair and later in the Bronx Zoo. Although their captors had described them as happy and satisfied upon their arrival, the July 19, 1904, edition of the *St. Louis Dispatch* soon carried the shocked headline "Enraged Pygmies Attack Visitor": "The African pygmies of the Fair took to the warpath late yesterday because a visitor took a photograph of one of them and would not indemnify them to the extent that they deemed meet. They gave the photographer a scare he will remember. . . . They attacked him and were handling him roughly and were attempting to take everything he had away from him when whit men rescued him." Two years later, the *New York Daily Tribune* of September 26, 1906, reported, "Ota Benga, the pygmy at the New York Zoological Gardens, the Bronx, made a desperate attempt to kill one of the keepers yesterday afternoon with a knife."

The refusal to speak was yet another powerful method of resistance. Captured warriors were particularly likely to use silence as a way of maintaining their dignity in the midst of extremely dehumanizing conditions. The *Illustrated London News* described how Nonsenzo, one of the Zulu warriors exhibited at St. George's Gallery, Knightsbridge, refused to engage his captors: "He stands six feet without shoes, and is a very powerful man. He has a violent temper if excited. He left his country nine months ago. He talks little. Though he appears to be a man who has seen and done much in his time, he will never speak of his past life."[51] That same year, the February 15 edition of the paper described how another group of subjects "sat quietly smoking and laughing while our correspondent sketched them. . . . Their deportment was easy and unconstrained, and they seemed to place considerable confidence in their European captors, although they were firm in refusing to give any information calculated to injure the cause of their country."[52] Likewise, the *St. Louis Dispatch* of August 13, 1904, reported the following about the Anthropological Athletic Meet: "Thirteen different tribes were represented in the second Anthropological athletic meet at the Stadium Friday afternoon. All the contestants performed in their native costumes. . . . Geronimo, the old Apache chief, was on the field but took no part in the sports. He leaned silently against the track-rail looking on but gave no other sign that he was at all interested."

When individuals who were treated as objects within the purview of the ethnographic showcase were able to master English, it had a transformative effect. They were heard and their opinions were taken much more seriously. For example, Martinus and Flora, two "Earthmen" from South Africa, distinguished themselves by performing in English—having learned the language when they lived with a British family. As Lindfors explains, "audiences were most impressed by their mastery of a 'civilized' tongue. One provincial paper reported that 'the most interesting part of the séance is found to consist in the spritely conversation they carry on with their visitors.'"[53] The English were often shocked to find that Africans and Native Americans held less positive feelings about them. The chief of the Ojibwes, who were exhibited in London, declined the efforts of the London City Missions missionaries to convert them because of the poverty and distress they had witnessed in London.

> When we first came over to this country, we thought we should find the white people all good and sober people, but as we travel about we find this was all a mistake. . . . We see hundreds of little children with their naked feet in the snow, and we pity them, for we know that they are hungry, and we give them money every time we pass by them. In four days, we have given twenty dollars to hungry children—we give our money only to children. We are told that the fathers of these children are in ale-houses where they sell fire-water, and are drunk. . . . You talk about sending black coats among the Indians. Now we have no such poor children among us. We have no such drunkards or people who abuse the Great Spirit.[54]

In the early 1890s a troupe of South African singers toured London. Although not part of an ethnographic showcase, per se, they were required to dress in traditional African attire, even though they were mission educated and did not dress in this way at home. The *Christian Express* of November 2, 1891, complained, "one thing we do regret, the adoption, almost exclusively on the stage, of the old barbarian dress none of them ever wore at home." Thus, the conventions of the ethnographic showcase strongly informed how their managers staged their shows. For example, even though the choir members were described as having come to the group already speaking English and Dutch, with one young woman conversant in five languages, the *Ludgate Monthly* still described their achievements as inauthentic, arguing that "Kaffirs are very fond of mimicry, and are always ready to pick up anything to imitate."[55]

Further, the missionaries who arranged the European tour and brought the group together saw themselves as having the right to exert absolute and complete control over the singers, their lives, their destinies, and their identities. Mr. Letty, who organized the group, was quoted as saying, "We had plenty of applications, but had to be very careful in the selection. We wanted representatives of the principal southern tribes, people with good moral characters, good education, good musical ability, and as far as possible good looking as well."[56] A female member of the choir expressed sentiments at odds with her white benefactors when she was asked what she would like to say to the English people "on behalf of her race," she agreed that her ultimate goal was to build a school for Africans in South Africa. However, her vision of what that school would do and the role it would play in African lives was very different from that of most missionaries, who saw education as serving to further integrate Africans into European society and commerce (often in a position of near permanent inferiority). She saw schools as providing the foundation for Africans' social and economic independence: "Help us to found the schools for which we pray, where our people could learn to labour, to build, and to acquire your skill with their hands. Then could we be sufficient unto ourselves. Our young men would build us houses and lay out our farms, and our tribes would develop independently of the civilization and industries which you have given us."[57] She went on to echo the Ojibwe chief by disputing one of the most fundamental tenets of missionary ideology and the civilizing mission—mainly that the Europeans had been an unequivocally positive influence on African culture by requesting that the English "shut up the canteens and take away the drink." She also made an indirect reference to the hypocrisy of British colonialism when she asked, "can you not make your people at the Cape as kind and just as your people are here? That is the first thing and the greatest."[58]

The Return of the Look

In her book *Black Body*, Radhika Mohanram makes the important point that there is a "metonymic link" between surveillance and knowledge: "If knowledge formation is Panoptic in structure—the discipline which comes with being always visible—so also is colonial identity predicated on vision. Within the structure of surveillance the one who sees is invisible, but the one who is seen, the colonized in this case, is always subject to scrutiny."[59]

The complex power dynamics that surrounded the phenomena of looking, observing, and critically evaluating are aptly expressed by bell hooks, who writes, "To be fully an object then was to lack the capacity to see or recognize reality. These looking relations were reinforced as whites cultivated the practice of denying the subjectivity of blacks (the better to dehumanize and oppress), of relegating them to the realm of the invisible. . . . To look directly was an assertion of subjectivity, equality."[60] Aptly capturing the arrogance of the white subject in the face of the "return of the look," hooks writes, "Racist thinking perpetuates the fantasy that the Other who is subjugated, who is subhuman, lacks the ability to comprehend, to understand, to see the working of the powerful. . . . In white supremacist society, white people can 'safely' imagine that they are invisible to black people since the power they have historically asserted, and even now collectively assert over black people, accorded them the right to control the black gaze."[61]

Despite the fact that the power relations, which had adhered in the ethnographic showcase, dictated that the Indigenous people take on the role of silenced objects, subject to the whims of the European spectator, they found ways to refuse this dehumanizing role. Those denied the opportunity to express themselves verbally used their bodies, facial expressions, and other nonverbal forms of communication to show that they were sentient beings who knew how humiliating their circumstance was and who wished to live differently. Those who mastered the language and mores of English society were more direct. They challenged the supremacy of English culture and values. They demonstrated their awareness of the shortcomings of English society. And they, like their silenced brethren, insisted on the necessity of independence and self-determination. Others chose the path of silence—showing their displeasure through a deliberate refusal to engage. And still others, like Ota Benga, chose death. Ten years after his arrival in America, Benga committed suicide in Lynchburg, Virginia.[62] Appearing shortly after Benga's death, an article in the July 16, 1916, edition of the *New York Times* explained, "Finally the burden of the white man's civilization became too great for him to bear, and he sent a bullet through his heart. . . . [H]e was one of the most determined little fellows that ever breathed . . . a shred little man who preferred to match himself against civilization rather than be a slave."

Notes

1. Gossip, *Athenaeum*, May 1853, 650.

2. Anne Fausto-Sterling, "Gender, Race, and Nation: The Comparative Anatomy of 'Hottentot' Women in Europe, 1815–1817," in *Deviant Bodies*, ed. Jennifer Terry and Jacqueline Urlan (Bloomington: Indiana University Press, 1995), 32.

3. *Kaffir* is an Arabic term meaning *infidel* and became a term of racial abuse similar to *nigger* in the American vernacular.

4. "The Zulu Kaffirs at the St. George's Gallery, Knightsbridge," *Illustrated London News*, May 28, 1853.

5. *Illustrated London News*, June 12, 1847, 381.

6. *Illustrated London News*, September 14, 1859, 236.

7. *Illustrated London News*, May 28, 1853, 410.

8. Bernard Magubane, *The Political Economy of Race and Class in South Africa* (New York: Monthly Review Press, 1979), 38.

9. *Illustrated London News*, September 14, 1850, 236.

10. *Illustrated London News*, May 28, 1853, 410.

11. "The Ojibbeway Indians at Manchester," *Phrenological Journal* 78 (1844): 210.

12. *Illustrated London News*, June 12, 1847, 381.

13. *Proceedings of the Academy of Natural Sciences of Philadelphia* 4 (1848): 5–6.

14. *Illustrated London News*, June 12, 1847, 381.

15. *Illustrated London News*, June 12, 1847, 381.

16. *Illustrated London News*, June 12, 1847, 381.

17. Charles Dickens, "Cape Sketches," *Household Words* 1 (1850): 58–59.

18. Raymond Corbey, "Ethnographic Showcases, 1870–1930," in *The Decolonization of Imagination*, ed. Jan N. Pieterse and Bhikhu Parekh (London: Zed Books, 1995).

19. Veit Erlmann, "Spectatorial Lust: The African Choir in England," in *Africans on Stage: Studies in Ethnological Show Business*, ed. Bernth Lindfors (Bloomington: University of Indiana Press, 1999), 110.

20. *Illustrated London News*, May 28, 1853, 410.

21. *Illustrated London News*, June 12, 1847, 381.

22. David Livingstone, *Missionary Travels and Researches in South Africa* (New York: Johnson Reprint Company, 1858), 49.

23. Robert Moffatt, *The Lives of Robert and Mary Moffatt* (London: T. Fischer Unwin, 1885), 223.

24. Adam Sedgwick and William Monk, ed. *Dr. Livingstone's Cambridge Lectures* (London: Bell and Daldy, 1858), 25.

25. Thomas Aveling, *The Missionary Souvenir* (London: Paternoster Row, 1850), 126.

26. *Illustrated London News*, May 28, 1853, 410.

27. A Friend and a Brother, "Thoughts on the Savage Lions of London," *Punch*, July 23, 1853, 38.

28. Z. S. Strother, "Display of the Body Hottentot," in Lindfors, *Africans on Stage*, 25.

29. *Athenaeum*, May 1847, 33.

30. Timothy Mitchell, "World as Exhibition," *Comparative Studies in Society and History* 31 (1989): 236.

31. Mitchell, "World as Exhibition," 219.

32. Mitchell, "World as Exhibition," 232.

33. Mitchell, "World as Exhibition," 222.

34. Mitchell, "World as Exhibition," 235.

35. Mitchell, "World as Exhibition," 232.

36. Strother, "Display of the Body Hottentot," 43.

37. Edward Hyde East, *Report of Cases Argued and Determined in the Court of the King's Bench* (London: Steven and Sons, 1910), 104:344.

38. East, *Report of Cases*, 344.

39. *Illustrated London News*, June 12, 1847, 381.

40. *Illustrated London News*, May 28, 1853, 410.

41. *Illustrated London News*, September 14, 1850, 236.

42. "An Affair with the (Knightsbridge) Caffres," *Punch*, October 8, 1853, 154.

43. Anne McClintock, *Imperial Leather: Race, Gender, and Sexuality in the Colonial Contest* (New York: Routledge, 1995), 40.

44. *Illustrated London News*, September 14, 1850, 236.

45. Johannes Fabian, "The Other Revisited: Critical Afterthoughts," *Anthropological Theory* 6 (2006): 143.

46. *Illustrated London News*, September 14, 1850, 236.

47. Tracey Denean Sharpley-Whiting, *Sexualized Savages, Primal Fears, and Primitive Narratives in French* (Durham NC: Duke University Press, 1999), 24.

48. *Illustrated London News*, June 12, 1847, 381.

49. East, *Report of Cases*, 345.

50. East, *Report of Cases*, 345.

51. *Illustrated London News*, May 28, 1853, 410.

52. *Illustrated London News*, February 15, 1853, 90.

53. Bernth Lindfors, "Hottentot, Bushman, Kaffir: Taxonomic Tendencies in 19th Century Racial Taxonomy," *Nordic Journal of African Studies* 5 (1996): 15.

54. R. W. Vanderkiste, *Notes and Narratives of Six Years Mission, Principally among the Dens of London* (London: James Nisbet, 1852), 118–19.

55. E. Scopes, "The Music of Africa," *Ludgate Monthly* 2 (1891): 111.

56. Scopes, "Music of Africa," 109.

57. "Native Choristers from South Africa," *Review of Reviews* 4 (1891): 256.

58. "Native Choristers from South Africa," 256.

59. Radhika Mohanram, *Black Body: Women, Colonialism, Space* (Minneapolis: University of Minnesota Press, 1999), 67.

60. bell hooks, *Black Looks: Race and Representation* (Boston: South End Press, 1992), 168.

61. hooks, *Black Looks*, 168.

62. Phillips Verner Bradford and Harvey Blume, *Ota Benga: The Pygmy in the Zoo* (New York: St. Martin's Press, 1992).

3

Reinventing George Heye

*Nationalizing the Museum of the
American Indian and Its Collections*

ANN MCMULLEN

Nothing but Stories

The year 2004 was important for the Smithsonian Institution's National Museum of the American Indian (NMAI). For many, NMAI's opening on Washington DC's National Mall marked the fulfillment of overdue obligations and long-awaited dreams. Few recognized that 2004 also marked a forgotten anniversary: a century had passed since George Gustav Heye began cataloging the objects in the museum's collection. Press coverage repeatedly mentioned NMAI's roots in New York's Museum of the American Indian but referred to Heye as a "passionate," "obsessive," and "rapacious" collector and a "buccaneer." Directly or indirectly responsible for removing treasured objects from Native hands or lands, Heye's contributions could hardly be commemorated. However, Mr. Richard Kessler noticed this treatment and addressed himself to the *Washington Post*: "The Smithsonian is ignoring and . . . demeaning the contribution of its chief benefactor. . . . Mr. Heye, whom *The Post* disdainfully called a 'boxcar' collector, . . . contributed his entire collection for public use and exhibition. . . . But for his 'boxcar' collection, we'd have no Museum of the American Indian today. . . . It is high time for the ingrates in charge of this museum . . . to acknowledge and credit their benefactor." It is doubtful that NMAI staff members would have disagreed with Kessler's remarks, because the image of Heye portrayed by the press was delivered to reporters in their NMAI press kits.[1]

Few at the NMAI think or speak about Heye except to repeat similar second- and thirdhand anecdotes and sound bites that are learned by watching and emulating others. As Thomas King suggests in *The Truth about Stories: A Native Narrative*, "The truth about stories is that that's all we are."[2] And like any mythology, stories told about Heye have grown over generations, and their roots are often shadowed or unknown. As defined by Eric Hobsbawm, this is the stuff of invented traditions, those "invented, constructed and formally instituted . . . within a brief and dateable period."[3]

Here I explore the invention of George Heye and how his image has been shaped by NMAI's need to serve a different mission than Heye himself espoused. Because NMAI simultaneously holds part of the national collections and supports Native empowerment, explicating Heye's collection involves both U.S. and Indigenous nationalism and generates interesting rhetoric.

Regarding rhetoric—the persuasive use of language—others have used the same texts I employ here to support very different interpretations of George Heye. Ideas for this essay arose during my work on NMAI's collections planning documents.[4] Struck by NMAI rhetoric about Heye, I sought alternative background materials. At first I only hoped to understand Heye's transition from collector to museum founder but was caught up in uncovering a very different story. At this point, I make no claim to exhaustive research on George Heye and his intent; but given readily available material that contradicts prevailing NMAI stories, I suggest that those who have described Heye only as an obsessive and even nefarious collector have done so based on their own preconceptions or disregard for contradictory evidence. Nonetheless, while I believe George Heye's story is more complex and more honorable than how it has been told, I doubt my version will totally rehabilitate him. He was—like anyone—a man of his time. However, for the NMAI, he remains an inconvenient truth and has become a victim of its self-told history.

There is more to this than simply correcting Heye's biography. While discussing this essay with a group of coworkers, I explained Heye's intent in creating his museum. Among the dissonant voices, I heard a Pawnee man who escorts Native and non-Native collections researchers say, "What do you mean? I thought he was just a crazy white man—*that's what we tell everybody!*" He realized that labeling George Heye as an obsessive collector who accumulated objects solely to own them also dehistoricized the collections and implied that they grew randomly. He recognized that NMAI could—and should—take responsibility for understanding Heye's motivations and how the collection was formed.

Investigation of collectors and their impact on museums—including how collections were assembled, how collectors have shaped what is preserved in museums, and how collections can be integral to knowledge projects—is not a new subject. Susan Pearce and James Clifford suggest that we cannot let our interest in objects and collections obscure the histories of how they were accumulated since this is part of the deeper history of museums and colonialism.[5]

There is no single path to understanding connections between collecting and museums. Much scholarship has focused on large-scale, individual collectors; but George Stocking rightly suggests that we examine their lives in the context of wealth, since objects represent wealth and making collections implies possession of the resources needed for their care, maintenance, and display.[6] The names and biographies of collectors who epitomize this—Hearst, Horniman, and Pitt Rivers—are reasonably familiar. However, the attention paid to individual collectors—whether personal or scholarly—has been rather unequal, with more attention paid to individuals who collected for their own purposes rather than research. Far less notice has been given to collectors working in service to anthropology and how their work affects what museums hold today. This imbalance is somewhat contradictory, since Anthony Shelton suggests that museums prefer systematic collectors—those focused on the increase of collective knowledge—and that other collectors often disappear in museums' self-representations. Shelton and Clifford suggest that this results from the perception that these good, controlled, systematic collectors seem rational while the others—whose intents are less transparent—are cast as obsessive or inscrutable.[7]

For many, collectors—especially those of the impassioned variety—are a kind of stereotype. Jean Baudrillard, in particular, suggests that collectors are incomplete human beings who create an alternate reality through their collections. Others focus on the guilty and almost sexual pleasure collectors take in acquiring things and arranging, handling, or even fondling them.[8] Altogether, this emotional involvement with objects seems at odds with museums' scholarly objectivity, so we should not be surprised that museums often shy away from delving too deeply into collectors' motivations. However, because these collections carry their own intellectual burdens, we need to unpack the collectors' agendas rather than hiding them behind those of museums themselves.

In studying collectors and collections, Susan Pearce suggests that collectors' assemblages can be characterized as souvenirs, fetish objects, and systematic collections; but this is based largely on contemporary collectors. In contradiction, Brian Durrans notes that we should not assume that we can confidently understand the motivations of colonial and modern Euro-American collectors, because concepts like self, other, identity, scientist, and collector have shifted over time. He further suggests that nineteenth-century collectors' cognitive and conceptual distance from us (as modern-day analysts) may be as great as that between them and the people from whom they collected and that—from our own viewpoint—collectors may be a kind of "Other."[9]

Durrans's argument encourages reexamination of collectors who are perceived as irrational or obsessive and reinterpretation of their collections. Often, those of us who study such collections view them as small slices of reality and compare them to our own, presumably broader, cultural conceptions. However, Chris Gosden and Chantal Knowles, discussing collecting in Melanesia, suggest that we examine collections not as partial records but instead as "complete, although particular, outcomes of individual sets of colonial practices."[10] This should remind us that any individual's collection may represent a complete image of what that collector envisioned and that identifying that imagined whole is primary to understanding the collector.

Altogether, this means that studying collectors and their collections is about more than biography. To understand collectors' legacies, we must understand what they intended to create, how they did it, and what they said and recorded about their collections. At the same time, we must also examine museums' motives and intents and how they have made use of collections for their own purposes, even when the museums' purposes are vastly different than those of collectors themselves.

Museums, Colonialism, Anthropology, and the Primacy of Objects

Much has been said about museums and colonialism, but the subject deserves some brief repetition here. Early European museums focused more on nature and antiquity, but works by non-Western people, who were encountered during exploration and conquest, soon followed. Later public museums, and how they ordered and explained "curiosities," helped create ways of thinking about people represented by objects. With collections swelled by military souvenirs, museums vacillated between representing others, colonial and imperial rule, and Western hegemony.[11] Museums and their ideological cousins—world's fairs and Wild West shows—brought the world to visitors for consumption. Museums offered concrete representations of travel writing, presenting panoptic views of time and geography that could be comprehended as they were traversed. While world's fairs offered synchronic views, museums were seen as representing the past.[12]

The anthropology that grew up in museums was equally predicated on the past; and by creating the "ethnographic present," it temporally distanced Indigenous people from colonizers and museum visitors. Salvage anthropology and primitive art collecting irrevocably placed Indigenous objects in museums, where they were preserved and used to create images of the vanquished.[13] Because Native works did not fit art museums' focus on high culture, anthropology museums helped make Native cultures accessible to the public; but, for some, museums represented "the final ugly and unadorned edge of Manifest Destiny."[14] Collecting by individuals and museums prolonged colonial patterns and cultivated nostalgia for the lost past. Museums' disregard for Native arts made for sale fostered images of unchanging Native people and made the museum "a shrine to the premodern."[15]

While anthropology shed its dependence on objects along with its museum roots, objects remained museums' central focus. They were "real things" fixed in time and worked well as the basis for representation. And because ethnology's focus was on nonliterate peoples, objects became primary texts for understanding Native people. For "prehistory" represented by archaeological collections, this was equally true: the Smithsonian's Otis Tufton Mason states that it was a "story written in things."[16]

It is at this moment in anthropological thinking—the earliest years of the twentieth century—that George Gustav Heye comes on the scene.

Will the Real George Heye Please Stand Up?

First, I should relate facts about George Heye that cannot be contested; everything else can be considered spin, either my own or others. George Gustav Heye was born in 1874 to Carl Friedrich Gustav Heye, a U.S. emigrant from Germany, and Marie Antoinette Lawrence Heye, whose family were longtime New Yorkers. Carl Heye made his money in oil, and George Heye's upbringing was considered privileged. He graduated from Columbia University's School of Mines in 1896 with a degree in electrical engineering. His employer sent him to Arizona in 1897, where he observed the wife of his Navajo foreman chewing her husband's shirt to kill the lice. He said, "I bought the shirt, became interested in aboriginal customs, and acquired other objects as opportunity offered, sending them back home. . . . That shirt was the start of my collection. Naturally when I had a shirt I wanted a rattle and moccasins. And then the collecting bug seized me and I was lost. . . . When I returned to New York . . . I found quite an accumulation of objects . . . and I began to read rather intensively on the subject of the Indians."[17]

From 1901 to 1909 Heye worked in investment banking, which he left to focus on collecting. He had already moved from buying single objects to large collections and had 10,000 objects by 1906, maintaining a catalog on three-by-five-inch cards.[18] He bought collections, sponsored expeditions and publications, and traveled and collected himself. The collection's rapid growth—and its directions—were influenced by Marshall Saville at Columbia and by George Pepper of the American Museum of Natural History (AMNH). By 1908, having filled his apartment and a warehouse, Heye made arrangements with the University of Pennsylvania's University Museum to exhibit his collection but hired his own staff. His mother died in 1915, and he inherited an estimated $10 million. That year, he married his second wife, Thea Page, honeymooning at Georgia's Nacoochee Mound excavations, which he funded with the Bureau of American Ethnology.

In 1916, with the collection totaling 58,000 objects, Heye was offered a building site at 155th and Broadway in New York in a complex of cultural organizations.[19] Supported by affluent friends, the Museum of the American Indian (MAI) was built; and Heye deeded his entire collection to it, endowed the museum, and was named director for life. The museum opened in 1922, and Heye built a professional staff and kept collecting. By 1926 he had filled his museum and built a separate storage facility in the Bronx. However, with the deaths of two major benefactors in 1928, Heye had to dismiss most of his staff. With more than 163,000 objects by 1929, Heye continued purchasing collections assembled by others. At his death in 1957, the collections numbered over 225,000 catalog numbers, representing perhaps 700,000 individual items. These represent approximately 85 percent of the NMAI's current object holdings.[20]

In the Eyes of His Contemporaries: 1957–1960

Heye's official biographer, J. Alden Mason of the University Museum, identifies 1903 as the beginning of Heye's professional work: "Collecting as a hobby was now at an end, and [he] proceeded to fulfill that destiny which the Fates had ordained at his birth . . . the most comprehensive collections of the American Indian in the world." Samuel K. Lothrop, who worked for Heye before departing for Harvard, stresses Heye's contributions: "He occupied a unique place in . . . New World anthropology, because he assembled the largest existing collection representing the aboriginal cultures of this hemisphere. . . . Heye never studied anthropology but . . . was not a dilettante and, by experience in handling the material, he became a connoisseur in many phases of native art. . . . From 1904 onward, he was not satisfied with mere purchases of specimens, but sent out well-financed expeditions."[21] Others, including E. K. Burnett, who worked as Heye's administrator, considered him a collector: "As with all dedicated collectors, George Heye was ruthless in his dealings."[22]

In 1960 Kevin Wallace of the *New Yorker* published a less adulatory piece, largely based on quotes from an anonymous professor who spoke freely and somewhat bitterly: "I doubt . . . his goal was anything more than to own the biggest damned hobby collection in the world. . . . George didn't buy Indian stuff . . . to study the life of a people . . . it never crossed his mind. . . . He bought all those objects solely . . . to own them—for what purpose, he never said. He . . . was fortified by sufficient monomania to build up a superlative, disciplined collection."[23]

As a whole, Heye's friends and contemporaries provided what were probably intended as humorous anecdotes, but ultimately they have been accepted as judgments. Much of what later became legend stems from these anecdotes, including characterization of Heye as "a boxcar collector" with a "genius for being indiscriminate."[24]

The Museum of the American Indian: 1960–1989

Frederick J. Dockstader (Oneida and Navajo) became director of the MAI in 1960 and seldom mentioned Heye. In his *Indian Art of the Americas,* Dockstader simply mentions the excellent collection Heye had assembled. For a book of museum "masterworks," Dockstader reprises Heye's life, noting his "primary desire was . . . to provide a complete picture of Indian life . . . a simple stirring stick was . . . as significant . . . as the most elaborately carved and painted totem pole."[25]

Following Dockstader's dismissal in 1975, the museum tried to increase its visibility with exhibitions at Manhattan's U.S. Customs House; but the self-image it presented was that of a magnificent collection of Native heritage and not George Heye's lifework. In their publications, curators Anna Roosevelt and James Smith ignore Heye. A 1978 article by Vince Wilcox focuses on the collection—"considered by many to be the legacy of a single man and his obsession"—and calls Heye, "first and foremost a collector, not a true scholar . . . the Museum was for him the most expedient method to develop a major collection." Roland Force's *The Heye and the Mighty,* which recounts the MAI's struggle to relocate and the Smithsonian transfer, entitled his chapter on Heye with one word: "Obsession."[26]

The National Museum of the American Indian: 1989–Present

The early years at the NMAI saw little concentration on George Heye. With the opening of New York's George Gustav Heye Center (GGHC), an accompanying book called Heye "the epitome of the obsessive collector," while another suggested that the collection "reflects the monumental—and ultimately unfathomable—desire of George Gustav Heye to possess as many objects as possible."[27] In 1999 Clara Sue Kidwell acknowledged that Heye knew the value of systematic collecting and documentation but focused on his "idiosyncratic passion" for older material.[28]

With the 1999 opening of the Cultural Resources Center in Suitland,

Maryland (where the collections would be housed), and the groundbreaking for the NMAI Mall Museum, attention shifted to Washington. In 2000, Smithsonian secretary Larry Small authored an article entitled "A Passionate Collector." Rather than discuss the value of the collection, he focuses on Heye as an individual collector, drawing heavily on anecdotes provided by Wallace's 1960 article, including one anecdote where Heye was said to have "quizzed small-town morticians about their recent dead who might have owned Indian artifacts." Drawing on Wallace, Small calls Heye a "great vacuum cleaner of a collector" but credits him with saving a "legacy of inestimable worth" through his "life of focused accumulation."[29]

In 2003 NMAI director Rick West summarized Heye's work: "he collected diligently, indeed, some would say almost obsessively, dispatching teams . . . to the far reaches. . . . They sent Native objects back . . . literally in railway boxcars because the volume was so great." Other references to a "small army of collectors" made Heye's motives imperial.[30] However, most replayed now common characterizations: "obsessive," "rapacious," "inveterate," and "boxcar collector."[31] Curator Mary Jane Lenz repeats the same stories but attempts to explain Heye, identifying his aim of creating "the leading institution in this country devoted to the scientific study of American Indian archaeology and ethnology." She also quotes Heye to suggest that his interest was not solely possession: "They are not alone objects to me, but sources of vistas and dreams of their makers and owners. Whether utilitarian or ceremonial, I try to feel why and how the owner felt regarding them." *Native Universes*, the major publication that accompanied the opening of the NMAI Mall Museum, never mentions George Heye.[32]

Through press coverage during the 2004 opening, specific images of Heye were developed, fed largely by the museum's press releases.[33] The biography in the press releases called Heye's first object, "the beginning of his passion for collecting" and described his life's work as "buying everything in sight."[34] The press reveled in Heye as a passionate collector who was driven by unexplained motives and indifferent to living Native people, as opposed to the founder of a large museum that was taken over by the Smithsonian.[35] Quotes from director West compounded the mystery: "he loved the stuff. [But] it was never quite clear how much he really thought about the people who made [it]." All-absorbing passion was a common theme: "collecting Indian objects was his passion in life, plain and simple." Insanity and consumption were equally prevalent: "The extraordinary collection was formed by the monomaniacal passion of George Gustav Heye. . . . His eclectic taste devoured with equal fervor both the artistically exquisite and the ploddingly mundane." Harking back to the whispered "Rosebud" of *Citizen Kane*, Heye was compared to William Randolph Hearst in his "obsession for hunting and gathering other peoples' stuff."[36]

External Views

Recent scholarly discussions of Heye are much the same, referring to him as "an institution in himself" and as "the greatest collector of all."[37] While he did support expeditions and excavations, he is said to have done so, "for the enhancement of his private collections."[38] However, the collection's size and how it was acquired are inflated, making Heye's behavior look even more extreme. Some set Heye within the context of early twentieth-century anthropology and museums but labeled him "a wealthy individual with a passion for rapidly buying a huge collection," which became a "monomaniacal dedication."[39] Edmund Carpenter's study identifies Heye as compulsive, secretive, and driven to "amass the greatest collection, *ever*," suggesting that "Robber Baron bargaining" — rather than the objects themselves — was Heye's driving desire.[40] Unfortunately, suggesting that Heye's goal was to amass a huge collection identifies his motives by matching them with his results, rather than understanding the goals he set for himself.

*A Different View of George Heye and the
Museum of the American Indian*

All these stories may be true, but they are not the whole story. The authors I cite have often overemphasized aspects of George Heye's life — multiple marriages, epicurean tastes, fast driving, and love of cigars — because he left so few personal writings. I believe we need to extract George Heye from this cult of personality and examine his intent in building a collection, sponsoring research and publications, and founding and running a museum. Again, my goal is not to valorize Heye but to understand what values shaped the collection and how it might be used by the NMAI, Native people, and Native nations.

First, we need to deal with George Heye as a collector, and he clearly spent part of his life thinking of himself as a collector.[41] Because Native objects inspired Heye's interest and started his studies, we can conclude that his early collections stood for Indian people; but this does not tell us what Native people or objects meant to his identity. He did object to having his collection or his museum absorbed by others, suggesting that he valued its identification with himself. However, the museum was not Heye's primary self-identification: some acquaintances—and even his own son—were said to be unaware of its role in his life. And, despite repeated references to his "accumulation," he differed from individuals who secretly fill their homes with old newspapers or hundreds of cats: he shared his collection with visitors.[42]

George Heye thus began as a collector and may have maintained that tendency; but, as Shepard Krech has said of collectors who found museums, it is "difficult to separate what drove them to collect from what propelled them to build museums . . . after a certain point they collected to fill their museums." Additionally, we should not underestimate the intellectual role of gentleman scientists: in England, two exceptional collectors—Frederick John Horniman and Augustus Henry Lane Fox Pitt Rivers—are honored primarily as museum founders, although their lives closely resemble Heye's. I believe that George Heye's role as museum builder—rather than collector—deserves further examination.[43]

Heye did not initiate his collections catalog until 1904, soon after he purchased a significant southwestern ceramic collection. This turn to systematic collecting and documentation marks the beginning of his museum idea. Although the museum was founded in 1916, Heye had been talking about it at least since 1906, when he appealed to Archer Huntington. With support from his mother, Heye had already funded important excavations in Mexico and Ecuador, the beginning of a long-term Latin American research plan laid out by Marshall Saville and undertaken long before the museum became reality. Here, Heye's support for systematic Latin American research predated the American Anthropological Association's 1907 identification of the region as a priority. By 1908 the name "Heye Museum" was being used on letterhead and by those who visited.[44]

The collection's 1908 move to the University Museum was noted in a *Science* announcement, indicating that it was considered scientifically important.[45]

Aims and Objects of the Museum of the
American Indian, Heye Foundation

Although anthropology's twentieth-century transition from museums to universities is now seen as a matter of course, it could not have been foreseen when Heye began planning his museum in 1903, several years before Franz Boas turned his complete attention to anthropology at Columbia University. Steven Conn has shown that nineteenth-century studies of Native people shaped American intellectual and disciplinary development, including history, literature, and anthropology. American archaeology was particularly important to anthropology's growth but was later replaced by an emphasis on salvage ethnography and Western civilization's Middle Eastern origins. At the University Museum and the American Museum of Natural History—which Heye may have considered models—American archaeology was increasingly marginalized. Although the Smithsonian and Harvard's Peabody Museum of Archaeology and Ethnology retained strong programs, New York museums did not serve Heye's interest in archaeology. Simultaneously, museums began to move toward public education, often collecting to develop exhibits rather than pursue science.[46]

By contrast, Heye's interests were specifically New York, adult education, and American Indians; in a 1915 letter to Boas, he explained, "When I started my collections I was in business downtown. . . . When I endeavored . . . to find some place to go . . . [to] be directed in the science I wished to take up . . . there was no place in the city where a man could go and get elementary training, or . . . any training at all unless he entered a regular college course. . . . Since there are many men in New York . . . placed as I was . . . [I will establish] an institution . . . open to them in the evening where they can be taught at least the rudiments of Anthropology."[47] With Archer Huntington's offer of a building site at Broadway and 155th Street, Heye's dream would soon become reality in New York.[48]

By signing the 1916 trust agreement, Heye created "a museum for the collection, preservation, study, and exhibition of all things connected with the anthropology of the aboriginal people of the North, Central, and South Americas, and containing objects of artistic, historic, literary, and scientific interest."[49] That year, George Pepper wrote, "a new institution has been founded . . . whose object will be the preservation of everything pertaining to our American tribes."[50] Pepper placed great emphasis on systematic collecting and scholarly purpose: "[the] sole aim is to gather and to preserve for students everything useful in illustrating and elucidating the anthropology of the aborigines of the Western Hemisphere, and to disseminate by means of its publications the knowledge thereby gained."[51] Collections purchases and donations were justified as valuable to building the collection—bringing together "specimens that have never been duplicated"—and special emphasis was placed on organic items preserved in caves or sacred bundles.[52] Preservation and study were also emphasized by Heye in a 1935 letter to a Hidatsa man who requested return of a sacred bundle: "The primary object of the Museum is to preserve and to keep safely for future generations anything pertaining to the life and history of the American Indians . . . where the descendants of the old Indians, as well as students and the public, can see and study these objects of veneration, beauty and historical or scientific interest."[53]

Heye's work has often been explained by reference to Boas's salvage anthropology paradigm; and although Boas urged Heye to focus on salvage, Heye resisted. While preservation was important to Heye, accumulating early objects was primary. Anthropologists, including Frank Speck and Edward Sapir, who documented "memory culture" could not understand Heye's frequent disregard for recent works they offered. These pieces were contradictory to Heye's agenda—he purchased them solely to document organic items or precontact technologies. Heye seldom explained himself; and most did not recognize his interest in early Native life, perhaps best illustrated by a museum publication: "Cuba before Columbus."[54]

The museum's exhibits were much like those of its contemporaries. Cases focused on tribes related by geography or linguistics, such as "Central Algonkians" or the "Southern Siouan Group." The museum's entrance—representing New York—was literally a gateway to the hemisphere: mid-Atlantic tribes flanked the doorway, and visitors moved through the continents as they traveled further. Archaeology and ethnology were separated, and special cases focused on object types or technologies such as silverwork, wampum, quillwork, and "Modern Bead-work."[55]

Despite the popularity of dressed mannequins and life groups at the AMNH, MAI exhibits relied on closely packed objects with few labels. Printed guidebooks provided cultural context, using present tense for Indian people and objects and past tense to describe traditional lifeways. Cultural variation was explained largely by geography and habitat. Visitors may have understood only the recent past and the more distant, "prehistoric" past as temporal frameworks.[56]

After its early years, the MAI suffered through the Depression, and the exhibits probably did not change significantly. Following the loss of its backers in 1928, the museum drastically cut research and publications; Heye personally supervised what entered and left the collection, filling in perceived gaps. However, the events of 1928 cost Heye and the museum much more than funding. From the beginning, Heye had relied on professional advice; but in dismissing his staff, he lost the knowledge and manpower to organize and research collections. Academic influences on his thinking were also lost; and, as American anthropology grew by leaps and bounds, Heye continued to rely on objects as primary texts.

Where the museum once possessed a grand interpretive potential based on a massive material archive and individuals who knew what to make of it, the collection ended up an orphan. The later struggles of the MAI are well known, and in 1989 the museum — Heye's monument — ceased to exist as the Smithsonian's National Museum of the American Indian was born.[57] What lived on was the collection Heye had built, and the question has become how it can be understood as something more than a monument to one man's work, especially when it has continually been read as a private and unexplained obsession.

Narratives of Nationalism: National Capital versus Cultural Capital

While Heye's museum certainly did not support Indigenous nationalism, the NMAI implicitly encourages cultural sovereignty.[58] However, the NMAI's mission effectively obscures the political ground on which the museum negotiates in serving both the American people and Native interests. Speaking about the NMAI's 1994 opening of the George Gustav Heye

Center, Cheyenne and Arapaho filmmaker Chris Eyre puts this succinctly: "The concept of the museum is that [for] America this is *their* history, but it isn't really, it's Native history."[59]

The debate over nationalism began not in Washington but in New York. Heye's focus on American Indians may indicate that he felt they contributed to national character, yet he never said so. But after 1975 the MAI — or its collection — became the prize in an odd tug-of-war between the cultural capital in New York and the national capital in Washington DC. Under Roland Force's direction, the museum sought to relocate to the U.S. Customs House near Battery Park, arguing that the collection deserved a more prominent location. Resistance by local neighbors and the mayor's office brought competing offers from the AMNH, Oklahoma City, Las Vegas, Indianapolis, and others; but the most widely publicized came from H. Ross Perot, who offered $70 million to move the museum to Dallas. However quickly that offer faded, it succeeded in turning up the rhetoric about the collection as a "national treasure." New York newspapers were filled with stories, and in 1985 the United Airlines passenger magazine ran the story, "The Fight for the Greatest American Art Collection." In 1987 the *Washington Post* published remarks by Senators Daniel Patrick Moynihan and Daniel Inouye. The headline for Moynihan read, "Why Should New York Let the Smithsonian Abscond with It?" Inouye's remarks were entitled, "It Belongs on the Mall, America's Main Street."[60]

With the 1989 passage of the National Museum of the American Indian Act (Public Law 105-185), the MAI collections became part of American national heritage and patrimony; its merger with the Smithsonian's Native holdings purportedly gave "all Americans the opportunity to learn of the cultural legacy, historic grandeur, and contemporary culture of Native Americans." In other comments, memorialization and pluralism were twin themes. In a Senate address, Inouye stated, "The time has come to honor and remember the greatness of the first Americans, their wisdom, their leadership, their valor, and their contributions to the people of the United States." In signing the act, President George H. W. Bush remarked, "The nation will go forward with a new and richer understanding of the heritage, culture and values of the peoples of the Americas of Indian ancestry," and the Senate Committee on Indian Affairs chairman, John

McCain, stated, "The Indian Museum will show that a dynamic, pluralistic society can celebrate distinctiveness without fostering separatism."[61]

Senator Moynihan may have been the only person to publicly acknowledge George Heye: "We may all anticipate the day that George Gustav Heye's gift to the world will be displayed in a manner reflective of the great and living cultures of the American Indian." Ironically, this came at the moment when "Heye's gift" joined American national heritage and the Smithsonian's national collections, known for Dorothy's ruby slippers, Archie Bunker's chair, and Fonzie's leather jacket. Still, some Native people looked to the hope that "tribal people *could* assume control of the . . . Native objects left in George Heye's rapaciously acquired collection."[62] The trick was how the collection could be redefined as the collective property of Native nations.

I doubt Congress foresaw growth of "a national tribal museum" from the Smithsonian transfer. What might have happened, as Paul Chaat Smith suggests, is that Indians would have been "explained and accounted for, and somehow fit into the creation myth of the most powerful, benevolent nation ever."[63] However, discussions of the collection's potential Native repossession began in the 1980s, when then MAI's Native trustees—including Vine Deloria and Suzan Shown Harjo—began to talk about the collection as "an irreplaceable heritage." Speaking to the board in 1984, Deloria said, "This is a struggle to control our collection." Lloyd Kiva New stated, "No matter what you do, just take care of the collection. It is our Fort Knox."[64] Discourse on control continued throughout the Smithsonian transfer and into debates over the NMAI's 1991 repatriation policy, which was read as indicating that collections were the "sole property" of affiliated tribes. This was clarified to cover only items successfully claimed for repatriation, but the discussions threw light on what Native control meant to different constituencies.[65]

Cultural Sovereignty and Indigenous Nationalism
at the National Museum of the American Indian

By 1994, with the opening of the George Gustav Heye Center, Native voice had become the NMAI's leading trope for exhibit practice. In an accompanying book, one author wrote, "Much has been written about us from the perspective of the outsider, but our own story—written by our own people with an inside perspective—remains to be told."[66] Since then, Native voice—allowing Indigenous people to "show and tell the world who we are and to use our own voices in the telling"—has been the NMAI's primary means of assuring cultural sovereignty.[67]

At the same time, the NMAI addressed Native ambivalence over museum possession of Native objects. As Rick West states, "There was . . . this historic love/hate relationship between museums and Native communities. We . . . value them . . . because they have our stuff, and we hate them because they have our stuff."[68] Indian visitors to the collections grudgingly acknowledge that without George Heye's interference many objects would now be lost. Delaware Grand Chief Linda Poolaw notes, "If . . . Heye hadn't collected those things back then, we would not have them today. . . . Over 100 years later, my people can see what we had."[69] By soliciting recommendations about care of collections and their movement from New York to Washington, the NMAI extended the bounds of tribal sovereignty over the collections as a "moral and ethical responsibility."[70]

Beyond work on exhibitions and collections, others see the NMAI's very existence as Native cultural sovereignty. Amanda Cobb suggests that the National Museum of the American Indian Act symbolizes Native cultural resurgence and has given it greater visibility. She calls the act significant because museums' representations of Native people have seldom been recognized as colonial forces, noting that the NMAI's importance lies in the fact that "Native Americans have *again* turned an instrument of colonization and dispossession . . . into an instrument of self-definition and cultural continuance."[71] Nevertheless, a few things remain to be said about the problems and prospects of cultural sovereignty as it might be expressed within the NMAI or any other museum.

First, we must question whether creating a separate Indian museum at the Smithsonian embodies essentialism.[72] Like the planned National Museum of African American History and Culture, the NMAI provides a "separate but equal" place for telling American history outside the national museum that is dedicated to that purpose. Yet visitors probably do not expect a big dose of American history to be taught at the NMAI any more than they expect it at the National Air and Space Museum: each Smithsonian museum is constituted by *subject matter* and is not intended as a place for perspective-based history. And, if the NMAI is seen as a subject-matter museum, the public expects that subject to be Native culture, with the emphasis on the singular, rather than on plural cultures.

Tony Bennett has suggested that what is perceived as national heritage is universally supported, and the adoption of the NMAI into the Smithsonian family has ironically made it part of American national patrimony.[73] But this does not account for how Americans—Native and non-Native—look to the NMAI to support their perspectives on Indian people and culture. Bennett also suggests that museums run the risk of creating an image of the past as counterpoint to and retreat from the present. The NMAI wants to become an "international center that represents the totality of Native experiences," focusing on living people and cultures; but that does not deter visitors' perceptions of NMAI collections as images of the frozen past, sources of nostalgia, or resources for the future.[74] The extent to which the NMAI serves those seeking an essentialist, "spiritual" alternative to contemporary crises of personal identity, family life, and environmental degradation only reinforces a newer but still potentially treacherous master narrative.[75]

In presenting living cultures, the NMAI rests too often on working with "traditional elders" to illustrate how traditional culture is lived today, resulting in an uncomfortable nostalgia that implies that Native people live only through reference to tradition and must constantly explain how their present-day lives remain traditional.[76] This is far from how many Native people, especially those who do not call themselves "traditional," want to think about the present and the future of cultural sovereignty, regardless of objects or museums. If the NMAI is to successfully combat the misperception that it only narrates the past, I suspect it needs to engage with those who are revolutionizing diverse bodies of scholarship, reclaiming them, and making them relevant to the Native present and future through Native intellectual sovereignty.[77]

Jacki Thompson Rand has recently spoken about how early dominance by male Native artists has left a mark on the NMAI by privileging art and material culture.[78] Though I agree with Rand, I believe the larger issue for museums' problematic reliance on material culture may be Native scholars' own neglect of visual culture. Museums have long created flawed images of Native cultures; but most Native scholars have—like early twentieth-century anthropology—abandoned museums, seeking the more visible and potentially independent university atmosphere.[79] I recognize that museums — aimed at the public — remain marginal to intellectual life, but they do retain considerable power and can be valuable to increasing understanding of cultural sovereignty. While contemporary Native artists and photographers have reinterpreted art, objects, and images in the name of cultural sovereignty, the greatest intellectual attention paid to material culture is often for repatriation — the literal rather than the symbolic repossession of what museums hold.[80]

My point here is not to criticize Native scholars for lack of involvement in museums but to ask why. If sovereignty, as Scott Lyons suggests, is the "strategy by which we aim to best recover our losses from the ravages of colonization" and Native communication and resistance have always taken textual and nontextual forms, why has reinterpretation and repossession of visual culture fallen so far behind writing in Native self-representation? One difficulty may be that what museums ask of Native people is often a literal reading of objects, hence museums' recourse to elders whose traditional knowledge is expected to provide a Rosetta stone.[81] While such readings may sometimes suffice, they cannot substitute for recontextualizations supplied by Native scholars working across disciplines, such as reading and writing history through art.[82]

What Next?

Returning to George Heye, we must still question whether the collection he built can serve Native cultural sovereignty at the NMAI or elsewhere. As I have suggested, Native ambivalence about museums has many sources, including possession of what once was theirs. However, as an anonymous member of a Native consultation, which was held during early architectural program meetings for the NMAI, once stated, "My grandparents were my collection."[83] This quote suggests that museums' dependence on material culture continues to reduce Native culture to its physical products, often permanently separated from related knowledge. To better serve its Native and non-Native constituencies, the NMAI plans to develop its collections by moving away from physical objects and toward documentation of intangible culture, both associated with physical objects and as separate expressions. Without this step, the NMAI can never begin to represent Native experiences and serve Native communities in ways they themselves define.[84]

But we must also recognize the prospects and limitations of the collection George Heye built and of the objects subsequently acquired by the MAI and the NMAI. Despite the NMAI's plans to expand what it considers collections, the collection is what it is for the moment; and many will not find the right materials and texts to carry out cultural sovereignty projects. Only time will tell whether sufficient building blocks exist for work that Native people want to do in museums. Heye's interest in documenting the precontact Native past has left an indelible mark, both in how objects were removed from Native hands and, because deposition in museums has authenticated these objects as "typical," "proper," or "the best," freezing images of Native culture that retain their potency for consumption and replication. This is a problem for all museums, whose origins in collecting Western civilization's antiquities still frame a perception that everything and everybody represented in museums are equally antique.[85] The NMAI's attempt to move from the classical museum to a place of living people and cultures requires changing a global mind-set on both public and academic levels.

Future use of collections and resources can only succeed when collections are understood as the selectively accumulated and reified products of outsiders' perceptions. The ideological burdens that museum objects carry, whether cultural, institutional, or personal, must be understood; and there is still considerable work needed to answer the question posed by Patricia Penn Hilden and Shari Huhndorf: "How did these objects climb into their glass case in the National Museum of the American Indian?" From that point forward, cultural studies can then deal with material culture as just one kind of text for intellectual and cultural sovereignty projects, including the strategically anticolonial and overtly nationalistic as well as those focused on the future rather than the past. Lloyd Kiva New articulated this while pondering the value of the NMAI collections: "I began to wonder what . . . [the NMAI] could do. . . . While I agreed with . . . preservation of Indian culture, I hoped . . . this did not mean some kind of cultural embalming process wherein obsolete cultural ways are kept going beyond their time. . . . 'Conservation' or 'preservation' means that the museum should take impeccable care of patrimonial objects in its collection. But a more important task should be . . . using the objects . . . to help Indian culture develop new ways to respond to the dynamics of an ever-changing social environment."[86]

From his perspective as an artist, Lloyd New saw beyond current readings of Native objects as art. While potentially useful to tribal national pride, transformation of ethnological and archaeological objects from artifact to art remains problematic. Their elevation may have increased respect for Native artistry, but it also promises to strip objects of cultural contexts and continues to privilege physical over intangible cultural expressions. Introduction of Native objects into art worlds has simultaneously elevated their status as desirable commodities, again emphasizing material and commercial value and potentially encouraging neo-imperial collection and consumption of objects and the people they metonymically represent.[87]

I am not suggesting that aesthetics are not part of the picture; aesthetics are still how collectors and museums often see objects. George Heye was no exception; although he did not consider objects as art, he privileged some objects as "fine examples."[88] Ruth Phillips calls this Heye's "privileging of rarity and age," but this perception of the collections and Heye's work results from how the MAI and the NMAI have historically overemphasized "masterworks" at the expense of other aspects of the collection and emphasized art rather than culture or history. Since 1970 approximately 8,500 objects have been published or exhibited, often three or four times; and this does not include loans of these same "masterpieces" to other institutions. What of the quarter-million other objects, including 568 items simply identified as "stick" in the NMAI's collections? These items of everyday life do not feed anyone's wonderful master narrative of Native life. But they are important, and their preponderance indicates they were equally important to George Heye. Although he probably loved those masterpieces, he also appreciated things that other collectors and museums ignored, including those 568 sticks.[89] The collection's strength grew from Heye's interest in materials that escaped archaeological preservation and other collectors' notice, but it has been dismissed by the boxcar-collector metaphor and by the misrepresentations of his intent, which has been read as simply amassing a huge collection.

. . .

Research for this essay was completed in 2007, the fiftieth anniversary of George Heye's death; and the intervening years have not been kind to his legacy. As I have suggested, the NMAI has seen fit to emphasize and magnify his role as a collector, masking him and his intent in a cloak of insanity and consumption. Ultimately, Heye's image has been so thoroughly wrapped and packed that he is no longer perceived as anything but a man who was singularly obsessed with the simple desire to collect and possess Indian stuff. He is not remembered as a man who funded countless expeditions and excavations, who funded research and publications, or who assembled a professional staff the likes of which few museums have ever seen. Most of all, he is not remembered as a man who built a museum that rivaled its contemporaries in scope and scholarly production. The NMAI's own origin story can seldom admit that it grew out of that other museum—the MAI—or that the collection results not from the "boxcar" metaphor but from a definitive intellectual basis and how it was carried out. George Heye the museum founder cannot be a culture hero in the NMAI story because it is easier for many to deal with him as "just a crazy white man." Simultaneously, systematic erasure of Heye's purpose and intent in assembling a collection and founding the MAI has allowed the NMAI to create a new, ahistoric foundation for the collection that rests on a belief that Heye's expansive collecting encompassed everything rather than the very specific interests he developed for sixty years. Contrary to this trajectory, I believe that interpreting NMAI collections cannot proceed without understanding George Heye, and that it is time to tell better-informed stories of Heye's life's work and its impact on the museum's past, present, and future.

Notes

This essay originates in a paper of the same name delivered at the Newberry Library's September 2007 symposium "Contesting Knowledge: Museums and Indigenous Perspectives," and I am indebted to the staff of the library's D'Arcy McNickle Center for American Indian History and the Committee on Institutional Cooperation–American Indian Studies Consortium for their support. I am equally indebted to Bruce Bernstein and my coffee klatch colleagues—Patricia Nietfeld, Mary Jane Lenz, Tom Evans, Lou Stancari, and Cynthia Frankenburg—for ongoing discussions on George Heye and the NMAI collections. My thoughts on Native intellectualism would not be what they are without benefit of conversations with Paul Chaat Smith. I also owe thanks to Lisa M. King for discussions on rhetorical sovereignty and for introducing me to its literature and to Kylie Message for her suggestion that I look to the history of the Frederick Horniman collection and museum for parallels with George Heye's life. For their comments on this paper or discussions on its substance, I thank Bruce Bernstein, Ruth Phillips, and Ira Jacknis.

1. For characterizations of Heye, see Jerry Reynolds, "The Struggle to Save the Heye Collection," *Indian Country Today*, September 18, 2004, http://www.indiancountry.com/content.cfm?id=1095516461; and Francis X. Clines, "The American Tribes Prepare Their National Showcase," *New York Times*, March 28, 2004, http://query.nytimes.com/gst/fullpage.html?res=9A03EFD81030F93BA15750C0A9629C8B63. Richard F. Kessler, "A New Museum, an Ancient Heritage," *Washington Post*, September 18, 2004; this article referred to an earlier piece by Jackie Trescott, "History's New Look: At the Indian Museum, a Past without Pedestals," *Washington Post*, September 13, 2004. For the NMAI's 2004 press release, see NMAI, "George Gustav Heye: Founder of the Museum of the American Indian (1916) in New York City," http://www.nmai.si.edu/press/releases/09-16-04_heye_biography.pdf.

2. Thomas King, *The Truth about Stories: A Native Narrative* (Minneapolis: University of Minnesota Press, 2003), 122.

3. Eric Hobsbawm, "Inventing Traditions," introduction to *The Invention of Tradition*, ed. Eric Hobsbawm and Terence Ranger (Cambridge: Cambridge University Press, 1983), 1.

4. NMAI, *Intellectual Framework for the Collections and Collecting Plan*, adopted by NMAI Board of Trustees, October 2006; and NMAI, *Scope of Collections Description*, 2007.

5. Susan M. Pearce, *Museums, Objects, and Collections: A Cultural Study* (Washington DC: Smithsonian Institution Press, 1992); and Susan M. Pearce, *On Collecting: An Investigation into Collecting in the European Tradition* (London: Routledge, 1995); James Clifford, "Objects and Selves" afterword to *Objects and Others: Essays on Museums and Material Culture*, ed. George W. Stocking Jr. (Madison: University of Wisconsin Press, 1985), 236–46.

6. George W. Stocking Jr., "Essays on Museums and Material Culture," in Stocking Jr., *Objects and Others*, 3–14.

7. Anthony Shelton, "The Return of the Subject," introduction to *Collectors: Expressions of Self and Other*, ed. Anthony Shelton (London: Horniman Museum and Gardens; Coimbra: Museu Antropológico da Universidade de Coimbra, 2001), 11–22; Clifford, "Objects and Selves."

8. Jean Baudrillard, "The System of Collecting," trans. John Cardinal, in *The Cultures of Collecting*, ed. John Elsner and Roger Cardinal (London: Reaktion Books, 1994), 7–24. On the sexual aspects of collecting, see Werner Muensterberger, *Collecting:*

An Unruly Passion; Psychological Perspectives (New York: Harcourt, Brace, 1994).

9. Pearce, *Museums, Objects, and Collections*; and Brian Durrans, "Collecting the Self in the Idiom of Science: Charles Hose and the Ethnography of Sarawak," in *Collectors: Individuals and Institutions*, ed. Anthony Shelton (London: Horniman Museum and Gardens; Coimbra: Museu Anthropológico da Universidade de Coimbra, 2001), 189–201.

10. Chris Gosden and Chantal Knowles, *Collecting Colonialism: Material Culture and Colonial Change* (New York: Oxford University Press, 2001), xix.

11. American museums' collections often include masses of weapons collected during American military campaigns, almost to the exclusion of other items from conquered peoples. For instance, some American Plains and Philippines collections are almost entirely weaponry—clubs, bows and arrows, and bladed weapons—and represent the literal disarming of Indigenous people during the Indian Wars and the Spanish-American War. On museums' simultaneous presentation of others and colonial rule or hegemony, see Aldona Jonaitis, "Franz Boas, John Swanton, and the New Haida Sculpture at the American Museum of Natural History," in *The Early Years of Native American Art History*, ed. Janet Catherine Berlo (Seattle: University of Washington Press, 1992), 22–61.

12. On world's fairs and Wild West shows, see Burton Benedict, "The Anthropology of World's Fairs," in *The Anthropology of World's Fairs: San Francisco's Panama Pacific International Exposition of 1915*, ed. Burton Benedict (Berkeley CA: Lowie Museum of Anthropology, 1983), 1–65; L. G. Moses, *Wild West Shows and the Images of American Indians, 1883–1933* (Albuquerque: University of New Mexico Press, 1996); and Robert W. Rydell, *All the World's a Fair: Visions of Empire at American International Expositions, 1876–1916* (Chicago: University of Chicago Press, 1984). For relations between museums and travel writing, see Tony Bennett, *The Birth of the Museum: History, Theory, Politics* (London: Routledge, 1995); Stephen Greenblatt, *Marvelous Possessions: The Wonder of the New World* (Chicago: University of Chicago Press, 1991); Mary Louise Pratt, *Imperial Eyes: Travel Writing and Transculturation* (London: Routledge, 1992); and David Spurr, *The Rhetoric of Empire: Colonial Discourse in Journalism, Travel Writing, and Imperial Administration* (Durham NC: Duke University Press, 1993). On museums and representations of the past, see David Lowenthal, *The Past is a Foreign Country* (New York: Cambridge University Press, 1985); and Ann McMullen, "Relevance and Reflexivity: The Past and the Present in Museums" (unpublished manuscript, 2006).

13. On temporal distancing, see Johannes Fabian, *Time and the Other: How Anthropology Makes Its Object* (New York: Columbia University Press, 1983). For the role of anthropology and primitive art collecting in museum representations, see Janet Catherine Berlo and Ruth B. Phillips, "Our (Museum) World Turned Upside

Down: Re-presenting Native American Arts," *Art Bulletin* 77, no. 1 (1995): 6–10; Jonaitis, "Franz Boas, John Swanton, and the New Haida Sculpture"; and Christina F. Kreps, *Liberating Cultures: Cross-Cultural Perspectives on Museums, Curation and Heritage Preservation* (London: Routledge, 2003).

14. W. Richard West Jr., "Museums and Native America: The New Collaboration," (paper, presented at the International Council of Museums–Germany conference, Berlin, November 2003), http://icom-deutschland.de/docs/washington_west.pdf. Art museums' inclusion of Native objects came with the 1930 Exposition of Indian Tribal Arts and the 1941 exhibition at the Museum of Modern Art. Both exhibitions included objects borrowed from Heye's MAI. See John Sloan and Oliver La-Farge, *Introduction to American Indian Art* (New York: Exposition of Indian Tribal Arts, 1931); and Frederic H. Douglas and Rene D'Harnoncourt, *Indian Art of the United States* (New York: Museum of Modern Art, 1941).

15. Ruth B. Phillips, "Why Not Tourist Art? Significant Silences in Native American Museum Representations," in *After Colonialism: Imperial Histories and Postcolonial Displacements*, ed. Gyan Prakash (Princeton NJ: Princeton University Press, 1995), 115. On museums, colonial collecting, and nostalgia, see Margaret Dubin, "Native American Imagemaking and the Spurious Canon of the 'Of-and-By,'" *Visual Anthropology Review* 15, no. 1 (1999): 70–74; and Margaret Dubin, *Native America Collected: The Culture of an Art World* (Albuquerque: University of New Mexico Press, 2001).

16. On anthropology's withdrawal from museums, see Stocking, "Essays on Museums and Material Culture"; and Ira Jacknis, "Franz Boas and Exhibits: On the Limitations of the Museum Method of Anthropology," in Stocking Jr., *Objects and Others*, 75–111. On objects and representation, see Pearce, *Museums, Objects, and Collections*; and Steven Conn, *Museums and American Intellectual Life, 1876–1926* (Chicago: University of Chicago Press, 1998). Mason is cited in Steven Conn, *History's Shadow: Native Americans and Historical Consciousness in the Nineteenth Century* (Chicago: University of Chicago Press, 2004), 9. Speaking about the peoples of the Americas, George H. Pepper (George Heye's right-hand man) states, "Having no written language, [they] left no records that can be woven into a consecutive story. . . . The student must evolve the story of the various prehistoric tribes from what they have left behind them." George H. Pepper, "The Museum of the American Indian, Heye Foundation," *Geographical Review* 2, no. 6 (1916): 405–6.

17. J. Alden Mason, "George G. Heye, 1874–1957," *Leaflets of the Museum of the American Indian, Heye Foundation* 6 (1958): 11. It is difficult to know what Heye read at this early point, but by 1904 he was said to have purchased the anthropological publications of the AMNH and was interested in those of the Peabody Museum of Archaeology and Ethnology at Harvard. George Pepper to Frederick Ward Putnam, June 19, 1904, NMAI Archives, box OC87, folder 11. Notably, he does not

appear to have succumbed to romantic notions about Indian people such as the "myth of the Mound Builders" and instead probably concentrated on up-to-date scientific-anthropology literature. For more on that myth, see Robert Silverberg, *Mound Builders of Ancient America: The Archaeology of a Myth* (New York: New York Graphic Society, 1968); and Conn, *History's Shadow*.

18. Bruce Bernstein has noted that Heye's use of three-by-five-inch cards, like those used in library card catalogs, was a distinctly modern museum development. Bruce Bernstein, e-mail message to author, October 9, 2007. In the late nineteenth century, most museums used large-format, bound ledgers for cataloging. While a few museums have retained this system (or have kept it only for recording accessions), others switched to the complete use of cards or used cards as an adjunct to ledger-book cataloging. Heye's use of cards rather than a ledger may have had instrumental purposes: it is easier to delete an object or recatalog objects using a card system. Duplicate sets of cards can also be arranged according to category or geography, thus allowing a particular aspect of the collection to be seen at a glance; but there is no evidence that Heye did this. His motivations for using cards rather than a ledger for cataloging remain unclear. For early professional museum discussions on accession—and catalog-card systems, see *Proceedings of the American Association of Museums*, Records of the Sixth Annual Meeting Held at Boston, Massachusetts, May 23–25, 1911 (Baltimore: Waverly Press, 1911), 31–42.

19. These included the Hispanic Society of America, the American Geographical Society, the American Numismatics Society, and the American Academy of Arts and Letters.

20. This summary of Heye's life is based on the professional obituaries J. Alden Mason, "George G. Heye, 1874–1957"; and Samuel K. Lothrop, "George Gustav Heye, 1874–1956," *American Antiquity* 23, no. 1 (1957): 66–67, which agree on all major facts of Heye's life. The figure of $10 million for Heye's inheritance comes from a more informal article, Kevin Wallace, "Slim-Shin's Monument," *New Yorker*, November 19, 1960. Figures for collections totals are derived from the NMAI's *Scope of Collections Description* and were calculated using the museum's computerized collections database. The NMAI's current object holdings are estimated at 266,000 catalog records, representing 825,000 items. Each catalog number may represent a single object or thousands of beads, hence the difference in the totals.

21. Mason, "George G. Heye, 1874–1957," 11; Lothrop, "George Gustav Heye, 1874–1956," 66.

22. E. K. Burnett, "Recollections of E. K. Burnett" (transcripts of tapes, 1964), NMAI Archives, box vw, folder 13.

23. Edmund Carpenter identifies the anonymous professor—who provided this and other quotes in Wallace, "Slim-Shin's Monument"—as anthropologist Junius Bird, who participated in expeditions funded by Heye and, after 1931, was curator of South American archaeology at AMNH. See Edmund S. Carpenter, "9/3428: Three

Chapters from an Unfinished, Two-Volume Study of George Heye's Museum of the American Indian," *European Review of Native American Studies* 15, no. 1 (2001): 1–12; and Edmund S. Carpenter, *Two Essays: Chief & Greed* (North Andover MA: Persimmon Press, 2005). Bird's animosity may stem from the fact that he was among those dismissed when the MAI lost funding after 1928 and that Heye chose to invest remaining funds largely in continued collections purchases rather than in staffing or expeditions. However, Bird was part of an MAI-funded expedition to Greenland in 1930.

24. Wallace, "Slim-Shin's Monument." Some sources suggest that Heye created the MAI as a tax shelter, but I can find no basis for this conclusion.

25. Frederick J. Dockstader, *Indian Art of the Americas* (New York: Museum of the American Indian, 1973); and Frederick J. Dockstader, introduction to *Masterworks from the Museum of the American Indian* (New York: Metropolitan Museum of Art, 1973), 10.

26. Anna Curtenius Roosevelt and James G. E. Smith, eds., *The Ancestors: Native Artisans of the Americas* (New York: Museum of the American Indian, 1979); U. Vincent Wilcox, "The Museum of the American Indian, Heye Foundation," *American Indian Art Magazine* 3, no. 2 (1978): 40; Roland W. Force, *The Heye and the Mighty: Politics and the Museum of the American Indian* (Honolulu HI: Mechas Press, 1999), 3–4.

27. Tom Hill, "A Backward Glimpse through the Museum Door," introduction to *Creation's Journey: Native American Identity and Belief*, ed. Tom Hill and Richard W. Hill Sr. (Washington DC: Smithsonian Institution Press), 19; Natasha Bonilla Martinez, "An Indian Americas: NMAI Photographic Archive Documents Indian Peoples of the Western Hemisphere," in *Spirit Capture: Photographs from the National Museum of the American Indian*, ed. Tim Johnson (Washington DC: Smithsonian Institution Press, 1998), 29. Later exhibitions at the Heye Center do not mention Heye except to note that specific items were purchased by him; see Joseph D. Horse Capture and George P. Horse Capture, *Beauty, Honor, and Tradition: The Legacy of Plains Indian Shirts* (Washington DC: National Museum of the American Indian, 2001). In beginning this research, I suspected NMAI rhetoric would differ depending on whether New York or national audiences were addressed. However, available documents indicated only slight differences. Texts for national consumption focus on the NMAI as a Native place emphasizing Native voice while those intended for New York audiences focus on the city as a cultural capital, a Native place (contrasted with Ellis Island, the Statue of Liberty, and diverse ethnic neighborhoods), and a center of intercultural world commerce; see John Haworth, "New York City in Indian Possession: The George Gustav Heye Center," in *Spirit of a Native Place: Building the National Museum of the American Indian*, ed. Duane Blue Spruce (Washington DC: National Museum of the American Indian, 2004), 133–49; and Gabrielle Tayac, "From the Deep: Native Layers of

New York City," in *New Tribe New York: The Urban Vision Quest*, ed. Gerald Mc-Master (Washington DC: National Museum of the American Indian, 2005), 12–19. The old MAI is now often described in terms of New Yorkers' fond memories of its crammed cases, and they are said to sorely miss the presence of Heye's collection and look forward to its return to New York in planned exhibitions. Some NMAI staff at the GGHC use the word *repatriation* to refer to use of the collections—permanently housed in Suitland, Maryland—in New York–based exhibits and make the rather unlikely suggestion that the MAI and its collections figure as largely in New Yorkers' cultural consciousness as the more iconic American Museum of Natural History, the Metropolitan Museum of Art, or the Museum of Modern Art.

28. Clara Sue Kidwell, "Every Last Dishcloth: The Prodigious Collecting of George Gustav Heye," in *Collecting Native America: 1870–1960*, ed. Shepard Krech III and Barbara A. Hail (Washington DC: Smithsonian Institution Press, 1999), 237. In 1917 MAI fieldworker Donald Cadzow recorded what he called Heye's "Golden Rule": "*Every object collected add field tag*/Material must be *old*/Hunting outfits/fishing outfits/costumes/masks and ceremonial objects, also dance objects/household utensils *particularly stone and pottery dishes and lamps*/Talismans, hunting charms, all *ivory carvings (old)/NO TOURIST MATERIAL*." Field notes by Donald Cadzow, 1917, NMAI Archives, box OC24, folder 22. Although many stress this aspect of Heye's collecting, early twentieth-century anthropologists and the large museums that purchased their collections maintained the same attitudes, privileging earlier works over more recent pieces, including "crafts" made for sale; see Phillips, "Why Not Tourist Art?"

29. Lawrence M. Small, "A Passionate Collector," *Smithsonian Magazine*, November 2000, http://www.smithsonianmag.com/history-archaeology/small_novoo.html. The Smithsonian accepted the personal collections of Charles Lang Freer (1854–1919), Dr. Arthur M. Sackler (1913–1987), and Joseph H. Hirshhorn (1899–1981) and made them into separate Smithsonian museums that include their names, but these benefactors have never been spoken of as Heye has been. Origins of the Smithsonian's National Museum of African Art in the personal collection of Warren H. Robbins and his Museum of African Art are almost completely invisible; see Smithsonian Institution Archives, "Histories of the Smithsonian Institution's Museums and Research Centers," Smithsonian Institution, http://siarchives.si.edu/history/exhibits/historic/history.htm.

30. West, "Museums and Native America"; and James Pepper Henry, "Challenges in Managing Culturally Sensitive Collections at the National Museum of the American Indian," in *Stewards of the Sacred*, ed. Lawrence E. Sullivan and Alison Edwards (Washington DC: American Association of Museums, 2004), 105–12.

31. Bruce Bernstein, "The National Museum of the American Indian Collections," *American Indian Art Magazine* 29, no. 4 (2004): 52–55; Douglas E. Evelyn, "The

Smithsonian's National Museum of the American Indian: An International Institution of Living Cultures," *The Public Historian* 28, no. 2 (2006): 50–55; and Liz Hill, "A Home for the Collections: The Cultural Resources Center," in Blue Spruce, *Spirit of a Native Place*, 117–31. By now, readers should recognize "boxcar" as a theme. However, no MAI employee ever mentioned collections being shipped from the field in boxcars, and I doubt it ever occurred. However, after Wallace's anonymous professor characterized Heye as "what we call a boxcar collector," the phrase has been repeated so often that it has taken on the flavor of fact, as evidenced in NMAI director Rick West's quote.

32. Mary Jane Lenz, "George Gustav Heye: The Museum of the American Indian," in Blue Spruce, *Spirit of a Native Place*, 99, 115; and Gerald McMaster and Clifford M. Trafzer, *Native Universes: Voices of Indian America* (Washington DC: National Museum of the American Indian, 2004).

33. Elsewhere, Patricia Hilden has suggested that the NMAI is extremely protective of its image. Hilden observes that negative feedback on exhibits and programs were quickly removed from comment books left to gather visitor responses, leaving only positive comments for visitors to read before adding their own. Patricia Hilden, "Race for Sale: Narratives of Possession in Two 'Ethnic' Museums," *The Drama Review* 44, no. 3 (2000): 33n7, http://www.csun.edu/~vcspc00g/603/race forsale.pdf .

34. Drawing on Heye's obituary, Mason, and Wallace, the NMAI biography of Heye also recounts the MAI's 1938 return of a Hidatsa sacred bundle, calling it "an unknown predicator of the repatriation section of the legislation establishing the National Museum of the American Indian"; NMAI, "George Gustav Heye." See also "George Heye Dies: Museum Founder — Authority on Indian Tribes Endowed a Foundation for Scientific Collections," *New York Times*, January 21, 1957; Mason, "George G. Heye, 1874–1957"; Wallace, "Slim-Shin's Monument." As Ira Jacknis suggests, this event was "not what it appeared to be." Ira Jacknis, "A New Thing? The NMAI in Historical and Institutional Perspective," in "Critical Engagements with the National Museum of the American Indian," ed. Amy Lonetree and Sonya Atalay, special issue, *American Indian Quarterly* 30, nos. 3–4 (2006): 533. Kidwell further suggests that Heye's agreement to return the bundle was a public relations ploy, and Carpenter indicates that the publicity angle was suggested by none other than John Collier. Kidwell, "Every Last Dishcloth"; and Carpenter, *Two Essays*, 105. The museum's board stated, "This is in no way a recognition on our part of any legal or moral obligation to return the bundle." Carpenter, *Two Essays*, 106.

35. Though NMAI director W. Richard West Jr. is often referred to as its "founding director," this tends to erase the MAI and its museum functions as the NMAI's predecessor and George Heye as that museum's founding director.

36. Richard West, "Native Treasures," interview by Jeffrey Brown, *NewsHour with Jim Lehrer*, September 21, 2004, http://www.pbs.org/newshour/bb/entertainment/

july-dec04/museum_9-21.html; Reynolds, "Struggle to Save the Heye Collection"; Ellen Herscher, "A Museum to Right Past Wrongs," *Archaeology*, December 6, 1999, http://www.archaeology.org/online/features/amindian/index.html; and Clines, "American Tribes Prepare Their National Showcase," and see also Kidwell, "Every Last Dishcloth." Press coverage was voluminous and repeated many of the same themes and phrases. See also Francis X. Clines, "A Gathering of Treasures and Tribes," *New York Times*, March 27, 2000, http://query.nytimes.com/gst/full page.html?res=9A04E4DC113DF934A15750C0A9669C8B63; Herman Lebovics, "Post-Colonial Museums: How the French and American Models Differ," *History News Network*, September 13, 2004, http://hnn.us/articles/6939.html; Judy Nichols, "Sharing Tradition with the World," *Arizona Republic*, September 18, 2004; Elizabeth Olson, "A Museum of Indians That Is Also for Them," *New York Times*, August 29, 2004, http://query.nytimes.com/gst/fullpage.html?res=9500E0 D7113FF93AA2575BC0A9629C8B63; John Roach, "At New American Indian Museum, Artifacts Are 'Alive,'" *National Geographic News*, September 21, 2004, http://news.nationalgeographic.com/news/2004/09/0914_040913_indians_exhibits.html; and Lyric Wallwork Winik, "To Reconcile a Tragic Past," *Parade Magazine*, September 5, 2004.

37. Douglas Cole, *Captured Heritage: The Scramble for Northwest Coast Artifacts*, (Seattle: University of Washington Press, 1985), 216; and Berlo and Phillips, "Our (Museum) World," 7.

38. James E. Snead, "Science, Commerce, and Control: Patronage and the Development of Anthropological Archaeology in the Americas," *American Anthropologist* 101, no. 2 (1999): 264.

39. Jacknis, "A New Thing?," 516; Cole, *Captured Heritage*, 217. On the inflation of the collection's size, see Hilden, "Race for Sale"; Patricia Penn Hilden and Shari M. Huhndorf, "Performing 'Indian' in the National Museum of the American Indian," *Social Identities* 5, no. 2 (1999): 161–83; and Shari M. Huhndorf, *Going Native: Indians in the American Cultural Imagination* (Ithaca NY: Cornell University Press, 2001).

40. Edmund Carpenter, who has examined Heye's life and motives, denies that much of the collection was stolen from Native owners: "Such pieces exist, of course, but are much rarer than one might suppose. . . . There are certainly stolen objects in the Heye collection, but I know of none stolen from Indians. Stealing from reservations just wasn't George Heye's style. He loved to acquire in bulk, and that meant from existing collections. Above all, he loved to buy and sell." Carpenter, "9/3428," 15.

41. Freud suggested that fetishistic collecting resulted from the redirection of surplus libido; and since Heye was said to be a man of appetites, fetishism may be a possible explanation. Pearce, *Museums, Objects, and Collections*. On the other hand, Roy Ellen suggests that fetishists transform persons or social relations into objects

to control them, and Heye's perceived disinterest in living Indians may rule out true fetishism. Roy Ellen, "Fetishism," *Man* 23, no 2. (1988): 213–35. For other studies on collectors and collecting, see Pearce, *On Collecting*; Muensterberger, *Collecting*; and John Elsner and Roger Cardinal, eds., *The Cultures of Collecting* (London: Reaktion Books, 1994).

42. True collectors are defined by their vision of what a complete collection might be; their enjoyment in building, ordering, and classifying their collections; and their understanding of how items fit into the whole. On Heye's attitudes toward his collection, see Lothrop, "George Gustav Heye, 1874–1956"; Mason, "George G. Heye, 1874–1957"; Burnett, "Recollections of E. K. Burnett"; Wallace, "Slim-Shin's Monument"; and Force, *Heye and the Mighty*. For collectors' visions, see Pearce *Museums, Objects, and Collections*; and Susan Stewart, *On Longing: Narratives of the Miniature, the Gigantic, the Souvenir, and the Collection* (Durham NC: Duke University Press, 1993).

43. Shepard Krech III, introduction to Krech and Hail, *Collecting Native America*, 10. Horniman began collecting in the 1860s, filling his house and opening it to the public and, in 1901, opening a separate building. Pitt Rivers's life closely resembles Heye's. Beginning somewhat modestly, the collections of Pitt Rivers and Heye both grew rapidly following inheritances, and both men sought alliances with existing museums but wanted independence and hired their own staff. Heye, Horniman, and Pitt Rivers all began by buying individual items and later focused on purchasing many large collections that had been made by others. On Frederick John Horniman, see Ken Teague, "In the Shadow of the Palace: Frederick J. Horniman and His Collection," in Shelton, *Collectors: Expressions of Self and Other*, 111–36; and Anthony Shelton, "Rational Passions: Frederick John Horniman and Institutional Collections," in Shelton, *Collectors: Expressions of Self and Other*, 205–24. On Pitt Rivers, see William Ryan Chapman, "Arranging Ethnology: A. H. L. F. Pitt Rivers and the Typological School," in Stocking Jr., *Objects and Others*, 15–48.

44. Purchase of the southwestern ceramic collection from Henry Hales — and creation of the catalog — was prompted by anthropologists George Pepper and Marshall Saville. Jacknis also recognizes purchase of the Hales collection and the beginning of the catalog as significant to Heye's move from private to systematic collection. The value Heye placed on the Hales collection is indicated by the fact that the first object in the catalog is from that collection and not the Navajo shirt that began his personal collection. See Kidwell, "Every Last Dishcloth"; Lenz, "George Gustav Heye"; and Jacknis, "A New Thing?" In 1916 George Pepper indicated that Heye had become serious about a museum fifteen years earlier, and Force cites correspondence between Heye and Huntington. See Pepper, "Museum of the American Indian"; and Force, *Heye and the Mighty*. On Heye's Latin American research, see Carpenter, *Two Essays*; Pepper, "Museum of the American In-

dian"; MAI, "Aims and Objects of the Museum of the American Indian, Heye Foundation," *Indian Notes and Monographs* 33 (New York: Museum of the American Indian, Heye Foundation, 1922); Kidwell, "Every Last Dishcloth"; and Jacknis, "A New Thing?"

45. In 1908 George Gordon of the University Museum agreed to house and exhibit Heye's collection. Until 1916 Heye served on the University Museum board and funded North American expeditions and excavations. Despite the fact that the work was done under the auspices of the University Museum and potentially to benefit it, the materials collected were cataloged using Heye's numbering system rather than Penn's, which suggests that Heye never intended to merge his collection with the University Museum. Heye collections were withdrawn and moved to New York after 1916. See "Scientific News and Notes," *Science* 29, no. 736 (1909): 225; Carpenter, *Two Essays*; Kidwell, "Every Last Dishcloth"; Force, *The Heye and the Mighty*; and Lucy Fowler Williams, *Guide to the North American Ethnographic Collections at the University of Pennsylvania Museum of Archaeology and Anthropology* (Philadelphia: University of Pennsylvania Museum of Archaeology and Anthropology, 2002).

46. See Conn, *History's Shadow*; Snead, "Science, Commerce, and Control"; Williams, *Guide to the North American Ethnographic Collections*; Jacknis, "A New Thing?"; and Jonaitis, "Franz Boas, John Swanton, and the New Haida Sculpture." The Brooklyn Museum may have competed with the AMNH and Heye, but it maintained an ethnographic art focus and lacked Heye's resources. Diana Fane, "New Questions for 'Old Things': The Brooklyn Museum's Zuni Collection," in Berlo, *Early Years of Native American Art History*, 62–87. The *Anthropological Papers of the American Museum of Natural History* between 1907 (the series' inception) and 1916 indicate ethnographic and ethnological emphasis over archaeology.

47. Kidwell, "Every Last Dishcloth," 243. Heye maintained a penchant for hiring non-academics, like himself, as well as individuals outside his own class, potentially avoiding an ivory-tower mentality or simply hiring those he liked. Before the Bronx Annex was built, staff members were divided between "upstairs" and "downstairs." George Heye, Frank Utley, Jesse Nusbaum, William C. Orchard (an English artist and formerly an AMNH preparator), Edwin F. Coffin (a former race-car driver), Charles Turbyfill (a livery stable worker picked up during the Nacoochee Mound excavations), Amos Oneroad (A. B. Skinner's Dakota informant and driver), Donald Cadzow, and Foster Saville (Marshall's brother) were upstairs; more academic types were downstairs: Frederick Webb Hodge (formerly chief ethnologist at the Bureau of American Ethnology), Marshall Saville (first curator of Mexican and Central American Archaeology at the AMNH and later at Columbia), George H. Pepper (AMNH), Alanson B. Skinner (Columbia, Harvard, and AMNH), and Mark Raymond Harrington (AMNH and Columbia). On MAI employees, see Carpenter, *Two Essays*; Kidwell, "Every Last Dishcloth"; Jacknis, "A

New Thing?"; and Mark Raymond Harrington, "Memories of My Work with George G. Heye," n.d., NMAI Archives, box OC 79, folder 5. We should also remember that the MAI had no women as professional staff members and, as a workplace, seems to have resembled a private men's club. This air of masculinity may have been a sign of the times, but it may also have encouraged focus on "old Indians" who—as warriors—were male as well as a lack of attention on later works, including commercial crafts made by women. Phillips, "Why Not Tourist Art?" On anthropologists' interest in men's objects versus collectors' interest in those made by women, see Marvin Cohodas, "Louisa Keyser and the Cohns: Mythmaking and Basket Making in the American West," in Berlo, *Early Years of Native American Art History*, 88–133.

48. Serving New York was important, both for Heye and others. The AMNH was built by those who wanted to "bring glory to their city," including Collis Huntington and his son Archer, who supported Heye and his museum; see Jacknis, "Franz Boas and Exhibits." Collections exchanges between Heye or MAI and New York museums—such as AMNH and the Brooklyn Museum—were rarer that those with other institutions. Carpenter suggests that AMNH and George Heye made many exchanges, but these occurred largely around 1905. Likewise, Brooklyn Museum exchanges with MAI occurred only during Dockstader's tenure. For public auctions, Heye and the Brooklyn Museum, AMNH, and the University Museum were said to avoid competition; see Carpenter, *Two Essays*; and Burnett, "Recollections of E. K. Burnett." I suspect that Heye's goal was to bring collections to New York; he did not feel compelled to secure objects from New York museums for the sake of adding them to MAI.

49. Force, *Heye and the Mighty*, 10.

50. Pepper "Museum of the American Indian," 401.

51. Pepper "Museum of the American Indian," 415. Pepper reiterates the public emphasis of the museum, stating, "The founding of the Museum of the American Indian marks the end of personal effort and opens up a broad field wherein all who are interested in the American Indian can work," and "from a private undertaking, superintended and financed by an individual, it has become a great public benefaction—a benefaction that needs the assistance of all who are interested in the preservation of material that will help . . . better understanding of the primitive tribes of the two Americas." Pepper, "Museum of the American Indian," 416, 418.

52. MAI, "Aims and Objects," 3. Publications that were funded by Heye before MAI's creation—such as this one, from which this section takes its name—were subsequently reprinted by the museum, reinforcing perception of the museum's scholarly contributions at its inception; see MAI, "List of Publications of the Museum of the American Indian, Heye Foundation," *Indian Notes and Monographs* 36 (New York: Museum of the American Indian, Heye Foundation, 1922). After Heye's

death the museum's purpose shifted and was stated, "collection and preservation of material culture objects made by the natives of the western hemisphere . . . [to] afford serious students at the undergraduate and graduate levels every facility for research." MAI, "The History of the Museum," *Indian Notes and Monographs*, misc. ser., 56 (New York: Museum of the American Indian, Heye Foundation, 1964): 3–4.

53. Carpenter, *Two Essays*, 85. In Heye's obituary, Samuel K. Lothrop makes clear that staff members saw their work as building a museum, not supporting a private collection: "We were all of us, I think, drawn towards Heye by the prospect of a new dream museum." Lothrop, "George Gustav Heye," 66.

54. Kidwell, "Every Last Dishcloth"; Phillips, "Why Not Tourist Art?"; Mark Raymond Harrington, "Cuba before Columbus," *Indian Notes and Monographs*, misc. ser., 17 (New York: Museum of the American Indian, Heye Foundation, 1921).

55. MAI, "Aims and Objects"; MAI, "Guide to the Museum," *Indian Notes and Monographs*, unnumbered (New York: Museum of the American Indian, Heye Foundation, 1922).

56. While Heye was developing his museum, major changes in exhibition occurred elsewhere. The Pitt Rivers Museum focused on evolutionary typologies, while the Smithsonian's National Museum of Natural History—opened in 1910—followed culture areas. The Smithsonian and AMNH included life groups and dioramas, drawn from trends at the 1893 Chicago World's Fair. See Bennett, *Birth of the Museum*; and Tony Bennett, *Pasts Beyond Memory: Evolution, Museums, Colonialism* (London: Routledge, 2004); Chapman, "Arranging Ethnology"; John C. Ewers, *A Century of American Indian Exhibits in the Smithsonian Institution*, Smithsonian Report for 1958, 1959, 513–52; Jacknis, "Franz Boas and Exhibits"; and Rydell, *All the World's a Fair*. The MAI did not include life groups, although some models illustrated artists' conceptions of prehistoric village and home life. As in other things, Heye had his own ideas about what exhibits ought to do and eschewed those that did not fit his sense of museum economy, which invested much more in accumulating collections than creating visitor-friendly exhibits for an unlettered public. Where other museums depended on labels to educate, lack of labeling at MAI—and emphasis on "study collections" for "serious students"— probably created a sense of elitism. For his museum, Pitt Rivers emphasized autodidactic exhibit experiences, allowing visitors to teach themselves without reading; but MAI exhibits probably required considerable familiarity with the subject matter and materials, emphasizing research rather than pedagogy. Portable MAI school exhibits in the 1940s included much more labeling than the museum's permanent exhibits. Study collections were also used elsewhere, probably beginning with the British Museum in the 1850s; see Bennett, *Birth of the Museum*.

57. On Heye's control over the collection, see Carpenter, *Two Essays*; Mason, "George G. Heye, 1874–1957"; and Burnett, "Recollections of E. K. Burnett." Without his

staff, Heye also lost contacts to locate collections; regions where he could not identify appropriate collections for purchase are notably weaker than areas where anthropologists assisted him. As time went on, fewer anthropologists were involved in material culture research and collection, thus Heye could probably not have attracted the same kind of staff even if he had had funding for them. On specific collections strengths, see NMAI, "Scope of Collections Description." For the MAI's later history, see Force, *Heye and the Mighty*, 362, 381–82.

58. The NMAI's mission statement reads, "The National Museum of the American Indian is committed to advancing knowledge and understanding of the Native cultures of the Western Hemisphere, past, present, and future, through partnership with Native people and others. The museum works to support the continuance of culture, traditional values, and transitions in contemporary Native life."

59. Hilden and Huhndorf, "Performing 'Indian,'" 163.

60. Force, *Heye and the Mighty*, 381–82; see also Suzan Shown Harjo, "NMAI: A Promise America Is Keeping," *Native Peoples*, 9, no. 3 (1996), 28–34, http://www.native peoples . com / article / articles / 223 / 1 / NMAI-A-Promise-America-Is-Keeping / Page1 .html. Force states that Inouye's involvement stemmed from his initial proposal to reinter all Native American human remains from Smithsonian collections on the National Mall to create a Native American memorial. Force's narrative privileges Inouye's efforts to create the NMAI, while Suzan Shown Harjo suggests Inouye's first concern was repatriation of human remains and other cultural objects and that saving the MAI was secondary.

61. See U.S. Senate, *An Act to Establish the National Museum of the American Indian within the Smithsonian Institution, and for Other Purposes*, Public Law 101-185, 101st Cong., 1st sess. (1989), http://anthropology.si.edu/repatriation/pdf/nmai _act.pdf; and Force, *Heye and the Mighty*, 402, 445. John McCain, Guest Essay, *Native Peoples* 8, no. 1 (1995), quoted in Harjo, "NMAI." For a comparison of nationalist tactics used for the NMAI and France's Musée du Quai Branly, see Lebovics, "Post-Colonial Museums."

62. Moynihan, 101st Cong., 1st sess., *Congressional Record* (November 14, 1989), quoted in Force, *Heye and the Mighty*, 443–44; on assuming control, see Hilden and Huhndorf, "Performing 'Indian,'" 167.

63. Jacknis, "A New Thing?"; and Paul Chaat Smith, "Ghost in the Machine," in *Strong Hearts: Native American Visions and Voices*, ed. Peggy Roalf (New York: Aperture, 1995), 9. An early architectural planning document does not articulate Native control over the museum: "The objectives of NMAI continue the Smithsonian's mission to increase and diffuse knowledge, and to interpret the pluralistic nature of this nation's social, ethnic and cultural composition"; Venturi, Scott Brown, and Associates, *The Way of the People, NMAI Master Facilities Programming, Revised Draft Report* (Philadelphia: Venturi, Scott Brown, and Associates, 1991), 30.

64. On Deloria and Harjo, see Reynolds, "The Struggle to save the Heye Collection"; Lloyd New and Vine Deloria are quoted in Force, *Heye and the Mighty*, 203, 83.

65. William C. Sturtevant, "Repatriation Policy and the Heye Collection," *Museum Anthropology* 15, no. 2 (1991): 29–30; W. Richard West Jr., "The National Museum of the American Indian Repatriation Policy: Reply to William C. Sturtevant," *Museum Anthropology* 15, no. 3 (1991): 13–14; and Edmund Carpenter, "Repatriation Policy and the Heye Collection," *Museum Anthropology* 15, no. 3 (1991): 15–18. NMAI repatriations can also support Indigenous sovereignty, especially where it has traditionally been ignored. A newspaper article documenting the NMAI's repatriation of human remains to Cuba made this apparent: "For the first time in over 500 years, the Taíno descendant population of Caridad de los Indios will be recognized in a formal international encounter. On behalf of their community, Cacique Panchito Ramirez and the elders of la Rancheria, will receive the human remains of seven of their ancestors." "Smithsonian's NMAI Returns Taíno Remains to Cuba: After 500 Years the Taíno Community Continues to Gain Recognition and Respect," *La Voz del Pueblo Taíno* 5, no. 3 (July–September 2002): 1.

66. Manuel Ríos Morales, "Community as Identity," in *All Roads Are Good: Native Voices on Life and Culture* (Washington DC: Smithsonian Institution Press, 1994), 158. Repossession of narrative and history is significant to the regrowth of nationalist expression. The nineteenth-century move toward making science and ethnology the only way to write about Indians both dehistoricized and denationalized Native people, because only nations could be expected to have histories; see Conn, *History's Shadow*, 23.

67. Richard West, quoted in Marilyn Christiano and Shelley Gollust, "This is America—National Museum of the American Indian," *Voice of America* broadcast, September 20, 2004, http://www.voanews.com/specialenglish/archive/2004-09/a-2004-09-20-2-1.cfm. The NMAI's philosophical perspective of Native self-representation through direct self-expression has been most widely disseminated by director Rick West in his writings and interviews; see W. Richard West Jr., "Research and Scholarship at the National Museum of the American Indian: The New 'Inclusiveness,'" *Museum Anthropology* 17, no. 1 (1993): 5–8; W. Richard West Jr., "The National Museum of the American Indian: Perspectives on Museums in the 21st Century," *Museum Anthropology* 18, no. 3 (1994): 53–58; West, "Museums and Native America"; Brown, "Native Treasures"; Clines, "Gathering of Treasures and Tribes"; Herscher, "Museum to Right Past Wrongs"; and Amanda J. Cobb, "Interview with W. Richard West, Director, National Museum of the American Indian," in "National Museum of the American Indian," ed. Amanda J. Cobb, special issue, *American Indian Quarterly* 29, nos. 3–4 (2005): 517–37; and Amanda J. Cobb, "The National Museum of the American Indian as Cultural Sovereignty," *American Quarterly* 57, no. 2 (2005): 485–506. On the difficulties of successfully carrying out this strategy, see Cynthia Chavez Lamar, "Collaborative Exhibit Development

at the Smithsonian's National Museum of the American Indian," in *The National Museum of the American Indian: Critical Conversations*, ed. Amy Lonetree and Amanda J. Cobb (Lincoln: University of Nebraska Press, 2008); Hilden and Huhndorf, "Performing 'Indian'"; Julia Klein, "Native Americans in Museums: Lost in Translation?" *APF Reporter* 19, no. 4 (2001), http://www.aliciapatterson.org/APF1904/Klein/Klein.html; and McMullen, "Relevance and Reflexivity." For similar work by other institutions, see essays in Laura Peers and Alison K. Brown, eds., *Museums and Source Communities* (New York: Routledge, 2003); Laura Peers, *Playing Ourselves: Interpreting Native Histories at Historic Reconstructions* (Lanham MD: AltaMira Press, 2007); and Ann McMullen, "The Currency of Consultation and Collaboration," *Museum Anthropology Review*, 2, no. 2 (2008).

68. Cobb, "Interview with W. Richard West."

69. NMAI, "George Gustav Heye."

70. On NMAI collections care, see Craig Howe, "Sovereignty and Cultural Property Policy in Museums" (paper presented at the Property Rights and Museum Practice workshop, University of Chicago Cultural Policy Center, winter 2000), http://culturalpolicy.uchicago.edu/workshop/howe.html; Nancy B. Rosoff, "Integrating Native Views into Museum Procedures: Hope and Practice at the National Museum of the American Indian," *Museum Anthropology* 22, no. 1 (1998): 33–42; and Henry, "Challenges in Managing Culturally Sensitive Collections." Tom Biolsi notes that such steps are increasingly common as tribal sovereignty — understood as dominion over bound lands — is extended to other domains of power and influence outside those boundaries. He also suggests that the NMAI has become a "national indigenous space," over which collective Native sovereignty has been cast; Thomas Biolsi, "Imagined Geographies: Sovereignty, Indigenous Space, and American Indian Struggle," *American Ethnologist* 32, no. 2 (2005): 248. The degree to which tribal nations in the United States have contributed financially to the NMAI may also indicate the museum's perception and designation as a national Indigenous space; see Harjo, "NMAI."

71. Cobb, "National Museum of the American Indian as Cultural Sovereignty," 486.

72. Paul Chaat Smith has suggested that the NMAI, with Indian gaming and repatriation legislation, is a very large payment on America's "moral debt" to Native people; personal communication with the author, August 7, 2007. Ruth Phillips has also questioned whether museum collaborations with Native communities represent "symbolic restitution." Ruth B. Phillips, "Community Collaboration in Exhibitions," introduction to *Museums and Source Communities*, ed. Peers and Brown, 157–70.

73. Bennett, *Birth of the Museum*.

74. NMAI, *Strategic Plan: 2006–2008* (Washington DC: National Museum of the Ameri-

can Indian, 2005); NMAI, "Intellectual Framework for the Collections and Collecting Plan."

75. Hilden and Huhndorf, "Performing 'Indian,'" 162. On master narratives, see Edward M. Bruner, "Ethnography as Narrative," in *The Anthropology of Experience*, ed. Victor Turner and Edward M. Bruner (Urbana: University Illinois Press, 1986), 135–55.

76. Robert Warrior suggests that Native writings that stress idealism and essentialism and overemphasize authenticity and tradition are potentially dangerous and limiting; I suggest that similar museum products are equally limiting and present the public with images that fit preconceptions but do little to serve Native people and sovereign expressions; see Robert Allen Warrior, *Tribal Secrets: Recovering American Indian Intellectual Traditions* (Minneapolis: University of Minnesota Press, 1995). Scott Lyons notes that desire to repossess tradition and culture admits loss and can prompt a sense of guilt. This suggests that the traditional—however reclaimed or reintroduced—remains a desired state for many, thus furthering dependence on older models rather than negotiation of new Native expressions. See Scott Richard Lyons, "Crying for Revision: Postmodern Indians and Rhetorics of Tradition," in *Making and Unmaking the Prospects for Rhetoric*, ed. Theresa Enos (Mahwah NJ: Lawrence Erlbaum Associates, 1997), 123–31.

77. I cannot do justice here to this expanding body of literature, but on intellectual sovereignty, see Georges E. Sioui, *For an Amerindian Autohistory: An Essay on the Foundations of a Social Ethic*, trans. Sheila Fishman (Montreal: McGill-Queen's University Press, 1992); and Robert Allen Warrior, *Tribal Secrets and the People and the Word: Reading Native Nonfiction* (Minneapolis: University of Minnesota Press, 2005). On appropriations of spirituality, see Lisa Aldred, "Plastic Shamans and Astroturf Sundances: New Age Commercialization of Native American Spirituality," *American Indian Quarterly* 24, no. 3 (2000): 329–52; and Laurie Ann Whitt, "Cultural Imperialism and the Marketing of Native America," in *Contemporary Native American Cultural Issues*, ed. Duane Champagne (Walnut Creek CA: AltaMira Press, 1999), 169–92. For reclaiming Indigenous tribal names, see Cornel Pewewardy, "Renaming Ourselves on Our Own Terms: Race, Tribal Nations, and Representation in Education," *Indigenous Nations Studies Journal* 1, no. 1 (2000): 11–28. On rhetorical sovereignty, see Lyons, "Crying for Revision"; and Scott Richard Lyons, "Rhetorical Sovereignty: What Do American Indians Want from Writing?" *College Composition and Communication* 51, no. 3 (2000): 447–68. For literary nationalism, see Jace Weaver, *That the People Might Live: Native American Literatures and Native American Community* (Oxford: Oxford University Press, 2007); Jace Weaver, Craig S. Womack, and Robert Warrior, *American Indian Literary Nationalism* (Albuquerque: University of New Mexico Press, 2006); and Craig S. Womack, *Red on Red: Native American Literary Separatism* (Minneapolis: University of Minnesota Press, 1999). On political sover-

eignty, see Taiaiake Alfred, *Peace, Power, and Righteousness: An Indigenous Manifesto* (Oxford: Oxford University Press, 1999).

78. Jacki Thompson Rand, "Why I Can't Visit the National Museum of the American Indian: Reflections of an Accidental Privileged Insider, 1989–1994," *Common-Place* 7, no. 4 (2007), http://www.common-place.org/vol-07/no-04/rand. In many ways, the NMAI has reemphasized old museum traditions of dependence on objects as storytelling devices or illustrations. This dependence results in major parts of the Native story remaining untold or being accompanied by items that visitors do not find worthy of inclusion in what they have been told is the world's best collection of "Indian stuff"; see Chavez, "Collaborative Exhibit Development." The NMAI's continued reliance on objects is especially surprising considering the points included in an early programming document: "Although . . . objects held by the Smithsonian are unsurpassed . . . Native American people are not 'object-oriented.' . . . The picture of Native American life should . . . not . . . over-emphasize the objects themselves over the people and culture." Venturi, Scott Brown, and Associates, *Way of the People*, 40.

79. Elizabeth Cook-Lynn, *Why I Can't Read Wallace Stegner and Other Essays: A Tribal Voice* (Madison: University of Wisconsin Press, 1996). The intellectual freedom of university scholars, as compared to those in museums, may be no small matter in this decision; political and intellectual structures of existing museums may not allow complete expression of Native cultural sovereignty, except perhaps in tribal museums. See McMullen, "Relevance and Reflexivity"; and McMullen, "Currency of Consultation". However, following Robert Warrior's thoughts on Native intellectualism, Native museum work must remain engaged with the wider world and not be conducted only in tribally controlled domains; see Warrior, *Tribal Secrets*.

80. Native artists have used their own art and others' to talk about political and cultural sovereignty, but more striking examples come from contemporary Native photographers' readings of historic Native imagery and their interpretations of survivance—as Anishinabe author Gerald Vizenor has used it—and of sovereignty strategies visible therein. See Gerald McMaster and Lee-Ann Martin, eds., *Indigena: Contemporary Native Perspectives in Canadian Art* (Vancouver: Douglas and McIntyre, 1993); Theresa Harlan, "Creating a Visual History: A Question of Ownership," in Roalf, *Strong Hearts*; Theresa Harlan, "Indigenous Photographies: A Space for Indigenous Realities," in *Native Nations: Journeys in American Photography*, ed. Jane Alison (London: Barbican Art Gallery, 1998), 233–45; Jolene Rickard, "Sovereignty: A Line in the Sand," in Roalf, *Strong Hearts*, 51–54; Jolene Rickard, "The Occupation of Indigenous Space as 'Photograph,'" in Alison, *Native Nations*, 57–71; Hulleah Tsinhnahjinnie, "When Is a Photograph Worth a Thousand Words?" in Alison, *Native Nations*, 41–55; and Dubin, "Native American Imagemaking."

81. Lyons, "Rhetorical Sovereignty," 449. See also Weaver, *That the People Might Live*; and Womack, *Red on Red*. Native people put in the position of "reading" objects often refuse to comment on items they have identified as "not ours," suggesting that they recognize that culturally specific, literal readings are desired and decline to offer comment or interpretation on a culture other than their own.

82. Warrior, *Tribal Secrets*. Ruth Phillips and others in the Great Lakes Research Alliance for the Study of Aboriginal Arts and Cultures (GRASAC), based at Carleton University in Ottawa, Ontario, are currently drawing on museums and archives to create a shared Web-accessible database of objects and resources to encourage interdisciplinary research on Great Lakes visual culture. While some individuals involved in these research projects are not "material culture specialists," work already underway on the relation of Indigenous diplomacy, rhetoric, wampum belts, and treaties promises to lay new ground for intertextualization of material culture and other expressive forms.

83. Venturi, *Way of the People*.

84. As Hupa tribal member Merv George Jr. said of the NMAI, "They have these items. But they don't have the stories that go along with the items"; interview with Merv George Jr. quoted in Klein, "Native Americans in Museums." Despite the richness and complexity of the collections, Heye's collecting and curatorial practices and often pervasive disregard for objects' documentation can limit the collections' potential. Descriptions of MAI work during his lifetime recount confusion, loss, or destruction of field notes, excavation records, and other documentation, characterized as a luxury Heye could not always afford to maintain. These losses significantly reduce the collections' value for almost all uses. NMAI, "Intellectual Framework for the Collections and Collecting Plan"; and NMAI, "Scope of Collections Description."

85. This is connected with Fabian's "denial of coevalness," which suggests that ethnography temporally distances its object from its recorder by making it impossible for both to exist in the same place at the same time. Living peoples whose works are placed in museums as ethnology or primitive art face the same difficulty of bridging the time gap created by this distancing and museum objectification of material culture as frozen life. See Fabian, *Time and the Other*; Janet Catherine Berlo, "The Formative Years of Native American Art History," introduction to *The Early Years of Native American Art History*, ed. Janet Catherine Berlo (Seattle: University of Washington Press), 1–21; and Jonaitis, "Franz Boas, John Swanton, and the New Haida Sculpture."

86. Hilden and Huhndorf, "Performing 'Indian,'" 170; Lloyd Kiva New, "Translating the Past," in *All Roads Are Good*, 42.

87. On the treatment of objects as art, see Ruth B. Phillips, "Disrupting Past Paradigms: The National Museum of the American Indian and the First Peoples Hall at the Canadian Museum of Civilization," *Public Historian* 28, no. 2 (2006): 75–80;

Jacknis, "A New Thing?" For the commodification of Native objects, see Hilden, "Race for Sale"; Hilden and Huhndorf, "Performing 'Indian'"; and Dubin, *Native America Collected*.

88. MAI histories describe Heye's overemphasis—as a collector rather than a scientist—on whole ceramic vessels and other complete items and his specific disregard for potsherds; see Lothrop, "George Gustav Heye, 1874–1956." I suspect that, lacking the knowledge or imagination to mentally reconstruct them into complete objects, Heye did not find potsherds and other fragmentary objects "readable."

89. Pearce summarizes Michael Thompson's "rubbish theory," which divides material culture into rubbish (objects of no value), transients (commodities and items that move within capitalist systems and whose value declines over time), and "durables" (things whose value appreciates and is often spiritual, scientific, or artistic); see Pearce, *Museums, Objects, and Collections*, 34. Heye seemed uninterested in transients in this system, but he obviously valued both durables and rubbish in his attempts to understand Native lifeways. This presentation of Thompson's theory does not account for transient objects in collectors' and museums' hands that move into the durable category as they age and become appreciated as art or artifacts; see Ann McMullen, "See America First: Tradition, Innovation, and Indian Country Arts," in *Indigenous Motivations: Recent Acquisitions from the National Museum of the American Indian* (Washington DC: National Museum of the American Indian, 2006), 19–25.

4

Ethnographic Elaborations, Indigenous Contestations, and the Cultural Politics of Imagining Community

A View from the District Six Museum in South Africa

CIRAJ RASSOOL

On April 3, 2001, in a landmark moment in the history of cultural display in South Africa, the bushman diorama, exhibited in the South African Museum (SAM) since 1960, was shut down. Amid strong feelings expressed by some staff members that the act of closure smacked of political correctness and that it appeared to be a knee-jerk reaction, the diorama was boarded up and "archived," symbolizing the museum's commitment to change.[1] A few days before, on March 30, 2001, delegates of the Khoisan communities of South Africa had gathered together at Oudtshoorn for the first time in their memory to deliberate over various issues at a consultative conference, titled "Khoisan Diversity in National Unity." At this conference, the tribes, their leaders, researchers, and academics assembled to discuss "how the Khoisan people and their leaders" would be "accommodated constitutionally."[2] But the central purpose of the conference was to take discussions forward, regarding "the next step in the National Khoisan Legacy Project, which strove to develop heritage resources significant to the Khoisan people."[3] On June 7, 2001, the Sixty-fifth Annual Conference of the South African Museums Association (SAMA) was held in Port Elizabeth around the general theme of museum ethics. At this meeting, representatives of three of the key museums in South Africa that hold collections of human remains, especially of the Khoisan, declared the interest and willingness of their institutions to pursue a discussion about repatriation.[4]

These processes and events reflect the tensions and contestations that are emerging over the place of Khoisan history and culture and the appropriate terms and frameworks of their representation, in the domain of heritage and public culture after apartheid. These struggles have occurred amid centralized processes of transforming old national museums and museum collections as well as attempts by the state to spearhead official heritage projects, in the form of the Legacy Project program, geared toward the transformation of heritage. At certain times these moves represented attempts to transcend older frameworks of ethnography and racial science; at other times they represented a quest to recover an Indigenous cultural history that had been distorted and obscured by colonialism and apartheid. Sometimes this has meant the reinvention of ethnicity in the name of Indigenousness. Often, as we shall see, these seemingly contradictory moves, of challenging ethnography and of appealing to ethnic identity, have occurred simultaneously. It is necessary for us to understand when and under what conditions ethnic frameworks are reproduced and when they are (potentially) transcended.

These contradictions are reflective of broader challenges and contests unfolding in the sphere of heritage in the public domain more generally. Contrary to what some historians in South Africa might think,[5] almost every sphere of heritage production has seen complexity, controversy, and contestation in relation to dominant discursive frames that have been crystallizing. Among the elements of this dominant discourse has been the framing device of the "rainbow nation," where the concept of culture is largely in primordial terms. These dominant discursive forms have been contested. In significant cases, particularly in community museums and local cultural projects, certain initiatives had begun to push beyond these dominant narrations and to contest the constitutive elements of the nation, the cultural politics of tourism, as well as the signage systems and forms of memorialization that are attached to urban and rural landscapes. It is here that the concept of community has been approached outside of ethnic discourses of diversity.[6]

The discourse of many cultures, through which culture and heritage are more easily commoditized as spectacle, has continued to unleash itself upon the South African landscape. New cultural villages are positioning themselves for tourism virtually every day.[7] While this has been the main character of cultural tourism, cultural festivals and cultural campaigns run by newspapers have also been characterized by the search for authentic culture. Elsewhere, the leading documentary photographer of the social conditions of apartheid and resistance, Peter Magubane, is now free from having to document the struggle and is thus able to focus on neglected heritage, continuing to promote his recently published book of photographs, *Vanishing Cultures*, which is little more than a collection of studies on tribes that are now addressed as authentic cultures.[8]

As cultural tourism continues to present itself as the passport to tourism's democratization, South Africa continues to be depicted as a world in one country, with visitors being invited to gaze on the ancient rituals of old Africa and to explore a culture as fascinating as it is diverse. In a dazzling array of cultural villages, culture and history remain frozen in a timeless zone as a kaleidoscope of frozen ethnic stereotypes that correspond with the predominant tourist images of Africa. Each cultural village reproduces a specific ethnic stereotype, whose roots lie in colonial administration and in nineteenth- and early twentieth-century imperial exhibitions. Notions of authenticity and being close to the real Africa are generated by the correspondence between nineteenth-century images of pulsating tribes and the performance of ethnographic spectacle.[9] The case of the Makuleke of Limpopo Province, where a tourism development project has been created as a means to give effect to a successful land claim, reflects the possibilities of creating cultural villages without reproducing and indeed memorializing static notions of culture and ethnicity. Reflecting an awareness of the dangers of stereotyping and conforming to outsider views of Africa, the Makuleke proposals called for the creation of an interpretive center, thus creating the possibility of challenging ethnic fixing and culture depicted as timeless essence.[10]

In our research, we have referred to the dominant framework for the depiction of South African cultural heritage as often perpetuating frozen ethnic stereotypes, much of which was constructed in the colonial gaze. Elsewhere we have also referred to the rainbow narrative and to the discourse on many cultures. It is possible to utilize a similar analytical frame to understand the contradictory moves that occurred from March through June of 2001 to place the issue of Khoisan heritage and culture on the public history agenda in South Africa. These cases imply a contest unfolding over the legacy of ethnography in postapartheid South Africa, which extends these constructs. Ethnography is seen here as a knowledge system that seeks to classify and order society on the basis of supposed racial or ethnic grounds.

In the history of the museum, the life of ethnography saw the presumed application of science to the collection and display of objects and artifacts in pursuit of the study and depiction of racial and cultural difference. The early category that was used in South African museums and universities was, of course, ethnology, which was used to refer both to the scientific study of native races and to the sociology of primitive societies.[11] Later, under the rubric of the supposedly more acceptable category of ethnography, the focus shifted from an interest in bodies to an interest in cultural difference, often making use of visual representations of the racialized native body, placed in invented cultural scenes. South African museums were indeed characterized by the familiar colonial classificatory division between ethnography and cultural history, which separated static depictions of supposed primitive societies from depictions of the stages of development of supposedly civilized societies. Under apartheid this division was given added force through the operation of governmental funding structures, with cultural history deemed to be a white own affair.[12] The creation of Iziko Museums of Cape Town from the old national collections and museums represents more than just a new institutionalized centralization of resources. In Iziko, especially with the creation of the new Social History Collections division, the institutional circumstances have arguably been created for the possibility of putting to rest the classificatory division between cultural history and ethnography.[13]

But the discourse of ethnography has gone on to have life outside the museum as well. Cultural villages represent a new genre of living museum, in which an overnight hotel-type experience is arranged in the guise of ethnic authenticity. Sometimes the cultural encounter in such invented settings takes on qualities of anthropology lessons. Carolyn Hamilton has drawn attention to the immersion of visitors inside a tourist anthropology of Zulu identity at Shakaland in KwaZulu-Natal and to the Zulu cultural lessons that are given inside the Great Hut by a cultural advisor, who explains the Zulu way of doing things.[14] But more than being a replication of the museum, or an approximation of the circumstances of an anthropological field encounter or anthropology classroom, ethnographic discourse has also found expression in the cultural politics of Indigenous identity assertions, as evidenced in the proceedings and discussions of the National Khoisan Consultative Conference at Oudtshoorn.

Ethnography has also continued to have life in successful land claims on national park land, which were lodged in the mid-1990s under the terms of the Restitution of Land Rights Act Twenty-two of 1994. The successful land claim launched in 1995 by the Southern Kalahari San (many of whom were performing as bushmen in the setting of a private game park, Kagga Kamma, at the time of the claim) resulted in the South African government handing over 50,000 hectares of land from the former Kalahari Gemsbok National Park. This claim was based indirectly on the ethnological and anthropometric research that was conducted in 1936 by a team of University of the Witwatersrand anthropologists and linguists in preparation for the display of bushmen at the Empire Exhibition. This claim emphasized continuities with an Aboriginal past, closeness to nature, and the racialized identity of a people who were "frozen in artificial time"; it was first performed in Johannesburg in 1936 and later transferred to Kagga Kamma.[15] Thus, just as the demise of apartheid has created enormous possibilities for ethnographic discourses to be overcome, this period has paradoxically also seen new ethnographic elaborations on older systems of thought and classification.

When news broke that the closure of the Khoisan diorama at the SAM was imminent, some unhappiness was expressed in certain staff quarters. Retired taxidermist Reinhold Rau, who was still in the employ of the museum, described the closure as ridiculous. Completely missing the point, he stated that he himself had "made a cast of a European [which was] on display in this same natural history museum." He went on to describe the argument that you could not have people in the same museum as animals as being "rubbish."[16] Later, the SAM restaurant staff bemoaned the drop in museum attendance, which they attributed to the closure of the diorama, which was once described as the most popular museum exhibit in South Africa.[17] Without any investigation or analysis and in the service of a rather naive sense of journalistic balance, *Cape Times* journalist Melanie Gosling attempted to canvass Khoisan opinion. From the conference in Oudtshoorn, whose proceedings had just been finalized, a view was expressed that supported the diorama's closure, because it "did not depict indigenous people as human"; while in Windhoek, where a meeting of the San Cultural Heritage Committee had just taken place, the closure of the diorama was supposedly condemned, based on the argument that it was important that "their past be preserved."[18] This latter view was strongly reminiscent of David Kruiper, who then lived in Kagga Kamma and who paid homage in 1995 to the central cast of the bushman diorama, perceived to be the image of the *stamvader*, (tribal patriarch) Ou Makai.[19]

The intention to close the diorama was first made known on a public television news broadcast in October 2000 by Jack Lohman, who was then newly appointed as director of Iziko. Unbeknownst to his senior colleagues, who were caught a little unaware, Lohman, as someone with a good sense of the media sound bite, went on television to proclaim on behalf of the museum that the diorama had seen its final season and that the museum was closing its shutters on this exhibit.[20] Ben Ngubane — the then Minister of Arts, Culture, Science, and Technology — personally entered the fray soon after, expressing support for what he thought was the movement of the controversial displays. After Ngubane had called on Iziko to urgently investigate this issue, Fidel Hadebe, Ngubane's spokesperson, said, "the ideal situation is that such displays should be put where they belong, in the cultural history museum, and not among animals."[21] In this limited view, concern was not expressed about the objects and artifacts that comprised the diorama, especially about the casts and their history, their acquisition, and their lives within the museum's collections and exhibitions.

Senior staff members in the SAM had recognized for years the controversial nature of the diorama, through research on the diorama's intellectual history as well as research on its audiences.[22] Over the years, some attempt at contextualization was created — initially with a limited display on the making of the casts, including information about the people who were cast — amid academic debates on the creation of the category of bushman. For a time, the late-eighteenth-century artwork by Samuel Daniell depicting a San camp, on which the design of the diorama had been based, was exhibited alongside the diorama.[23] Later, in the wake of the controversial but powerful exhibition Miscast: Negotiating Khoisan History and Material Culture, curator and artist Pippa Skotnes created an accompanying display that attempted to depict San intellectual traditions, much like some of the intentions of Miscast. This was achieved, however, through the depiction of the relationship between /Xam subjects and those early anthropologists Wilhelm Bleek and Lucy Lloyd—who studied them in the mid-nineteenth century—as an instance of remarkable cooperation and mutual respect. In this framework, the Bleek and Lloyd archive was celebrated as "a 13,000-page record of a series of relationships between two European scholars and a group of /Xam and !Kung individuals whose common aim was to preserve the memories of culture and traditions which were fatally threatened."[24]

The contextual effects of these parallel exhibitions were, however, quite limited. Despite their awareness of the diorama's shortcomings, senior staff members in the SAM seemed to be largely paralyzed at any prospect of altering Margaret Shaw's legacy. Amid this simultaneous discomfort and paralysis, the diorama, left to itself, continued to perform the function of being the place where tour groups and school students came to view images of primitiveness and ecological soundness. For students in museum studies, the diorama came to be a kind of meta-ethnography exhibit, as an exhibition displaying a particular time, thus giving effect to Davison's idea that the casts were, "authentic artefacts of scientific attitudes and museum practice in the early twentieth century."[25]

Amid internal confusion in Iziko among staff members who were suddenly caught in the maelstrom of transformation, and in response to the criticism from a tourist industry that felt deprived of one of its prime destinations, the SAM felt compelled to issue a statement explaining the diorama's closure. The statement explained that, under the new banner of Iziko, the SAM and the South African Cultural History Museum were once again part of a single organization. An institutional cleavage between them had been created under apartheid in the 1960s, as a means of separating colonial history from Khoisan and other anthropology collections, which remained with natural history in the SAM. The SAM viewed the diorama as part of an exhibition system, which did not "demonstrate that anthropology includes all humankind." The diorama's closure represented a decision to "archive" the exhibit while its future was reviewed. The statement also hinted at future directions and modes of work: "Instead of showing only 'other cultures', new exhibitions will focus on themes that embrace all people." According to the statement, the diorama's closure represented the museum's commitment to change. It sought to encourage debate within the museum; and it invited the public, and especially *"people of Khoisan descent,"* to participate in these debates.[26] At the SAM a notice on the boarded-up diorama expressed a similar desire. The diorama, the notice said, "will be left in place while a process of consultation with *affected communities* takes place. We are committed to *working in partnership with Khoisan people* in developing new exhibitions [emphasis mine]." But how was this partnership and process of consultation with the Khoisan to be accomplished?

The answer to this question is perhaps to be found in the conference rituals and cultural constructions that unfolded at the Oudtshoorn conference. This gathering was attended by more than five hundred people, most of whom were Khoisan delegates from thirty-six communities and organizations as well as from different regions. "Never before had individuals and leaders from nearly all Khoisan communities and organizations in South Africa come together in huge numbers to deliberate on their future." The conference was opened by deputy president Zuma, who started by referring to the "special role" of Khoisan people in the history of the struggle against colonialism. He made special mention of Autshumato, who was Robben Island's first political prisoner and "the only man to escape from the island and survive." The conference is said to have reflected "the enduring strength of the Khoisan people," who "waged the first wars of resistance against the colonial onslaught of the seventeenth century." Among the themes that were discussed at the conference were religious values, culture and identity, education and the representation of Khoisan in the media, land rights, Khoisan NGOs (non-governmental organizations) and economic empowerment, intellectual property, Indigenous knowledge systems, and the role of Khoisan women.[27]

A focus on the possibilities of the National Khoisan Legacy Project as well as on the question of Khoisan constitutional accommodation enabled "the aspirations of Khoisan unity and for a national South African identity" to be "elevated."[28] The conference was made possible by what Henry Bredekamp has called, "an upsurge in Khoisan revivalism." Great pride was expressed in being Khoisan, with Khoisan identity and culture enthusiastically embraced. Delegates also applauded traditional Khoisan dancing, singing, and speech in Khoisan languages, while many wore clothing with Indigenous motifs, such as a leopard motif. In addition, the conference "provided an opportunity for Khoisan to network and to foster a common vision and approach to the future."[29] It was reported in the press that outside the conference center, "people of the Inqua, !Xu, Griekwa, Nama, Hessequa and other Khoisan tribes embraced each other warmly," while inside the conference, Inqua choirs and dance groups performed as San children "portrayed traditional tribal stories through dance routines."[30]

The state's program of Legacy Projects was explained as "a national initiative for nation-building designed to fill in gaps in South Africa's heritage resources created by colonialism and apartheid policies in the past." It was noted that the ideal Khoisan Legacy Project needed to be inspirational to the Khoisan and had to build an understanding of Khoisan heritage; a number of suggestions to accomplish these goals were made, including "a statue, memorial or monument to the Khoisan" and a "national institute and museum for Khoisan heritage studies." It had been decided that, in order for the largest number of people and communities to benefit, the Khoisan Legacy Project would be structured around a National Khoisan Heritage Route, which would incorporate oral history and intangible heritage. It would also include buildings and other structures and sites such as natural features of the landscape, rock art, graves, and memorials. Attention had to be given to "the past and/or present spiritual and/or social value of the site for Khoisan communities," as well as to the aesthetic and historical values of the site. "All Khoisan interest groups" were intended to "participate in the identification and justification of sites for development"; and it was stressed that all Khoisan communities were to be encouraged to "establish their own 'house of memory,' where oral histories, written records and heritage objects could be collected to form a core legacy collection unique to that community."[31]

Though ethnography had hitherto considered and framed Khoisan heritage, when viewed in these ways, the potential exists for the framework of ethnography to be transcended. Amid a guiding principle in Oudtshoorn of recovering Indigenous heritage, of simultaneously "advancing unity amongst the Khoisan and advancing a South African national identity," and of rearticulating and reconstituting "the realms of identity and culture," it is significant that the closure of the diorama was supported with the argument that it did not depict Indigenous people as being human.[32] It is also significant that the idea of a National Khoisan Heritage Route as a "set of tourist attractions" was felt to be in need of more careful evaluation.[33] More generally, in being reclaimed, the category "Khoisan," despite its origins as a racial concept in anthropology, has the potential to enable more specific ethnic claims to be sidestepped while also enabling an Indigenous identity to be refashioned.

Despite these possibilities, there were other characteristics to the consultative conference that reflected a rebirth and recoding of ethnography and colonial identities rather than their transcendence. This was evident nowhere more than in the deliberations around constitutional accommodation. Making use of United Nations discourses on Indigenousness, it was claimed that the Khoisan could rightly aspire to a special status "because of the fact that they were Aboriginal and/or first indigenous of the country." Groups such as the Griqua, for example, had "an unbroken basis of leadership which stretched over centuries." Khoisan culture and religion were claimed to be distinctive; and it was also asserted that Khoisan people were unrepresented in various public offices and structures such as the Office of the Public Protector, the Human Rights Commission, the Commission for Gender Equality, the Youth Commission, the Independent Broadcasting Corporation, and even the Independent Electoral Commission. National recognition needed to be obtained through a proposed National Council of Indigenous People (NCIP), which would consist of the Chief-leaders of all the first Indigenous groups. As the real engine, the executive of the NCOP would liaise with various parliamentary standing committees, as well as the Council of Traditional Leaders. A proposed model for constitutional accommodation was drafted by the National Griqua Forum. In this model the Council of Indigenous Peoples, with representation by the Griqua, Nama, Korana, San, and Cape Khoi, would be the basis of accessing the National Assembly and the NCIP. Furthermore, out of a link with the entirely separate Bantu-speaking Council of Traditional Leaders, a joint standing committee on Indigenous and traditional affairs would be created.[34]

Thus, alongside the potential for a post-ethnic framework for Khoisan identity and heritage, a belated pitch for an accelerated route to ethnic formation in the name of Indigenous identity was being made after apartheid. Khoisanness was no longer Indigenousness merely as Aboriginality in South Africa. Now what was being claimed was Khoisan Indigenousness as ethnicity. What was being called for was a preferential classificatory category, with Indigenous identity as the basis of access to state resources. This ethnic framework was also ethnographic, based on claims of cultural specialness and distinctiveness (*eiesoortigheid*). Identity and constitutional representation were further subdivided into discrete subethnicities, each of which would have an equal number of representatives. And all over this proposed system of classification and representation were chiefs and *stamhoofde*, or "tribal heads," and members of royal houses who would be remunerated as cabinet ministers and as members of Parliament, "since they are leaders of the first Indigenous people and deserve to be treated as such."[35]

This Khoisan political elite would occupy seats in a reinvented, belated colonial system of native affairs with its origins in the system of indirect rule, a system from which the Khoisan in South Africa had largely been excluded. Just as the potential for ethnography to be transcended had been elaborated upon, in almost the same breath it was being reproduced on nearly the same terms as colonialism. Also being highlighted was the ever-present shadow of colonial construction in assertions of Indigenousness. But what was being proposed was a shift from physical anthropology to native affairs, from race to ethnicity.

So, these are the contradictory claims on identity and heritage—simultaneously challenging and reproducing, questioning and asserting ethnography—that the SAM would face in its efforts to consult with Khoisan people over the future of its diorama and ethnographic collections. While consultations and partnerships with emerging elite Khoisan constitutional and cultural forums might hold the possibility of setting the SAM on a new path of responsiveness to Indigenous audiences, the museum could well find itself immersed in Indigenous definitions and ethnographic elaborations that perpetuate the very intellectual frameworks and cultural histories they wish to overcome.

Even so, the focal point of the diorama as the indicator of museum transformation seemed to be missing the point. For while the diorama has occupied a symbolic space as the visual expression of colonial taxonomy, ethnography, and racial science in South African museums, it is but the tip of the ethnographic iceberg. In considering the history and ethnographic dilemmas of the SAM—especially the legacy of Louis Peringuey, an early director of the museum, and his assistant, James Drury, the museum modeler—our discussions have tended to overemphasize the legacy of cast making. It can be argued that in closing the diorama, the SAM had perhaps diverted attention away from a more nefarious legacy. Our research shows that far more than casts, Peringuey's legacy is that of the collecting of skeletons. Human remains lie at the center of the emergence of museums in South Africa as institutions of order, classification, and knowledge at the turn of the twentieth century. Human remains provided the basis of the founding of the McGregor Museum in Kimberley and was central to the development of the SAM in the age of anthropology.[36]

Most people might assume that these human remains were excavated by professional archaeologists and that they are fossilized remains of long-dead people, collected, perhaps, as part of research on prehistory, evolution, and human origins. What has been largely left unexamined in the history of anthropology, archaeology, and museums is the way that many of these remains were acquired, particularly around the turn of the century.[37] Our research reveals a little of the evidence of an incipient trade in human remains at this time, between grave robbers and South African museums as well as museums in Europe. It reveals, moreover, that there was intense rivalry and competition among museums about any future possession of the skeletons of still-living persons, as well as the digging up of very recently buried bodies.

Our study examines the ethics of these exhumations and, in the light of this, questions the appropriate steps for placing the issue of human remains in museums on the agenda of both the academy and museums. At the heart of the institutional history of the museum in South Africa in the twentieth century was a competitive and insatiable trade in human remains, to a significant extent of the newly dead, and in some cases, of the still living. This trade involved very close connections by men and women of science in South African museums and beyond with gross acts of plunder and the defilement of human bodies.[38] The southern Kalahari and the Northern Cape more generally were part of an enormous field site, stretching from southern Namibia across to then Bechuanaland, for the acquisition of human remains that were central to racial research in South Africa and Europe. The failure of the academy and museums to examine these political questions squarely derived from a perpetuation of the idea that the bones and skulls of Khoisan people, in the twentieth century, were natural history fossils, referred to as relics at the beginning of the twentieth century.

In stating the case for repatriation and reburial, we ask what interest the state has in the remains of recently dead people being kept in its institutions. Repatriation could take a number of forms, and the National Heritage Resources Act proposed one method. This would require a claim being made by a "community or body with a bona fide interest" for such a "heritage resource" held in a publicly funded institution as apart of the "national estate."[39] The onus thus lies on such communities or bodies to make claims on skeletons from museums. Such a method, we argue, would create a piecemeal process and is not based on any understanding on how human remains were acquired in the first place.[40] This framework also implicitly encourages ethnic claims on bones as the basis of the expression of a bona fide interest. Such an ethnic framework would ensure that the bones be returned in precisely the same framework in which they were first collected.

The method of repatriation and reburial for which we argue is a mass reburial in a public ceremony and the construction of a national memorial site. Human remains were collected from the most decimated sections of the Indigenous population. Apart from the Khoisan, there was no harvesting of the human remains of the Indigenous on the scale of that which took place in the United States or Australia. White colonizers were probably far too scared of Bantu speakers to attempt to rob their graves en masse. To represent the interests of the majority and to act on behalf of the Indigenous, the state should assert their prior rights against any museum collection, provenanced or unprovenanced, and act decisively to ensure repatriation.

When Mike Raath, in his address to the 2001 SAMA Conference, and Francis Thackeray, in personal communication, expressed the desire of their institutions to engage in a process of repatriation, they drew on the research and arguments contained in *Skeletons in the Cupboard*. In conducting fresh audits of the skeletal collections inside their museums, they discovered that, indeed, just like the SAM and the McGregor Museum, a substantial percentage of their bones were ill begotten and indeed fell into the category that *Skeletons in the Cupboard* had described. There was no question in their minds that consultation needed to occur. The SAM, on the other hand, had understood that the curatorship of these sensitive collections needed to change, and proposals were being formulated for special keeping places with restricted access for the "respectful treatment" of human remains. Continued retention on this basis, however, did not adequately recognize the extent to which ethnographic museums were institutions of atrocity. Museum collecting involved more than the epistemic violence of classification, ordering, and the hierarchical systems of racial science. It involved literal violence and violation of the body.

In arguing for an approach to repatriation, community engagement, and a public that refuses to be contained in ethnic frameworks, we have implicitly tried to find a way of transcending ethnographic discourse, both in and outside the museum. This argument recognizes that a culture war has been unfolding over the legacy of ethnography: as a museum discipline, as a practice of collecting and archiving, and as a discourse of classification in identity assertions and in heritage constructions more generally. In South Africa, where the struggle against race opened the possibility that ethnography itself could be questioned, we have seen ethnography come into its own with renewed vigor. Nevertheless, even within the Khoisan Legacy Project, the potential is being explored of approaches to culture and heritage that draw on the resources of language and memory for the public inscription of landscapes with Indigenous histories and cultural emblems and for the mapping of personal and community histories. Dealing with the diorama should surely be part of a broader project to address the history of ethnography at the SAM. Repatriation of museum skeletons through public reburial, rather than claims of ethnicity, would ensure that the legacy of ethnography might not only be understood but overcome. The skeletons of ethnography could still be put to rest.

Finally, it remains for me to provide some ideas on how the experience of the District Six Museum in Cape Town enables us to approach the question of community and museum publics beyond frames of ethnography and atonement.[41] From a variety of perspectives, the category of community museum is one that has been used to describe the District Six Museum. It is also a concept that is deployed deliberately by the museum to define the cultural politics of its memory work. The museum's use of "community" is not one that is naive, but one that is conscious and strategic. The museum insists on utilizing this concept as an organizational device in asserting a particular politics of governance and institutional orientation, in expressing a particular commitment to social mobilization, and in constructing and defending independent spaces of articulation and contestation in the public domain. This strategic position emanates from a complex museum institution that has created a hybrid space of cultural and intellectual production of contests and transactions among activist intellectuals, purveyors of academic knowledge, museum professionals, and performers of authentic voice. These features of the District Six Museum as a space of knowledge draw on a genealogy of forums of intellectual, cultural, and political expression in District Six, which came into existence during the 1930s, as well as on the politics of community organizing from the 1980s.

The idea of a community museum tends to conjure notions of authenticity and representativeness in a local institution that supposedly works with an audience that is considered to be a bounded community. The interests and worldview of the community museum are supposedly circumscribed by locality. With a history of racialized group areas in South Africa, this concept of community, defined by seemingly natural ethnic markers, is an ever-present danger. In a typological system of museums, community museums are sometimes understood as almost one of the simplest units of museum structures when considered along a continuum of museums of different rank, a hierarchy in which national museums are seen as more complex.[42] In this framework, the notions of community and community museum invite a paternalistic sentiment and ideas of innocence and naïveté, as the community now has access to modes of cultural and historical expression from which it had previously been excluded. The community museum also raises the idea of a museum as a focus of educational and cultural services. Here the museum seeks to reach certain audiences and to deliver "benefits to specific, geographically defined communities" through strategies of inclusion, within a framework of atonement and service.[43] The museum here is understood as being distinct from such communities with whom it may wish to extend formal relations of service and consultation and with whom it may even introduce forms of partnership, joint management, and relations of reciprocity.

The concept of the community museum has posed a range of difficulties in the District Six Museum and has been the focus of much debate. In the first place, the concept of community has been the subject of much suspicion because of its uses under apartheid, tending to be used in racialized, bounded ways to refer to racial and ethnic units of the population. Community was defined in racial and ethnic ways through the workings of the state and its apparatuses. Even when understood in geopolitical terms to refer to localities and neighborhoods where people lived, it was racialized because of the operation of racial legislation. One of the ironies of the postapartheid period is that ethnic forms of community identity and identification have had new life as primordial and static cultures, reproduced either for tourism or in search of state benefits through land claims.[44]

The District Six Museum defined itself as a community museum because it sees its work as a locus of social organizing and mobilization. This definition also signaled a desire to create a participatory and enabling framework of interpretation and empowerment and to generate the museum project as an ongoing process. A community museum wishing to influence the identity-making processes of re-creating and redefining a community from the ruins of apartheid's destruction required a strong museum infrastructure and more decisive means of balancing social activism with professional museum skills. The work of balancing these productive tensions strategically and finding the appropriate means of determining priorities under rapidly shifting cultural and political conditions remains one of the most important challenges of the District Six Museum's creative development.

Finally, the community museum as a project can only have longevity and sustainability through the generation of internal institutional capacity and expertise and through enhancing internal processes of debate and argumentation. While the museum's existence parallels the prosecution and ongoing settlement of the land claim by a legally defined claimant community, the notions of "community-ness" with which it works are not determined by descent, mere historic claims, or spatial presence. Instead, the museum's idea of community is strategic and expresses a desire for particular forms of social reconstruction. Community itself is an imagined identity of commonality and interest. Its parameters are the very essence of contestation. Through its exhibitions, programs, and forums, and in its internal processes of negotiation and brokerage, the District Six Museum is constantly involved in redefining and reframing its notions of community. It continues to be a site where postapartheid identities are being imagined and self-fashioned and not simply being imbibed passively from those that have been produced by colonialism and apartheid.

Notes

1. Melanie Gosling, "Controversial Khoisan Exhibition to Close," *Cape Times*, April 2, 2001; "Museum defends closure of 'bushmen' exhibition," *Dispatch Online*, April 6, 2001, http://www.dispatch.co.za/2001/04/06/southafrica/MUSEUM.HTM. For a discussion of these events see Leslie Witz, "Transforming Museums on Post-apartheid Tourist Routes," in *Museum Frictions: Global Transformations/ Public Cultures,* ed. Ivan Karp and others (Durham NC: Duke University Press, 2006), 107–34.

2. Bureaugard Tromp, "Zuma Praises Khoisan 'Wars of Resistance,'" *Independent Online*, March 30, 2001, http://www.iol.co.za/index.php?setid=1&clickid=124&artid=ct200103300_9401489K000126 (accessed October 8, 2008).

3. Institute for Historical Research, *National Khoisan Consultative Conference, Oudtshoorn: March 29 to April 1, 2001*, Conference Booklet, (Cape Town: Institute for Historical Research, University of the Western Cape, 2001).

4. Mike Raath (Johannesburg, South Africa: University of the Witwatersrand), "Human Material in Collections: Airing the Skeletons in the Closet," and Graham Avery (Iziko Museums of Cape Town), "Dealing with Sensitive Issues and Material: South African Museum's Experience and Ideas," papers presented to the 65th Conference and Annual General Meeting of the South African Museums Association (SAMA), June 5–7, 2001; a third position was outlined for me in personal communication by Francis Thackeray of the Transvaal Museum, Northern Flagship Institution. The theme of the SAMA conference was "A Question of Museum Ethics: Hayi bo! Shu! Eina! Ouch!"

5. See for example the posting by Jane Carruthers, in which she attempted to point out the dangers posed for history, inter alia by heritage—a zone that for her was almost inherently exaggeration, myth making, omission, and error and that she suggested should not be "the domain of historians." Jane Carruthers, "Heritage and History," Africa Forum #2, H-Africa, October 20, 1998, http://h-net.msu.edu/

cgi-bin/logbrowse.pl?trx=vx&list=h-africa&month=9810&week=c&msg=sv82D
ZpkATFzGc7zqbkFKA&user=&pw.

6. For a discussion of these contests and the ways in which heritage projects and sites such as the District Six Museum, Western Cape Action Tours, and the Makuleke community in the Limpopo Province reflect the potential to challenge dominant heritage discourses, see Ciraj Rassool, "The Rise of Heritage and the Reconstitution of History in South Africa," *Kronos*, no. 26 (2000): 1–22.

7. According to a *Sunday Times* report, one of the more recent sites to emerge is the Shangana Cultural Village, which opened in Hazyview in Mpumalanga alongside the Kruger National Park in March 1999. Largely the result of efforts of former advertising executives Robert More and James Delaney, who had set out "to create authentic Shangaan villages," the village was built "with the help of the local community" and with wood sourced from alien tree clearing in the Sabie Valley. See *Sunday Times* (London), August 22, 1999. Soon after, the Cape Metropolitan Council announced its decision to develop an "African Theme Park" on the outskirts of the city. The park would contain Xhosa, Zulu, and Ndebele villages as well as a restaurant, museum, auditorium, curio shop, and parking area; *Cape Times*, August 23, 1999.

8. Peter Magubane, *Vanishing Cultures in South Africa: Changing Customs in a Changing World* (Cape Town: Struik, 1998). In a remarkable and ironic twist, a number of scholars such as Sandra Klopper, Andrew Spiegel, Chris van Vuuren, and Debora James, who had been called in at a late stage of the book's production as specialists to rescue the book from simplistic tribalism, found themselves listed as consultants on the book's contents page. This served to give authority to the book's tribal focus, which tourists in search of African tribes demand and publishers of coffee table tourist books, such as Struik, eagerly provide. This book further carries the seal of approval of no less than Nelson Mandela, who wrote a foreword. Magubane's quest to corner a tourist market is seemingly unquenchable. His second book, *African Renaissance*, reproduces the tribal categories of the former book, as if this is the only means of scripting Indigenousness.

9. For an extended discussion of these issues, see Leslie Witz, Ciraj Rassool, and Gary Minkley, "Repackaging the Past for South African Tourism," *Daedalus* 130, no. 1 (2001), 277–96.

10. Lamson Maluleke (in collaboration with Eddie Koch), "Culture, Heritage and Tourism: Proposals for a Living Museums Project in the Makuleke Region of the Kruger National Park, South Africa," *Proceedings of the Constituent Assembly of the International Council of African Museums-Africom* (Lusaka, Zambia: Africom, October 3–9, 1999), 101–5; see also David Bunn and Mark Auslander, "Owning the Kruger Park," *Arts 1999: The Arts, Culture and Heritage Guide to South Africa*, 60–63.

11. Patricia Davison, "Redressing the Past: Integrating Social History Collections at Iziko," *South African Museums Association Bulletin*, 2005, 101–4.

12. The 1983 Tricameral Constitution in apartheid South Africa created a racialized government structure with areas of political, social, and cultural life defined as "own affairs" and "general affairs." Own affairs referred to the affairs of a particular racial group as defined under apartheid.

13. Davison, "Redressing the Past."

14. Carolyn Hamilton, "Authoring Shaka: Models, Metaphors and Historiography," (PhD diss., Johns Hopkins University, 1993), 540–42.

15. For a discussion of the cultural politics of the southern Kalahari land claim and the genealogy of "bushman" cultural performance, see Ciraj Rassool, "Cultural Performance and Fictions of Identity: The Case of the Khoisan of the Southern Kalahari, 1936–1937," in *Voices, Values and Identities Symposium*, ed. Yvonne Dladla (Pretoria, South Africa: South African National Parks, 1998), 73–79; see also Ciraj Rassool and Patricia Hayes, "Science and the Spectacle: /Khanako's South Africa, 1936–37" in *Deep Histories: Gender and Colonialism in Africa*, ed. Wendy Woodward, Patricia Hayes, and Gary Minkley (Amsterdam: Rodopi, 2001), 117–62.

16. Melanie Gosling, "Controversial Khoisan Exhibit to Close." *Cape Times*, April 2, 2001. It is interesting to note that Gosling reported on this story, whose Khoisan-related journalism is always accompanied by the description of her as the "environmental reporter."

17. Pippa Skotnes, "The Politics of Bushman Representations," in *Images and Empires: Visuality in Colonial and Postcolonial Africa*, ed. Paul Landau and Deborah Kaspin (Berkeley: University of California Press, 2002), 253–54.

18. Melanie Gosling, "Controversial Khoisan Exhibit to Close."

19. Rob Gordon, Ciraj Rassool, and Leslie Witz, "Fashioning the Bushman in Van Riebeeck's Cape Town, 1952 and 1993," in *Miscast: Negotiating the Presence of the Bushmen*, ed. Pippa Skotnes (Cape Town, South Africa: UCT Press, 1996), 269.

20. Interview with Jack Lohman, South African Broadcasting Corporation, October 4, 2000, cited in Patricia Davison, "Typecast: Representation of the Bushmen at the South African Museum," *Public Archaeology* 2, no. 1 (2001): 8.

21. *Independent Online*, "Ngubane wants to move disputed San display," November 2, 2000, http://www.iol.co.za/general/newsprint.php3?art_id=qw97317942089B223 (accessed October 8, 2008); African National Congress Daily News Briefing, November 3, 2000, http://70.84.171.10/~etools/newsbrief/2000/news1103.txt.

22. See for example, Patricia Davison, "Human Subjects as Museum Objects: A Project to Make Life-Casts of 'Bushmen' and 'Hottentots,' 1907–1924," *Annals of the South African Museum* 102, no. 5 (1993): 165–83; as well as Patricia Davison, "Rethinking the Practice of Ethnography and Cultural History in South African Museums," *African Studies* 49, no. 1 (1990): 149–67.

23. Davison, "Typecast," 3–20.

24. Skotnes's veneration of especially Lucy Lloyd is explained in Pippa Skotnes, introduction to Skotnes, *Miscast*, 22–23; the apogee of this fetishism can be found

in her book on the making of the archive, Pippa Skotnes, *Claim to the Country: The Archive of Wilhelm Bleek and Lucy Lloyd* (Johannesburg: Jacana, 2007). This approach to the Bleek-Lloyd Archive, couched within a politics of atonement and paternalism, is also expressed in the work of Janette Deacon. See Janette Deacon, "A Tale of Two Families: Wilhelm Bleek, Lucy Lloyd and the /Xam San of Northern Cape," in Skotnes, *Miscast*; and especially Janette Deacon and Craig Foster, *My Heart Stands in the Hill* (London: Struik Publishers, 2005). This is also the framework for Iziko South African Museum's Rock Art Exhibition, "!Qe: The Power of Rock Art," which was curated by Deacon and which perpetuated a dominant shamanist and neuropsychological paradigm. For a contrary view on this intellectual legacy, see the work of Andrew Bank, "Evolution and Racial Theory: The Hidden Side of Wilhelm Bleek," *South African Historical Journal* 43 (2000): 163–78; and especially Andrew Bank, *Bushmen in a Victorian World: The Remarkable Story of the Bleek-Lloyd Collection of Bushman Folklore* (Cape Town: Double Storey, 2006). For a discussion of the different approaches to the Bleek-Lloyd Archive, see Ciraj Rassool, "Beyond the Cult of 'Salvation' and 'Remarkable Equality': A New Paradigm for the Bleek-Lloyd Collection," *Kronos* 32 (2006): 244–51.

25. Patricia Davison, "Human Subjects as Museum Objects," 182.
26. "Debating the Diorama," http://www.museums.org.za/sam/resource/arch/bush debate.htm (accessed July 24, 2002, in author's possession).
27. Michael Besten and Henry C. Jatti Bredekamp, *Report on the National Khoisan Consultative Conference (NKCC) Held in the Oudtshoorn Civic Centre, March 29–April 1, 2001*, April 2001.
28. Besten and Bredekamp, *Report on the National Khoisan Consultative Conference*, emphasis mine.
29. Besten and Bredekamp, *Report on the National Khoisan Consultative Conference*.
30. Bureaugard Tromp, "Zuma Praises Khoisan 'Wars of Resistance.'"
31. Janette Deacon, *Report on the Workshop to Discuss the DACST Khoisan Legacy Project, Jointly Organised by SAHRA and the UWC Institute for Historical Research at the McGregor Museum, Kimberley, 1–3 December 2000*; and Janette Deacon, "Draft Business Plan for a National Khoisan Legacy Project," in *National Khoisan Consultative Conference, Oudtshoorn*, Conference Booklet.
32. Besten and Bredekamp, *Report on the National Khoisan Consultative Conference*.
33. Besten and Bredekamp, *Report on the National Khoisan Consultative Conference*.
34. Anthony le Fleur, "Khoisan Grondwetlike Akkommodasie," in *National Khoisan Consultative Conference, Oudtshoorn*, Conference Booklet, 113–21. The quotations from this work are my own translation.

35. Anthony le Fleur, "Khoisan Grondwetlike Akkommodasie," in *National Khoisan Consultative Conference, Oudtshoorn,* Conference Booklet, 113–21.

36. This research is contained in Martin Legassick and Ciraj Rassool, *Skeletons in the Cupboard: South African Museums and the Trade in Human Remains, 1907–1917* (Cape Town: South African Museum, 2000).

37. A partial exception is Alan Morris, "Trophy Skulls, Museums and the San," in Skotnes, *Miscast,* 67–79.

38. For an extensive study of this nefarious trade in Khoisan human remains from southern Africa for racial research in South Africa and Europe, which included purchases of bones of the recently dead and people's skeletons before they had died, see Legassick and Rassool, *Skeletons in the Cupboard,* esp. 1–40.

39. National Heritage Resources Act No. Twenty-five of 1999.

40. It is interesting to note that even the deputy president, Jacob Zuma, in his address to the National Khoisan Consultative Conference, did not understand the history of the acquisition of bones by South African museums. He referred to "Khoisan skeletons found accidentally during construction work" and to those that had been "excavated in the course of archaeological research."

41. Here I draw upon my recently published article, Ciraj Rassool, "Community Museums, Memory Politics and Social Transformation: Histories, Possibilities and Limits," in Karp and others, *Museum Frictions,* 286–321.

42. For an example of this idea of community museums as being local and simple as opposed to national and more complex, considered in a hierarchy of importance and stature, see Khwezi ka Mpumlwana and others, "Inclusion and the Power of Representation: South African Museums and the Cultural Politics of Social Transformation," in *Museums, Society, Inequality,* ed. R. Sandell (London: Routledge, 2002), 244–61.

43. Richard Sandell, "Museums and the Combating of Social Inequality," in Sandell, *Museums, Society, Inequality,* 7.

44. Witz, "Transforming Museums"; David Bunn, "The Museum Outdoors: Heritage, Cattle, and Permeable Borders in the Southwestern Kruger National Park," in Karp and others, *Museum Frictions,* 357–91.

2

Curatorial Practices:
Voices, Values, Languages,
and Traditions

Museums and Indigenous Perspectives on Curatorial Practice

JACKI THOMPSON RAND

If there was a time when museum exhibitions were designed solely to entertain and engage the imagination, it is no more, at least on the topic of Indigenous peoples. The following four papers that center on curatorial practice illustrate the point. The papers show that exhibitions serve not just a curator's creativity and judgment but rather many masters, and the potential occupants of those roles represent a sea change in museum culture and practice.

West Side Stories, an exhibit on northwestern Saskatchewan Metis, and a Huichol exhibit at the National Museum of the American Indian (NMAI) share two common goals: to address colonial historical narratives and to buttress political and legal claims in the respective lands of the Metis and the Huichols. Two other papers, "A Dialogic Reaction to the Problematized Past: The National Museum of the American Indian" and "The Construction of Native Voice at the National Museum of the American Indian," analyze the NMAI as a solution to offensive traditional museum practices concerning Indigenous topics and objects. Each author asks if the NMAI has succeeded as a response to a long history of museum abuses.

Exhibiting both Metis history and Huichol ideas about cosmological territoriality are performance in a contact zone with a view to similar ends. Both Metis and Huichol engage in struggles with respective states that would rather not acknowledge them. Their self-representations are literal attempts to reverse invisibility, educate others about their ancestral ties to land, and make a case for their own humanity. Indigenous peoples throughout the world have carried on this work since the invasion of their lands. Sharing power with museum professionals to exhibit their stories with their political agendas in plain view is a new twist. Each exhibit involved Indigenous stakeholders whose participation not only provided Native voice but also exerted content control. The Native collaborators shared power and control over the exhibits in substance, exhibition technique, and curatorial decisions. The painstakingly constructed Metis and Huichol exhibits are examples of the seriousness with which Native peoples exploit the museum as a contact zone. Both exhibits chart the wide gulf between Native experience and memory and the superficial knowledge of a non-Native audience, which would not matter if not for the fact that, at least for the Indigenous, much is at stake.

The essays on the NMAI speak directly and indirectly to problematized traditional museum practices and the politics of museums in a national context. Brady discusses how the NMAI leadership has presented the museum as a response to a troubled history between Native and non-Native people, a solution to a litany of longstanding Native resentments against the museum establishment. Collaboration between museum and Native consultants has been a cornerstone of the "Museum Different," a slogan adopted by the NMAI leadership to signify a new kind of relationship between Native people and a national museum. As one might predict, the inclusion of Native people as collaborators produced a schism among museum departments over Native control (versus benign Native voice). Shannon's analysis shines a bright light on the difference between professional hubris and resentment against Native interlopers, a long-standing museum tradition, and a productive understanding of using Native voice in the development of an exhibit. Shannon's discussion of the use of raw transcript text and the necessity of interpretive intervention illustrates a productive collaborative moment between project equals that transcends the patronizing spirit of inclusion. The transformation of raw Native text into exhibit text by a museum professional who possesses a nuanced understanding of the question and solution suggests respectful and trusting relationships between the collaborators. This is a goal to which museums should aspire.

Brady brings us home with a reality check on the NMAI as solution. Like an experienced detective, she doggedly ferrets out the resistant strains of tradition and naturalized processes that have evaded the NMAI's "Museum Different" solution and are now structurally embedded in it. The NMAI, sitting on the National Mall in sight of the Capitol, unresistingly has become absorbed, colonized if you will, in a nation-making process. It is a storage and exhibition facility for the material culture of one of the other peoples of the United States. Exhibits, gift shops, and restaurants serve a non-Native audience. Most Native people will never see the NMAI. The NMAI has compensated them with a "Fourth Museum" that will reach out to them via the Internet and traveling programs, projects that will never substitute for the real thing. Brady's assessment of the NMAI as a neoliberal formation makes a strong case that an opportunity to bring Native people into the national consciousness has resulted in a watered down amusement on the National Mall.

5

A Dialogic Response to the Problematized Past

*The National Museum of
the American Indian*

MIRANDA J. BRADY

Over the past several decades, museum practices and associated legislation have been shifting to reflect newer understandings about self-representation and the exhibition of Indigenous material and non-material
cultures. Museums like the Smithsonian Institution's National Museum
of the American Indian (NMAI) on the National Mall have adopted more
reflexive and collaborative models to ostensibly include the perspectives
of those being (re)presented. The NMAI's new dialogic form and practices are responses to the problematization of its predecessors, including
the U.S. Army Medical Museum (AMM), which was the source of some
of the National Museum of Natural History's (NMNH) collections, and
the George Gustav Heye Museum of the American Indian (MAI) in New
York, from which the NMAI's collections were acquired.[1] In other words,
certain aspects of museum form and practice have been troubled, and the
NMAI has arisen as a solution. One of the ways in which the NMAI denat-
uralizes past approaches is in its own self-understanding and approach
to communication. While previous sites proposed to advance a priori
knowledge via a static transmission model, the NMAI questions dominant
history through a more dialogic approach to communication.[2] Using collections, technology devices, architecture, and telepresence to help visitors connect with the lived spaces of a largely remote constituency, the
NMAI understands its role as a platform for "giving voice" and as a site of
"multicultural dialogue."[3] Dialogic approaches to communication have
marked several phases in the creation of the museum ranging from ar-

chitectural design to the curatorial process to other methods of working in "consultation, collaboration, and cooperation" with American Indians and Natives of the Western Hemisphere.[4] However, while the NMAI considers itself a solution to troubled museological approaches to communication, other practices remain naturalized. Although for many American Indian people the NMAI represents an unprecedented expression of cultural sovereignty, the museum has a number of problematic aspects that have yet to be questioned, including its role in reproducing national identity, the fund-driven majority museum, and the collection of Native culture for a largely non-Native audience.[5]

The following explores the emergence and constitution of the NMAI and some of the ways in which it has arisen as a response to the practices of its predecessors. This paper will discuss not only the museum's most celebrated capacities but also the residual museological practices that accompany them; the goal is to ask why particular contradictions persist despite major shifts in understanding regarding the representation of Native cultures. This paper will apply Michel Foucault's notion of problematization to museological study; explore the historically situated condition of the NMAI's predecessors; detail the ways in which the NMAI and associated legislation were a responses to problematized practices, assuming more dialogic approaches to communication as a solution; and will finally question why particular contradictions continue in the NMAI's approach.

Troubling the Past

Many traditional museum practices have been troubled over the past thirty years in academic discussions, professional organizations, and legislation. One major change has affected Native human remains. Once considered to be national cultural patrimony, policy has prescribed their deaccession from national collections to culturally affiliated groups as a result of the 1989 National Museum of the American Indian Act and the 1990 Native American Graves Protection and Repatriation Act (NAGPRA). It took many years of activism to denaturalize dominant culture's understanding of human remains as national cultural patrimony because their systematic collection was historically justified by scientific and nationalistic discourses.

However, other museological practices remain naturalized, and still others are new responses to past practices that are now considered unethical, impractical, or misrepresentative. For example, the NMAI still works to maintain the largest collection of the material cultures of Native people of the Western Hemisphere for the enjoyment of a largely white audience in a majority museum.[6] Why does the collection of Native material culture in the nation's capital remain naturalized? One reason might be that it was not the national museum complex itself that was questioned.

We can understand problematization as a process of making naturalized occurrences, phenomena, or practices problematic in light of the establishment of the conditions that make particular solutions possible.[7] Also included in this process are the conditions under which it becomes natural to question certain practices and the discursive formations that make particular lines of questioning available. As Michel Foucault explains, "It is problematization that responds to these difficulties, but by doing something quite other than expressing them or manifesting them: in connection with them, it develops the conditions in which possible responses can be given; it defines the elements that will constitute what the different solutions attempt to respond to. This development of a given into a question, this transformation of a group of obstacles and difficulties into problems to which the diverse solutions will attempt to produce a response, this is what constitutes the point of problematization and the specific work of thought."[8]

The problematization of the traditional museum has provided the conditions of response, what is understood as a reappropriation, decolonization, or subversion of the museum form.[9] However, it is important to emphasize that while problematization is an analytic that places the novelty of response in reaction to historical circumstances that circumscribe and limit the range of response, it does not wholly make a determination. It also means that while certain solutions became apparent, they were not inevitable and were largely influenced by the kinds of questions that were being asked.

Two major complaints launched against the majority museum of the past by Native American activists were (1) the collection of Native human remains, sacred and funerary objects, and other material culture as patrimony for use by majority culture and (2) the ways in which majority culture disadvantaged participation by American Indian people in representing their own cultures and lives. These complaints came to the fore when it became apparent that George Gustav Heye's MAI, an exemplar of these offenses, might become nationalized. As Laura Dickstein Thompson points out, curatorial input from American Indian employees was largely ignored at the MAI, and the museum's model privileged museum professionals who were schooled in more traditional curatorial approaches.[10] However, it was ultimately because the largest collection of Native objects in the world faced financial instability and possible dismantling that the Smithsonian Institution saw an opportunity to address such concerns. It was under these conditions, with pressure from MAI trustees and the state of New York to keep the collection together, that a deal was struck with the Smithsonian Institution to create the NMAI and to annex the collection into that of the Smithsonian.[11]

While some objects have been repatriated, a major contingency of the legislation was always to keep the collection intact. Many important figures at the MAI and the Smithsonian were also quite nervous about the prospect of repatriation being opened by the new policies. For example, Julie Kidd, director of the MAI at the time of the collection transfer, reprimanded the MAI's American Indian trustees for agreeing to the return of some of the collections as she believed "funerary" and "sacred" objects might be too broadly construed. Kidd writes in a 1991 memorandum, circulated to trustees, "Forgive me, but you, as the Indian leaders of the NMAI board have let your people down. You have made yourselves the heroes of the moment—but you have sacrificed the future."[12]

Although the agreement established that some of the collections be repatriated despite internal anxiety, Kidd's comments reflect the broader drive. The NMAI Act did address parts of the two major concerns listed above, including the return of human remains and sacred and funerary objects from the MAI's collections as well as from the broader Smithsonian collection. It did insist that American Indian people play an integral role in self-representation. However, what remained unaddressed was the majority culture's tendency to collect and exhibit Native culture for mostly non-Native audiences. The NMAI's planning documents indicate that, while the museum will be serving Native people indirectly as "constituents," the vast majority of the "audience" for the Mall Museum will be non-Native.[13] Several scholars have expressed concern about the abstract treatment of polemical issues within the NMAI, like genocide and repatriation; and its planning documents indicate the NMAI was well aware of its audience when determining the "tone" of the museum:[14] "The museum has both a *constituency* and an *audience*. Although there is some amount of overlap, these groups have different concerns and relationships with the museum. The *constituency* is the Indigenous peoples of the western hemisphere. With this museum the government of the United States is offering Native people a place of respect and the opportunity to tell their own stories. The *audience* will be the millions of annual visitors of all ages and levels of education. Most of these people will be non-Indian citizens of the United States and from abroad."[15]

Unlike a tribal museum, which is generally located near the tribe or American Indian nation where the residents can enjoy it, the NMAI is located in the nation's capital, across the country from the homes of the vast majority of people who identify as American Indian (Oklahoma, California, New Mexico, Arizona, etc.).[16] Planning documents of the NMAI indicate museum organizers were well aware of this distance.[17]

While the NMAI Act was a response to the problematization of certain Western paradigms, it responded to another question as well: how can we keep this collection together and annex it into the collection of national cultural patrimony? The NMAI Act addressed some of the major concerns of American Indian activists and was seen, along with the NAGPRA legislation, in many ways as a major victory. However, it also further naturalized the voyeuristic treatment and commodification of Native culture by the majority, as it supported national identity on the mall. Although some aspects of collection had been troubled, the conditions under which the NMAI came about were not conducive to the problematization of the representation of Native culture in the national museum complex in general. It was seen as self-representation without consideration of the ways in which working within such a venue might frame American Indian issues or delimit the potential for deep critical engagement with past and continuing government policy.

Despite the shift in the NMAI's self-understanding, the tendency to compile and maintain othered cultures to bolster nationalism continues as a long tradition on the National Mall. For example, while the AMM was founded to study battle wounds and illnesses, it eventually became interested in Native crania and invested great effort in comparative analysis between Native skulls and those of different races.[18] At first, the AMM largely collected the dead from battle sites, but it later made a concerted effort to acquire Native remains from burial sites or through trades with the Smithsonian.[19] George Otis, assistant surgeon and curator for the AMM proudly explains in 1876 that remote army outposts also had a new opportunity to contribute to the museum and the advancement of knowledge: "many medical officers at remote posts, who had infrequent opportunities of contributing to the pathological material of the Museum, but earnestly shared in the general desire of members of the corps to promote its welfare, forwarded donations of Indian crania, of specimens of native history, and of objects of ethnological or archaeological interest. The minerals, fossils, stone implements, pottery, etc., and the Indian curiosities, were exchanged with other museums for objects more immediately connected with the purposes of the Army Medical Museum."[20]

The AMM sought to advance nationalism through medical and scientific discovery in addition to assisting other national offices in achieving these same goals.[21] As part of an effort to demonstrate its scientific research, the AMM participated in the 1876 Philadelphia Centennial Exhibition, celebrating America's ingenuity and technology.[22] Various skeletal remains and demonstrations were prepared to show the latest breakthroughs in anatomical and ethnological understanding made by the national institution.

Certainly, collecting was not a new phenomenon, and it often took the form of pilfering other cultures to augment "national patrimony."[23] But the widespread, systematic collection and scientific study of human remains to bolster nationalism was a newer phenomenon.[24] At the most basic level, the AMM demonstrated the legitimacy of westward expansion and progress by proving it could physically control the bodies of American Indian people despite their resistance. The nation also indicated it could better manage these bodies on a micro level by studying and diagnosing them, connecting their collection and scientific study with a deterministic national moralism. Collections were acquired and organized into taxonomies that were consistent with the discourses of scientific inquiry, unlike cabinets of curiosities and collections of the past; this was in direct juxtaposition with "uncivilized" American Indian people and many of their understandings about burial and the appropriate treatment of their ancestors.[25]

The point in drawing this quick comparison is to emphasize the ways in which national museums serve national goals, as Robin Marie DeLugan similarly argues.[26] Although the AMM and the NMAI represent dramatically different missions, it is important to note that they both worked to naturalize the phenomenon of collecting Native people and culture as patrimony for national identity. And yet, it is only limited aspects of collecting (human remains and sacred and funerary objects) and the ways in which collections are presented that become problematic with the NMAI Act rather than the phenomenon of the national American Indian museum itself.

The Floyd Favel video in the NMAI exhibit Our Peoples and the accompanying passage by former Smithsonian secretary Lawrence Small both work to justify the initial compilation and maintenance of the collection. As Favel suggests, "Much that is preserved would have disappeared," had the white businessman George Gustav Heye not had the "wealth, the wherewithal, and the desire" to gather the massive, 1 million–object collection.[27] Nearby, a panel attributed to Small acknowledged that we now understand Heye's motivations differently in a contemporary context, but "In his unstoppable course, Heye saved an irreplaceable living record that might otherwise have gone to oblivion. Out of his acquisitive passion has come a legacy of inestimable worth, to heirs on whom he never reckoned. Had he been someone other than who he was, he would have left us all poorer."[28]

Small's statement is ironic and perhaps self-serving in light of his legal trouble over a personal collection of rare-bird feathers.[29] It also reflects an identification with those enjoying the objects preserved in the museum rather than with those who might enjoy them in their lived communities.

However, as mentioned, these naturalized practices emphasize the novelty of the dialogic model. The NMAI has a number of productive capacities, and the dialogic model assumed by the museum is an important aspect of its productivity. Clearly, NMAI predecessors like the AMM, the NMNH, and the original MAI did not assume this dialogic model. Not only does the NMAI emphasize the importance of conceptualizing its role on the mall in dialogic terms, it has further encouraged dialogue in conversations, extending into various micro-moral domains from general and tribal press to academic discussions, political discourse, and conversations among tourists. It represents a major transformation in traditional museological understanding.

The MAI Becomes the NMAI

The national museum's shift from the scientifically oriented "universal" museum to a site of self-articulated history signifies a shift in power-knowledge relations.[30] The NMAI offers alternative modes of engaging with objects, including nonlinear object placement. The building's curvilinear architecture and use of sandstone and landscaping juxtapose with more neoclassical designs on the mall. According to Dickstein Thompson, the NMAI's mission was likely informed by recent museum scholarship and emerging trends in interpretive practices, including self-presentation and the concept of "decolonizing" social institutions.[31]

Communications technologies were used throughout and in conjunction with the NMAI Mall Museum to augment its dialogic function. The museum works to (re)create "Indian Country" on the mall, using television monitors and computer screens, and to authenticate its claim to American Indian voice through video and pictorial testimonials. These work in tandem with museum collections; lighting; aural cues; and use of landscape, space, architecture, and movement. The use of multisensory devices throughout the museum (from climate control to sounds and lighting) helps to evoke an affective reaction on the part of museum visitors. In essence, visitors are invited to use this (re)presentation to project themselves into Indian Country.

In addition "cultural interpreters" or Native guides lead tours throughout the museum. While tour talks seem somewhat scripted, they vary depending on the individual experiences of the cultural interpreter. Each interpreter has a different talk and tour prepared. They work performatively to "give voice" to Native concerns.[32] Where cultural interpreters are not an embodied presence, they are made available via telepresence. Video monitors throughout exhibits enable visitors to access prerecorded messages and interviews with Native people speaking about their experiences as members of particular groups and as part of their broader understanding of what pan-Native identity means.

Digital kiosks are also used throughout the Mall Museum to augment a more "interactive" experience. For example, rather than using wall labels to present particular facts about an object (including its country of origin, creator, catalogue number, and the materials that comprise it), the NMAI utilizes virtual kiosks in front of Window on Collections display cabinets on the third and fourth levels. Visitors often go through two or three layers to access information about an object, scrolling through a virtual menu of other objects and then selecting the object for a closer look. In limited cases, video and audio options are available through which users might learn more about particular objects that are grouped into themes like projectile points, beads, dolls, peace medals, containers, animals, and so forth.

The NMAI offers several filmic presentations each day, which typically include *Welcome Home* and *A Thousand Roads* in the Rasmuson Theater on the first level, as well as a multisensory presentation *Who We Are* in the fourth-level Lelawi Theater. Museum planners called the Lelawi a preparation theater and hoped visitors would start with this multimedia presentation and work their way down from the fourth floor.[33] According to Beverly Singer, who was involved in the production of *Who We Are*, "The prep theatre was always viewed in the museum planning as the gathering place to prepare visitors to shed their preconceived ideas of 'Indians' by immersing them in a full-bodied experience of contemporary Indigenous life."[34] Included in the multisensory presentation is a projection of images onto a variety of surfaces depicting practices, important beliefs, and the environments in which various Native groups live. At the end of the presentation, a montage of Native public figures is shown with a crescendo of pop-rock music, and the beat of a drum ends the show as the dim lights are turned up. Visitors often say things like "Cool!" after the presentation is over, and they shuffle out into the Our Universes gallery.

The gallery is dark with a simulated fiber-optic night sky overhead, so the flow is not disrupted as visitors exit the theater into the first of three permanent galleries containing both culturally specific alcoves and areas addressing more common themes. The topics of colonization, identity construction, and connection with the universe are addressed throughout the museum's galleries, although many have argued that the museum's approach toward such topics is ambiguous and abstract.[35] In a video shown in the Our Peoples exhibit, First Nations actor Floyd Favel recites a script written by Paul Chaat Smith (Comanche) and Herbert R. Rosen. The video, perhaps more explicitly than any other text in the museum, explains the purpose of the museum. Favel states, "This is about history and about the past. Two different things. The exhibit that surrounds you now examines the alchemy that changes the past into stories. The histories we tell about it. The past never changes, but the way we understand it, learn about it, and know about it changes all the time. . . . And over time, the way others see us has changed as well."[36] Favel ends by challenging museumgoers: "This gallery is making history. And, like all other histories, it has a point of view, an agenda. . . . So view what's offered with respect, but also skepticism. Explore this gallery, encounter it, reflect on it, argue with it."[37]

Favel's invitation for visitors to argue with the museum provides an example of the NMAI's self-understanding as dialogic. His own appearance in the video and the aural, pictorial, and video evidence of contemporary Native people augmented with the presence of a small but visible group of Native cultural interpreters from throughout the Western Hemisphere also work to produce this overarching dialogic theme throughout the museum.

The NMAI sees itself as a communications technology. It attempts to convince visitors that the version of "truth" that has been privileged by traditional museums is only one possible version among many, and it is one that reflects the imperatives and power relations of that particular historical conjuncture. But, though the NMAI responds to the problematic static model of its predecessors, it continues to naturalize a number of traditional museological practices while also creating some more troubling effects of its own.

Residual Practices and Contradictions

While the appearance of the NMAI reflects a shift in power and knowledge formation, there are still many contradictions that are apparent upon closer investigation; these hearken back to museological understandings of the past. Perhaps the most serious of such residual practices within the NMAI Mall Museum is its audience. The majority of American Indian people will never make it to the museum, and as discussed, a distinction is made in the NMAI's planning documents between those native "constituents" who will be served by the museum and the mostly white "audience," who will comprise the visitors to the mall.[38] Alternative goals were suggested in focus groups conducted with Native people by NMAI planners prior to the opening of the museum. For example, one participant commented, "Programs that reach Indian communities are more important than buildings."[39] However, the importance of a museum on the National Mall went largely unquestioned, despite its distance from the majority of American Indian people.

[To address this issue, the NMAI purports to bring the collections to American Indian people through interpersonal and technological networking, thus augmenting the museum's three physical structures with an effort that has been termed the "Fourth Museum."] Director Richard West has been fond of referring to the project as "the museum without walls" and has emphasized the importance of extending the museum beyond its "proverbial bricks and mortar."[40] As part of the program, digital versions of each collection item will be accessible remotely online. According to the NMAI Cultural Resources Center (CRC) collections manager, Dr. Patricia Neitfeld, this task will be completed in 2008. (The entire collection has been imaged, and the virtual images may be viewed at the CRC in Suitland, Maryland.)[41]

[One of the difficulties of the Fourth Museum concept is the commercial nature of the Internet and the threat of such a medium to traditional lifestyles.[42]] In addition, though most contemporary museums work to integrate digital media into their offerings from Web sites to interactive devices, many Native and non-Native people have difficulty accessing the Internet.[43] Although this gap is closing and many Indigenous people are using the Internet in a variety of unprecedented ways, we can still question the ways in which communications technologies are touted as a democratic panacea to social inequalities.[44] The lives of Native people have been voyeuristically documented and staged with every different emerging medium for the majority culture, from the AMM's composite craniology photographs taken in 1884 to *Nanook of the North*.[45] In addition, as Michael Brown suggests, new media like the Internet are particularly conducive to sharing sensitive information with outsiders.[46]

The digital media within the NMAI Mall Museum are also problematic. Although virtual kiosks are considered more interactive, they provide the same kinds of information generally available on a wall label in many cases. Information is provided through merely another medium in the Window on Collections displays, for example. That the users choose the sequence in which to access information says little about whether they feel a greater connection with American Indian people. Interactive kiosks do not allow for idiosyncratic details that do not fit into the particular information categories provided (e.g., date, place of origin, artist, materials), with the exception of limited cases in which video or audio options are available. Moreover, although NMAI planners worked to create a less object-oriented and more people-oriented experience for museumgoers, the Window on Collections displays make objects the focal point, whether they be virtual or physical objects, because they have been removed from their cultural contexts and grouped according to themes like "beadwork" and "projectile points."[47] My own observations during the summer of 2006 revealed that children are especially prone to access digital kiosks, often without taking time to focus on the actual objects themselves from the physical collections. Pushing buttons seems to become the focus in many cases, and visitors also complained of limited kiosks being crowded by children and other patrons.[48]

The drive to preserve Heye's collections is a kind of residual practice, despite alternative grouping. Although the new understanding does not work according to the same "salvage ethnography" that drove the compilation of the collection, rather than encouraging more progressive repatriation legislation, the museum exerted a great effort in creating facilities that employ modern technology "to control lighting, temperature, dust, and pests." Other factors are controlled as well. For example, while one participant suggested, "Plant life has power," *The Way of the People* explains that plants should not be used inside the building as they might attract pests.[49] It suggests that costumes and "theatrical props" should be "sealed and located away from collections" and that "windows, unless required for egress or access, should be non-operable and sealed and doors should be provided with weather stripping to control environmental conditions and dust and also provide pest control."[50] Some focus group participants emphasized the importance of being able to smell the wood and the feeling of being within a wooden structure, stating that "You should smell sage, wood, fish" and that the museum should be "a giant 'scratch and sniff.'" Yet the museum opted wherever possible to minimize the use of wood and smells that might attract pests.[51]

In an NMAI focus group, one American Indian participant said he kept an important object, his father's pipe, in a building that was "alive." He stated, "The pipe is kept in a frame building without environmental controls—I don't call it a museum. . . . It is still alive."[52] Despite such advice, the NMAI continues to store its collections in climate-controlled environments in the CRC and the NMAI to prevent their decay, while generally only virtual versions will have the opportunity to be "lived" in American Indian communities. Indeed, this drive to preserve objects still reflects Heye's original mission from 1916, which sought to "gather and preserve for students everything useful in illustrating and elucidating the anthropology of the aborigines of the Western Hemisphere."[53]

Another major residual practice within the NMAI is the use of expressionless mannequins and dioramas throughout several NMAI displays, including the Hupa, Mapuche, and Anishinabe cultural areas in Our Universes. Planners of the NMAI were well aware that such practices had been troubled as these concerns were articulated in the 2000 *The Changing Presentation of the American Indian: Museums and Native Cultures*, a collection of essays resulting from an NMAI-hosted symposium of the same name in 1995.[54] Rick Hill, a Tuscarora artist and writer and former special assistant to the director of the Smithsonian's NMAI, writes in one chapter, "But the dioramas are in themselves a throwback to the old-style museums that freeze Indians in the past. . . . The dioramas become a big toy for adults."[55] He asks, "Will museums forever associate Indians with dioramas containing life-size figures?"[56]

If consultants to the NMAI were concerned with the implications of dioramas and life-size, lifeless-looking mannequins, why does the museum continue to include them? One explanation for the persistence of the dioramas in the NMAI and other residual practices is that while community curators were given the opportunity to self-present, their understanding of such self-presentation comes from the traditional museum form with which they are accustomed. In such museums, the diorama is standard. S. Elizabeth Bird had similar findings when she invited American Indian people to write a television show about themselves.[57] While all participants agreed that television shows generally portray American Indian people in misleading ways, the shows they created fit the confines of the television genre and its commercial form. While participants were free to create any kind of text, they typically created situation comedies or dramas. These were the television texts with which they were familiar, despite the many problematic aspects of such forms, like their tendency to solve complex social problems in half an hour or hour-long segments and the pervasive flow of commercials and self-promotion.[58] Similarly, despite the collaboration and inclusion employed by the NMAI, we must ask what really changes when American Indian people themselves are working within the confines of the cultural form.

The use of the identity category "Indian" is also a residual practice that was first invented by Europeans to lump together all disparate groups of non-Europeans of the Americas.[59] We can even understand the NMAI's overarching mission to represent all those people who are "Native to the Western Hemisphere" as a residual practice shaped by George Gustav Heye in his mission to collect the material cultures of those groups. Heye articulated an "aborigine" identity for his collection, and the NMAI continues to construct "Native" identity in terms of the geographic delimitations defined by Heye.[60] Had Heye wished to include in his collections the material cultures of different groups, we would have a different articulation of "Native" within the NMAI.

While the NMAI works to dislodge iconographic images of American Indians perpetuated by Hollywood (as Favel states in the Our Peoples video), the museum partnered with and accepted donations from entities that have clearly worked to perpetuate them. This raises a difficult set of concerns between critical scholars and majority museum fund-raising practices. For example, the museum accepted money from a benefit sponsored by Orion Pictures from the opening of the movie *Dances with Wolves* and even invited actor Kevin Costner to serve as one of thirty-seven Honorary Committee Members of the NMAI's National Campaign. Scholars have argued that the film, like many Hollywood texts, reflects a kind of imperialist nostalgia, which works to validate white experience and suggests an inevitable decline of American Indian people.[61] In addition, the NMAI partnered with Atlanta Braves owner Ted Turner in exchange for free airtime on his cable television network to promote the museum's fund-raising drive.[62] The museum entered into the partnership despite the fact that the team's symbolic "tomahawk chop" and mascot were widely criticized by American Indian activists; included in this criticism was Charlene Teters, who said of Turner, "He just doesn't get it."[63] Although somewhat indirectly, the museum's affiliation with such parties suggests it endorses them by deeming them worthy of partnership.[64]

Finally, the NMAI museums won their locations after competing with other historically marginalized groups for representation. The George Gustav Heye Center in New York's Custom House was originally slated for a Holocaust museum, and the NMAI Mall Museum spot was also highly coveted by leaders promoting the Smithsonian Institution's National Museum of African American Art and Culture.[65] Such a phenomenon reflects the political nature of voice and national recognition.

The preceding discussion should be couched in a broader set of concerns over neoliberal museum conditions.[66] While the examples provided above might be some of the most egregious contradictions to the museum's self-articulated goals and have been selected in order to further the point, they do illustrate the broader conditions under which the museum became manifest. The point of raising all of these difficulties is not to dispute the fact that the NMAI provides a great sense of pride for many people who identify as American Indian or the fact that interpretive practices are shifting to include alternative, non-Western-centered perspectives for the better. On the contrary, the NMAI provides unprecedented opportunities for disparate Native groups to enter into public discourse on a large scale and to assume an expert position on their own cultures and lives. It en- courages a new inclusive and dialogic model for doing so. However, this shift is accompanied by its own problems. Inclusion can mean accommodation in a more pejorative sense. The rise of the museum within its current neoliberal formation meant great pressures to fund this massive-scale project and facilitated what I will call a series of unfortunate compromises, for lack of a better term.[67]

While the NMAI was a response to problematized museological practices, like the collection of human remains and static notions of public education and "truth," there is no doubt that the contradictions in the rise of big-budget national ethnic museums like the NMAI will be the focus of future museum studies concerns.

As Dickstein Thompson suggests, many staff members at the NMAI believe the main difference between the new NMAI museums and museums of the past, like Heye's MAI, is the conscious inclusion of "Native American perspectives."[68] Such inclusion might take varying forms and represent different degrees of emancipation from past conventions. I would argue the self-reflexive nature of the museum does question educational institutions as static transmitters of information to emphasize communication as a dialogic process. However, at the same time, it naturalizes the importance of the museum complex and nation building in general in lieu of programs that more directly benefit American Indian people.

It is useful to remember that while now considered problematic the practices of the AMM were also, at one time, considered deeply patriotic. Beginning in the 1960s, the sharp increase in ethnic museums and the disappearance of the AMM from the National Mall into obscurity illustrates the problematization of the earlier model as discussed above.[69] However, both forms of national museum have taken part in the process of nation building and represent a confluence of influences. And while some museological practices have been problematized and discursive formations made some solutions available, other residual forms and practices continue.

The implications of attaching American Indian identity to the national museum as a technology for entrance into public discourse are yet to be seen. Moreover, the simultaneous construction of national identity and partnership with corporate interest go largely unquestioned within the contemporary national museum complex. Current conditions are made possible through neoliberal formation in the midst of which the museum has manifested and constituted itself. It is doubtful the museum's avowed goals can be seamlessly integrated into a national museum that is defined by these tensions. While it is perhaps too hasty to dismiss the emancipatory potential of the museum and its dialogic function, it is only through critical examination that we might better understand the myriad ways in which the museum is productive.

Notes

I would like to thank the Newberry Library's D'Arcy McNickle Center for American Indian History and the Committee for Institutional Cooperation for their generous graduate fellowship during the summer of 2007. Additionally, I would like to thank Michigan State University for sponsoring the "Indigenous Past and Present" First Annual Symposium, from which this paper comes. Excerpts of this paper are included in my PhD dissertation, "Discourse, Cultural Policy, and Other Mechanisms of Power: The National Museum of the American Indian" (Pennsylvania State University, December 2007).

1. The NMAI Act (1989) addresses the practices of all three of these museums. Specifically, NMAI legislation suggests much of the NMNH collection of Native human remains was acquired from the AMM.

2. For more on a dialogic model of communication, see James Carey, "A Cultural Approach to Communication," in *Communication as Culture: Essays on Media and Society* (New York: Routledge, 1989), 13–36.

3. Anna McCarthy describes "telepresence" as the use of television to help viewers figuratively project themselves into alternate spaces. See Anna McCarthy, *Ambient Television: Visual Culture and Public Space* (Durham NC: Duke University Press, 2001); First Nations Plains Cree actor Floyd Favel uses the term "giving voice" in a video in the Our Peoples exhibit. The script he recites is attributed to Paul Chaat Smith (Comanche) and Herbert R. Rosen; NMAI director Richard West used the term "multicultural dialogue" in a speech to the National Press Club two weeks prior to the opening of the NMAI. In a speech broadcast on C-SPAN, West cited former Smithsonian secretary Robert McCormick Adams when he emphasized the museum's role in "the encouragement of a multi-cultural dialogue." See Richard West, "The National Museum of the American Indian: A Historical Reckoning," (speech, National Press Club, Washington DC, September 9, 2004), transcript online at http://www.nmai.si.edu/press/releases/09-09-04_NPC_remarks _by_rick_west.pdf.

4. The wording "consultation, collaboration, and cooperation" is from the NMAI's mission statement. See Laura Dickstein Thompson, "The Mission Statement and Its Relationship to Museum Interpretive Practices: A Case Study of the National Museum of the American Indian," (PhD diss., Columbia University, 2001); West, "National Museum of the American Indian." The NMAI's mission statement delimits its representation to "Natives of the Western Hemisphere." George Gustav Heye actually first delimited the collection in his 1916 mission statement to "aborigines of the Western Hemisphere" according to Dickstein Thompson.

5. Amanda Cobb, "The National Museum of the American Indian as Cultural Sovereignty," *American Quarterly* 57 (2005), 485–506.

6. I borrow the term "majority museum" from James Clifford, who places such a

large-scale museum in juxtaposition with local, tribal museums. See James Clifford, "Four Northwest Coast Museums: Travel Reflections," in *Exhibiting Cultures: The Politics of Museum Display*, ed. I. Karp and S. D. Lavine (Washington: Smithsonian Institution Press, 1991).

7. Michel Foucault, "Polemics, Politics and Problematizations," in *Essential Works of Foucault*, vol. 1, *Ethics*, ed. P. Rabinow (New York: Free Press, 1997).

8. Foucault, "Polemics, Politics and Problematizations."

9. In the text of several display panels, the NMAI calls such subversion "survivance," a concept coined by American Indian scholar Gerald Vizenor to indicate survival with dignity. The "We're Still Here" narrative articulated throughout the museum also links to this discourse. See Gerald Vizenor, "Native American Indian Literatures: Narratives of Survivance," in *Native North America: Critical and Cultural Perspectives*, ed. R. Hulan (Toronto: ECW Press, 1999).

10. Dickstein Thompson, "Mission Statement."

11. Roland Force, *The Heye and the Mighty* (Honolulu HI: Mechas Press, 1999).

12. Memorandum from Julie J. Kidd to Indian Members of the NMAI Board of Trustees, "Re: Repatriation," March 6, 1991, accession 04-170, box 4/8, Smithsonian Institution Archives.

13. *The Way of the People: National Museum of the American Indian EMP*, Progress Report Executive Summary (n.d.). This report was accessed through archives of the National Museum of the American Indian Cultural Resources Center in Suitland MD.

14. See Amy Lonetree, "Missed Opportunities: Reflections on the NMAI," in "Critical Engagements with the National Museum of the American Indian," ed. Amy Lonetree and Sonya Atalay, special issue, *American Indian Quarterly* 30, nos. 3–4 (2006): 632–45; Amy Lonetree, "Continuing Dialogues: Evolving Views of the National Museum of the American Indian," *Public Historian*, 28 (2006): 57–61; and Sonya Atalay, "No Sense of Struggle: Creating a Context for Survivance at the NMAI," in "Critical Engagements with the National Museum of the American Indian," ed. Amy Lonetree and Sonya Atalay, special issue, *American Indian Quarterly* 30, nos. 3–4 (2006): 597–618; *Way of the People*, Progress Report Executive Summary. Sonja Atalay describes the overall "tone" of the NMAI, and I borrow this term from her.

15. *Way of the People*, Progress Report Executive Summary.

16. Clifford, "Four Northwest Coast Museums."

17. Venturi, Scott Brown, and Associates, *The Way of the People: A Detailed Architectural Program for the Museum on the National Mall, Appendix. Master Facilities Programming, Phase 2 Final Report*, Smithsonian Institution Office of Design and Construction (Philadelphia: Venturi, Scott Brown, and Associates, September 15, 1993). This report was accessed through the archives of the National Museum of the American Indian Cultural Resources Center in Suitland MD.

18. J. S. Billings, "On Composite Photography as Applied to Craniology," *Thirteenth Memoir, Memoirs of the National Academy of Sciences*, vol. 3, pts. 1–2, (n.p., 1884), as cited by National Anthropological Archives and Human Studies Film Archives: United States Army Medical Museum Composite Photographs of Skulls, http://www.nmnh.si.edu/naa/guide/_uv.htm#jrg514. J. S. Billings and W. Matthews, "On a New Cranophore for Use in Making Composite Photographs of Skulls," *Fourteenth Memoir, Memoirs of the National Academy of Sciences*, vol. 3, pts. 1–2, (n.p., 1884), as cited by National Anthropological Archives and Human Studies Film Archives: United States Army Medical Museum Composite Photographs of Skulls, http://www.nmnh.si.edu/naa/guide/_uv.htm#jrg514.

19. AMM, *Check List of Preparations and Objects in the Section of Human Anatomy of the United States Army Medical Museum for Use during the International Exhibition of 1876 in Connection with the Representation of the Medical Department of the U.S. Army* (Washington DC: U.S. Government Printing Office, 1876). As recently as the 1980s, Smithsonian Institution public affairs specialists emphasized the fact that the AMM collections were comprised of fallen soldiers gathered in order to advance medical knowledge about injuries. For example, in an internal Smithsonian Institution Office of Public Affairs memorandum titled "Some of the Most Outrageous Statements That Have Been Made by Indians Concerning Remains," director Madeleine Jacobs instructs her colleague: when speaking to reporters, "Please remember that the Army Medical Museum surgeons were collecting battlefield remains to study injuries so that they could improve medical practices"; memorandum, August 17, 1989, accession 04-170, box 2/8, Smithsonian Institution Archives. However, it is clear from the inventory list of the International Exhibition of 1876 that battle sites were not the museum's only interest, as many of the Native remains came from burial sites and were obtained through trades that the AMM made in a conscious effort to grow its collection.

20. *Check list*, 3–4.

21. From its inception in 1846, the Smithsonian Institution worked to legitimize its place as a leader in international scientific work. When the Bureau of American Ethnology was founded by the institution in 1879 as a result of director John Wesley Powell's advocacy, it helped to further legitimize and professionalize the field of ethnology in the United States. See Curtis Hinsley, *Savages and Scientists: The Smithsonian Institution and the Development of American Anthropology 1846–1910*, (Washington DC: Smithsonian Institution Press, 1981).

22. Items from the exhibition helped the Smithsonian Institution to build its collection base. Similarly, the Field Museum of Chicago, first known as the Columbian Museum of Chicago, also built its collections through the 1893 World's Columbian Exhibition in Chicago. Field Museum, "Museum Information: An Introduction to the Field Museum," http://www.fieldmuseum.org/museum_info/. An area ripe for analysis is the way in which the Field Museum is now incorpo-

rating elements of a more dialogic model by including quotations from contemporary American Indians and communications technologies throughout its Ancient Americas exhibition, opened in March 2007. One portion of the exhibit is blocked off, and a notice simply hangs in place of a display that is now considered inappropriate, explaining the museum's compliance with newer understandings.

23. See Tony Bennett, *The Birth of the Museum* (New York: Routledge, 1995); and Elazar Barkan and Ronald Bush, *Claiming the Stones/Naming the Bones: Cultural Property and the Negotiation of National and Ethnic Identity* (Los Angeles: Getty Research Institute, 2002).

24. According to director Madeleine Jacobs's August 1989 memorandum, the comparison had been drawn between the collection of American Indian remains by the state and the practices of Nazi Germany. Among other items on the list of "outrageous statements" was that "we are like Nazi Germany. Suzan Harjo says, [the collecting of Indian remains was] 'the first precursor of genetic experiments in Nazi Germany.' To which we don't say anything."

25. See Carol Duncan and Alan Wallach, "The Universal Survey Museum," in *Museum Studies: An Anthology of Contexts*, ed. Bettina Messias Carbonell, (Malden MA: Blackwell, 2004); and Rebecca Tsosie, "Indigenous Rights and Archaeology" in *Native Americans and Archaeologists: Stepping Stones to Common Ground*, ed. N. Swidler, K. Dongoske, R. Anyon, and A. Downer, Society of American Archaeology (Walnut Creek CA: AltaMira Press, 1997).

26. Robin Marie DeLugan, "'South of the Boarder' at the NMAI," in "Critical Engagements with the National Museum of the American Indian," ed. Amy Lonetree and Sonya Atalay, special issue, *American Indian Quarterly* 30, nos. 3–4 (2006): 558–74.

27. These quotes appear in the Our Peoples exhibit video.

28. This quotation has been taken from a panel in the Our Peoples exhibit, shown in 2000.

29. Elizabeth Olsen, "Smithsonian's Chief Admits to Endangered Bird Violations," *The New York Times*, January 24, 2004.

30. See Duncan and Wallach, "Universal Survey Museum."

31. See Dickstein Thompson, "Mission Statement"; and Linda Tuhiwai Smith, *Decolonizing Methodologies: Research and Indigenous Peoples* (New York: Zed Books, 1999).

32. The Our Peoples exhibit video suggests that the museum is engaged in the process of "giving voice" to Native people of the Western Hemisphere.

33. Beverly Singer, "The Making of Who We Are, Now Showing at the NMAI Lelawi Theater," in "National Museum of the American Indian," ed. Amanda J. Cobb, special issue, *American Indian Quarterly* 29, nos. 3–4 (2005): 466–77.

34. Singer, "Making of Who We Are," 468. It is important to note that the NMAI uses

media performatively to help troubled past media practices. For example, in the Our Peoples video, Favel singles out media like paintings and photographs as well as Hollywood for essentialist, stereotypical representations of American Indian people as "saviors of the environment, barbarians, and noble savages. The lowest form of humanity. Sometimes all at once." One of the NMAI's goals is "debunking stereotypes"; see Richard West, "From the Director" *National Museum of the American Indian Magazine*, Summer 2007, 17.

35. See Amy Lonetree, "Missed Opportunities"; Amy Lonetree, "Continuing Dialogues"; Sonya Atalay, "No Sense of Struggle."

36. Our Peoples exhibit.

37. Our Peoples exhibit.

38. *Way of the People*, Progress Report Executive Summary.

39. Venturi, Scott Brown, and Associates, *The Way of the People: National Museum of the American Indian, Master Facilities Programming, Phase 1, Revised Draft Report*, Smithsonian Institution Office of Design and Construction (Washington DC: Venturi, Scott Brown, and Associates, November 22, 1991), 17.

40. Richard West, "From the Director" *National Museum of the American Indian Magazine*, Spring 2007, 17.

41. Patricia Neitfeld, personal communication with the author, October 23, 2006.

42. Barbara Monroe, "The Internet in Indian Country" *Computers and Composition* 19 (2002): 285–96.

43. Lianne McTavish, "Visiting the Virtual Museum: Art and Experience Online," *New Museum Theory and Practice*, ed. Janet Marstine (Malden MA: Blackwell, 2006); Rachel Anderson, "Native Americans and the Digital Divide," Benton Foundation, 1999, http://www.benton.org/publibrary/digitalbeat/db101499.html.

44. Kyra Landzelius, introduction to *Native on the Net: Indigenous and Diasporic Peoples in the Virtual Age*, ed. Kyra Landzelius (New York: Routledge, 2006).

45. See J. S. Billings, "On Composite Photography"; J. S. Billings and W. Matthews, "On a New Cranophore"; and *Nanook of the North*, film, directed by Robert J. Flaherty (Revillon, France: Les Frères, 1922).

46. Michael Brown, *Who Owns Native Culture?* (Cambridge MA: Harvard University Press, 2003).

47. Douglas E. Evelyn and Mark G. Hirsch, "At the Threshold: A Response to Comments on the National Museum of the American Indian's Inaugural Exhibitions," *Public Historian* 28 (2006): 85–90; and Gwyneira Isaac, "What Are Our Expectations Telling Us? Encounters with the NMAI" in "Critical Engagements with the National Museum of the American Indian," ed. Amy Lonetree and Sonya Atalay, special issue, *American Indian Quarterly* 30, nos. 3–4 (2006): 574–96.

48. This assessment comes from interviews conducted by the author with NMAI visitors during the summer of 2006.

49. Venturi, Scott Brown, and Associates, *Way of the People*, Phase 2 Final Report,

3:105; Venturi, Scott Brown, and Associates, *Way of the People*, Phase 1, Revised Draft Report, 18; Venturi, Scott Brown, and Associates, *Way of the People*, Phase 2 Final Report, 4:51–52.

50. Venturi, Scott Brown, and Associates, *Way of the People*, Phase 2 Final Report, 4:52, 53.

51. Venturi, Scott Brown, and Associates, *Way of the People*, Phase 1, Revised Draft Report, 18; Venturi, Scott Brown, and Associates, *Way of the People*, Phase 2 Final Report, 4:51–52. However, some wood is used in the museum, including replicas in the Hupa and Yup'ik cultural areas in Our Universes, the floor in the Potomac, and wall adornments in the café.

52. Venturi, Scott Brown, and Associates, *Way of the People*, Phase 1, Revised Draft Report, 20.

53. As cited by Dickstein Thompson, "Mission Statement."

54. Richard W. Hill Sr., "The Indian in the Cabinet of Curiosity" in *The Changing Presentation of the American Indian: Museums and Native Cultures* (Washington DC: National Museum of the American Indian; Seattle: University of Washington Press, 2000).

55. Hill, "Indian in the Cabinet," 105.

56. Hill, "Indian in the Cabinet," 105.

57. S. Elizabeth Bird, "Imagining Indians: Negotiating Identity in a Media World" in *The Audience in Everyday Life* (New York: Routledge, 2003).

58. Todd Gitlin, *Media Unlimited: How the Torrent of Images and Sounds Overwhelms Our Lives* (New York: Henry Holt, 2002).

59. Robert Berkhofer, *The White Man's Indian* (New York: Vintage Books, 1979).

60. Dickstein Thompson, "Mission Statement."

61. Shari M. Huhndorf, *Going Native: Indians in the American Cultural Imagination* (Ithaca NY: Cornell University Press, 2001).

62. Turner Broadcasting, "Turner Broadcasting expands Native American initiative," news release, April 7, 1993.

63. Bunty Anquoe, "Turner Praises Indians with One Hand, Chops with Other" *Indian Country Today*, December 10, 1992.

64. The NMAI felt financial pressures from its inception, as the NMAI Act required planners to seek funding for one-third of the building costs of the Mall Museum from private sources (approximately $36.7 million). The museum actually raised about $70 million in the first campaign, and a second campaign pushed the NMAI to raise another $50 million, reaching the "ultimate private goal" of $120 million. Memorandum, *Mall Brochure*, September 17, 2000, accession 171, box 4, Smithsonian Institution Archives.

65. Force, *Heye and the Mighty*; Dickstein Thompson, "Mission Statement"; and Toby Miller and George Yúdice, *Cultural Policy* (London: Sage, 2002).

66. For more on museums and neoliberal conditions, see Jeremy Packer and Mary

Coffey, "Hogging the Road: Cultural Governance and the Citizen Cyclist," *Cultural Studies* 18 (2004): 641–74.

67. The presence from 2000 to 2007 of former Smithsonian secretary Lawrence Small, a businessman and the first nonacademic, nonscientist secretary at the institution, demonstrates the shift of concentration to financial concerns. See J. Trescott and J. V. and Grimaldi, "Smithsonian's Small Quits in Wake of Inquiry" *Washington Post*, March 27, 2007.

68. Dickstein Thompson, "Mission Statement," 174.

69. Faith Davis Ruffins, "Culture Wars Won and Lost: Ethnic Museums on the Mall, Part I: The National Holocaust Museum and the National Museum of the American Indian," *Radical History Review* 68 (1997): 79–100.

6

West Side Stories

*The Blending of Voice and
Representation through a
Shared Curatorial Practice*

BRENDA MACDOUGALL
AND M. TERESA CARLSON

On May 26, 2007, after months of research, consultation, and negotiation, an exhibit entitled West Side Stories: The Metis of Northwestern
Saskatchewan, depicting the social, cultural, political, and economic life
of eighteen subarctic Metis communities (see map 2) opened at the Diefenbaker Canada Centre (DCC) in Saskatoon, Saskatchewan.[1] The idea for
West Side Stories emerged from a need to communicate and disseminate
some of the results gathered from a large, interuniversity research project, "Otipimsuak—the Free People: Métis Land and Society in Northwest
Saskatchewan," which is currently funded through the Social Sciences and
Humanities Research Council of Canada's (SSHRC) Community University Research Alliance (CURA) program.[2] The nature of the collaboration
that went into the development of West Side Stories challenges the manner in which Aboriginal communities, museums, and academic scholarship can forge collaborative relationships. Conceived by three cocurators
from the University of Saskatchewan—Teresa Carlson, acting director of
the DCC; Brenda Macdougall, Department of Native Studies; and Keith
Carlson, Department of History—the purpose for designing the exhibit
was to locate an alternative means of communicating research findings to
a mixed audience of nonacademics, youths, scholars, and Aboriginal and
non-Aboriginal individuals in a way that was both informative and visually appealing. It was especially important to represent the more intangible aspects of cultural heritage, such as the voice, values, language, and

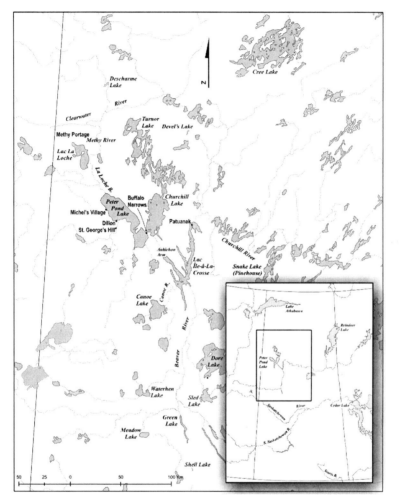

2. Saskatchewan, Canada. Map by Elise Pietroniro, GIServices, Department of Ge-
ography, University of Saskatchewan. *Projection*: UTM Zone 13N, NAD1983. *Source*:
National Atlas of Canada. Vector level: 2,000,000, Natural Resources Canada.
Courtesy Brenda Macdougall.

traditions of an Indigenous people—those aspects of life that are rarely given prominence within museum exhibitions, which are typically more artifact-centered in design. The resulting exhibit relied heavily upon text panels to showcase the research findings, which were augmented by photographic and artifact displays, as well as thematic reproductions. The emphasis upon text rather than visuals within an exhibit was unusual and set West Side Stories apart from more traditional museological practice. What emerged through the process of negotiating our shared curatorial practice was an active assertion of ownership, governance, and voice by each stakeholder as represented by the people of northwestern Saskatchewan, scholars from the University of Saskatchewan, and the DCC—something that was permitted only by the equitable sharing of both power and responsibility.

The SSHRC's CURA program is predicated upon collaboration between university and communities with shared research interests and goals. The "Otipimsuak" project is engaged in documenting the history of Metis communities of northwestern Saskatchewan and is engaged in capacity-building projects by training local people in various aspects of the research program.[3] By the time the exhibit was conceived in early 2006, much of the CURA's research effort had focused on traditional land-use studies, on analysis of the political and legislative processes by which the Metis were alienated from their lands, and on the overall economic history of the region—the areas typical of Aboriginal research in recent years. Although research focused on the economic, legal, and political history of the region was significant, the communities also wanted the stories about their relationships to one another, to their spirituality, and to the landscape to have a place in the project, providing a more intimate and human portrait of Metis life in both historical and contemporary terms. These stories became the foundation of the West Side Stories exhibit. The collaboration to document this particular area of research by the Metis communities of northwestern Saskatchewan, scholars from the University of Saskatchewan, and the staff of the DCC represents a new methodology for telling the story of a people in a way that reflects their cultural values, beliefs, and sensibilities.

One of the most compelling reasons for mounting the West Side Stories exhibit was revealed early in the research project, challenging the existing paradigm in which Metis history is captured. Within the larger research enterprise, which focuses on political, legal, and economic topics, little effort had been made to reflect the social and cultural history of the Metis community, including concepts about their ethnogenesis as a people of the subarctic. But these origins are in fact part of what differentiates them from the Metis of the south, demarcated by the histories of the Metis of Red River and the Metis of the western plains, whose economy was dominated by the buffalo-based trade. Instead, the moment of northwestern Saskatchewan Metis ethnogenesis can be traced back to the eighteenth-century fur trade, when independent traders from Montreal competed with the Hudson's Bay Company (HBC) for economic supremacy in the rich subarctic and arctic fur regions.[4] Northwestern Saskatchewan Metis identity was forged independent of the well-known and often-discussed events of southern Canadian Metis nationalism, namely the Battle of Seven Oaks in 1817, the mid-to-late-nineteenth-century history of the Red River, and the events at Batoche, Saskatchewan, in the 1880s. Therefore, this exhibit attempts to highlight historical moments, cultural expressions, and economic and political processes that contributed to making West Side Metis society a simultaneously distinct but integral part of greater Metis history. As a result, West Side Stories challenges the public to reconsider their understanding of who the Metis are and reflect upon the diversity of Metis experiences within Canada.

The manner in which Metis history and society are interpreted has undergone significant and important changes in recent years. Earlier generations of scholars interpreted Metis culture as though it consisted of the worst aspects of First Nations and European societies, as though in coming together the two cultures gained little and lost much. Alternatively, other historians discussed Metis society as a static relic of the past, unable to find relevance in a world no longer dominated by the buffalo hunt or the fur trade.[5] Early Metis scholarship also tended to focus on prominent figures such as Cuthbert Grant, Louis Riel, or Gabriel Dumont, who led the Metis in their struggles for independence in the nineteenth century.[6] However, such biographical portrayals seldom presented a sympathetic or balanced perspective that accounted for collective Metis sensibilities or cultural beliefs.

Since the mid-1980s, scholars have forged new paths of historical inquiry. Increasingly, the focus has been on understanding Metis cultural diversity through studies of interrelated subjects such as class and religious distinctions, the borderlands experience between Canadian and American Metis people, economic and cultural diversity between individuals and communities, and, perhaps most importantly, Metis family life.[7] As a result, Metis history is now beginning to be understood in terms of theoretical concepts of *metissage*, *hybridity*, *aboriginality*, and *syncretism*, which allow for cultural continuity to coexist alongside a dynamic historical progression. It is now broadly accepted that while Metis society was built on a foundation of cross-cultural sharing, it consists of much more than the sum of its First Nations and European parts. While the Metis of northwestern Saskatchewan appreciate the bicultural roots of their society, they recognize themselves as a separate people—with both traditions reflected in their history. For example, they continue to value First Nations ideas about the centrality of family and individual and community identity, as reflected in the Cree concept of *wahkootowin*. This notion in turn also respects Roman Catholic ideas pertaining to the expansiveness of family, as seen in the relationship between the godparents and the birthparents of baptized children.[8] The Metis further acknowledge the legacy of broad regional economic ties, which so clearly influenced the corporate social system and commercial trade that were introduced. While these influences characterized the HBC, the Metis simultaneously participated in traditional, subsistence-based harvesting activities.

Metis origins are now conceived as having emerged from within a dynamic contact zone that was more than just a cultural middle ground, where economic opportunity coexisted with social convenience. Rather, Metis history is the story of community and nation building, as well as of how a new people can emerge. Metis origins may have begun in the fur trade, but the nation and its people were shaped by a series of unfolding historical events and processes. The story of Metis emergence in northwestern Saskatchewan is a part of this unfolding narrative and historiography.

The Community

Undeniably, Metis ethnogenesis in northwestern Saskatchewan occurred in the closing decades of the eighteenth century as a result of fur trade expansion across Canada and the northern United States. During the eighteenth and nineteenth centuries, Metis communities emerged in these regions within a generation of the trade's establishment. The ethnogenesis of this new people was dynamic, occurring in different regions at different times as the trade expanded and contracted.

Île à la Crosse is one of the oldest, most culturally homogeneous Metis communities in the Canadian subarctic and rose in prominence during the competitive race between fur traders to reach the Mackenzie and Athabasca trade regions. It became a hub for Metis sociocultural development in the subarctic. Independent traders Thomas and Joseph Frobisher from the Montreal-based St. Lawrence trade network established the first post at Île à la Crosse as an outpost for their anticipated Athabasca-based trade ventures. While the Montreal traders were the first to move into northwestern Saskatchewan, they were quickly followed by the HBC in the 1780s. On these initial excursions, French Canadian, English, and Scottish traders from the XY, North West, and Hudson's Bay companies, respectively, began to establish, as part of their trading experience, intimate and often long-lasting relationships with local Cree and Dene women.[9] These initial unions between non-Aboriginal men and Indian women are best characterized as that of a protogeneration who, while not Metis, sparked the creation of this new society. The result of these unions was the ethnogenesis of the Metis and the region's formation of communities such as La Loche, Green Lake, Beauval, Dillon, and Pinehouse, all located across northwestern Saskatchewan. The West Side consequently became home to a group of Metis who worked in the fur trade for generations, in occupations ranging from traders and servants to freemen, subsistence hunters, and fishermen.

Roman Catholic missionaries from the Order of Mary Immaculate (otherwise known as the Oblates or as the OMI) arrived in the region in 1845 to establish, at Île à la Crosse in 1846, the first western mission outside of Red River. Subsequent missions were permanently established at Green Lake in 1875 and La Loche in 1890. In addition to these three permanent mission stations, other Catholic missions operated in various communities as needed, and itinerant priests regularly traveled throughout the region.[10] Upon their arrival in the mid-nineteenth century, the Oblates encountered a people who already understood and practiced the holy sacraments, observed the Sabbath regularly, and acknowledged the powers of the saints over their lives. Just as the Metis incorporated the fur trade into their cultural development on the West Side, they also created a flourishing socioreligious lifestyle marked by periods of both intense revelry and religious piety.[11] Within this milieu, the church worked to establish itself among these people, acculturating to the demands of Metis identity while striving to improve the rudimentary teachings of Catholicism, which had been held by residents since the early the nineteenth century.

Over the next five generations, Metis families of the West Side worked within the economy of the fur trade, intermarried with one another as well as with nearby Cree and Dene community members and incoming traders, adhered to a new form of Catholicism, and, in turn, shaped the region into a homeland. The extension of Treaty Six and Treaty Ten into the region in the late nineteenth and early twentieth centuries and the concurrent issuance of scrip marked the beginning of a new era in the north, as Canadian legal and political structures extended into the region. For the first time, there was an imposed and arbitrarily created legal and jurisdictional distinction separating Indians from Half-Breeds: the former group took treaty, while the latter was issued scrip; one group were now wards of the federal government and had their lives regulated by the Indian Act of 1867, while the other were citizens of the state; one had treaty rights protected by law, while the other had ceded all rights to the lands and resources and therefore enjoyed no such protection, either real or theoretical. These legal distinctions, however, had minimal impact on the people of the region until the provincial government of Saskatchewan obtained jurisdictional authority over natural resources via the Natural Resource Transfer Agreement in 1930.[12] With no constitutional protection as an Aboriginal people, the Metis were, for the first time, effectively marginalized within their own homeland.

The Research

Although the Metis are now officially recognized as one of three Aboriginal societies in the Constitution Act of 1982 — alongside First Nations (Indians) and Inuit — with existing and, more importantly, protected Aboriginal rights, Canadian legislation neither defines their term "Métis" nor the scope of their rights. These two issues are important considering that Canada's northern regions are rich in natural resources that have become integral to provincial economies since the late 1940s. The mining sector and the oil and gas industry have, in recent decades, become increasingly significant to Saskatchewan, once an agrarian-based province.

Through most of the twentieth century, the provincial north's 320,000 square kilometers have been extensively explored, developed, and processed by mining and forestry companies, as well as by other resource-extraction industries such as the commercial and sport fishing and hunting industries. Ownership of most of the land and all of the mineral, oil, and gas rights is held by the government and managed from the provincial capital, Regina, a city located approximately 1,300 kilometers to the south. The region's largely Aboriginal population—Cree, Dene, and Metis—have historically had very little participation in this lucrative economy and have not shared in the wealth extracted from their territories.[13]

Although few of the northern Aboriginal peoples in the province have prospered during this era of internal colonialism, the Metis have been at a far greater disadvantage. For instance, while they have participated in both commercial and subsistence hunting, trapping, and fishing sectors for generations, as provincial citizens in the postwar era, Metis have had to obtain issued licenses to continue to pursue their livelihood and feed their families (theoretically, registered Indians have had no such impediments and, as treaty signatories, have received much greater protection for their traditional livelihood). In a region that has been historically low on cash, purchasing a license can be too great a financial burden to overcome for many Metis. Consequently, many Metis become "criminals," arrested and charged with poaching under provincial wildlife legislation.[14] Furthermore, unlike their First Nations relatives, the Metis were not compensated when additional limits were placed on their ability to engage in traditional economies. In 1953, for example, the Primrose–Cold Lake Air Weapons Range, a cold war facility for training American and Canadian bomber pilots, was established. Straddling the border between Alberta and Saskatchewan, the range was organized so as to avoid Indian reserves. However, the range encompassed traditional First Nations and Metis hunting, fishing, and gathering sites. For the Metis Nation, four Metis communities—Beauval, Jans Bay, Cole Bay, and Île à la Crosse—were adversely affected socially and economically when residents were prevented from accessing traditional harvesting sites within the range. Citing inadequate compensation and a loss of Aboriginal rights to hunting, trapping, fishing, and gathering, the Metis demanded redress but received no compensation until 2007. By contrast, First Nations groups who had lost their access to areas within the range were compensated a decade earlier.[15]

The legacy of the pre-1982 era, during which time the Metis were truly Canada's forgotten and ignored Aboriginal people, fueled the passions of contemporary communities to adequately research and document their history as a people. As a result, in the past decade, the Metis of northwestern Saskatchewan have been engaged in research projects to improve their political and economic situation in the hope that this will, in turn, secure their social and cultural well-being. Through engagement with academic researchers in the larger CURA project, it is intended that an atlas representing Metis history, society, and land use in northwestern Saskatchewan will be created. To that end, research topics were pursued that could be easily integrated into regional maps. This approach, however, produced uneven results, as the bulk of the initial research was focused in the fields of historical geography, rural economies, and land use, with emphasis on policy analysis and archival research. Researchers engaged with community members to conduct traditional land-use (TLU) interviews, mostly with male community members. The presumption was that, because men were hunters, trappers, and fishermen, traditional land use revolved around those particular male economies. However, since traditional harvesting activities would have required an entire family's participation, research on those activities could have produced a great deal of data about family and community structure and organization. Regardless, the roles of women and young people in the various levels of production were secondary considerations. Similarly, the archival research focused on the collection of scrip records for the Metis in northwestern Saskatchewan, on files from the Department of Justice relating to the distribution of scrip in the region and across Canada, and on fur trade records that provided insight into the historical resource economy of the region. Again, by and large, these areas of research exclude women because of the focus on typically public and political—and therefore male—zones of interaction.

Perhaps not surprisingly, then, the bulk of the CURA research almost exclusively focused on the stories of men, whether political or economic in nature. It became clear that the narratives of women were embedded in the social life and cultural heritage of the communities themselves. These stories also needed to be told for the research project to be balanced and truly representative of Metis society in northwestern Saskatchewan. As a result, in the summer of 2006 two of the researchers—Keith Carlson and Brenda Macdougall—organized a research team of five students, trained them in community-based research methodologies, and took them north to conduct interviews. The purpose of the summer research program was, first and foremost, to locate stories that reflected issues of importance to these communities and that detailed the sociocultural traditions of their nation. The five students—MacKinley Darlington, Kevin Gambell, Jodi Crew, Katya MacDonald, and Amanda Fehr—selected topics from issues that had been raised during initial meetings held with the researchers and community leaders. Gambell and Fehr, who were employees of the center, intended to eventually develop an exhibit based on research at the DCC. In this way, the collaboration between the DCC and the CURA began in earnest.

The topics presented to the students were broadly conceived to cover issues related to spirituality and religion, social organization, and northern farming or horticultural practices. Throughout the summer, as they visited communities, interviewed residents, and read secondary literature, the students narrowed and refined their topics. Furthermore, they chose topics from those broadly presented that heavily reflected their personal interests, thereby creating a synergy between the community, the topic, and themselves. This synergy resulted in the following research projects: the influence of the Virgin Mary on the West Side's form of Catholicism; the emergent and distinctive form of traditional spirituality expressed in public shrine sites and apparitions; the cultural, social, and political meanings embedded in the organization and maintenance of local cemeteries; the role of communal gardening practices on social cohesion and support; and community spatial organization as a means of gaining insight into the values and ethos of a people. Each of these research projects had a significant impact on the conceptualization, creation, and message eventually conveyed within the exhibit.

The Pedagogy

An integral aspect of the research process is, of course, the dissemination of results. For scholars, this typically involves writing papers and monographs for an academic or educated audience as well as presenting at conferences. Too often, research conducted in Aboriginal communities has had very little lasting impact on or contribution to the well-being, intellect, or needs of the people who shared their knowledge, hospitality, stories, values, and artifacts. Accordingly, it was the ambition of those involved in this project to see the research data made accessible to the Metis in a manner that they could appreciate, share, and enjoy. It was essential that, as ethically responsible researchers, we produce useful materials for the communities from which the shared knowledge originated. This decision was just as imperative for Teresa Carlson, acting director of the DCC. Providing access to a broader population within Saskatchewan and contributing to the University of Saskatchewan's centennial celebrations, which were planned for the fall of 2007, were two aspects of the center's greater mandate. The decision to produce a multifaceted exhibit reflective of the varied research efforts that went into the CURA atlas project was unanimous. All that remained was to mount the exhibit as it was envisioned.

Like scholarly writing, by definition and intent, both permanent and temporary museum exhibits are factually based, well-researched, and, generally, developed with the same types of processes and principles that are applied in academic scholarship. In this sense, what we attempted at the DCC with West Side Stories did not, in and of itself, contribute to the development of new methodological approaches to innovative cultural heritage displays. Even the concept of partnering with Indigenous communities was not methodologically transformative. Indeed, recent scholarship in the field of museum studies has invested greatly in examining the often tense and rather problematic relationship that has existed between museums and Aboriginal communities.[16] The reasons for examining this relationship are by now obvious. As part of the colonial enterprise, material objects, physical remains, and even the people of Indigenous communities were collected, catalogued, and displayed in order to educate and entertain the citizens in colonial centers of power. Historically, museum exhibits dealing with Aboriginal collections were seldom culturally sensitive to the societies of origin. Museums often displayed "artifacts" such as ancestral remains, funerary items (i.e., religious artifacts and regalia that were highly personalized and symbolic in nature, such as medicines, pipes and bundles, masks, and clothing), and other personal talismans representing the spiritual guardians of individuals. These items, central to a society's material culture, were often forcibly removed or stolen from their home communities, a practice that is disturbing to living members of the communities.[17] The purpose of these displays was to inform and entertain the viewing public with curios from "primitive" cultures rather than to respond to the cultural sensitivities, ideologies, or belief systems of the other. The secondary purpose for these displays, unstated but undeniably clear to any Aboriginal person who has ever been to a museum, was to reinforce the power and authority of colonial regimes by displaying the collected, and often times confiscated or stolen, possessions of the dispossessed.

There has been an increasing awareness among curators that these types of displays are not simply insensitive but are relics of a colonial past without a place in a postmodern, global society. Increasingly, efforts have been made by various museums, often because of the demands of Indigenous communities, to return to specific, identifiable, and locatable communities many religious artifacts, human remains, and other culturally sensitive objects.[18] Where repatriation is not possible, museums have often removed culturally or spiritually sensitive items from permanent displays, leaving in their place descriptions of the objects and reasons for their exclusion. Part of this growing sensitivity of museums and other cultural heritage agencies to the inappropriateness of previous representations of Aboriginality has been greater efforts to engage and collaborate with Aboriginal peoples in the development of new research and curatorial practices.

Increasingly, there are Aboriginal people on staff at mainstream museums to assist in redesigning existing displays as well as to create new, appropriate displays that include Aboriginal perspectives and voices. Typically, these employees work closely with local communities and elders to ensure that displays of objects, therefore the message of exhibits, reflect cultural sensibilities and values. In Saskatchewan, two instances of Aboriginal participation in museological practice have emerged at, first, a regional cultural heritage center and, later, at a national historic site. Near Saskatoon, Wanuskewin Heritage Park is a regional cultural heritage site located on the banks of the South Saskatchewan River in an area that was an ancient buffalo jump site, making it a place with a high degree of archaeological, anthropological, and historical significance. Wanuskewin is operated under the leadership and guidance of First Nations people and non-Aboriginal academics and organizations to increase public awareness, understanding, and appreciation of the cultural legacy of the northern plains First Nations people. As such, its board of directors consists of representatives from the University of Saskatchewan, the Federation of Saskatchewan Indian Nations, the city of Saskatoon, the governments of Canada and Saskatchewan, the Meewasin Valley Authority, and the Friends of Wanuskewin organization. The creation of Wanuskewin was possible because of the involvement of local First Nations people at the conceptualization phase of development. Because they have been involved since the beginning, Wanuskewin is now viewed as a proper Aboriginal enterprise. Conversely, the Batoche National Historic Site is a part of the national parks system and depicts the history of the armed Metis resistance against the Canadian government in 1885. In recent years, however, Batoche has benefited from hiring a Saskatchewan-born, Metis site manager, who has worked to ensure Metis participation at the park through living history and theatrical performances and through the establishment of a genealogical center staffed by an elder. In turn, the site manager has also partnered with scholars in research projects and conferences. While Batoche is still a federally owned and operated site, the emerging relationship between the park and the Metis community is transforming the way in which it operates.

Clearly, there is a growing trend within Aboriginal communities to create and build their own museums or "keeping houses." Aboriginal societies' adoption of the museum as an idea has been transformative for a people who had no historical practice of collecting and displaying objects as a means of relating their history and sense of nationhood. Teresa Carlson has had first-hand experience in witnessing and assisting this kind of transformation. In the early 1990s the Stó:lō of British Columbia realized that, although their traditional territory encompassed twenty-one individual reserves within almost 800,000 hectares, many non-Aboriginal people in the area had no idea who the Stó:lō were, where they lived, what their traditions were, or even that they continued to exist. The provincial education curriculum mandated no teaching about the Stó:lō people, and instead it emphasized study of Aboriginal societies from other regions of

Canada. So several departments within the collective Stó:lō Nation (primarily the Aboriginal Rights and Title and the Education and Community Development offices) as well as cultural advisors, Stó:lō government officials and elders, local museums and archives, and the Chilliwack School District developed a Stó:lō Nation education and cultural center.[19]

As a professionally trained museologist, Teresa Carlson, with Stó:lō community members, created Shxwt'a:selhawtxw—the House of Long Ago and Today—a cultural center that houses exhibits of past and present traditions, utilizing historical artifacts as well as contemporary objects. The primary role of Shxwt'a:selhawtxw is not that of a museum but rather of an educational center.[20]

Hands-on exhibits and experiences educate visitors of all ages in the traditional practices and current lifestyles of the Stó:lō. The Aboriginal staff of Shxwt'a:selhawtxw teach visitors not only that the history of encounters between the Stó:lō and the non-Aboriginal people is important but also that shared traditions are threads that continue to link the present with the past. What has resulted is a stronger relationship between the Stó:lō and the non-Aboriginal communities within their territory. Non-Aboriginal people now not only know of the Stó:lō and their past but are also more aware of how they continue to live and contribute to their present, shared communities. This results in more empathetic understanding toward spiritual, cultural, and ritual practices of the living community. The sharing of this knowledge has, in turn, resulted in greater numbers of returned artifacts and objects from "personal collections" and small local museums, in greater respect for areas accessed for spiritual and resource gathering practices, and in interest by non-Aboriginal people in the protection of archaeological sites.

While processes may be changing, the fact of cultural heritage sites being artifact centered has not received similar critical appraisal. Aboriginal and non-Aboriginal cultural heritage institutions have focused on archaeological, historical, contemporary, and environmental resources in the forms of landscapes, monuments and sites, material-culture collections, and archival-quality documents. Regardless of the type of facility—traditional museum or Aboriginal-controlled keeping house—they all begin with the collection of artifacts, objects, or documents as the basis of the displays. It is safe to say that most collections begin with objects that are gathered from a particular era or part of the world and are organized into like categories such as "beadwork" or "clay pots." These objects are then utilized to re-create large-scale reproductions of the natural environment, villages, or camp sites. In all instances, the objects tell the story. Material goods are usually described in a scientific or anthropological manner—this is what it is, this is what it was used for, this is who made it or owned it, this is when it dates from, this is the material that it is made of. The result is an emphasis on the object, while the people who created it are a secondary consideration. This is not surprising, as the cultural heritage being managed, preserved, and interpreted are tangible resources that can be easily used to represent a storied past. This reality has led to the general practice of museum exhibitions being created around artifacts with very little textual information provided by academic research rather than from objects located and used to corroborate the research-based story being told.

It is the manner in which we began this project that has set West Side Stories apart from other displays of its kind. Beginning with a research project that, while community-based, was fairly standard in form and approach within the scholarly world, the pedagogy that informed West Side Stories approached the creation of an Aboriginal-society exhibit from a different place. Instead of beginning in the past or with artifacts, West Side Stories started with a community of living people who wanted to share their history, stories, values, and ideas about who they were and how their community existed with outsiders who were not familiar with them. Arguably, this is what would happen within the environment of a keeping house, owned and operated by Indigenous people such as the Stó:lō Shxwt'a:selhawtxw is. However, the difference here is that none of the people involved were employees working to fulfill a specific mandate generated by a community or members within the community. The three cocurators of West Side Stories—Teresa Carlson, Brenda Macdougall, and Keith Carlson—are all employees of the University of Saskatchewan. Only one, Teresa Carlson, has previous experience with museology and curatorial practices; and only one, Brenda Macdougall, is Metis (although the West Side is not her territory).[21] However, the community heavily shaped the exhibit, because its members controlled much of the research that went into the displays by choosing the themes, by directing the student researchers to areas and topics that mattered to them, and by framing the story that was told with their needs and interests. Consequently, West Side Stories began with words, not objects; and it is, therefore, as another institution's curator observed, "text-heavy."[22]

The Exhibit

The approach we took with West Side Stories placed agency for the storytelling with the community, whether the text was fashioned from historical records, from the narratives of ancestors embedded in the historical documents, or from first-person interviews that revealed the contemporary voice and historical interpretation. The development of West Side Stories began in January 2007; and while funding had merely come in promises of support, the opening date was set to coincide with the arrival on campus of over 5,000 scholars from across Canada and the United States, as the University of Saskatchewan hosted Congress 2007 (the largest joint annual meeting of all major academic organizations belonging to the Canadian Federation for the Humanities and Social Sciences, held in Canada). It was hoped that the exhibit would be widely seen and commented upon by Congress attendees, which, indeed, is what occurred. Another central element during the development of West Side Stories was to design it as an exhibit that, after its time in Saskatoon, could travel to northern Saskatchewan to be displayed and permanently housed in the Metis communities that originally participated in the project. Additionally, the summer of 2007 marked the one hundredth anniversary of the final Half-Breed Claims Commission that traveled to La Loche to issue scrip.[23] Taking West Side Stories north at the end of August would coincide with this anniversary.

The three cocurators along with two graduate students—MacKinley Darlington and Kristina Duffee, master's students in history and Native studies respectively—began conceptualizing the form of the exhibit. The overall scope of the exhibit would examine the processes of ethnogenesis over time—how the communities not only emerged from but also shaped relationships within the territory since the late 1700s as well as how unique character and historical forces shaped their form of being Metis. As such, the exhibit was not chronologically ordered in the linear manner that usually directs exhibits. Visitors could move throughout the exhibit in any direction, between past and present and from theme to theme, without losing sight of the overall story. For instance, the history of the mission was located next to more contemporary examples of religious influence—such as a Marian shrine re-creation that demonstrated how Catholicism and traditional spirituality work in concert today—which in turn was next to a PowerPoint presentation of how communities have created a unique typology for their homeland. Centrally located is a series of maps and other visual displays that are intended to orient visitors to the Metis spatial conceptualization of the region in general and to Île à la Crosse specifically. The placement of this element in a central location was a conscious decision meant to encourage visitors to revisit the land and relate to the stories of the people.

The central, overarching thematic structure for West Side Stories hinges on a representation of the in-depth role of family in the emergence of a new culture and in how individuals and groups of Metis related to one another, influenced the fur trade, transformed Catholicism and traditional spirituality into a new religious experience, shaped political relations with others, and formed the basis of stories that became fundamental to our research. We decided to prominently feature the students' research projects as three-dimensional displays. In this way, we re-created a Marian shrine and cabin (with various items identified by their Michif names); a display highlighting the local, often humorous names for various locations and neighborhoods in the village of Île à la Crosse; garden and cemetery displays, highlighted through an examination of the history of economic and spatial relationships of families in the region; and a scrip display that encompassed the narratives about how Canadian legal definitions disrupted relationships between family members.[24] Along with three-dimensional displays of this research, each student drafted the content for text plates and selected photographs to accompany their work.

Unable to confirm funding for the exhibit until the end of March, the real activity of building the exhibit did not actually begin until about six weeks prior to its opening. Until then, our time was spent planning exactly what we wanted to see in the exhibit, despite our collective anxiety that we would not be able to fulfill our vision or, worse, that we would be left constructing displays made of papier-mâché and crayons. Regardless, the exhibit planning pushed forward, and the team worked to appropriately transform the research and generate ideas about the overall content of West Side Stories. Although many individuals conducted the research, the overall presentation of the exhibit required a unified stylistic approach. As a result, it was determined that Teresa Carlson and Brenda Macdougall would handle layout and design. Carlson's experience working for the Stó:lō Nation museum in British Columbia gave her the skills to design the text-plate backgrounds and create an overall unified design element. While drafting the text plates, Macdougall consciously ignored all the museological rules regarding how much text is permissible to maintain the average person's interest. Although advised that the average visitor will not read more than about fifty words per text plate, many of our plates exceeded that limit. However, most of the text on each plate was interspersed with images in an attempt to establish a visual interest.

Because the exhibit was designed around text, the breaking of this cardinal rule of museology was necessary. As text plates were drafted, they were sent to both Teresa and Keith Carlson for editing and review. Teresa also began fashioning the layout for new plates. When gaps in the research were identified, students conducted additional, secondary research and located appropriate images or photographs to fill out the content, and additional text plates were drafted.[25]

The strengths of each cocurator were drawn upon, and each heavily influenced the overall look and content of the exhibit. For instance, in addition to Teresa Carlson's museum experience and knowledge of design, her internal university contacts ensured that necessary items, such as vestments and other items from the Roman Catholic Church as well as a poem and letter written by Metis-leader Louis Riel, were a part of the exhibit design.[26] Keith Carlson had strong technical skills, such as information technology (IT) and mapping capabilities, necessary to turn the research on place names into the dynamic audiovisual PowerPoint presentation that was the central point for the entire exhibit. Brenda ensured that, as the exhibit unfolded, appropriate and authentic artifacts (beaded moccasins, vests, coats, and other items of material production, along with tools and utensils) and artwork were collected from northwestern Saskatchewan community members. Every item included in the exhibit was worn and used in the work life of people, constructed by a Metis artisan, and, as much as possible, manufactured in the north by Metis people.

1. Beaded smoked hide vest on display at Diefenbaker Canada Centre. Photo courtesy M. Teresa Carlson.

2. Detail of *Batoche* by Christi Belcourt. Photo courtesy M. Teresa Carlson.

Additionally, Brenda's broader contacts with Metis artisans and historic sites, such as the Batoche National Historic Site, provided for the inclusion of paintings and historic artifacts and reproductions in the exhibit. While not necessarily from the north, these items enhanced the textual focal points of the display. Only those items that could support and illustrate the textual content were sought. So, while there is an element of reproduction and viewing of material culture as is found in more traditional museum settings, these items were never the primary focal point for West Side Stories. Significantly, no single item is more important or is given more prominence in the exhibit than any other. These items were not chosen because they were the oldest, the most beautiful, the most representative, or the rarest—they were chosen only in so far as they enhanced (and did not detract from) the textual focus of the exhibit.

Significant to the overall look of the exhibit was its need to convey a sense of theater or artistic atmosphere. The right ambience, more than artifacts, was the ingredient that became the backdrop for the textual content. Finding just the right template for the text plates became a major

3. York boat on display at Diefenbaker Canada Centre. Photo courtesy Brenda Macdougall.

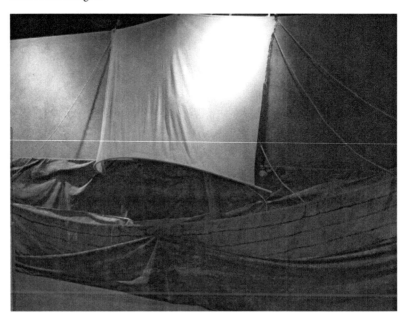

concern. A great deal of effort went into designing different backgrounds with distinct colors and textures. Selecting appropriate fonts and sizes and images was also part of the overall look of the exhibit. After some effort, we settled upon using a hide vest as the background for the text plates, altering it slightly to give it a more stylized representation (see fig. 1). The goal was to make the text appear as though it was printed upon stretched, smoked hide, making the exhibit appear as though it was a part of the region's traditional economy and, therefore, cultural aesthetic.

Additionally, representations of intricate flower-patterned beadwork on the text plates that introduced various sections were a subtle means of both highlighting that form of Metis art as well as marking intellectual or thematic shifts in the display itself. Instead of using actual beadwork, we utilized the paintings of Metis-artist Christi Belcourt, which reproduce beadwork using intricate patterns of painted dots (see fig. 2).

With this foundational work completed, we hired the artistic director of the Saskatchewan Native Theatre Company (SNTC), Mark Erickson, and his assistant, Jesse Gerard, to collaborate on designing and constructing the three-dimensional portions of the exhibit, including many of the backdrops upon which the text plates were hung.

After consultations with the SNTC crew, they took our ideas about authenticity and our desire to set a more theatrical ambiance and applied them to the design elements of the exhibit so that there was a singular artistic statement and mood. Erickson further created backdrops, built theatrical sets, and produced creative renderings of items that we otherwise would have had no means of replicating. For instance, the SNTC crew created a three-dimensional mural of a York boat with canvas sails and renderings of water (see fig. 3).[27]

An actual York boat reproduction would have had to have been borrowed and shipped, a prohibitive cost. Furthermore, because York boats were over forty feet in length, there would have been insufficient gallery space to display a boat. The SNTC crew also constructed a cabin in which household items were displayed, built picket fences like those surrounding people's homes in many northern communities, and built a Marian shrine with a mural of trees for a backdrop, as is commonly found throughout northwestern Saskatchewan (see figs. 4 and 5).

The purpose for these three-dimensional pieces was not so much to represent a real item but to set a mood for audiences that provided a sense

4. Marian Shrine replica at Diefenbaker Canada Centre. Photo courtesy Brenda Macdougall.

5. Replica of cabin at Diefenbaker Canada Centre. Photo courtesy
Brenda Macdougall.

of how people lived and interacted as well as how they created and defined their cultural ethos.

It was important that the overall design and layout reflect the culture that was being represented and provide the sensation of being permitted to view a side of the northern Metis that is largely private and unknown. To that end, the emphasis on the northern way of life was paramount. As such, we avoided thematically or theatrically recreating the typical symbols associated with southern Metis culture — the l'Assumption sash, the particular shade of blue that adorns the Metis national flag, buffalo and Red River carts, and the iconography of Louis Riel and Gabriel Dumont. Some of these symbols do appear in the exhibit, but only when they are a part of the history or cultural objects created within the communities. These types of images are commonly used on most promotional materials and displays for Metis people, and as such they have become indelible symbols of the Canadian Metis essence. However, two particular aspects made them inappropriate for our purposes. First, for the most part, they represent southern, plains-based Metis societies; and second, perhaps

6. Riel genealogy display at Diefenbaker Canada Centre. Photo courtesy Brenda Macdougall.

more importantly, they are symbols of masculinity. It was critical that West Side Stories provide a more balanced approach to gender and not simply fall into the reproduction of stereotypical, masculine images. By not recreating these iconic images, this exhibit attempted to challenge people to rethink their ideas about who Metis people were, how they lived, and what the culture is today.

However, because subarctic Metis identity contributes to and supports concepts of the Metis Nation as a whole, there are instances when the most iconic symbols of Metis culture appear in the exhibit. As already noted, we included the poem and letter written by Louis Riel, but we did so only because it enhanced and contributed to an important component of the region's history and highlighted the issue of relatedness as a driving force in Metis community and cultural formation (see fig. 6).

While Louis Riel himself was never known to have been in northwestern Saskatchewan, his grandfather had been sent there by a Montreal trading firm to work; and while there he married a local Dene woman. Consequently, Louis Riel's father, Jean Louis Riel, was born in Île à la Crosse. Furthermore, after entering the sisterly order of the Grey Nuns, Riel's younger sister Sara served as a missionary in Île à la Crosse until her premature death in 1883. Because she was a nun, Sara did not marry while in the region; but she did become a godmother for almost a dozen children who were born while she was serving the mission and was thus drawn into the family structure in a more personal manner than typical for clergy. Had the Riel family not been so intimately connected with the region, the letter and poem of Louis Riel would not have been included in the text.[28] Accordingly, the brief history of the Riel family is told from a subarctic rather than a plains perspective.

The exhibit ends by raising some difficult contemporary issues with which northern Metis communities must contend. Their continued tense relationship with the Canadian government has come to the fore recently and old wounds have been opened as the government seeks to settle claims for residential school abuses. Home to the oldest mission station in Saskatchewan, Île à la Crosse was also home to one of the oldest boarding schools in western Canada.[29] However, the government under the current prime minister, Stephen Harper, has declared without foundation that this school was not a "residential" school funded by the federal government.

Instead, it has been declared a provincial (and church-funded) boarding school; and therefore, former Metis students are not entitled to compensation, even if they suffered the same abuses as their First Nations cousins who went to the federal residential school at Beauval, a community located about thirty miles to the south.[30] The injustice of this decision speaks to the power that the scrip and treaty processes of the late nineteenth and early twentieth centuries continue to have on shaping Canada's conceptions of who is Indian and who is Metis. Not far from this portion of the exhibit is the scrip and treaty display that deals with those very same issues and demonstrates that even the treaty and scrip commissioners had a difficult time distinguishing between the people in any meaningful way. As pictures taken at the time demonstrate, cultural or physical markers that could have distinguished Indian from Metis did not exist; and yet today we have rigid legal categories that impact people in profound ways.

The exhibit, however, did not end with a story of betrayal but rather with an assertion of identity and power through the use of community mem-

7. Samples of infinity beadwork at Diefenbaker Canada Centre. Photo courtesy Brenda Macdougall.

ber Rita Bouvier's poem, "Land is the Politic," and a collection of northern beadwork that has transformed the Metis infinity symbol into a local assertion of culture (see fig. 7).[31]

West Side Stories ended as it began, with stories of the land and images of the people who call it home. Our hope, though, is that this exhibit does not end there. We still hope to see it travel to the north and become a part of the cultural legacy that the Metis communities shared with us.

In many respects, West Side Stories was an experiment. It was an attempt by all three cocurators to explore new media and methods for telling the story of a people and disseminating research data. The power of the exhibit, however, lies with the people in the communities who directed the types of research that were conducted and their hope to have their story faithfully told. In this instance, the community did not simply have input into the types of stories being told — they framed the content of the entire exhibit through expressions of their values, ideals, and worldview, all which became the exhibit's text. Our goal as cocurators and researchers was to be faithful first to the culture being represented rather than to museological practice. The comment that the exhibit was text-heavy affirmed for us that we achieved what we set out to do. We located a new, transformative means to disseminate research results to a larger audience than could have been achieved with conference papers, articles, or monographs alone. When people of the West Side attended the opening of the exhibit, they commented on how profoundly touched they were by what we had done, on how so many of the displays invoked memories long forgotten, and on how satisfied they felt that it would be seen by the young people of Saskatchewan. Similarly, noncommunity members also conveyed their sense that West Side Stories was aesthetically attractive and that the story being told was fresh and innovative. Significantly, West Side Stories touched people both emotionally and intellectually because it is an account of a people's humanity.

Notes

The support of the northwestern Saskatchewan families and the Northwest Métis Council made both the exhibit and this article possible; to all, we thank you for your kindness and generosity. Financial assistance for this research and exhibit came from the Métis National Council (MNC), the University of Saskatchewan, and the CURA project "Otipimsuak—the Free People: Métis Land and Society in North-west Saskatchewan," funded through the Social Sciences and Humanities Re-search Council of Canada (SSHRC). Thank you to co-leads Dr. Frank Tough, Dr. Lawrence Martz, and Clément Chartier for your help and support. A special thanks to all of those individuals who loaned us their personal art and artifacts so that West Side Stories was a success. The writing of this article would not have been possible if not for you all.

1. The Metis communities in northwestern Saskatchewan are all linked to one an-other by family ties and shared histories. They include Île à la Crosse, Green Lake, La Loche, Dillon, Turnor Lake, Buffalo Narrows, Dore Lake, Beauval, Patuanak, Pinehouse, Sled Lake, Canoe Narrows, Cole Bay, Jans Bay, Michel Village, De-scharme Lake, Bear Creek, and St. Georges Hill.

2. The "Otipimsuak—the Free People" project received three-year funding in 2004 and then received a one-year extension to complete the research. The princi-pal investigators for this project are Dr. Frank Tough, University of Alberta; Dr. Lawrence Martz, University of Saskatchewan; and Clément Chartier, former pres-ident of the Métis National Council. It also involves various faculty and student researchers from those two universities as well as trained community researchers in those communities.

3. Throughout this paper the term *Metis*—without an accent—is used to denote mixed-descent people who forged for themselves separate and distinct commu-nities from either of their Indian and European ancestors. The use of the term without an accent over the *e* signifies that it is being used to encompass all mixed-descent people in the region. The reason for this choice is that *Métis* typically implies specific historical circumstance associated with French and Catholic in-fluences that originated with the eastern trade routes prior to the fall of New France and the Scottish takeover of the St. Lawrence trade. The term *half-breed*, also known as "the country born," has historically referred to English and Scot-tish mixed-bloods who came out of the Hudson's Bay Company trade. The Me-tis of northwestern Saskatchewan are predominantly, although not exclusively, from French and Cree forebears. So we use the term to be inclusive of all mixed ancestry people in the area. However, Métis has modern legal and political usage, as it was spelled this way in the Canadian Constitution Act of 1982. For consis-tency's sake, this spelling has been adopted by Métis political organizations such as the Métis National Council (MNC) and, therefore, is used as the spelling in the CURA project.

4. Jacqueline Peterson was the first to coin the word ethnogenesis in her PhD re-search, "The People in Between: Indian-White Marriage and the Genesis of a Métis Society and Culture in the Great Lakes Region, 1680–1830," (PhD diss., University of Illinois at Chicago Circle, 1980). The term refers to the birth of a culture, which, she notes, in the case of the Metis occurred in the Great Lakes

during the fur trade; although, she also argues that notions of being a separate people with a national consciousness did not occur until the end of the Pemmican Wars and the Battle of Seven Oaks in 1815 at Red River.

5. Perhaps the two best examples of this type of scholarship are Marcel Giraud, *The Métis in the Canadian West*, 2 vols., trans. George Woodcock (Edmonton: University of Alberta Press, 1986); and George Stanley, *The Birth of Western Canada: A History of the Riel Rebellions* (1936; repr., Toronto: University of Toronto Press, 1992). Giraud and Stanley both interpret Metis history as being the result of a collision of civilization and savagery on the southern plains. As with all frontier paradigm scholarship, Giraud and Stanley explain the outcome of colonial conquest and rationalize the relationship of the state to those cultures ill prepared for the modern world. A similar, although more sympathetic, rendering of events and treatment of the Metis can be found in John Kinsey Howard, *Strange Empire* (New York: William Morrow, 1952).

6. Cuthbert Grant, a North West Company employee, led Metis traders and hunters in their first resistance against the Hudson's Bay Company in the early nineteenth century, an act that resulted in the Battle of Seven Oaks. Louis Riel and Gabriel Dumont are the two most celebrated Metis leaders having challenged the Canadian state's right to colonize western Canada. Through the formation of the Provisional Council in 1869–70, Riel negotiated the creation of the Province of Manitoba and secured land and cultural rights for the Metis within that province. In 1885 Riel and Dumont attempted to do the same along the south Saskatchewan River valley although their efforts resulted in an armed conflict known as the Northwest Resistance. Riel was subsequently hanged for high treason, while Dumont fled Canada and traveled in the American West and Europe as a part of Buffalo Bill's Wild West Show before returning to Saskatchewan, where he remained until his death in 1906. See Don McLean, "Cuthbert Grant: First Leader of the Métis," *Fifty Historical Vignettes: Views of the Common People* (Regina SK: Gabriel Dumont Institute, 1989); Denis Combet, ed., *Gabriel Dumont: The Memoirs as Dictated by Gabriel Dumont and Gabriel Dumont's Story*, trans. Lise Gaboury-Diallo (Saint-Boniface MB: Éditions du blé, 2006); George Woodcock, *Gabriel Dumont* (Don Mills ON: Fitzhenry and Whiteside, 1978); George F. G. Stanley, ed., *The Collected Writings of Louis Riel* (Edmonton: University of Alberta Press, 1985); and Maggie Siggins, *Riel: A Life of Revolution* (Toronto: Harper Collins, 1994).

7. Jennifer S. H. Brown, *Strangers in Blood: Fur Trade Company Families in Indian Country* (Vancouver: University of British Columbia Press, 1980); Frits Pannekoek, *A Snug Little Flock: The Social Origins of the Riel Resistance* (Winnipeg MB: Watson and Dwyer, 1991); Irene Sprye, "The Métis and Mixed-Bloods of Rupert's Land Before 1870," in *The New Peoples: Being and Becoming Métis in North America*, ed. Jacqueline Peterson and Jennifer S. H. Brown (Winnipeg: University of Man-

itoba Press, 1986), 95–118; Gerhard J. Ens, *Homeland to Hinterland: The Changing Worlds of the Red River Métis in the Nineteenth Century* (Toronto: University of Toronto Press, 1996); Sylvia Van Kirk, *Many Tender Ties: Women in Fur Trade Society in Western Canada, 1670–1870* (Winnipeg MB: Watson and Dwyer, 1980); Martha Haroun Foster, *We Know Who We Are: Métis Identity in a Montana Community* (Norman: University of Oklahoma Press, 2006); Susan Sleeper-Smith, *Indian Women and French Men: Rethinking Cultural Encounter in the Western Great Lakes* (Amherst: University of Massachusetts Press, 2001); Tanis C. Thorne, *The Many Hands of My Relations: French and Indian on the Lower Missouri* (Columbia: University of Missouri Press, 1996); Lucy Eldersveld Murphy, *A Gathering of Rivers: Indians, Métis, and Mining in the Western Great Lakes, 1737–1832* (Lincoln: University of Nebraska Press, 2000); Heather Devine, *The People Who Own Themselves: Aboriginal Ethnogenesis in a Canadian Family, 1660–1900* (Calgary: University of Calgary Press, 2004); Brenda Macdougall, "Wahkootowin: Family and Cultural Identity," *Canadian Historical Review* 87, no. 3 (2006): 431–62; and Nicole St-Onge, "Uncertain Margins: Métis and Saulteaux Identities in St-Paul des Saulteaux, Red River 1821–1870," *Manitoba History* 53 (October 2006): 1–9.

8. *Wahkootowin* is a Cree term used to express the sense that family was the foundational relationship for pursuing any economic, political, social, or cultural activities and alliances. See Brenda Macdougall, "Wahkootowin," as well as Brenda Macdougall, "Socio-Cultural Development and Identity Formation of Metis Communities in Northwestern Saskatchewan, 1776–1907," (PhD diss., University of Saskatchewan, 2005).

9. The XY Company's actual name was the New North West Company; but because of the confusion that would have caused, it was referred to as the XY Company. The term *XY* was taken from the company's brand, which they used to mark their fur and supply bundles. See Lawrence J. Burpee, *The Search for the Western Sea: The Story of the Exploration of North Western America*, 2 vols., rev. ed. (Toronto: Macmillan Company of Canada, 1935); Edith I. Burley, *Servants of the Honourable Company: Work, Discipline, and Conflict in the Hudson's Bay Company, 1770–1879* (Toronto: Oxford University Press, 1997); Gordon Charles Davidson, *The Northwest Company* (Berkeley: University of California Press, 1918); and Arthur S. Morton, *A History of the Canadian West to 1870–71*, 2nd ed. (Toronto: University of Toronto Press, 1973). Despite a lack of firm demographic sources, archaeologists and anthropologists have endeavored to trace the ethnohistorical and material culture of the subarctic Woods Crees and Denes in northwestern Saskatchewan to determine which people first occupied the region around Île à la Crosse. It is generally accepted that the Churchill River is the dividing line between Cree and Dene territory and that Île à la Crosse was the frontier between those two societies. See Robert Jarvenpa, *The Trappers of Patuanak: Towards a Spacial Ecology of Modern Hunters* (Ottawa ON: National Museum of Canada, 1980); Robert Jarvenpa and Hetty Jo Brumbach, *Ethno-Archeological and Cultural Frontiers: Atha-*

bascan, Algonquian, and European Adaptation in the Central Subarctic (New York: Peter Lang, 1989); David W. Friesen, *The Cree Indians of Northern Saskatchewan: An Overview of the Past and Present* (Saskatoon sk, 1973), 7; and Morton, *History of the Canadian West*.

10. The mission's significance to the community is evident when considering the mission's remarkable growth. Within a few decades, the Île à la Crosse mission became a large, thriving religious and economic center in the region, housing a contingent of Oblate priests, lay brothers, and Sisters of Charity ("Grey Nuns"), who arrived from Montreal in 1860 to establish the school and hospital. By 1867, missionaries had expanded the Île à la Crosse mission to include the Grey Nuns' school for girls, an orphanage for boys, a small home for the elderly and infirmed, and a hospital for anyone in need of medical services. Gaston Carrière, omi, "The Oblates and the Northwest, 1845–1861," *The Canadian Catholic Historical Association Study Sessions* (Ottawa on: Canadian Historical Association, 1970): 35–66; Thérèse Castonguay sgm, *A Leap in Faith: The Grey Nuns Ministries in Western and Northern Canada* (Edmonton: Grey Nuns of Alberta, 1999), 2:17; Martha McCarthy, *From the Great River to the Ends of the Sea: Oblate Missions to the Dene, 1847–1921* (Edmonton: University of Alberta Press, 1995); and Raymond J. Huel, *Proclaiming the Gospel to the Indians and the Métis* (Edmonton: University of Alberta Press, 1996).

11. The observance of Catholic rituals in the English River District has been attributed to the efforts of Catholic Francophones in the employ of, first, the North West Company (nwc) and then the hbc, who adhered to these rituals in an effort to maintain, and also to re-create, familiar sociocultural values within a foreign space. According to voyageur scholar Carolyn Podruchny, experienced voyageurs ritually baptized novice Canadian fur traders in the St. Lawrence River at three sites to mark their entrance into the West and, symbolically, the beginning of their new lives. The third and final site of the voyageurs' ritual baptisms was at Portage La Loche, the northernmost post in the English River District, where the men began the dangerous, thirteen-mile Methye Portage, a trail that covered a succession of hills before arriving at the edge of a steep precipice demarcating the continental divide. Just as baptisms were performed without clergy, hbc records note that by the 1820s the local population acknowledged the power of the saints over their lives and regularly observed the Sabbath. While not a mandatory religious obligation, Metis people of the district annually observed All Saints Day—a holy day on November 1 for remembering martyrs. Furthermore, Sunday services for the populace were held at the chief factors' house at the post throughout the early 1800s. See Carolyn Podruchny, *Making the Voyageur World: Travelers and Traders in the North American Fur Trade* (Toronto: University of Toronto Press, 2006); Carolyn Podruchny, "Baptising Novices: Ritual Moments among French Canadian Voyageurs in the Montreal Fur Trade, 1780–1821," *Canadian Historical Review* 83, no. 2 (2002): 173–74; Carolyn Podruchny, "'Dieu, Diable, and the Trick-

ster': Voyageur Religious Syncretism in the *pays d'en haut, 1770–1821*," *Etude Ob-
lates de l'Ouest* 5 (2000): 75–92; McCarthy, *From the Great River*, 32–33; Carrière,
"Oblates and the Northwest," 45–46; Huel, *Proclaiming the Gospel*; and A. G.
Morice, OMI, *History of the Catholic Church in Western Canada: From Lake Supe-
rior to the Pacific* (Toronto: The Masson Book, 1910). See also *Île à la Crosse Post
Journals, 1819–1820*, November 1, 1820, HBC Archives, B.89/a/4, Winnipeg; *Île à
la Crosse Post Journals, 1824–1825*, November 21, 1824, HBC Archives, B.89/a/8,
Winnipeg.

12. When Rupertsland became incorporated into Canada in 1870, only the very small,
postage-stamp province of Manitoba was accorded the same status as the other
provinces in the confederation. Until 1905, when the provinces of Alberta and
Saskatchewan were created, the majority of what are now the western provinces
were collectively the North West Territory and as such were governed as a colonial
frontier by Ottawa. However, these provinces did not gain the full governing rights
granted to other provinces until 1930, when they gained control over their natural resources and resource revenue. Until 1930 development of those provincial
natural resources and any income derived from that development belonged to the
federal government, which would, in turn, transfer monies to Alberta and Saskatchewan accordingly.

13. According to 1997 statistics, Aboriginal people made up 87 percent of northern
Saskatchewan's population of 40,000. There has not been a significant shift in the
population in the last decade; and, overall, the entire provincial population has
held steady at just over or just under 1 million since the 1960s. Graham F. Parsons
and Ron Barsi, "Uranium Mining in Northern Saskatchewan: A Public-Private
Transition," in *Large Mines and the Community: Socioeconomic and Environmental Effects in Latin America, Canada, and Spain*, ed. Gary McMahon and Felix
Remy, http://www.idrc.ca/en/ev-28034-201-1-DO_TOPIC.html.

14. See F. Laurie Barron, *Walking in Indian Moccasins: The Native Policies of Tommy
Douglas and the CCF* (Vancouver: University of British Columbia Press, 1997);
and David Quiring, *CCF Colonialism in Northern Saskatchewan: Battling Parish
Priests, Bootleggers, and Fur Sharks* (Vancouver: University of British Columbia
Press, 2004).

15. While it was announced in 2005 that the Metis were to be compensated, no monies were paid out at that time. In 2007 the federal government again reassured
the Metis that they would be compensated, although to date no funds have been
released. "Métis Receive $20M in Bomb-Range Compensation," *CBC News*, March
18, 2005; "Ottawa Pledges $15M for Métis Communities Affected by Air Weapons
Range," *CBC News*, January 22, 2007. The Buffalo River Dene Nation, however,
have not been satisfied with the compensation and since 2001 have opposed what
they deem to be the theft and destruction of their traditional territory and have
actively asserted their rights to hunt there.

16. Deborah Doxtator, "The Home of the Indian Culture and Other Stories in the Museum," *Muse* 6, no. 3 (1988): 26–29; Assembly of First Nations and Canadian Museum Association, *Turning the Page: Forging New Partnerships Between Museums and First Peoples: Task Force Report on Museums and First People* (Ottawa, 1992); Moira McLouglin, "Of Boundaries and Borders: First Nations History in Museums," *Canadian Journal of Communication* 18 (1993): 365–85; and Danielle LaVaque-Manty, "There Are Indians in the Museum of Natural History," *Wicazo Sa Review* 15 (2000): 71–89.

17. Majorie Halprin, "Museums Marketing and Modern Anthropology," *Reviews in Anthropology* 17 (1991): 99–110; Julia D. Harrison and Bruce G. Trigger, "'The Spirit Sings' and the Future of Anthropology," *Anthropology Today* 4, no. 6 (1988): 6–9; and Richard Atleo, "Policy Development of Museums: A First Nations Perspective," BC *Studies* 89 (1991): 48–61.

18. Unlike the United States, Canada has no Repatriation Act. Any removal of artifacts from public viewing or return of remains and objects is done only at the inclination of the museum or cultural heritage site.

19. The Stó:lō Nation education and cultural center was established in 1994. Within a few years, the group's work resulted in publishing two books with accompanying teaching guides and syllabi, which could replace antiquated and irrelevant core curriculum, as well as an award-winning historical atlas, which was on the provincial best-sellers list for four consecutive months. See Keith Thor Carlson, ed., *A Stó:lō Coast Salish Historical Atlas* (Vancouver BC: Douglas and McIntyre, 2001); and Keith Thor Carlson, ed., *You Are Asked to Witness: The Stó:lō in Canada's Pacific Coast History* (Chilliwack BC: Stó:lō Heritage Trust, 1997).

20. Shxwt'a:selhawtxw was born from a need for teachers and students to experience aspects of the Stó:lō way of life, philosophy, technology, and culture through a hands-on approach. By touring the longhouse in which the Shxwt'a:selhawtxw is housed, people can participate in demonstrations of fishing, weaving, and carving. See "Chilliwack," British Columbia Tourism Travel Guide, http://www.britishcolumbia.com/regions/towns/?townID=3357; Meagan Easters, "Repatriation as a Reflection of Stó:lō Cultural Values: *Tset Tháyeltxwem Te lálém S'olhetawtxw* (We Are Building a House of Respect)" (master's thesis, Carleton University, 2004); and "Field Trip Information," Fraser River Sturgeon Conservation Society, http://www.frasersturgeon.com/pdf/HSBCSchool/fieldtrip.pdf.

21. With a postgraduate diploma in cultural resource management, Teresa helped to develop the Shxwt'a:selhawtxw by both working with the artifacts and designing the hands-on portions of the museum's exhibits. She additionally worked in the Stó:lō Nation's archeological repository. Since being at the University of Saskatchewan, Teresa has done the same work with the DCC, which mounts various exhibits throughout the year and oversees the development of educational curriculum about those exhibits so tours of school children are able to learn about issues and ideas that they may not have had exposure to otherwise.

22. The expression used was a descriptive observation rather than a negative criticism, although it may have been a subtle assessment of our approach to the exhibit. The speaker of that phrase also noted that the cultural heritage site where he worked would never have used as much text to identify the collections being represented and would have included more artifacts.

23. Scrip, either in the form of land or money, was offered to the Metis of western Canada in order to extinguish their Aboriginal title. To qualify for scrip, an individual applied to the Half-Breed Claims Commission during travel to different regions. Scrip was issued first in Manitoba in 1875 and then in the rest of western Canada between 1885 and 1921. Some of the most comprehensive descriptions and analyses of the scrip system can be found in Frank Tough, *"As Their Natural Resources Fail": Native Peoples And the Economic History of Northern Manitoba, 1870* (Vancouver: University of British Columbia Press, 1996); and D. N. Sprague, *Canada and the Métis, 1869–1885* (Waterloo ON: Wilfred Laurier University Press, 1988).

24. Michif, a blended language of Cree (or Saulteaux) and French, has received a great deal of scholarly attention in recent years. To a lesser degree, scholars have also examined Bungi, a blend of Cree and Gaelic spoken by British Half-Breeds in the Red River area in the nineteenth century. There is some debate among linguists as to whether the language on the West Side is indeed Michif. However, the people are firm in their assertion that they speak a form of Michif that is unique to their community—it is more Cree than French in both content and structure. See Peter Bakker, *A Language of Our Own: The Genesis of Michif, the Mixed Cree-French Language of the Canadian Métis* (New York: Oxford University Press, 1997); John Crawford, "What is Michif? Language in the Metis Tradition" in *The New Peoples: Being and Becoming Metis in North America*, ed. Jacqueline Peterson and Jennifer S. H. Brown (Winnipeg: University of Manitoba Press, 1981), 231–42; Patrick C. Douaud, *Ethnolinguistic Profile of the Canadian Métis* Mercury Series—Canadian Ethnology Service Paper 99 (Ottawa ON: National Museum of Man, 1985); Margaret R. Stobie, "Background of the Dialect Called Bungi," *Historical and Scientific Society of Manitoba* 3, no. 24 (1967–1968): 65–75; and Margaret R. Stobie, "The Dialect Called Bungi," *Canadian Antiques Collector* 6, no. 8 (1971): 20.

25. Photographs were selected from several archival repositories including the Saskatchewan Archives Board, the Société historique de Saint-Boniface, and the Gabriel Dumont Institute. Material relating to scrip in northwestern Saskatchewan was provided by the Métis Archival Project, directed by Dr. Frank Tough (http://www.ualberta.ca/NATIVESTUDIES/research/mapresearch.pdf), while research on more contemporary issues, such as residential schools and the Primrose Lake Air Weapons Range, were obtained from recent news coverage by the *Saskatoon Star Phoenix*, the Canadian Broadcasting Corporation (CBC), and the *Toronto Globe and Mail*.

26. Two weeks before being hanged in 1885, Louis Riel wrote a letter and poem to his jailer, Robert Gordon. Both the letter and the poem begin with apologies to Robert Gordon for keeping him waiting for the poem and for the author's poor English before dealing with themes of spiritual redemption and virtue. This letter and poem were in the possession of Edna Robinson, whose father was a newspaper owner in eastern Canada who came into ownership of the writing when he published it in his paper. The letter and poem are one of the few known pieces of Reil's writing to be in English, making it extremely rare. Mrs. Robinson left the letter and poem to the University of Saskatchewan in her will and the bequest was turned over in the fall of 2006. See Louis Riel to Robert Gordon, October 27, 1885, Special Collections, University of Saskatchewan Library.

27. The York boat was an inland boat used by the HBC to carry furs and trade goods along inland waterways in Canada. It was named after York Factory, the headquarters of the HBC, and modeled after Orkney Islands fishing boats, which descended from the Viking longboat. The York boat was preferential to the canoe as a cargo carrier because of its larger size, greater capacity, and improved stability in rough water. It was about fourteen meters long (forty-six feet), and the largest could carry over six tons (13,000 pounds) of cargo. It had a pointed bow, a flat bottom, and a forty-five-degree-angle stern, making beaching and launching easier. The boat was propelled both by oars and by a canvas sail, and it was steered with a long steering pole or with a rudder when under sail. It had a crew of six to eight men.

28. For an overview of the Riel family history, see Maggie Siggins, *Riel: A Life of Revolution* (Toronto: Harper Collins, 1994). The information about Sister Sara Riel was drawn from the Île à la Crosse mission records, Registres paroissiaux, 1867–1912, *Eglise catholique, Mission de Saint-Jean-Baptiste, Île à la Crosse, Saskatchewan*, Société historique de Saint-Boniface.

29. The boarding school at Île à la Crosse was established the same year that the Oblates arrived (1846). However, it grew in size; so by the twentieth century, the school boasted a separate school building and boys' and girls' dormitories. The facility was simply known as the Île à la Crosse boarding school and operated until it burned down in the mid-twentieth century. At that time, under pressure from the community, the province of Saskatchewan assumed responsibility for education in northwestern Saskatchewan and instituted a public school system.

30. The prime minister's comments actually demonstrate how little we know about the running and maintenance of the residential school system. We know from community members that some First Nations students attended school in Île à la Crosse, while some Metis students from the region attended school at Beauval.

31. Rita Bouvier, "Land Is the Politic," in *Blueberry Clouds* (Saskatoon SK: Thistledown Press, 1999). The infinity patterned beadwork came from the collections of Clément Chartier and Brenda Macdougall.

7

Huichol Histories and Territorial Claims in Two National Anthropology Museums

PAUL LIFFMAN

This paper represents a long walk before we get to the museum. That is, I first want to survey the wide field in which 20,000 Huichol (Wixarika) Indians, who live scattered over 4,000 square kilometers of canyons and mesas in the Sierra Madre of western Mexico, make different kinds of claims about their territoriality. This field includes commerce, courts, schools, and of course museums—where they sometimes represent territory in paradoxically opposed ways. It also, most profoundly for them, includes some of their sacred histories about the treks of their ancestors. In these seemingly disparate venues, Huichols claim land rights ranging from outright ownership of those 4,000 square kilometers (400,000 hectares or 1 million acres) to seasonal ceremonial, hunting, gathering, and commercial access to ancestral places spread over 90,000 square kilometers in five states surrounding the Sierra, a territory they call *kiekari*. Huichol shamans characterize this territory as a network of "roots" (*nanayari*) based on economic and ceremonial practices around the hundreds of extended family hearths.[1]

Therefore, to fully understand what Huichols do in museums, it helps to understand not only their formal legal and political claims but also their deeper histories of combining sacred and commercial practices and the fundamentally interethnic nature of certain sacred texts. Ultimately, understanding the point of view of Native American museographers may require reframing the museum as just one of several venues in which Huichols represent their identity and history. While museums are only one of several venues for Huichol claims, symbolic legitimation of the state is an ancient, constitutive function of their identity. That is, Huichol identity is less intrinsic than derived from producing symbols to reinforce, if not to reconstruct, the identities of specific shamanistic clients, consumers, and spectators of their art and ritual as well as of the nation as a whole. The central question, then, is how Huichols understand their role in museums as an outgrowth of their history as symbolic legitimators of the state, a gift for which they expect recognition of their material claims. This leads me to consider more generally the unequal exchange of symbolic and material goods between Indigenous minorities and the nation-states whose savage founding violated their rights in the first place.[2]

It is important to first consider the totality of a given people's cultural and political claims before analyzing a single exemplary one, like museums, in isolation. This is because you have to consider the relations among the histories and audiences for the whole set of offerings, gifts, petitions, or demands for rights, resources, and recognition. The immediate political conjuncture obviously influences which elements in this set of claims people decide to foreground and combine. Indeed, the very notion of "claims" cannot be neatly confined to any specific domain of practice. Instead it is more productive to consider that the general structure of exchange may have always and already encompassed (or at least provided the basis for) political, ritual, and museum representations of culture.

In short, the production of cultural texts is best treated as contingent on a historically deep and sociologically broad view that extends outward to consider the diverse audiences and inward to consider how representative the performers involved might be. In this, I am summarizing Charles Briggs's ethnography of traditionalization and his drawing out the literally spatial referents of the term *discursive cartographies* in two of his essays.[3] Where I differ from Briggs is that I do not distinguish a priori between claims made by Indigenous political brokers who perform their identities to the public or to the state from those made by shamans who petition with sacrifices for resources and other kinds of reciprocity from their sacred ancestors (who in turn were historically tied to Indigenous states, at least in the case of the Huichols). Briggs distinguishes between these two modalities because of their qualitatively different access to mass-mediated audiences and the means of representation required to reach them, even though he recognizes the formal similarities between their attempts to encompass the local in global terms. Instead, at least in a formal sense, they are all part of a performative and pragmatic dimension of culture. It is up to a further ethnography of communication to determine how differently situated local Indigenous people who produce such representations might distinguish among these modalities.

Indeed, in its broadest discursive sense, claims to define Huichol cultural property—what constitutes the territory called kiekari—extend beyond Huichols themselves to a whole field of overlapping interlocutors. You could say that Huichol symbolic production in the public sphere constitutes a kind of contact zone that is not so different from what Mary Louise Pratt and James Clifford describe for museums: a place where different narratives and practices overlap. These narratives and practices have been informed by philosophers' phenomenology of "place," historians' analyses of agrarian conflict, and anthropologists' approaches to land tenure and space. But, in the end, all of them in some sense reference Huichol shamans' characterization of kiekari as a network of "roots." In turn, Huichol political leaders have produced discourses about these roots that appropriate classical anthropological models of culture for the courts, local government, schools, and museums. And these discourses in turn give more grist to the shamans.

Here is how it works: through blood sacrifices, temple ceremonies, and treks to ancestral sacred places, Huichol household and temple groups produce and keep redefining kinship bonds and links to land. This network of people and places must then be "registered" by fasting and leaving sacrificial offerings with the ancestral owners of the landscape, who are seated in the San Luis Potosí desert. Shamans refer to this ritually instantiated territoriality as if it were a metaphysical bureaucracy in which the offerings are analogous to the bribes and petitions that are stereotypically consumed by police and functionaries. In a historical sense, these offerings can be seen as ceremonial tribute, which Huichols have been rendering in one way or another for a millennium or more—since they first traversed this vast region as seasonal hunter-gatherers and traders in precious goods, such as turquoise, feathers, and peyote.

Therefore Huichol commercial claims to museum space—which at first glance would seem to undercut the sacred nature of that territoriality—are intrinsically linked to it in deep historical and broad geographical senses.

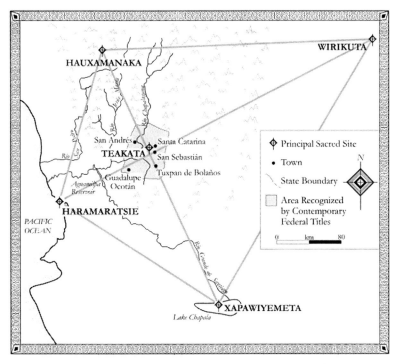

3. Huichol kiekari, a 90,000 sq km ceremonial territory encompassed by the five cardinal sacred places. The 4,000 sq km area belonging to the three Huichol comunidades recognized by the government is shaded, center left. Map by Susan Alta Martin.

Again, this system of ritual organization and economic practice has encompassed sacred places across 90,000 square kilometers over five states. Because the government treats contemporary Huichols as embodiments of the noble pre-Hispanic legacy that it claims as a source of legitimacy and since Huichols say their ancestors need sacrificial tribute at remote sacred places, Huichols insist that this territory must remain open to their commercial, hunting, and gathering activities. They argue that because of their antiquity and their crucial importance to the entire nation — indeed to the ecological balance of the planet as a whole — their sovereignty claims trump those of the Mexican nation.

However, that sovereignty is fragile because others keep invading Huichols' historical lands and otherwise challenging their territorial practices. Nowadays, religious and political leaders struggle to restore their lands in the Sierra and to regain access rights and protection for the ancestral sites that lie beyond it in the mestizo world, and so redefine their sovereignty as a people. Among those struggles are the aforementioned land claims in the courts and museums, sacred site disputes in regional politics, and a cultural revival movement in the local schools. By claiming land rights through these channels, Huichols not only have brought metaphors of national sovereignty into their rituals, but they have also introduced metaphors about themselves as brokers with the ancestral controllers of nature into national politics. This is why I do not want to distinguish between shamanistic and more conventionally conceived political claims. Indeed, by combining them, Huichols temporarily reconcile the tensions between anarchy and hierarchy, rainy and dry seasons, subsistence and commercial activity, and between the gender categories that correspond to that set of dichotomies in their own "cosmovision."[4] They also address Huichols' double image as exploited peasants and pre-Hispanic survivals in the public eye, so such claims can be seen as simultaneously addressing different social and cosmological interlocutors.

Red Gringo

Let me now turn to two episodes from Huichol sacred history that suggest where museums might fit into their worldview. The first of these episodes was related to me at a ceremony when I was doing anthropological fieldwork in San Andrés Cohamiata, a 750-square-kilometer *comunidad indígena* (Indigenous communal landholding) located in territory disputed by distinct ethnic communities and the state governments of Jalisco, Durango, Nayarit, and Zacatecas in the Sierra Madre Occidental of western Mexico. The second episode was told to interviewers from the National Museum of the American Indian (NMAI, where I would later work for a time as a translator and curatorial consultant). Sacred histories, as adapted for anthropological audiences, help tie together the broader senses of territory, representation, and interethnic collaboration that Huichols bring with them to museums. This explains why, in return, they may ask for kinds of reciprocity that initially strike the casual observer as odd, out of place, or incommensurate

To set the scene, since the colonization of the Huichol region began at the end of the sixteenth century and the predecessors of the current *comunidades indígenas* were set up, every year as part of the Feast of the Magi (los Reyes Magos, ideally held on January 6), each Huichol community holds a major ritual of political legitimation. The incoming civil-religious authorities, headed by the *tatuwani* or *gobernador* as an ascendant sun king, complete a long procession from the regional administrative capital (which was Colotlán but is now Mezquitic) back to the village plaza.[5] At this ceremony in 1995 during the height of litigation for the restitution of thousands of hectares of colonial and independence-era community lands, a shaman called Antonio, who lives in one of the most disputed areas of San Andrés, recounted the first of the two narratives to me.

Both narratives are about the primordial trek of the divine ancestors (*kakaiyarixi*) and santos (*xaturixi*), whose definitive actions created much of the landscape of western and northern Mexico. In general, Huichol sacred personages are objectified as places, and vice versa. The primordial trek of the santos, unlike many other Huichol origin accounts set in the eastern desert or western ocean, began in Spain and situates the sacred ancestors in relation to that colonial metropolis, the Aztecs, and Huichols' contemporary mestizo and gringo interlocutors, in that order.

On that particular day in January, Antonio told me the *historia* of Kiriniku Xureme (Blood Red Gringo). The original entourage of divine ancestors, who would create the physical features of the landscape of Mexico, departed from Spain. In Antonio's version, they then arrived in Wirikuta, the mountainous desert at the eastern edge of Huichol ceremonial territory, where the sun was born. There, they acquired a *tepari* (a stone disk used to cover an underworld offering chamber). The tepari was engraved with the image of an eagle eating a serpent. The entourage took this to Mexico City, where they gave it to the Aztecs. Antonio related that the Aztecs (not the Spaniards or the mestizos, as one might think) then placed the image of the eagle and serpent onto the currency of Mexico as the ubiquitous national seal. In exchange for this sacred value carved in stone, the Aztecs gave the ancestral Huichol delegation titles to the landscape they had just formed through the very act of traversing it. Unfortunately, these original land titles somehow were lost. Luckily, Red Gringo kept photocopies, but the loss remains. The ancestors' next stop was where the Huichols now live in the Sierra Madre Occidental.[6] Now, the shaman explicitly linked the tale to the key event of the ceremony, which was taking place while he told it to me. Even more pointedly, he indexed my presence there by way of Blood Red Gringo, who was accompanied by Teiwari Miyuawi (Blue Mestizo) and who was standing outside the *comunidad* with a camera as the ancestors arrived at San Andrés—the fifth and final place on their trek.

At the time, part of my role as an anthropologist included working with the community and a nongovernmental organization (NGO) as a consultant by assisting in territorial litigation through documenting the historical and cultural links between Wixarika people who were dispersed across the disputed boundaries. So it is no coincidence that this history was told to me during a ritual of legitimation, because it refers to the roles played in the definition of land tenure and the national space by the Huichol ancestral deer-person Kauyumarie; the Spanish santos; the pre-Hispanic and colonial political authorities; and by the contemporary mestizos—all of whom Huichols struggle with for land. In other words the shaman Antonio was indexing the participants in the ceremonial context; the main social actors in the broader historical context, of which the January 6 ceremony is part; the authorizing ancestors, whom Huichols believe determine historical and ecological processes; and the cosmological space in which those processes occur. In retrospect his narrative also can be taken to refer to the role of anthropological consultants in museum exhibits ostensibly under Indigenous direction: a sweeping, wide-angle view of the performative construction of territory. Lest it be thought that this narrative is an entirely positive account of interethnic collaboration, with the sunburned anthropologist as culture hero, let me hasten to add that the photographer Teiwari Miyuawi is an evil trickster figure associated with the onset of the chaotic rainy season and, more importantly, mestizo knowledge and power: a brilliant *cacique* (boss) who typically takes his clients' souls in return for his gifts.[7]

Returning to the ritual we were watching, the new hierarchy of the comunidad were making a grand solar entrance from the east. These incoming authorities represent the original ancestors; so at the very least this historia is a narrative of reciprocal legitimation between Huichols and the state, in which the Red Gringo serves a reproductive and documentary function. Antonio knew I had already been working as a historical and cultural consultant for the NGO that was representing the community's land claims. Did he also know that I might be going to work at a museum with other members of his community one day? Aside from how Antonio's narration encompassed me, it also encompassed the Spanish colonial state that gave out the primordial titles within the pre-Hispanic Indigenous state. As in official government *indigenismo*, the pre-Hispanic state in turn is encompassed by the contemporary Hispanic state. At the same time, Antonio's narration appropriated Spain as a land of Huichol ancestry up beyond the eastern horizon where the sun was born. The narrative thereby authorizes this Indigenous people to legitimate the state by virtue of seniority. This is a function that non-Indigenous others like me authenticate through graphic or photographic reproduction, even as Huichols recognize a sinister power lurking behind such semiotic processes.

Sacrificial Violence and Economic Value

The second narrative refers to a slightly later moment in Huichol history. Like the first one, it contains an Indigenous theory of political legitimacy. However, it also features a theory of the origins of economic value. That kind of value emerges from a violent ethnic split between the very heroes of the first narrative, but both narratives tell us about the role of intercultural relations in producing different kinds of value. This second Wixarika theory connects the economic value embodied in silver or gold, as well as the more profound cultural value and knowledge embodied in peyote, with the fundamental currency of sacrificial communication: blood. As the first history showed, the link between Huichol sacrifice and mestizo wealth and power is also made through shared Mexican symbols like the eagle perched on a nopal cactus (seen on both Mexican money and the flag).

In the second narrative, an important feature is that it conflates the figure of Kauyumarie (the promethean deer-person from the first history) with Tanana (Our Mother, one of two crucified Jesuses who reside in the town church of San Andrés Cohamiata) and Tayau (the sun risen from Burned Mountain in Wirikuta, where the primordial entourage mentioned above had first arrived). The key event is that the solar Jesus is murdered by the mestizo Santiago (the patron saint of the Spanish *recon-*

quista as well as of the invasion of the New World). This turns Tanana-Tayau into an ethnic symbol who stands for all Huichols at that moment. This mediation between contemporary Huichols, their sacred ancestor Kauyumarie, the sun, and Spaniards through an Indianized (and feminized) Jesus challenges attempts to distinguish separate autochthonous and Christian myth cycles, as the 1930s ethnographer Robert Zingg sought to do.[8] At the heart of this mediation is a speech genre that exemplifies what Richard Bauman calls the "traditionalization" of historical and institutional processes. A focus on context as well formal content enriches our understanding of myth and traditional knowledge. It also suggests the depth and complexity of what has recently been called "the Indigenous construction of nationality."[9] This history especially points to the complex and violent relationship between Huichol ancestral power and the non-Indigenous persona embodied in the Spanish patron saint of conquest, Santiago.[10] Of particular interest in the following exchanges is the generation of economic value by Santiago's murder of Jesucristo (which transforms the sun into gold) near the sun's very birthplace, Burned Mountain (Reu'unaxɨ or Cerro Quemado), located above the silver mines of Real de Catorce, San Luis Potosí. This cleft peak looms above the peyote-rich desert of Wirikuta and defines the eastern edge of the Huichol cosmological territory in one important set of contexts, although as we saw in the case of the Spanish santos, not all of them.

At this point, I would like to let some Huichols speak for themselves, albeit indirectly. The following exchanges include excerpts from various discussions between ceremonial experts from San Andrés Cohamiata and personnel of the NMAI. The personnel included me, when I was working for that institution as a translator and consultant for the Huichol ceremonial experts who had been invited there. The key expert is Catarino Carrillo, who had recently served as the tatuwani or gobernador of San Andrés and therefore knew what it means to lead the January 6 procession and embody the ancestors.

Catarino Carrillo says[11]:

Tsɨ mɨkɨ waɨkawa, tɨmɨ kename 'uwa mematinexɨa, Pariyatsutɨa mematinexɨa, Pariyatekɨa memakanexɨata 'ɨkɨ kenawanɨurɨ España.
[Well that's a lot (of ancestors), the ones who emerged here (in the Si-

*erra Huichol), the ones who emerged in Pariyatsutia (below, the west),
the ones who emerged in Pariyatekia (above, the east), that they say
(emerged in) Spain.]*

Xayuritɨni España memanexɨa; 'ena mehatinexɨa waniu Monterrey;
Monterrey memu'axɨa muwa 'aikutsi hatei muwa mematinexɨa.
*[If it's true they passed from Spain; here they say that they emerged in
Monterrey (Nuevo León); from Monterrey they arrived there in 'aikutsi
(an ancestral place in the desert) and they emerged there.]*

Monterrey memanexɨa muwa. Menetaxere Werika muwa kaneuyeikani
muwa. Netaxere niu'iyamani, muneuyuhayewa.
*[They passed there in Monterrey. They were there at the same time that
Werika (Eagle) lived there. At the same time he became accustomed
there, he stayed there.]*

Mumemaxirikɨ katɨaxɨ 'iyari rɨ, watamamuyuhayewaxɨ muwa waniu
tumini wewiyakai temixexeiya. Muniuyɨhayewa tatsɨrɨ Tatutsi Pɨrat-
sixiku. Neutikeni manari xeniu mɨkɨ muwa Reu'unaxɨ mana'unixɨ. Ku-
ruxite meme'unixɨ kename Reu'unaxɨ manata mɨkɨ kakeni.
*[Continuing to follow the path/life, they stayed there where we know they
say they made coins/money. Our Great-Grandfather Francisco stayed
there. (This refers to the Franciscan shrine complex at the Real de Catorce silver mines and mint, and by extension to Guadalupe, near the Zacatecas silver mines.) It is said that from there Reu'unaxi (the birthplace
of the sun) was destroyed. The varas (Brazilwood scepters of authority)
were destroyed, where Reu'unaxi stood.]*

Muwarɨ mekaxirixɨ Tamatsi xeniu muwa natikeni waxeiyati wariena
kanekaweni rɨki muwa mutaxerixɨ. Kauyumarie xeniu mutaxerixɨ mawa-
kanatiweni mina tewiyari xeikɨa maxa tewiyari muwa kanatikeni.
*[From there it is said they followed to where Our Elder Brother (deer)
stayed behind and watched (over) them. It is said that Kauyumarie became a mine-person and just stayed standing there, a deer-person.]*

Entonces muwa mɨkɨ mana waniu kename Tanana waniu, Tanana
waniu mɨkɨ Paritsika, Paritsika waniu miku'eiyakai, Santiago waniu
ha'akai mana memanexɨa.

['Then there they say that Tanana (Jesucristo), they say, Tanana, they say, answered Paritsika, Paritsika they say. (Paritsika is a metonym for Kauyumarie as the solar deer-mountain, Reu'unaxi.) They say Santiago got angry when they passed there.]

Entonces, Santiago mɨkitsi 'ukatiha'akai, mɨkɨ Paritsika xeikɨa mikue'iya-kai waniu teiwari hamatɨa Paritsika.
[Then that Santiago got very angry, that Paritsika, they say, that mestizo just answered Paritsika.]

Entonces, manari niuyeha'ani 'ana waniu kaniutsekieni Tanana. 'ena me nawaxawa pai'i, 'ena me Reu'unaxɨ rɨ mana me 'atihutɨ, mana 'atimietɨ niutsekieni, mana xuriya, neutaxiriexɨani muwa, muwa nehakuwie kɨ mamakatsie.
[Then, there then at that time they say he got angry, stabbing Tanana (Jesucristo). Here he was knifed then, here in Reu'unaxɨ falling flat lying there, falling flat stabbed, bleeding there, hanging there, tied up there by his hands.]

CATARINO CARRILLO: When he was stabbed there, he fell there on the ground. Then from there pure mines came out from the blood of that santito. . . . Then there are tourists working there, I don't remember very well. They made coins there, reales [a Spanish and Independence era unit equal to one eighth of a peso], Real de Catorce.

Now, a museum ethnographer summarizes:

Blood came out of the . . . *xaturi* [Jesucristo]. Here the earth sank. From here they arrive in Wirikuta, where Kauyumarie together with Maxa-kwaxi, Tunuwame, and Tseriekame stay. In this place there are some stones that they call gold and serve to make coins. Kauyumarie gathered those stones, took them to Mexico City and there in Mexico City they made coins, money, and the eagle on the coin.

What stands out here is the equivalence between sacrifice, wealth, and the roles of foreign observers at the place that is most identified with the emergence of the sun. These themes were already indicated in the earlier account of an eagle on a nopal becoming the image on the national currency, but here they receive their most dramatic treatment. The association of sacrifice and economic value comes out even clearer in a subsequent discussion.[12]

CATARINO CARRILLO: So Kauyumarie left the money in Mexico City so that people could buy things. From Mexico City, Kauyumarie returned to Wirikuta where there remained a mountain called Tamatsi Kauyumarie Muyewe together with the *santitos* [one of these being the patron saint of the community of study, San Andrés].[13]

JOSÉ AGUILAR: For that reason, we go each year to make a pilgrimage to Wirikuta. There our god remained. There they all are, including those that are in San Andrés. The food of the divine ancestors or their heart changed into peyote. . . . For that reason there is peyote, and the mestizo stayed in Mexico City so that he could make everything that Kauyumarie cannot make. The mestizo was smarter. . . .

No, well because Santiago was now on bad terms with the other companion, he separated there. Now he came along the whole river [the Río Grande de Chapalagana]. He passed there behind San Andrés until arriving there, where they call it Santiago [Ixcuintla, on the Pacific coast]. That *santito* has a lot of money; he's very rich. Tobacco, everything, corn; he has beans, amaranth. There we go to the coast to work. The money we earn, it stays there [ironic laughter erupts all around].

In sum, the sacred historical narratives described above trace the axis of power that leads inexorably southwest from Spain to the ancestors' point of arrival in Monterrey through Wirikuta and Mexico City; then northwest to Aguascalientes and Huejuquilla (Tatuwani Hapuripa), the Sierra Huichol, the Pacific lowlands; and finally back southeast to Lake Chapala (Xapawiyemeta) and Guadalajara. On this trek, Huichols displace—or rather, emplace—the uncontrollable violence of mestizo domination and capitalist exploitation into an articulated series of sacred places, a transnational circuit of value. They reproduce this circuit through a ritually mediated sacrificial violence normally under their control. In this vast scheme of territorialization, Huichols inhabit the geographical center and the narrative endpoint, but what Lomnitz calls the "'horizon of coercion' on which the social contract rests" is never far from view.[14]

Miguel Bartolomé, a theorist of Indigenous movements in Latin America, rightly points out that many analyses of such movements focus on specific causes and goals but overlook what he calls their *"processes of constructing nationality . . . the quest to constitute collective subjects that appeal to a shared social identity based on their own or an appropriated cultural tradition. . . .* [T]hey attempt to relate themselves on egalitarian terms with the other cultural groups that form part of the same state. . . . [M]obilizations . . . attempt for the ethnocultural communities to configure themselves as political subjects without this implying the necessary construction of their own state apparatus."[15]

But we have seen that Huichols do not seem to concede that they are a nation of people on an egalitarian footing with the other peoples of Mexico or even the very states that have constituted their principal political interlocutors. Instead, in the texts surveyed here, Huichols claim to be intrinsic to the constitution of the technologically and economically more-advanced mestizo people and the nation-state itself. They do this by providing their own ancestral shadow state in the desert with the sacrificial images and blood that in Huichol ritual are necessary for the propagation of all value. That blood is embodied in the gold appropriated by Santiago but also in the peyote that contains the knowledge still controlled by Wixarika ceremonial experts.

We might also note that, as Indians in a nation-state profoundly indebted to an indigenista imaginary for its ideological coherence, Huichols' mythological narrative is quite literally correct when it identifies them as a virtual caste of legitimizers and value creators, as well as blood givers.[16] Moreover, the genre of discourse glimpsed here is far from unique to Huichols and has been widely reported in central Mesoamerica and the Andes as "wealth narratives."[17] We might find comparable stances with deep roots in the ideological repertoires of many Indigenous peoples who have been facing off with states—and reappropriating each other in different kinds of supposedly reciprocal exchanges—for a very long time now.

Indeed, as Lomnitz has pointed out and as the betrayal depicted in the two histories examined here also shows, the roots of such forms of exchange are often entangled with violent appropriations of Indigenous lives and resources.[18] First, the Indigenous people give a gift of symbolic value to the state. Then, the state reciprocates by issuing an ever-unfulfilled debt that is inherited over generations in the form of disputed land titles. These titles only partially recognize the legitimacy of the Indigenous territoriality that preceded and indeed provided the material basis of that state. The parallel between the culture hero Kauyumarie in the Huichol histories and Lomnitz's key example of Juan Preciado, the betrayed son of the revolutionary boss Pedro Páramo (in turn, a twin of the Mephistophe-lean Teiwari Mïyuawi), in Juan Rulfo's landmark 1955 novel *Pedro Páramo* is striking. All that the Indians inherit is the unpaid debt of their land, thus setting off an unending series of claims and negotiations for reciprocity for their original "gift" of symbolic legitimacy (to say nothing of material resources). The hypocrisy of exchanging flawed documents for primordial legitimacy in the first history is foregrounded in the second one when Santiago, the leader of the Spanish santos whom the deer-person Kauyumarie guided throughout the national territory, later murders his follower Tayau-Jesucristo in order to appropriate a second form of value: gold. It is both classes of unpaid debt that Huichols would seem to be trying to redress when they design museum exhibits.

Museums

How then do Huichols represent their primordial claim to territory and cultural capital in museums that are predicated on incorporating Native history into a multicultural national narrative when the Indians consider the nation to depend on them instead? I am concerned with two national museums: the Museo Nacional de Antropología in Mexico City and the National Museum of the American Indian in Washington DC. What Huichols do there cannot be understood without considering what they have done simultaneously in their schools, the agrarian courts, and the regional political arena. In these and other seemingly unrelated domains Huichols and their allies have developed an anthropology that emphasizes cultural integrity, territorial extension, and continuity in archaeological and historical time for diverse, sometimes antagonistic publics.[19] These cultural, territorial, and historical claims in addition to commercial ones tied to Huichol ethnic art—another set of representations of sacred history—are linked by the more fundamental claim of ceremonial connection to the landscape.[20] All these performatively engendered indigeneities converge in Huichol representations in national-museum spaces.[21]

That is, the NMAI has provided a space for Huichols to connect art, ritual symbolism, and sacred-history narratives to a series of land claims in the courts, which began in the 1930s under the postrevolutionary agrarian reform.[22] With so many performative precedents, it should have come as no surprise that the community curators Catarino Carrillo and José Cayetano, who we just heard in the preceding interview transcripts, were so adept at visually representing their territoriality to a global audience in a country they had never visited until they arrived at the NMAI. In design sessions and surveys of the museum's collections, they conceived the exhibition as a total representation of kiekari as a cosmological territory.

In their thirty-square-meter end of the Our Peoples gallery, Charles Sanders Peirce's figure of iconicity (formal resemblance) and the classical trope of synecdoche (hierarchical metonymy) connect the objects on display to the kiekari in terms of their relative placement in the circular space, the directional color symbolism of the display cases, and the explicit narrative of the panels. In order to translate these figures and tropes, first enacted in rituals at domestic ceremonial patios and regional temples (*tukite*), into a museum context, they made them less performative and more denotative. Indeed, the performative aspects were displaced from the exhibit to other parts of the museum complex. Still, by undertaking this translation, Carrillo and Cayetano condensed 90,000 square kilometers—an area 300 million times larger than the space that was utilized in the exhibit. In short, despite being displaced to an exotic national space, the NMAI exhibit is more than a disembodied narrative because its very design is like a hyper-representational version of a Native temple: a performative space for revalidating territoriality, starting from the very site of the performance. Huichols have struggled for a long time in order that their cosmological sense of cultural geography and their claims for land ownership and cultural rights could be represented in so many venues across so much space.

One reason for this expansion of performative venues is the emergence of pan-hemispheric Indigenousness since the 1980s, a multicultural agenda which the NMAI explicitly embodies. Huichols—including the very community curators with whom I worked—are also active interlocutors in the Mexican pan-Indian movement that burgeoned after the Chiapas neo-Zapatista rebellion of 1994. The designation of Carrillo and Cayetano's village of Bancos de San Hipólito, Durango, and the 10,000 hectares of land surrounding it as a *comunidad autónoma* is integral to that hemispheric process as well. Yet the Huichol exhibit at the NMAI foregrounds the particularity rather than the universality of their culture and history—especially their brand of spatial encompassment—at the same time that it identifies Huichol territoriality with the agrarian problems shared with other Mexican peasants. James Clifford famously summed up these and other emerging functions of the museum as a "contact zone" when he wrote, "In this new, hybrid context the museum becomes a cultural center and a site of storytelling, of Indigenous history, and of ongoing tribal politics. It is also caught up with Fourth World tribal circuits, with 'cultural tourism' by natives and whites, and with commercial tourism at regional, national and international levels."[23]

In this final section of the chapter, we see how three of the aforementioned domains of cultural practice—ritual performance, legal strategies, and commercial artistic production—build on the sacred precedents that have been recounted in the preceding sections and inform each other. There is a more specific relationship between museums, the courts, and the market as institutional venues where Huichols make claims about their relationship to territory: the anthropological representations they prepare for land claims in the courts and the cultural claims in their art emphasize the ritual and symbolic aspects of their territoriality, whereas the anthropology they present in museums shifts the focus to more specifically legal concerns with constitutional issues and land boundaries. At the same time, they appropriate museum spaces for their own, nonpublic ritual ends.[24]

However, in terms of political context, the very existence of this ethnography reflects more than the emergence of pan-Indianism. A floodtide of globalizing economic and legal reforms to peasant and Indigenous peoples' relationship to the land throughout Latin America and beyond can be seen as its doppelgänger. That is, in 1992 the neoliberal government of Carlos Salinas de Gortari was engaging in a paradoxical pairing of institutional practices. It coupled constitutional amendments that terminated the revolutionary legacy of land reform (Article 27) and expanded the cultural and territorial rights of Indians (Article 4). The first amendment paved the way for the North American Free Trade Agreement (NAFTA), which has devastated the rural subsistence economy; the second made Mexico's signing of Convention 169 of the International Labor Organization (ILO) on the rights of Indigenous peoples into national law, at least in principle. Since then, Indigenous peoples (but not most mestizo peasants, for whom new claims are foreclosed) have been able to present claims in court for land restitution, usufruct, and temporary access, based on their *usos y costumbres*, or traditional cultural practices. Huichols in particular have made a sustained effort (both in the Mexican courts and in Geneva, when they appeal legal reverses to the ILO itself) to introduce their own history and anthropology of ancestral places, ritual hunting and gathering, ceremonial organization, and kinship links across officially recognized community and state boundaries. These arguments form part of claims for both outright ownership of land in the Sierra Madre where they live and seasonal access to sacred places in the vast region surrounding the Sierra.[25] Therefore even as their survival as *campesinos* was becoming more precarious, Huichol claims for land and autonomy connected traditional forms of territorialization to a growing sense of ethnic identity with other *indios* and to a codified set of practices and customs recognized by the state.

This new legal anthropology has helped win official recognition (if not full-fledged protection) of hunting and gathering practices over 750 square kilometers in the Wirikuta desert of San Luis Potosí that Huichols visit on arduous ceremonial treks from their temples in the Sierra (see fig. 8).[26] It has also contributed to the outright restitution of over 200 square kilometers of invaded lands in the Sierra that Huichols had inhabited until they were violently displaced during the later phases of the Mexican Revolution. These legal initiatives situate Huichols in the vanguard of Mexican Indigenous sovereignty claims.

As demonstrated earlier, commensurate with the size of the 90,000-square-kilometer kiekari, Huichols frame their demands for limited sovereignty over its ancestral sites in even more encompassing mythical-historical narratives about Huichol ancestors' primordial role in creating a big part of the national space when the santos arrived on the Gulf coast during the Aztec era. More important, as I also pointed out earlier, Huichol sovereignty depends on undertaking ritualized hunting and gathering throughout this vast region, leaving offerings for the land's divine owners and then "registering" the cycle in rituals back in the Sierra at the temples (tukite) that are near their homes, in order to revalidate cultural land rights.[27] In some key respects their museum experience extended this logic to a new institutional domain and an even broader geographical scale, but they faced resistance.

That is, the NMAI's official mission strikes a precarious balance between cultural conservatism and social change: "The National Museum of the American Indian is committed to advancing knowledge and understanding of the Native cultures of the Western Hemisphere, past, present, and future, through partnership with Native people and others. The museum works to support *the continuance of culture, traditional values, and transitions in contemporary Native life*."[28] This "continuance" is achieved in part by creating a venue for a multicultural identity politics of Indigenousness

8. Tukipa [temple] in Tuapurie (Santa Catarina Cuexcomatitlán), an architectonic representation of the ceremonial territory called kiekari and a prototype of their museum exhibitions. Photograph by Carl Lumholtz, ca. 1898. Reproduced by permission of the American Museum of Natural History.

based on shared, sacred, universal meanings of ceremonial connection to ancestral practices, a program which emphasizes cultural form over context. The Huichols sought to shift this emphasis by introducing into the exhibit a key land map that figures as a copy of the primordial titles. They also insisted on text panels that situate their history in the metanarrative of the Mexican Revolution. They specifically sought to have these panels describe the violent displacement of the Huichols of Bancos de San Hipólito from their historical lands and their ongoing legal battle with non-Indigenous peasants from San Lucas de Jalpa, Durango—a kind of museological agrarianism.

This emphasis on representing communal land struggle in museums resembles the widespread insistence by Mexican Indigenous community museums (which Huichols lack, however) on drawing attention to "the lineage between cultural patrimony, collective identity, and community survival."[29] While community museums may promote historical memory and the revitalization of traditional cultural practices among local people more directly than can a global project (like the NMAI), they also share with larger museums the challenge of comprehensively representing local values and voices against a backdrop of factional politics and conflicting economic interests.[30]

To address what might seem to be another contradiction at the NMAI, community curators José Cayetano and Catarino Carrillo had no difficulty combining their vision of museum display with claims on the ostensibly separate matter of commercial space in the museum. As Clifford observed in the "contact zones" passage quoted above, Indigenous people commonly conflate museology, politics, and commerce. Specifically, when museum curators asked Cayetano and Carrillo what they considered the chief goals of their exhibit to be, they replied that they wanted people to understand that there could be no sacred maize without land on which to grow it and (to the polite discomfort of some of those present) that they wanted to enhance sales of their people's art in the museum. However, the hybrid declaration of goals should not seem unreasonable considering Huichols' history of marketing ethnic art with a sacred aura, the proportion of NMAI floor space dedicated to commercial ends, and the percentage of museum funding derived from U.S. tribal gaming operations, even if it may have seemed literally out of place at the moment.

The compatibility of the market economy with Huichol ceremonial territoriality in a museum context had already emerged during the design of the National Museum of Anthropology in Mexico City in 1962 through 1964. At that time, chief museologist Alfonso Soto Soria had commissioned Huichols to make a statue of their fertility ancestor Takutsi Nakawe and other "*ídolos*" (idols). One Huichol brought him a Nakawe, saying he had found it in a cave, where it would have fulfilled a sacred function since caves are burial sites and portals to the underworld. Soto Soria relates that the Huichol explained to him that he had buried money to compensate for appropriating the figure and later replaced it with another idol, presumably of his own manufacture. "*La diosa había cambiado de sitio y siguió siendo su diosa*" (The goddess had changed places and continued being their goddess), comments Soto Soria, and he claims that Huichols continue to treat her as one in the museum.[31] This account either rationalizes museum acquisition practices or reflects the profound materiality of Huichol ceremonial practice in its attempt to encompass commodification, or both.[32] In addition, I hope the other evidence in this chapter now makes it clear that art is only the latest in a deep history of sacralized commercial exchanges tied to the original violence of ethnic relations and to sacrificial hunting and trading in western Mexico.

Returning to the paradox signaled at the outset of the previous section, the NMAI's multicultural mandate to enact a new mode of participation and advocacy that gives Indigenous people control of exhibitions about themselves led Huichol ceremonial experts to insist on augmenting the museum's homogenizing approach to Indian ceremonialism with both art-business savvy and just the kind of peasant agrarian history and artifacts that they insist on enhancing with ceremonial references in the courts.[33] The Huichols found elements from deep within their tradition to prepare themselves for this encounter; to lend a greater sense of sovereignty to their museological and legal collaborations; and to integrate the commercial, cultural, and political dimensions of those collaborations. To the degree Huichols have been successful in projecting this vision in their exhibit, one must take a nuanced rather than black-and-white view of the (in)capacity of "national minority museums" to overcome the oxymoron built into that very category.

A second seeming paradox is that Mexican agrarian courts have not yet fully recognized the implications of the federal government's adherence to ILO Convention 169 in the administration of rural justice. At the same time in Washington, despite strong support from the curators, not all the NMAI design staff immediately recognized much appeal in incorporating a text panel that describes events that are not entirely Indigenous, like the Porfirio Díaz dictatorship's disentailment of communal landholdings and the resulting 1910 revolution or the 1958 Plano Provisional Agrario of San Andrés Cohamiata, a monochromatic 1:250,000-scale, agrarian plat map. Yet such artifacts have crucial significance to Huichols since they effectively represent what they got in exchange for the tepari they gave to the Aztecs. This map in particular closely reflects the ritually sanctioned, eighteenth-century title boundaries of a landscape that is nearly twice as large as the 750 square kilometers that the federal government currently recognizes as a comunidad indígena confined to the *municipio* of Mezquitic, Jalisco.[34]

Despite the historical and cultural depth entailed in this ordinary-looking government blueprint, design-staff members objected that old land maps did not embody "exhibition values" in the way that aesthetically magnetic, ritual objects do and that panels with historic context threatened to exceed strict word limits. Both of these constraints seem to be general policy issues at the Smithsonian museums. Nevertheless, the museum honored its mandate, and the Huichol exhibit included a panel on the history of Indigenous agrarian struggle in Mexico and a shrunken reproduction of the map. Albeit only partially successful, these negotiations over content and form resulted in a museum display that reflects a new level of Mexican Indigenous agency in public representations of their identity and history.[35] The Huichol representation of their identity is only the second half of the story. This is because their identity initially derives from their primordial function as shamans and ceremonial legitimators who resolve the identities of others. This dialogical grounding explains why Huichols insist on depicting land titles and other material conditions of possibility in a government museum—the other side of the bargain that was struck when Kauyumarie presented the Aztecs with their symbol of sovereignty.

Not only did Huichols bring historical narratives and documents substantiating their territorial claims to the museum, they also brought their ritual practice of territorialization. To consecrate their work at the NMAI Cultural Resources Center in Suitland, Maryland, the two ceremonial experts conducted a brief ritual at the end of which a large candle was interred at the edge of the center's outdoor fire pit. Similarly, curator Ann McMullen recalls that "Catarino and José Cayetano also consecrated the NMAI Mall building site on September 20, 2004 by planting a candle studded with several dollars in U.S. quarters, many ribbons . . . sticks made into a cross and quarters applied to it with beeswax, then the whole wrapped in ribbons toward the eastern edge of the Mall property and near the edge of the pond. Perhaps they realized that the exhibit might not be permanent, but the candle—as planted—would stay."[36]

Historically, such gifts to the ancestral owners of the land consecrate land boundaries that are deemed to be "corners of the world."[37] They replicate the basic architectonics of the family ceremonial patio and the temple at the level of regional—and in this case transnational—geography. In this sense the NMAI community curators performatively expanded their territory even beyond the already vast 90,000 square kilometers in western Mexico that they call *takiekari* ("our homeland") in a modality that is simultaneously ritual and political. In the age of globalized, multicultural Indigenousness, takiekari vaults the border fence even as Indians and other peasants die trying to cross the northern desert.

Notes

My thanks to Dr. Susan Sleeper-Smith, the American Indian Studies Consortium, the staff of the Newberry Library, and the University of Nebraska Press for the opportunity to present this essay. The first part of this essay draws on a paper presented at the American Anthropological Association meetings in 2003, and the last part draws on a recent article in *Museum Anthropology*. I also gratefully acknowledge the support received from the National Museum of the American Indian, in particular from the curator of the Wixarika Our Peoples exhibit, Dr. Ann McMullen, who initially invited me to participate in its construction in 2002. The collegial assistance of Dr. Johannes Neurath of the Subdirección de Etnología of the Museo Nacional de Antropología in this research and his perspective on Mexican ethnology have been invaluable as well. Also, my colleague Laura Roush made valuable editorial comments. More generally, I want to express my gratitude to the Centro de Estudios Antropológicos of the Colegio de Michoacán for its support of my research on Mexican regional and national museums and to those people in Tateikie, San Andrés Cohamiata, who generously included me in their dialogue.

1. Paul Liffman, "Gourdvines, Fires, and Wixárika Territoriality," in "Ritual and Historical Territoriality of the Náyari and Wixárika Peoples," ed. Philip Coyle and Paul Liffman, special issue, *Journal of the Southwest* 42, no. 1 (2000): 129–66.

2. Claudio Lomnitz, "Sobre reciprocidad negativa/On Negative Reciprocity," *Revista de Antropología Social* 14 (2005): 311–39.

3. Charles L. Briggs, "The Politics of Discursive Authority in Research on the 'Invention of Tradition,'" *Cultural Anthropology* 11, no. 4 (1996): 435–69; and Charles L. Briggs, "Theorizing Modernity Conspiratorially: Science, Scale, and the Political Economy of Public Discourse in Explanations of a Cholera Epidemic," *American Ethnologist* 31, no. 2 (2004): 163–86.

4. *Cosmovision* is an expanded sense of "worldview" common in the Mesoamerican literature. Johannes Neurath, *Las Fiestas de la Casa Grande: Procesos Rituales, Cosmovisión y Estructura Social en una Comunidad Huichola* (Mexico City: Instituto Nacional de Antropología e Historia; Guadalajara: Universidad de Guadalajara, 2002).

5. Marina Anguiano Fernández, "El Cambio de Varas entre los Huicholes de San Andrés Cohamiata, Jalisco," *Anales de Antropología* 11 (1974): 169–88.

6. In another version, a mestizo took a photograph of the serpent-and-eagle tepari, and it is placed on the Mexican national flag. Huichol ceremonial experts, interview by NMAI staff and consultants, May 2001, interview MX-01:5B, transcript, NMAI. In a third version, the deer-person Kauyumarie found the flag at Xapawiyeme, an island in Lake Chapala identified as the southern cardinal point of Huichol sacred territory, before taking it to the island of Tenochtitlan, upon which Mexico City was built, where a mestizo took a photo of it. Huichol ceremonial experts, interview by NMAI staff and consultants, October 2002, interview DC.10/02, tape, NMAI; Huichol ceremonial experts, interview by NMAI staff and consultants, May 2001, interview tape 7.72, transcript, NMAI.

7. Johannes Neurath, "Lluvia del Desierto: el Culto a los Ancestros, los Ritos Agrícolas y la Dinámica Étnica de los Huicholes Tïapuritari," in *Cosmovisión, Ritual e Identidad de los Pueblos Indígenas de México*, ed. Johanna Broda and Félix Báez-Jorge (Mexico City: Consejo Nacional para la Cultura y Las Artes / Fondo de Cultura Económica, 2001), 485–526; and Johannes Neurath, "El doble Personaje del Planeta Venus en las Religiones Indígenas del Gran Nayar: Mitología, Ritual Agrícola y Sacrificio," *Journal de la Société des Américanistes* 90–91 (2004): 93–118.

8. Robert Mowry Zingg, *Report of the Mr. and Mrs. Henry Pfeiffer Expedition for Huichol Ethnography: The Huichols, Primitive Artists* (sponsored by the Depart-

ment of Anthropology of the University of Chicago and the Laboratory of Anthropology, Santa Fe, New Mexico, 1938; repr., Millwood NY: Kraus Reprint, 1977); and Robert Mowry Zingg, *Huichol Mythology*, ed. Jay C. Fikes, Phil C. Weigand, and Acelia García de Weigand (Tucson: University of Arizona Press, 2004).

9. Miguel Bartolomé, "Movimientos Indios en América Latina: Los Nuevos Procesos de Construcción Nacionalitaria," *Desacatos: Revista de Antropología Social* 10 (Autumn–Winter 2003) 167–80.

10. For more on this see, Neurath, "Lluvia del Desierto"; and Neurath, "El doble Personaje del Planeta Venus en las Religiones Indígenas del Gran Nayar."

11. Huichol ceremonial experts, interview by NMAI staff and consultants, May 2001, interview tape 5A:12, transcript, NMAI. These taped interviews were conducted in Mexico and at the NMAI. They included Huichol ceremonial experts and NMAI staff and consultants. A native speaking Huichol translator, the anthropologist Héctor Medina, and the author subsequently produced the transcripts and written translations.

12. Huichol ceremonial experts, interview by NMAI staff and consultants, October 2002, interview DC-10/2002, tape, NMAI; and Huichol ceremonial experts, interview by NMAI staff and consultants, March–April 2002, interview tape 5:885-920, transcript, NMAI.

13. Huichol ceremonial experts, interview by NMAI staff and consultants, May 2001, interview tape 5b:14, transcript, NMAI.

14. Lomnitz, "Sobre reciprocidad negativa," 325.

15. Bartolomé, "Movimientos Indios en América Latina," 150–51. Emphasis in the original, translation mine.

16. Louis Dumont, *Homo Hierarchicus: The Caste System and Its Implications*, trans. Mark Sainsbury (Chicago: University of Chicago Press, 1974).

17. See for example Michael Taussig, *The Devil and Commodity Fetishism in South America* (Chapel Hill: University of North Carolina Press, 1980).

18. Lomnitz, "Sobre reciprocidad negativa."

19. See by way of comparison Joanne Rappaport, *The Politics of Memory: Native Historical Interpretation in the Colombian Andes* (1990; repr., Durham NC: Duke University Press, 1998); and Haunani-Kay Trask, *From a Native Daughter: Colonialism and Sovereignty in Hawai'i* (Honolulu: University of Hawai'i Press, 1999).

20. See by way of comparison the following works by Liffman and Myers: Paul Liffman, "Huichol Territory: Land Conflict and Cultural Representation in Western Mexico" (PhD diss., University of Chicago, 2002); Paul Liffman, "Huichol Territoriality and the Mexican Nation," unpublished manuscript; and Fred R. Myers, *Painting Culture: The Making of an Aboriginal High Art* (Durham NC: Duke University Press, 2002).

21. See by way of comparison Robert Cantwell, *Ethnomimesis: Folklife and the Representation of Culture* (Chapel Hill: University of North Carolina Press, 1993.

22. Beatriz Rojas, ed., *Los Huicholes en la Historia* (Mexico City: Centro de Estudios Mexicanos y Centroamericanos; Zamora: El Colegio de Michoacán; Mexico City: Instituto Nacional Indigenista, 1993).

23. James Clifford, *Routes: Travel and Translation in the Late Twentieth Century* (Cambridge MA: Harvard University Press, 1997), 212.

24. I discovered this apparent paradox after working on two anthropologically based projects. First was my 1990s anthropological consultation for the comunidad indígena of San Andrés Cohamiata (a 750-square-kilometer expanse of mesas and canyons in the Sierra Madre that is inhabited by some 5,000 Huichol people) and the nongovernmental land rights organization Asociación Jalisciense de Apoyo a los Grupos Indígenas on boundary litigation in the agrarian courts of Nayarit and Durango and the antechambers of the International Labor Organization in Geneva. Later, in the early 2000s I was a consultant, translator, and interpreter working with two San Andrés Huichol community curators on the exhibit about their culture at the NMAI. This exhibit became part of the permanent gallery called Our Peoples: Giving Voice to Our Histories, which occupies roughly half of the fourth floor of the NMAI. It is one of three major permanent-exhibition areas and includes a total of over thirty peoples from the Amazon to Alaska.

25. International Labor Organization, *Report of the Committee Set Up to Examine the Representation Alleging Non-observance by Mexico of the Indigenous and Tribal Peoples Convention, 1989, 1998, no. 169,* made under Article 24 of the ILO Constitution by the Trade Union Delegation, D-III-57, Section XI of the National Trade Union of Education Workers (SNTE), Radio Education, regarding documents GB.270/16/3 and GB.272/7/2, htp://www.ilo.org/ilolex/cgi-lex/single.pl?query=161998MEX169@ref&chspec=16 (accessed on 11/16/2007).

26. San Luis Potosí, *Periódico Oficial,* 57, special issue, September 22, 1994.

27. Liffman, "Gourdvines, Fires, and Wixárika Territoriality."

28. NMAI, "Mission," http://www.nmai.si.edu/subpage.cfm?subpage=press&second=mission, emphasis mine.

29. Patricia Pierce Erikson, "'So My Children Can Stay in the Pueblo': Indigenous Community Museums and Self-Determination in Oaxaca, Mexico," *Museum Anthropology* 20, no. 1 (1996): 40.

30. For a critique of the NMAI's combination of a community model with a museology that incorporates more varied curatorial voices, see Amy Lonetree and Sonya Atalay, eds., "Critical Engagements with the National Museum of the American Indian," special issue, *American Indian Quarterly* 30, nos. 3–4 (2006). Lonetree bases her distinction between these two models on Ruth B. Phillips, "Community Collaboration in Exhibitions," introduction to *Museums and Source Communities: A Routledge Reader,* ed. Laura L. Peers and Alison K. Brown (London: Routledge, 2003), 155–70.

31. Alfonso Soto Soria, interview with the author, Mexico City, December 14, 2006.

32. See by way of comparison Howard Morphy, "Sites of Persuasion: *Yingapungapu* at the National Museum of Australia," in *Museum Frictions: Public Culture/Global Transformations*, ed. Ivan Karp and others 469–99. (Durham NC: Duke University Press, 2006), 480.

33. Even though conventional land claims focus precisely on subsistence issues, legal discourse (obeying Western philosophical separations between matter and spirit) often requires Indigenous people to background the possible economic benefits that access to sacred parts of the geography might bring, as in the Huichol access claim on the heavily touristed Isla de Alacranes in Lake Chapala. Paul Liffman, "The *Historia* of Islands: New Huichol Territorial Claims to Ancestral Places," in *Heritage of Resistance: The Tarascan and Caxcan Territories in Transition*, ed. Andrew Roth-Seneff and Robert V. Kemper (Tucson: University of Arizona Press, forthcoming). However, for Huichols, as for premodern Europeans, there is little hypocrisy in the idea of extending their lives through both ceremonial offerings and remunerative activities on a pilgrimage trek. Karl Polanyi, *The Great Transformation* (1944; repr., New York: Octagon Books, 1975).

34. The map was one of the few things, aside from a change of clothes, that Carrillo and Cayetano brought with them on their trek from their mountain *rancherías* in Bancos de San Hipólito, Durango, to the NMAI's Cultural Resources Center in Suitland, Maryland.

35. Museum curators carried out this contextualization — the selection and placement of Indigenous verbal texts in the spatial syntax of display cases; and the community curators and anthropological consultants reviewed it before installation.

36. Ann McMullen, personal communication with author, Chicago, September 24, 2007.

37. See María de los Angeles Arcos García, "Las Velas Tateikietari . . . Invocando la Lluvia y la Lucha de un Pueblo" (master's thesis, Universidad Autónoma de México-Xochimilco, 1998).

8

The Construction of Native
Voice at the National Museum
of the American Indian

JENNIFER SHANNON

In September of 2004 the National Museum of the American Indian
(NMAI)—the newest and last Smithsonian museum to be built on the
National Mall in Washington DC—presented its inaugural exhibitions to
the public. The NMAI is described as, "the culmination of nearly 15 years
of planning and collaboration with tribal communities from across the
hemisphere."[1] According to Richard West, the founding director of the
NMAI, "From the start, our new museum has been dedicated to a fresh
and, some would say, radically different approach to museum exhibitions.
To put it in the most basic way, we insist that the *authentic Native voice
and perspective* guide all our policies, including, of course, our exhibition
philosophy."[2] Therefore, it is not only "Native voice" that is being presented
by the museum, it is a more "authentic" representation. Similarly, Ruth
Phillips explains, "what collaborative exhibits seek, in contrast to those
they replace, are more accurate translations."[3]

The quintessential collaboration of the NMAI is its community-curated
exhibits, in which NMAI staff members work closely with Native communities to develop the content of the galleries. Native community members
were most involved in the development of exhibit themes, exhibit label
text, and video interviews. This is evidenced in the exhibits through authored text; for example, on general introductory panels, text is attributed
to Chicago cocurators as a group. For specific quotations, a person's name
and his or her tribal affiliation are displayed (figure 9).

I would argue that the NMAI's identity resides in this collaborative process and authored representations. It is the community curators' faces

and words on the walls, their knowledge and consent to be on display, that gives the museum its legitimization as a Native museum, one which ethically presents Native voice. In essence, their contributions give what many visitors seek: its "authenticity."

In this paper, I address the construction of "Native voice" within the NMAI through a focus on "community curating" (or collaborative exhibit making) museum representational strategies; and the changing relations between the subjects and objects presented in museum exhibitions. There are two moments represented in this account: the first part is based on an essay that was written in 2003 in anticipation of the opening of the NMAI, while the latter portion is based on an essay that was written in reflection two years after the museum opening, in 2006.

While I begin by examining evidence of Native voice in the exhibit text, after conducting my fieldwork I shift to a form of evidence that was explicitly *not* in the text.[5] In other words, I move from the construction of Native voice as evidenced in material signs and toward an understanding that it must also entail social commitment and advocacy.

Anticipation

In its rhetoric, the NMAI promises innovations in exhibit technology and ideology. One advertisement reads, "Any museum can invite you to look. A great one changes the way you see."[6] In *Native America Collected*, Margaret Dubin explains that "visitors need museums to validate their own experiences, to fill in the gaps in their knowledge of the world, and demonstrate proper ways of appreciating and understanding objects and events."[7] One of the goals of the NMAI is to fill in the gaps left by popular, inaccurate stereotypes of Native Americans through "authentic" representations of Native peoples. A loaded word, *authenticity* is one of the explicit promises of the museum.[8]

The construction of Native voice, and the NMAI's claim to authenticity, is substantiated both implicitly and explicitly through the work of uniquely embedded ethnographic text within the exhibit and the larger structure of the museum itself. In other words, the use of ethnographic evidence, specifically text derived from transcriptions of discourse, effects and is presented as authentic and authoritative cultural representation.

9. Part of the Chicago community exhibit panels in the NMAI Our Lives gallery, 2004. Photo courtesy Jennifer Shannon.

Native Voice in the New Museum

In *Museums, the Public, and Anthropology*, Michael Ames asks, "Are museums or anthropology really necessary anymore?"[9] The fact that Ames posed this question as a chapter heading in what is now considered to be a seminal work on the anthropology in museums and that it remained as a sign of the times in his later, revised compilation illustrates the real sense of unease in the discipline at that time.[10] Issues of representation, transparency, and authority in ethnography came under intense scrutiny in the 1980s, precipitating what has become known as the "crisis in representation."[11] The sheer amount of published, reflexive materials on the Smithsonian Institution by the Smithsonian regarding representation and collection issues since 1990 shows a similar trend in the field of museum studies.[12] It is during this time period, in 1989, that the Museum of the American Indian was incorporated into the Smithsonian Institution as the NMAI.

Ethnographic museums are seriously implicated by this critique or "crisis," as their main function is the representation of cultures or cultural products.[13] What, then, has been the museum response to this crisis? In *Reflections of a Cultural Broker: A View from the Smithsonian*, Richard Kurin provides a table entitled "What's In, What's Out" that offers some general insights. For example, "collectors" become "stewards," and "monologue" becomes "multilogue." However, in a list of some twenty-two museum features to be changed, the only one to remain the same, as an "institutional product," was "authenticity."[14]

Dubin suggests two specific responses that museums have made to the crisis: historical revision and change in exhibition-making practices to incorporate better communication between Natives and non-Natives.[15] She explains, "Ideally, the new museology demands a total overhaul of museum theory and practice. The primary goal is to open up space—discursive space as well as physical space—for indigenous objects to become speaking subjects who voice their own ideas and continue to (or even seize control of) their own representations."[16] The rhetoric and methodology of the NMAI suggests that it is a quintessential "new museum"; its mission statement focuses on "consultation, collaboration and cooperation with Natives."[17] Furthermore, its Web site states that the NMAI "empower[s] the Indian voice" and "actively strives to find new approaches to the study and representation of the history, materials, and cultures of Native peoples."[18]

Based on this mission, the 2004 inaugural exhibition of the NMAI included three permanent galleries—Our Universes, Our Peoples, and Our Lives—that each present eight communities reflecting on their own cosmologies, histories, and contemporary identities, respectively. The communities are represented as localities, rather than cultures, which is another response to the critiques of representation in cultural anthropology. For example, rather than an exhibit about Inuit identity, it is about the identity of the Inuit community of Igloolik, a town in the eastern Canadian Arctic.

In addition to addressing the crisis in representation, there are also visitor expectations that museums, as public institutions, must consider. They are expected to entertain and educate and to be authoritative and aesthetically pleasing.[19] These expectations invoke a number of different knowledge practices that come together in the making of a museum exhibit, including curatorial, design, marketing, and Native knowledge practices. These might include such materials as transcribed text, lighting effects, visitor polls, or instructions for how to properly display a pipe. It is the transcribed text, the ethnographic product of NMAI curatorial knowledge practices, on which I focus here through the examples of the Our Lives gallery.

Accessing Native Voice through Community Curating

Community curating is the method through which the NMAI constructs "Native voice." The Our Lives Native community cocurator committees were organized in various ways, depending on the community's preferences, and included between four and ten people. For example, the American Indian community of Chicago selected cocurators through nomination and election, a familiar process for them. For the Kalinago on the Caribbean island of Dominica, the chief of the Carib Territory selected the cocurator committee, making sure there was representation from each hamlet; for both males and females; and with basket makers, farmers, political figures, and cultural leaders.

The process of community curating for Our Lives, and for the inaugural exhibitions in general, was unique in that the NMAI curators spent a significant amount of time in each Native community, rather than only bringing the community members to the museum for consultation. There were regular meetings between the NMAI curators and the cocurator committees over the course of several years. For example, in Chicago, first there was an introductory meeting to invite the Chicago American Indian community to participate in the exhibition.[20] Once the community agreed to participate, periodic meetings between the NMAI staff and selected cocurators began.

These cocurator meetings were recorded, and the dialogue from these discussions as well as individual interviews with cocurators and other community members became the text of the exhibit. This process of visiting in the community, recording discourse, and talking with people about their life experience is what I refer to as ethnographic practice. In the first meetings, the NMAI curator listened to the cocurators as they began to formulate what it means to be a member of the American Indian community of Chicago today—for instance, activities like powwows that bring them together, community gathering places like the Anawim Center and the American Indian Center, and the various ways in which they maintain their Indian identity in the midst of a large metropolis. The cocurators' emphasis was that the Chicago community was a multitribal and a widely diverse group of people. The NMAI curator listened and returned to the community with themes that represented the various issues that were discussed. The cocurators then helped to further define these themes. Then the cocurators selected objects from within the NMAI collection as well as from their own community to represent these themes. The cocurators were later visited by a design team contracted by the NMAI and discussed their visions for presentation and reviewed the design team's sketches and layouts of the exhibit. An NMAI media team also visited the community later in the process, interviewing community members on video and recording important events during the week they were there, such as a powwow and a graduation ceremony. At each stage, people working on the exhibit came to the community to talk with community members, get a sense of place, and better represent them in the museum. Once there was agreement on the main themes of the exhibit, cocurators selected (or the NMAI curator commissioned) illustrative objects for the display.

Native Voice and the Shift to Narrative

The changing relations between subjects and objects within museums and an increasing incorporation of ethnographic text and practice reveal what I see as a shift in focus from objects to subjects and a consequent shift in the locus of authenticity. The Smithsonian's original and continuing mission, since the bequest of James Smithson in 1829, has been for the "increase and diffusion of knowledge." The original interpretation of this mission was to record and display for posterity dying Indian cultures that were becoming acculturated.[21] These early displays, exemplified by an exhibit labeled circa 1925 at the Museum of the American Indian, consisted of objects that were grouped together by type in glass cases, or in what I call object-to-object relations[22] (figure 10). These kinds of displays were closely tied to evolutionary and diffusionist theories in anthropology.

In the late nineteenth century, Franz Boas's notion of cultural groups and cultural relativism became influential in the field of anthropology. This approach focused on how objects are used and included cultural context (for example, through dioramas) to access the meaning of the object according to the people from whom it originated. The culture-area concept was thus developed at the Smithsonian as a means of classifying museum objects in order to better research and exhibit similarity and difference in the Smithsonian's extensive collections.[23] With this innovation in classification, objects at the Smithsonian were situated in a cultural context, in relation to subjects rather than simply to other objects, or what I call an object-to-subject relation.[24] In other words, the labels changed. For example, the object no longer is (only) an Eskimo oil lamp made of stone (and situated among similarly *functioning* objects), but it is (also) a stone oil lamp made by the grandfather of A. Ivalu in 1895 and used in the Return of the Sun Festival (and situated with clothing and items associated with that festival).

One example of a step further toward a Native point of view—though still maintaining the object-to-subject relation, where the object remains the focal point and is accompanied by a Native person's narrative—is the 1991 All Roads Are Good exhibit at the NMAI in New York. In this exhibition, "twenty-three Native Americans from throughout the Western Hemisphere—singers, storytellers, artists, elders, and scholars—were invited to select objects from the collections of the National Museum of the American Indian . . . and talk about the reasons behind their choices."[25]

Three years later, the NMAI presented the exhibit Creation's Journey, which was described as one of the "most elaborate attempts at multivocality to date," presenting displays of each object accompanied by explanatory texts grouped into the authorial categories of "art historian," "anthropologist," and "Native." It was a "curatorial experiment of monumental scale" that was "in tune to the sensitive political environment as well as the challenging postmodern aesthetic."[26] Jim Volkert, former head of the NMAI Exhibits Department, explains the experimental nature of this exhibit:

> the way that museums present information affects the way you perceive it. . . . So, for example, we had three of those famous decoys from Nevada. One was presented as if it were a piece of art. One was presented . . . in the way that it was discovered in the cave, as a piece of archaeology. And one was presented as if the duck, the decoy, were being used

10. *View of First Floor East Hall, Museum of the American Indian/Heye Foundation, 155th and Broadway, New York NY, February 1956.* Photo by Carmelo Guudagno. Courtesy NMAI Photo Archives. N28310.

floating in a creek, as a piece of natural history. And they were all set right side by side, that *same* object, in three different displays. And so you understood intuitively and immediately that the way the museum presents something affects how you perceive it. It's art, it's natural history, it's anthropology. . . . And so the point was not the supremacy of a Native perspective, but it's a piece that's been missing. . . . And that's what this museum is about. [And after seeing this exhibit] you *believed* the legitimacy of the Native voice.[27]

However, Dubin states that "the exhibit did not take into account the needs and expectations of the museum-going public, which still sought an authoritative experience."[28] It is in the interaction between the public and the museum where the "new museology" is most likely to break down. This is where the work of the museum, in response to the reflexive turn, can fail.[29]

The NMAI, as a "new museum," is going to display what I would suggest are subject-to-subject relations, particularly in the Our Lives gallery.[30] This gallery is much in line with the NMAI Exhibition Master Plan that was developed in 1995: "the museum intends for the exhibitions, for the most part, to be idea-driven: that is, that the exhibits will tell a story or communicate an idea, and the collections will be used to illustrate the story or illuminate the idea. The danger in this approach is that by definition the objects are subordinate to the idea of the exhibit instead of being the idea of the exhibit. This relegates the museum's most unique resource to a supporting role and may disappoint those visitors whose main goal is to connect with the objects."[31] For example, the Native groups in the Our Lives gallery are talking about *themselves*—their identities—what it means to be Inuit in Igloolik, or Mohawk in Kahnawake. These are situated identities, reflected upon and conveyed through the Native-authored text of the exhibit. It is about peoples' relations to each other, about *reflexive subjects*. The object, then, has become "illustration," accompanying the stories that Native people are telling about themselves. Unlike All Roads Are Good, the selection of objects is now at the endpoint of the exhibit-development process rather than at the beginning.

Therefore, there is a switch from evidence (and evidentiary claims) in *things* to evidence in *testimony* (or what I have been referring to as ethnographic evidence).³² It does not matter that the seal skin pants were created for the exhibit and never intended to be worn; the object is made authentic by its author, by the authority of the subject, by the "Nativeness" of the person who created it.³³ It is the authenticity of subject rather than the object that is now emphasized.

Embedded Representations

This authenticity of the subject is uniquely embedded in the NMAI within a concentric layering of signifiers that also indicate "Nativeness," including the museum institution itself. Although museum curators are moving from modernist-authoritative to postmodernist-interrogative positions as they attempt to erode the museum's position of authority, museum authority is not so easily undermined.³⁴ By its very nature, it legitimizes what it contains. Because it is a National Museum *of the American Indian*, Native authority is inherent in the institution.

An example from William Fitzhugh at the National Museum of Natural History illustrates the assumed authority of museums by the very nature of their being institutions of public learning. Fitzhugh explains how the simplistic and stereotyped image of the Eskimo, "has been created largely through museum representation"³⁵ (figure 11).

Fitzhugh goes on to say this is because visitors accept what is in the museum as *text*, as *truth*—even when it is what he describes to be an obviously outdated and underfunded exhibit.³⁶ In 1997, at Fitzhugh's suggestion, a Native of Kodiak Island, Sven Haakanson, conducted a review of the Eskimo exhibit. Haakanson concluded that the exhibit "does a wonderful job of demonstrating the types of tools, clothing and ritual materials. What the displays and text don't do is teach who the 'Eskimo' peoples really are. The visitors are taking the wrong information home, and this continues the misunderstandings of who the northern peoples are."³⁷

[The Our Lives exhibit, in contrast, is being constructed to address exactly that: who Native people are.] One way to illuminate how Native voice is constructed and embedded to achieve this outcome is to examine what Michael Lynch calls "localized praxis."³⁸ For instance, this concept "examine[s] how an activity comes to identify itself as observation."³⁹ In other words, how does the work of the curatorial staff and the Native community members come to be identified as, say, Native voice? I focus here on how ethnographic evidence, in the form of (entextualized) narrative, comes to be seen as Native voice and authority in the Our Lives exhibit.

As a field researcher for the NMAI in 2001, I worked with the Inuit community in Igloolik, Nunavut. I spent several one-to-two week visits with the community, during which I spoke with Inuit of all ages, organized cocurator workshops and youth presentations, and conducted one-on-one interviews to facilitate community participation as we worked together to develop the content for their exhibit. I tape-recorded all of the meetings and interviews and then, upon returning to the NMAI's Cultural Resources Center just outside of Washington DC, I transcribed the recordings.

Michael Silverstein and Greg Urban explain that the transcription of oral discourse can be seen as the production of a "text-artifact with a certain concreteness and manipulability"; they add parenthetically that "Perhaps these text-artifactual properties are suggestive—and surely have been suggestive—of museum specimens that can be transported back from the field and evaluated for their *authenticity* and cultural-aesthetic

11. Closed but visible Polar Eskimo exhibit at the National Museum of Natural History, October 2004. Photo courtesy Jennifer Shannon.

authoritativeness."[40] This analogy rang especially true to me. In fact, it did not seem like an analogy at all but rather an actual museum practice, for the recordings and transcriptions I made are now considered to be part of the NMAI's collection. Therefore, curators and fieldworkers collect *discourse* as well as objects.[41] But this discourse is no longer considered only an informational resource or reference for the curator to use in creating text panels or describing objects—it *is* the text panel. Portions of the transcript are used, deliberately verbatim, to represent the Native voice in the exhibit.

Once approved by a community's cocurator committee, the Our Lives curator and researchers assemble the text-artifacts and images of associated objects by theme into digital documents, complete with the dimensions of objects and numbers of words per label, and send it to the exhibit designers. It is important to remember that, while my account here is centered on text, the exhibit is a three-dimensional rendering that incorporates all five senses in its final form.[42] The role of technology and its possibilities in exhibits are significant, particularly in producing such effects as multivocality and multiple frames of reference. Therefore, the designers re-embed, or animate, the text-artifacts in a new context that can include not just text but also video, audio, projected winds and temperatures, smells, and lighting changes. The designers manipulate the objects and text-artifacts in space, their proximities and juxtaposition contributing in new ways to the production of authentic representation through the replication of forms.

Native voice is also embedded within a particular style of exhibit design within the gallery that facilitates an *implicit* relatedness among exhibits through the replication of form. In her discussion of the Women's Information Network newsletter in *The Network Inside Out*, Annelise Riles explains how a combination of textual information and graphics produced the effect of having "what looked like heterogeneity at one glance" and then "could be viewed as replication at the next."[43] This "aesthetic of controlled heterogeneity" can be seen in the distinctive forms taken by the Chicago, Igloolik, and Kahnawake community exhibits, for example.[44] These exhibits were distinct but at the same time were being grouped under a particular thematic structure of Our Lives and contained compositional similarities present in all eight community exhibits, such as text panels, video screens, and photographs.[45]

While it is important to consider the inevitable cross-cultural comparisons that will occur among these eight community exhibits that are juxtaposed within the gallery, it is equally essential to consider another comparison that also inheres in this gallery's form: the relationship between a Native community and its simulacrum, or "reality checking," so to speak.[46] The comparison becomes not between likenesses but between something "real," out there, and its representation — between the community in Igloolik and the exhibit of Igloolik on the gallery floor. The apparent match in this comparison is achieved at the NMAI through the representational strategies described above. The feeling that there is an adequate match may be considered as an authentic visitor experience.

A more *explicit* comparison — and on a much grander scale — exists at the level of the NMAI's curvilinear architecture in relation to other National Mall museums (figure 12). There is a luxury in starting from the ground up, in not having to create a "new museum" in an old space, where

12. Entrance of the NMAI. Photo courtesy Jennifer Shannon.

exhibits can become "rooted in the architecture" of the museum.[47] For, as Kurin describes, "In the museum, categories of knowledge are carved into the walls, chiseled in stone, and constructed with brick and mortar."[48] The architectural nature of the museum, and of the exhibit, usually creates certain limitations; but here, it provides new possibilities for representational strategies. According to the NMAI Web site, as a product of collaborative engagement with Native communities, the "museum's architecture and landscape design represent a distinctly Native approach."[49] It is clear that the NMAI has been deliberate about its form and presence on the mall, which is dominated by buildings with classical architecture. This contradiction is most notable in its juxtaposition to its next door neighbor, the National Air and Space Museum, with its white walls and box-like structure.

Preliminary Conclusions

As a new museum committed to a "new museology," the NMAI has been deliberate about distinguishing itself as a Native place through new engagements with and productions of authority, authenticity, representation, and Native voice in its inaugural exhibitions. It has shifted to a primacy of evidence of authenticity in ethnographic or discursive text rather than in objects or things. Representing subject-to-subject relations in the exhibit through embedded ethnographic text is, I suggest, intended to produce the effect of authority and authenticity of Native voice, or the authentic subject. The content of the exhibit, because it is a product and faithful entextualization of the authoritative subject, becomes authentic representation. Furthermore, the exhibits are enclosed by a structure that is described as a Native place. Because these moves are created in consultation with Native peoples, and through "transparent" methods, they are considered to be "authentic." The making of authentic representation, then, is a combination of form, content, and process that is perceived to be uniquely "Native." The NMAI therefore constructs Native voice through both implicit and explicit strategies of representation, replication, and comparison.

If we consider the text-artifact as ethnographic evidence embedded within the NMAI, according to Silverstein and Urban, "Politics can be seen, from this perspective, as the struggle to entextualize authoritatively, and hence, in one relevant move, to fix certain metadiscursive perspectives on texts and discourse practices."[50] In other words, the NMAI provides Native peoples with the means to take control of their own representations through their participation in the textualization of their voices, in the claim of authentic representation, and in the exhibiting of their cultures.

In the NMAI, as I have discussed in relation to the Our Lives gallery, the demands of the critiques of representation, the museum, the visiting public, and Native peoples appear to come together in a unique space and to mutually reinforce each other. There is no doubt that what I have found as evidence to produce these effects is a function of my attention to such devices as rhetoric and text, but that is what has been available to date. Only time would tell, as the museum opened in 2004, if the realization of these potentials was possible.

Reflection

It has been a few years since the opening of the NMAI.[51] I was present at the grand opening, the procession of over 20,000 Native people walking the National Mall, on September 21, 2004. I was present at the first viewing of the exhibits by the Our Lives community cocurators as well as for the first reception by NMAI staff of the reviews in the newspapers. In many ways, as is common once ethnographic fieldwork is underway—and in a way doubling the process at the NMAI—my account now becomes peopled, as did the exhibits, with the voices and perspectives of those involved in the production of Native voice.

The Definition of Native Voice

Native Voice is a phrase that continues to appear throughout NMAI written materials, including past mission statements and current exhibit labels. In the 2006 temporary exhibition about the Pacific Northwest Coast entitled Listening to Our Ancestors, NMAI staff attempted to be more transparent about the community-curating process through a series of panels at the end of the exhibit. One is labeled "Native Voice," and it begins with a quote by NMAI director Rick West: "Native peoples possess important and authoritative knowledge about themselves and their cultures, past and present, and deserve to be at the museological table of interpretation and representation." The panel continues, "The photos and text shown here provide a glimpse of our exhibition process and reveal how and why the museum shares authority with indigenous people to represent Native culture and history. . . . Exhibitions at the National Museum of the American Indian are developed in partnership with Native people. This practice is based on the belief that indigenous people are best able to teach others about themselves. Their understanding of who they are and how they present themselves to the world is what the museum calls 'Native voice.'"

⌈This exhibit panel seemed to answer the question I posed to many NMAI staff members at the time of the museum opening: what is Native voice? As we discussed in 2004, it was never defined, nor was community curating ever described to prepare the visitors, or critics, for what they were seeing in the exhibitions.⌋

Through the process of community curating, Native voice was produced by committee and resulted in a unified, authoritative voice in each exhibit, where community curators authored as a group each of the main thematic sections of their exhibits. This discussion and consensus process was not necessarily the original intention of the NMAI staff, who in a December 2000 vetting session of the Our Lives project had anticipated an atmosphere of "multivocality." There were individual quotes in the exhibits, but they are mainly illustrations, not rebuttals or varied experiences, of the main text panels.

When I first began my interviews with staff in 2004, around the time of the opening, there was no consensus about what Native voice is: does it mean Native perspective (and how do you go about accessing that) or does it literally mean the voices of Native peoples (as it was interpreted to be in the inaugural exhibitions, where the text on the walls represented excerpts from recorded interviews and discussion among community curators). I asked NMAI director Rick West for his thoughts on these definitions. He explained that curators have been "very disciplined about it." But with "some of the critique that's come back about the exhibitions," the "temptation" may be to "make it more, if you will, in terms of exhibition presentation, *perspective* rather than voice. I just want to make sure that we understand, just as we did on the *curatorial side* to begin with, what kinds of filters are being imposed and . . . what is the *cost* of that . . . [because] the farther you get from the words that were actually used, assuming that you were relying upon people who have capacity for expressing themselves to begin with, the *more* at risk you are of altering meanings, and changing meanings from the intention of the speaker."[52]

Institutional Dynamics of Native Voice

As West's comments intimate, there was an institutional divide at the NMAI: a curatorial side and an exhibitions side; each had different ideas about the community-curating process and the criteria for evaluating the success of exhibits. It seems the conflict between the Exhibits and Curatorial departments—and anyone working there readily acknowledges this struggle has been going on for many years, as it often does in other museums—is that, in this particular case, they look to different constituencies. The NMAI mission statement lists two: "Native communities and the non-Native public."[53]

As one NMAI staff member told me one afternoon,

I got the sense that Curatorial's main constituency were the Native communities, and they really at some level *apparently*—I'm not saying this as *fact*—it *seemed* to me that sometimes that that was the only constituency that they were particularly interested in. . . . And that the museum content that they were acquiring was important content, and that they had to sort of defend the interests of Native people. In some ways, I tended to look at some people in Curatorial as like the Indian agents—there seemed to me to be a kind of almost sort of paternalism, you know, Indian people can't take care of themselves so we have to take care of them. I think the tension on the other side was that, you know, we're here to create exhibits and tell people about Native people and the constituency for Exhibits was the public. And I think that dichotomy was very pronounced—again, this is very subjective, you need to talk to other people about this.[54]

Generally, I think this is a fair assessment from someone working in a public-oriented department.[55] The curatorial staff worried about doing things "the right way" and squarely faced and served Native communities in its philosophy and practice to accomplish this, while the Exhibits and

Education departments were more consistently mindful and directed toward doing appropriate "translation" for the museum-going public.

Under the direction of Craig Howe in the Curatorial Department in 1999, the curatorial staff was taught and internalized that success meant Native community members would walk into their exhibit (and staff did think of it as the community's exhibit) and say, "this feels right." And truly, if that is the measure of success, then the Our Lives exhibits were greatly successful. Community members with whom I have spoken do feel ownership over their exhibits, and they do recognize their ideas and words on the walls. All of the community members with whom I have spoken have expressed great pride and a sense of familiarity when they encountered their space in the exhibition.

But there has been much criticism of the process within the NMAI. One program manager in a public-oriented department stated that community curating "has value, but we went way too far in one direction . . . [and] abdicated our responsibilities" to the information that visitors want and the intellectual framing they need.[56] Similarly, like many public-oriented department members, the script writer–editor saw his job as bringing "clarity" to the exhibit process, making it easier for the visitors to understand the exhibits. He and I talked about how sometimes the cocurators would choose not to provide content for exhibits in which the museum staff was interested: "I felt we often acted as supplicants at times when we should have provided direction [to communities in curating]. And I don't think that was helpful. . . . I think that's probably heresy in Curatorial."[57] He discusses "paying the price" for just doing what the community wants and adds that it is the exhibition team to which you should have allegiance, not your department.

This common conception from outside the Curatorial Department — that there is a "cabal" as one museum consultant put it in 2006 during a discussion as to why the Curatorial Department needed to be "broken up" — is ironic since the curators did not have a single meeting as a department during the entire course of my fieldwork. Here, I think the public-oriented department members misinterpreted what was going on; there was not an allegiance among curatorial staff to their department, or perhaps even to each other, but rather — and fiercely — to the Native communities and individuals with whom they worked.

One curator explained to me that the curators' knowledge is key to determining what is important and relevant in the "raw transcripts," which "included a lot of sensitive information and a lot of irrelevant information." Knowing the difference was a curator's significant contribution, whereas others who were not in direct contact with communities "had no idea how the text and the things that were in the transcripts actually related to the *rest* of the exhibition as it had been developed so far."[58] To this curator, a request to turn over script-writing duties, "ran the risk of sort of just opening up the transcripts" and potentially displaying parts of conversations that community curators did not want in a public exhibit:

> Curatorial stands in a unique face-to-face position with the community, and being in the *best* position to actually, in some cases, *interpret* the feeling of the community when there's no possibility of going back and asking every single question. That *somebody's* got to take *responsibility* for that. And it seemed at that point that *at that time*, members of Curatorial, specifically the lead curators, were the only ones who recognized that it was a *responsibility*. And it was what we *owed* communities. . . . That you couldn't understand communities and what they wanted for their exhibits solely by what was recorded on paper, what was in the transcripts. . . . Part of it had to do with the development of personal relationships and *feelings* of community, of having *heard* them, of having heard their often emotional reactions to what they're talking about.[59]

This curator's comments are representative of the Curatorial Department's ethos in general, which includes a desire to follow community wishes, at times against other interests and actors within the museum bureaucracy, and a desire to shepherd the exhibit content that was developed through an intimate partnership with Native community members during the exhibit development process. In this process, content could be transformed by multiple other experts through script editing, the juxtaposition of images or objects, and use of colors and textual strategies of emphasis or de-emphasis.[60]

In other words, according to the NMAI curators and research assistants, they took on the role of community "advocates."[61] This responsibility to advocate is, in part, based on this particular kind of intimacy (or shared knowledge) curators have with cocurators. However, one curator revealed to me that in the museum bureaucracy, the Native communities often become pawns in interoffice power struggles, and that one way to assert themselves was to say, "the community wants it that way."[62] It was explained a number of times that a commitment to Native voice could also generate antagonism with other staff.

Therefore, participating in these community-curated exhibits had profound effects for NMAI staff within the museum; for instance, curators gained both trust in Native communities and reputations for being "obstructionist" or "protective" within the museum. Perhaps somewhat in consequence (along with other issues such as budget, timelines, and new business philosophies), about a year after the NMAI's opening the Curatorial Department was disbanded, and curators were reassigned to other departments during a massive organizational restructuring. There has also been widespread critical discussion in the museum about the merits and process of community curating.

The Reception of Native Voice

The individual community cocurators with whom I spoke felt empowered by the collaborative process and appreciated the work of the NMAI curators and staff to elicit and organize their discussions and to respect their wishes in the course of exhibit development. One community cocurator explained that the work of NMAI Curatorial staff was, during meetings with their committee, to guide "the discussion but in a very subtle way. They were more or less listening to the feedback and comments from the cocurators themselves."[63] A Kalinago cocurator described the collaborative process as similar to "creating a dance—you have people dancing and then you catch your steps and say, Guys! I love this one! Why don't we stick on this one. So, it was fun, to listen to the community people . . . but at the same time *capture* the main fundamental things you were looking [for] in the exhibit."[64]

As for the impacts on the Native communities as a whole, in places that are more remote and not in the United States, like Igloolik in the Arctic and the Carib Territory in the Caribbean, there was very little overall impact for having been a part of this exhibition. For Igloolik, they had worked with museums before and were frankly quite blasé about it (until they saw the final product, when they were beaming at seeing family members and friends in the videos on display). For the Kalinago in the Carib Territory, there was a sense of pride in being selected, but it was only realized in the few people who participated directly in the exhibit and had traveled to Washington DC for the opening.

On the other hand, for the St. Laurent Metis of Manitoba, it sparked a cultural center project, as they had won awards for their exhibit and were recognized in Canada for their contributions to the NMAI. Likewise, the Chicago urban Indian community recorded their experience attending the opening in an award-winning video entitled "From Wilson Ave to Washington DC," which is now being sold in their gift shop and in the NMAI. Furthermore, although over half of all American Indians live in cities, they are often overlooked and rarely if ever represented in museums. Their participation in the Our Lives exhibition gave members of the Chicago community a sense of validation, and they mention this participation in everything from grant applications to public gatherings.

Despite the communities' overwhelmingly positive reception, newspaper reviewers had an unexpectedly critical response to the exhibitions. Their descriptions of confusing exhibits or a lack of scholarship at the NMAI were often met with a common statement by NMAI staff: "They don't get it." As Ann McMullen and Bruce Bernstein explain in a memorandum to the board of trustees after the opening,

> What is clear from the reviews is that NMAI's dependence on Native voices—without "conceptual rigor" and without integration with other sources, versions, or voices—makes the exhibits and their content distinctly unpersuasive. The direct question posed is "Why should visitors believe what the museum says, including what Native people say?" This suggests that NMAI has failed to make a case for Native voice as an authentic source by not providing visitors a foundation in the essential subjectivity of all sources—Native or non-Native—and failed to explain its own epistemology in bringing forward Native voices and depending on them for the authority of the exhibits.[65]

Perhaps that is what Listening to Our Ancestors: The Art of Native Life along the North Pacific Coast exhibition attempted to correct through their panels describing Native voice as I mentioned earlier. While this co-curating process has been commended by both Native and non-Native scholars, the content of the exhibits, and especially the lost opportunity of emphasizing the colonial encounter and genocide, left a number of reviewers dissatisfied.[66]

As often happens at this institution, as staff turnover occurs, approaches to exhibit making and deciding what is best for Indian Country takes on new forms. It remains to be seen what is next for community curating at the NMAI or if other methods will be developed for constructing Native voice. But I can at least say that, according to cocurators who participated in the Our Lives gallery, the museum's commitment to Native voice through community curating was an empowering experience, if somewhat sheltered from the battles within the institution.

Conclusion

Many people, like myself, have perhaps entered a museum and reviewed its exhibits assuming that the display is as it was always meant to be. But over the course of my fieldwork, it became clear that each exhibition—through its multiple authors and multiple specialists as well as through its architectural, budgetary, and design requirements—represented instead a compromise of competing commitments, interests, and visions. While I had anticipated a uniquely successful intersection of postmodern engagement and authoritative representation, I found in the course of my fieldwork that the authority of the Native communities in these collaborative exhibits, while not contested, did not satisfy many reviewers both within and outside of the museum. It did, however, create ethical relationships for Our Lives contributors and accurate representations according to those who were closely partnered in the co-curating committee meetings.

By focusing on the practices of knowledge production, or the collaborative process of exhibition development, we can see how a "thing" like an exhibit acquired its "thingness," how text and imagery became Native voice, and consider whether these constructions satisfied the promises of authenticity and authority made by the museum. We can also see how discourses of paternalism versus advocacy and translation versus intimacy reveal different communities of expertise with different ways of knowing, understanding, and engaging with the reflexive subjects of museum exhibitions.

Finally, this form of inquiry leads us to better understand the role of the curators and their commitment to communities in this collaborative process. We see that Native voice is constructed not only through embedded material representations but also through the social relations of its producers, including the source communities and museum staff.[67] Native voice is not just the authored text in the exhibit; it is also the anxiety and commitment and advocacy that NMAI staff *and* Native cocurators bring to the process—each interacting with one another and being responsible for each other within their own communities.[68]

Notes

1. Smithsonian Institution Office of Public Affairs, "National Museum of the American Indian Announces Grand Opening on Sept. 21," news release, January 15, 2004.

2. Richard West, "A New Idea of Ourselves: The Changing Presentation of the American Indian," in *The Changing Presentation of the American Indian: Museums and Native Cultures*, ed. National Museum of the American Indian (Washington DC: National Museum of the American Indian, 2000), 7, emphasis mine.

3. Ruth B. Phillips, "Community Collaboration in Exhibitions," introduction to *Museums and Source Communities: A Routledge Reader*, ed. Laura L. Peers and Alison K. Brown (London: Routledge, 2003), 166.

4. My research has been dedicated to documenting the collaborative relationships and exhibit-making process of the NMAI Our Lives gallery and is based on fieldwork from June 2004 to June 2006, which was made possible by a dissertation-fieldwork grant from the Wenner-Gren Foundation. I conducted nine months of fieldwork at the museum from June to December of 2004 and from March to June of 2006. I also spent six months in each of two Native communities featured in the Our Lives exhibition: the urban Indian community of Chicago and the Kalinago (or Carib) community of the Commonwealth of Dominica. This research is rooted in my own experiences of working in the NMAI's Curatorial Department from August 1999 to May 2002 and as a contract fieldworker in 2003 and therefore provides a particular form of situated knowledge about museum practice and perspective. For a discussion about situated knowledge, see Donna Haraway, "Situated Knowledges: The Science Question in Feminism and the Privilege of Partial Perspective," in *Simians, Cyborgs, and Women: The Reinvention of Nature*, (New York: Routledge, 1991), 183–201. I would like to thank Hiro Miyazaki, Pa-

mela Smart, and Kim Couvson for their comments on earlier drafts. I would like also to thank the NMAI staff represented or quoted herein for their contributions through thoughtful conversations with me over the years, especially Dr. Cynthia Chavez, who was the lead curator of the Our Lives gallery and who encouraged me to embark on this work.

5. The 2003 version of this paper began as an experimental essay in 2002, which I later condensed and presented at the Cornell Department of Science and Technology Studies Conference, "Observing, Investigating, Reporting: Science Studies and Local Ethnographies," in April of 2003. It presents a perspective on museum practice that I certainly would not have imagined while working as a museum researcher. Using the notion of evidence to think differently about museum practice was inspired by a course taught by Hiro Miyazaki.

6. Margaret Dubin, *Native America Collected: The Culture of an Art World* (Albuquerque: University of New Mexico Press, 2001), 90.

7. Dubin, *Native America Collected*, 85.

8. West, "A New Idea of Ourselves."

9. Michael M. Ames, *Museums, the Public, and Anthropology: A Study in the Anthropology of Anthropology* (Vancouver: University of British Columbia Press, 1986).

10. Michael M. Ames, *Cannibal Tours and Glass Boxes: The Anthropology of Museums* (Vancouver: University of British Columbia Press, 1992). In anthropology, calls to reconfigure ethnography and anthropology and to renegotiate fieldwork are indicators of this crisis. See Douglas Holmes and George Marcus, "Cultures of Expertise and the Management of Globalization: Toward a Re-functioning of Ethnography," in *Global Assemblages: Technology, Politics, and Ethics as Anthropological Problems*, ed. Aihwa Ong and Stephen J. Collier (Malden MA: Blackwell Publishing, 2005); George Marcus and Michael Fischer, *Anthropology as Cultural Critique: An Experimental Moment in the Human Sciences* (Chicago: University of Chicago Press, 1999); George Marcus, *Ethnography through Thick and Thin* (Princeton NJ: Princeton University Press, 1998); and James Clifford, *Routes: Travel and Translation in the Late Twentieth Century* (Cambridge MA: Harvard University Press, 1997), esp. p. 89. Marcus and Fischer explain in *Anthropology as Cultural Critique* that this time of "crisis" is similar to that in the 1920s and 1930s and that it is apart of a cycle of paradigms; Marcus and Fischer, *Anthropology as Cultural Critique*, 8, 12. Dominic Boyer addresses the notion of crisis rhetoric in intellectual disciplines in his discussion of German intellectuals with a deep sense of cultural pessimism, who perceive a decline in intellectual and cultural traditions. This "language of crisis" intimates a loss of prestige and authority, while the status and security of the German intellectuals were quite high. Dominic Boyer, "The Social Life of German Cultural Bourgeoisie in the 'Long Nineteenth Century' and Their Dialectical Knowledge of German-Ness" in *Spirit and System: Media,*

Intellectuals, and the Dialectic in Modern German Culture (Chicago: University of Chicago Press, 2005). Similarly, consider the subsequent "museum boom" since this time in relation to Ames's and Sturtevant's "language of crisis." Compare Mary Bouquet, ed., *Academic Anthropology and the Museum: Back to the Future* (New York: Berghahn Books, 2001); with Ames, *Museums, the Public, and Anthropology*; Ames, *Cannibal Tours and Glass Boxes*; and William C. Sturtevant, "Does Anthropology Need Museums?" *Proceedings of the Biological Society of Washington* 182 (1969): 619–50.

11. Marcus and Fischer, *Anthropology as Cultural Critique*, 8; and Ames, *Cannibal Tours and Glass Boxes*, 168. With influence from the field of literary criticism, James Clifford and George Marcus's influential text *Writing Culture* took a critical approach to the main product of anthropological research—the ethnography; see James Clifford and George E. Marcus, eds., *Writing Culture: The Poetics and Politics of Ethnography* (Berkeley: University of California Press, 1986). Reflecting on their earlier work in *Writing Culture*, Marcus and Fischer conclude that this crisis arose with an "uncertainty about adequate means of describing social reality." Marcus and Fischer, *Anthropology as Cultural Critique*, 8. By regarding ethnography as invention rather than as the (direct) representation of cultures and by emphasizing it as a writing process, authors in *Writing Culture* brought into question the act of representation and the authority and authenticity of the writer and the written document, respectively. I would argue that Vine Deloria Jr., a board member of the NMAI and a notorious critic of anthropological engagements with Native peoples, was equally critical to the changing nature of the museum and of anthropology in North America. Deloria's *Custer Died for Your Sins* contributed significantly to the critique of anthropological literature, ethnographic practice, and contemporary museums. Vine Deloria Jr., *Custer Died for Your Sins: An Indian Manifesto* (Norman: University of Oklahoma Press, 1988); see also Thomas Biolsi and Larry J. Zimmerman, *Indians and Anthropologists: Vine Deloria, Jr., and the Critique of Anthropology* (Tucson: University of Arizona Press, 1997).

12. See for example, Ivan Karp and Steven D. Lavine, eds., *Exhibiting Cultures: The Poetics and Politics of Museum Display* (Washington DC: Smithsonian Institution Press, 1991); Ivan Karp, Christine Kreamer, and Steven D. Lavine, eds., *Museums and Communities: The Politics of Public Culture* (Washington DC: Smithsonian Institution Press, 1992); and Richard Kurin, *Reflections of a Cultural Broker: A View from the Smithsonian* (Washington DC: Smithsonian Institution Press, 1997).

13. I am sure that some NMAI staff members would bristle at my reference to the NMAI as an ethnographic museum; I use the term here because the process through which exhibit material was obtained was in part through (para)ethnographic practices. For those staff members with whom I spoke, when they called

an exhibit "too ethnographic," they considered this clearly to be a negative critique.

14. Kurin, *Reflections of a Cultural Broker*, 283. Discussions of authenticity regarding museums tend to focus on the authenticity of objects, or the valuation of art and artifacts or of art versus artifacts; James Clifford, *The Predicament of Culture: Twentieth-Century Ethnography, Literature, and Art* (Cambridge MA: Harvard University Press, 1988); Clifford, *Routes*, 211; Christopher Steiner and Ruth B. Phillips, *African Art in Transit* (New York: Cambridge University Press, 1994), 100–2; Michael O'Hanlon, *Paradise: Portraying the New Guinea Highlands* (London: British Museum Press, 1993), 62, 81; Ruth B. Phillips and Christopher Steiner, "Art, Authenticity and the Baggage of Cultural Encounter," in *Unpacking Culture: Art and Commodity in Colonial and Postcolonial Worlds*, ed. Ruth B. Phillips and Christopher B. Steiner (Berkeley: University of California Press, 1999), 19; Shelly Errington, *The Death of Authentic Primitive Art and Other Tales of Progress* (Berkeley: University of California Press, 1998); and Sally Price, *Primitive Art in Civilized Places* (Chicago: University of Chicago Press, 1989). Ames discusses how the Canadian Museum of Civilization has been shifting the focus away from authentic objects or "real things," to authentic visitor "experience." In other words, whether it is the "real thing," a replica, or a digital or graphic representation, it is the visitor's experience within the exhibit that is desired to be authentic. Ames, *Cannibal Tours and Glass Boxes*, 158–59.

15. Dubin, *Native America Collected*, 87.

16. Dubin, *Native America Collected*, 86.

17. *Native* is not only an adjective, but it is also a noun used by the NMAI to describe Indigenous, Aboriginal, and First Nations peoples. This is the language of the museum that I have chosen to follow in this essay.

18. NMAI, "The National Museum of the American Indian," Smithsonian Institution, http://www.nmai.si.edu/index.html (accessed December 12, 2002).

19. Dubin, *Native America Collected*, 85.

20. These meetings were held at the American Indian Center, which is a central place to access the community. But of course this also excluded many American Indians who do not participate in activities at the center. However, the issue of the limitations that this approach had for a broader representation of Chicago Native experience is beyond the scope of this particular paper. See James B. LaGrand, *Indian Metropolis: Native Americans in Chicago, 1945–75* (Urbana: University of Illinois Press, 2002).

21. William W. Fitzhugh, "Ambassadors in Sealskins: Exhibiting Eskimos at the Smithsonian," in *Exhibiting Dilemmas: Issues of Representation at the Smithsonian*, ed. Amy Henderson and Adrienne L. Kaeppler (Washington DC: Smithsonian Institution Press, 1997), 214.

22. Dubin, *Native America Collected*, 92. The Museum of the American Indian begun

by George Gustav Heye was later acquired by the Smithsonian, and it then became the NMAI.

23. Fitzhugh, "Ambassadors in Sealskins," 227.

24. See by way of comparison Eilean Hooper-Greenhill, *Museums and the Shaping of Knowledge* (New York: Routledge, 1992), 204.

25. NMAI, "All Roads Are Good," (Washington DC: Smithsonian Institution Press, 2002).

26. Dubin, *Native America Collected*, 89, 96.

27. Jim Volkert (former head of the NMAI Exhibits Department), personal interview with the author, Washington DC, July 8, 2004.

28. Dubin, *Native America Collected*, 92, emphasis mine.

29. For a discussion of what happens when a discipline's knowledge fails, see Hirokazu Miyazaki and Annelise Riles, "Failure as an Endpoint," in Ong and Collier, *Global Assemblages*, 320–32. See also numerous accounts of the exhibit Into the Heart of Africa, which was described as a failure to communicate with the audience, who misunderstood the "sophisticated" exhibit and became angry: Anna Laura Jones, "Exploding Cannons: The Anthropology of Museums," *Annual Review of Anthropology* 22 (1993): 211; Jeanne Cannizzo, *Into the Heart of Africa* (Toronto: Royal Ontario Museum, 1989); Jeanne Cannizzo, "Exhibiting Cultures: Into the Heart of Africa," *Visual Anthropology Review* 7, no. 1 (1991): 150–60; and Ames, *Cannibal Tours and Glass Boxes*, 157.

30. This lack of recognizable museum objects was emphasized by the Collections staff, referring to the Our Lives gallery as "Our Props" (as opposed to "Our Loans" for the Our Peoples gallery and "Our Objects" for the Our Universes gallery). In 2004 I overheard one senior manager call the Our Lives gallery "T-Shirts and Baseball Caps."

31. Gerard Hilferty and Associates, *National Museum of the American Indian Smithsonian Institution Mall Facility Exhibition Master Plan, Phase I Interim Report: Orientation and Research* (Washington DC, 1995), 3.

32. See Lorraine Daston, "Marvelous Facts and Miraculous Evidence in Early Modern Europe," in *Questions of Evidence: Proof, Practice, and Persuasion across the Disciplines*, ed. James K. Chandler, Arnold Ira Davidson, and Harry D. Harootunian (Chicago: University of Chicago Press, 1994), 274.

33. Ames asks in his discussion of the valuation and authenticity of Native art, is a work Indigenous because of its aesthetics or "is being Native enough, sharing in the indigenous experience?" Ames, *Cannibal Tours and Glass Boxes*, 82–83.

34. Dubin, *Native America Collected*, 84. See also Fred R. Myers, *Painting Culture: The Making of an Aboriginal High Art* (Durham NC: Duke University Press, 2002), 198–99; Ruth B. Phillips, "Apec at the Museum of Anthropology: The Politics of Site and the Poetics of Sight Bite," *Ethnos* 65, no. 2 (2000): 172; Brian Durrans, "The Future of the Other: Changing Cultures on Display in Ethnographic Mu-

seums," in *The Museum Time Machine: Putting Cultures on Display*, ed. Robert Lumley (New York: Routledge, 1988), 164; Ames, *Cannibal Tours and Glass Boxes*, 22.

35. Fitzhugh, "Ambassadors in Sealskins," 209. Fitzhugh and I are referring to the outdated "Eskimo" exhibit at the National Museum of Natural History in Washington DC. While this exhibit was still up, the Alaska Office of the National Museum of Natural History's Arctic Studies Program began creating more recent and collaboration-centered exhibitions.

36. Fitzhugh, "Ambassadors in Sealskins," 228. See also Clifford, *Predicament of Culture*, 25; David Dean, *Museum Exhibition: Theory and Practice* (New York: Routledge, 1994), 116.

37. Fitzhugh, "Ambassadors in Sealskins," 229.

38. Michael Lynch, *Scientific Practice and Ordinary Action: Ethnomethodology and Social Studies of Science* (New York: Cambridge University Press, 1997), 281.

39. Lynch, *Scientific Practice and Ordinary Action*, 280.

40. Michael Silverstein and Greg Urban, *Natural Histories of Discourse* (Chicago: University of Chicago Press, 1996), 3.

41. As anthropologist Pam Smart reminded me, there are other centers that specifically collect "discourse," such as the Smithsonian's Folklife Center.

42. See Mary Bouquet, "Thinking and Doing Otherwise: Anthropological Theory in Exhibitionary Practice," *Ethnos* 65, no. 2 (2000): 226.

43. Annelise Riles, *The Network Inside Out* (Ann Arbor: University of Michigan Press, 2001), 119.

44. Riles, *Network Inside Out*, 120.

45. For example, the fact that a multitribal, urban-Indian population will be displayed in the same manner as federally and state-recognized tribes, presented as a cohesive community, can be seen as intending to create a sense of legitimization or validation in viewers' perspectives of an often-overlooked but majority Native population.

46. This realism in exhibition design is similar to what Kirshenblatt-Gimblett describes as an "in situ" approach, in which the installation tries to "include more of what was left behind, even if only in replica." Barbara Kirshenblatt-Gimblett, "Objects of Ethnography," in Karp and Lavine, *Exhibiting Cultures*, 388.

47. Fitzhugh, "Ambassadors in Sealskins," 233.

48. Kurin, *Reflections of a Cultural Broker*, 279.

49. "The design of NMAI's facilities, including that for the new museum on the National Mall, reflects the museum's commitment to work in consultation, collaboration, and cooperation with Native people in all of the museum's activities. Between 1990 and 1993, NMAI and other Smithsonian offices conducted a series of twenty-four consultations with various constituency groups to determine what they wanted the new museum to be. The majority of the participants in these con-

sultations were Native people. . . . While consultations were oriented toward architectural and program issues, discussions often took the form of animated, emotional, and philosophical conversations about the condition and representation of Native people — past, present, and future." NMAI, "The National Museum of the American Indian," http://www.nmai.si.edu/mall/index.html (accessed December 12, 2002).

50. Silverstein and Urban, *Natural Histories of Discourse*, 11.

51. This portion of the essay is based on a conference paper prepared for the Central States Anthropological Association Meeting in Omaha, Nebraska, in April 2006.

52. Richard West (NMAI director), personal interview with the author, Washington DC, November 18, 2004.

53. NMAI, *Mission Statement*, (Smithsonian Institution, 2002).

54. Personal interview with an NMAI staff member, Washington DC, September 8, 2004.

55. I am in no way suggesting that public-oriented department staff do not also have a strong desire to do what is right for Native communities; but this divide in language, interpretation, perception, and practice about how to fulfill the NMAI's mission of Native voice among NMAI departments is a key part of the museum's internal dynamics.

56. Personal interview with an NMAI program manager, Washington DC, March 23, 2006.

57. Personal interview with an NMAI script writer–editor, Washington DC, September 8, 2004.

58. Personal interview with an NMAI curator, Suitland, Maryland, November 23, 2004.

59. NMAI curator, personal interview, November 23, 2004.

60. In general, Curatorial's direct and intimate contact with Native communities was coveted by other departmental staff members, who did not have such intimate experiences but who would say to me they wished they could. In this way, in a symbolic capital sense, Curatorial is at the top of the hierarchy, and its members are considered to be in a respected field. But in a power sense, as in decision-making capacity within the museum structure, they were far lower on the chain of command over time.

61. "All three [inaugural] exhibits are community curated, at least 70 percent. What we mean by that is the museum curators, the museum staff, whether Native or non-Native, serve as facilitators or advocates, that the *experts reside in the communities*." Bruce Bernstein (deputy assistant director of cultural resources), at the Our Lives vetting session, December 14, 2000.

62. Personal interview with an NMAI curator, Suitland, Maryland, October 29, 2004.

63. Personal interview with an NMAI cocurator, Carib Territory, Dominica, April 13, 2005.

64. Personal interview with an NMAI cocurator, Carib Territory, Dominica, April 25, 2005.

65. Ann McMullen and Bruce Bernstein, *Mall Museum Reviews: An Overview and Analysis* Unpublished Internal Document Created for the Board of Trustees, (National Museum of the American Indian, 2004). Used with permission of the authors.

66. Amy Lonetree and Sonya Atalay, eds., "Critical Engagements with the National Museum of the American Indian," special issue, *American Indian Quarterly* 30, nos. 3–4 (2006).

67. Laura L. Peers and Alison K. Brown, eds., *Museums and Source Communities: A Routledge Reader* (London; New York: Routledge, 2003).

68. P. Batty discusses the relationship between government advisors and Aboriginal communities in Australia as well as the need for Aboriginal authorization to conduct projects in their communities. He examines how Aboriginal people must endorse these advisors, investing them with cultural capital. Through a one-on-one relationship with a particular Aboriginal person (like a community liaison in the NMAI community curating process), the white individual's motivations, personal commitment, and alignment with the broader group could be explained and endorsed by his or her Aboriginal partner. In other words, confirmation that a hitherto "unknown white fella" was "on side" was facilitated through his or her demonstrable relationship with an Aboriginal person with the group. One could say that through these arrangements, the Aboriginal partner "empowered" his non-Aboriginal offsider to work on behalf of the Aboriginal community. P. Batty, "Private Politics, Public Strategies: White Advisers and Their Aboriginal Subjects," *Oceania* 75, no. 3 (2005): 217.

   While NMAI curators were both Native and non-Native, their relationship to Native communities as outside government advisors (in museum matters) can also be seen as being in need of endorsement by the community. Particularly in the process of interviewing and in other work outside of the community curator meetings, the liaison and Native cocurators were essential to NMAI staff being introduced to and having positive working relationships with additional community members.

3

Tribal Museums and the Heterogeneity of the Nation-State

Creation of the Tribal Museum

BRENDA J. CHILD

Tribal museums are unique institutions and their proliferation today is an affirmation of how history can empower Indigenous people. American Indian and First Nations peoples have not always been empowered by history or museums. In a number of ways, the tribal museum exists to contest and critique colonial notions of American and Canadian history that have been so disempowering to tribal nations. Revising history is not their only purpose. Tribal museums must serve the varied needs of Indigenous communities, whether that means undertaking historic and cultural preservation projects; teaching children from the tribe; restoring dignity to elders; or educating a broader public on Indian history, politics, culture, and sovereignty through tourism. Tribal museums remind us that North America is still a place of hundreds of diverse nations, each possessing distinct historical traditions and ways of interpreting and defining history, with dynamic cultural practices that predate the nation-states of the United States and Canada.

The tribal museum is not a new institution in Indian Country. The first tribal museums in the United States emerged in the mid-twentieth century. The Osage Tribal Museum in Pawhuska, Oklahoma, was constructed as a Works Progress Administration (WPA) and Civilian Conservation Corps (CCC) project that opened to the public in 1938 and today is on the National Register of Historic Places. And the Museum of the Cherokee in North Carolina opened a decade later. The Mille Lacs Indian Museum in Onamia, Minnesota, is located on Ojibwe land; but it has been a collaborative project between the band and the Minnesota Historical Society since the early 1960s and is a state historic site as well as a tribal museum. Like Mille Lacs, the Southeast Alaska Indian Cultural Center has developed a critical partnership outside of the community. The cultural center is a Tlingit nonprofit organization but is housed in a national park visitor center in Sitka after its establishment in 1969.

The tribal museum movement has steadily grown since the early days of the 1960s and 1970s—a crucial era when Indigenous leaders, activists, and intellectuals demanded change in historical narratives and when the first departments of American Indian studies organized in American universities. Now a whole generation has grown up with these ideas, and some have devoted careers to writing our own versions of history, telling our own stories in museum exhibits, for reasons important to our families, communities, and tribal nations. The tribal museum has flourished in that milieu. The second wave of tribal museums, including the Makah Cultural and Research Center on the Olympic Peninsula, opened in 1979 in the aftermath of the excavation of the remarkable archaeological site of Ozette. The Seneca-Iroquois National Museum in Salamanca, New York, dates from 1977; and the Yakama Nation Cultural Heritage Center in Toppenish, Washington, opened in 1980. The most recent wave of tribal museums has grown because of the impetus provided by the Native American Graves Protection and Repatriation Act of 1990. The material benefits made possible by gaming have also played a significant role, the most prominent example of this being the Mashantucket Pequot Museum and Research Center in Connecticut, whose tribal museum and research center is a 308,000-square-foot complex that consists of a gallery, classrooms, an auditorium, a library, and a children's library, as well as storage and conservation facilities.

Tribal museums share some of the same objectives as conventional museums, such as public history education; but the practice for which they are celebrated, extensive community involvement and collaboration, helps reproduce tribal values within the museum setting. Today we have well over one hundred of these institutions in the United States and Canada, and new tribal museums open every year. Tribal museums have been an important site of collaboration, one that has successfully engaged a new generation of tribal leaders and Indigenous intellectuals.

Brian Vallo, the former lieutenant governor of the Pueblo of Acoma and director of the Historic Preservation Office, was the founding director of the Sky City Cultural Center and Haak'u Museum, which opened in 2006. Vallo always emphasizes the importance of the seventy-nine focus groups they held at Acoma to develop the new museum, some of which included children, artists, elders, and spiritual leaders from the community. The meetings were crucial to every aspect of the museum, including the design, which incorporates historic pueblo architecture but also shows the influence of newer reservation architecture such as HUD houses and trailers. Design aesthetics that reflect Indigenous principles are a hallmark of tribal museums, a point of self-esteem for tribes, and an indication to visitors that they are on tribal ground. Community collaboration, an area in which tribal museums have been so innovative and successful, is a valuable model for mainstream institutions that also work with Indigenous communities and history.

These scholarly essays highlight the exciting history and present the vitality of tribal museums from all regions of Indian Country. Tribal museum research is a rich area of study, with the potential to be an important lens for understanding tribal communities' views of their own pasts, their conflicts and resolutions, and the dynamics of cultural and political sovereignty. Together, these essays point out that tribal museums are doing more than preserving a past and debunking outdated narratives of Indian history, as important as these goals may be. Tribal museums are Indigenous spaces that both reflect Native values and knowledge systems and languages, and work toward the preservation of living cultures. Tribal museums, while rooted in a Western institutional tradition, are furthering goals of decolonization and tribal sovereignty. They are museums, but they are also significant centers for community life today.

Gwyneira Isaac's essay, "Responsibilities toward Knowledge: The Zuni Museum and the Mediation of Different Knowledge Systems," presents an essential historical and cultural context for understanding the tribal museum on the Zuni Reservation in New Mexico. As Isaac explains, the Zuni system of knowledge values responsibility, from which ritual knowledge is inseparable. Zuni ideas have often come into conflict with twentieth-century anthropologists, many of whom intruded on Zuni beliefs and philosophy in dramatic ways through their ethnographic practices. Anthropologists collected knowledge from the Zunis by exhaustively photographing Zuni ceremonies, and scholar Frank Cushing went so far as to duplicate Zuni religious paraphernalia. Isaac argues that the tribal museum in Zuni is informed by this history. The work going on at the tribal museum in Zuni today includes the development of innovative "cultural maps," created by Zuni artists and elders. This supports the tribal museum's goal of transmitting Zuni knowledge of places in their landscape to young people in ways that respect Zuni ideas about responsibility. Only knowledgeable practitioners who privilege oral history interpret the maps to young people. The tribal museum in Zuni is able to meet the needs of the community by educating children in Zuni culture and philosophy, which protects their lands and resources for the future and advances Zuni sovereignty.

In "Reimagining Tribal Sovereignty through Tribal History: Museums, Libraries, and Archives in the Klamath River Region," Brian Isaac Daniels addresses three recent tribal museums, libraries and archives, the influence of two court cases in their development, and the tribes' need "to create and to control outward representations of their culture." Daniels studied the Hoopa Tribal Museum, a small museum open to the public, which preserves and cares for tribal objects in ways that are useful to the Hoopa. Unlike most mainstream museums, objects at the Hoopa are also for ceremony, not just display. Daniels' second case study is of the Yuroks, who like many tribes in Indian Country organized a Tribal Historic Preservation Office, and their attempt to identify and preserve historic, cultural, and sacred sites in the Yurok landscape. Daniels also considers Shasta, a non-federally recognized tribe with no reservation, which developed a tribal archive to house enrollment records; census materials; and scholarly, popular, and newspaper writings about Shasta people. Daniels argues that, whether located in a national capital or upon a remote reservation, tribal museums and archives share a similar aim in aspiring to "the dream of total knowledge," but this might be contested by the people he studied. Tribes in the Klamath River region, along with other American Indians, value the knowledge held by community members, elders, and others invested with sacred knowledge about their way of life, landscapes, and resources. As useful as tribes find tribal museums, libraries, and archives in their ongoing struggle for cultural and political sovereignty, knowledge still resides primarily in the community.

Kristina Ackley, a Wisconsin Oneida scholar, has written about her nation's tribal museum in the essay "The Oneida Nation Museum: Creating a Space for Haudenosaunee Kinship and Identity." Ackley reflects on the history of the Oneida Nation Museum in Wisconsin, founded in 1970, placing it in the context of Oneida history. The Wisconsin Oneidas maintain their identity as Haudenosaunee people, though their homeland and kin are in New York and the Northeast. The longhouse at the Oneida museum, Ackley writes, is part of a historical narrative that "testifies to an ongoing revitalization"; is a "marker of identity" that connects the nation to their past in the East; and presents an "official narrative" of Oneida history and culture. The museum has been a positive presence in the community; but controversies have emerged, including one issue resolved over time regarding the display of medicine masks. Ackley concludes, "the community is the context necessary to understand the exhibits" at their "museum for tribal people," though the museum also functions to educate the public about Wisconsin Indian history.

In "Museums as Sites of Decolonization: Truth Telling in National and Tribal Museums," Amy Lonetree calls for truth telling in museums, arguing that the National Museum of the American Indian, despite extensive collaborations with tribal communities throughout the Americas, fails on many levels because historical exhibits do not contain the "hard truths of the specifics of Native-white relations," leaving "Native people unable to heal from historical trauma." Lonetree and many critics have pointed out that the journey to the inauguration of the new museum has not been without its share of controversies and that many dissatisfied, talented Indian staff members departed the museum before its inauguration, feeling it fell short of its aspiration to be the "Museum Different." Lonetree finds that a better conduit for truth telling is the tribal museum, especially the Ziibiwing Center for Anishinabe Culture and Lifeways in Michigan, which she cites as a good example for its decolonizing practices. Ziibiwing succeeds, according to Lonetree, because oral histories form the basis for its historical interpretation and because its exhibits are organized in a way that is respectful of Ojibwe spiritual traditions and prophecies.

The development of so many new tribal museums in recent decades is unexpected, given the conflicts and contradictions that are involved in the adoption of this most Western of institutions. The tribal museum has provided another outlet for Indian creativity, remaking a colonial institution in ways that preserve the fundamental structures of tribal society and advance sovereignty. Kristina Ackley writes that the tribal museum directly confronts "the nationalizing intentions of Western museums." In my own state of Minnesota, the Mille Lacs Band of Ojibwe rebuilt and reinterpreted their tribal museum simultaneous to a case the tribe was pursuing over treaty rights, which appeared before the U.S. Supreme Court in 1999. In 1990 the Mille Lacs Band of Ojibwe sued the state of Minnesota, which argued that treaty rights to hunt, fish, and gather over ceded lands no longer existed once Minnesota entered the union. In 1999 the Supreme Court rejected the state's argument, which was a great victory for tribal sovereignty. The court case no doubt influenced the redevelopment of the tribal museum, especially how the tribe represented their history to visitors. The tribal museum at Mille Lacs is a reminder that Indian people live in a complex world, where politics often inform decisions and influence our narratives of history. In this struggle, the tribal museum is an important Indigenous space where Native people control and shape policies and exhibits with unprecedented tribal community cooperation and involvement.

9

Tsiʔniyukwalihoʔtʌ, the Oneida Nation Museum

Creating a Space for Haudenosaunee Kinship and Identity

KRISTINA ACKLEY

Visitors driving to *Tsiʔniyukwalihoʔʌ* ("This is our way"), the Oneida Nation Museum (ONM) in Oneida, Wisconsin, will notice several things as they approach.[1] The ONM is located just downhill from a tribal senior-housing facility and from a row of low, vacant buildings that used to house the former Oneida Health Care Center. Turning into the driveway, a pink neon Open sign is visible just above the ONM front door, somewhat incongruous with the otherwise-understated wood building that is surrounded by trees. A small garden is well tended in the back of the museum, and at the end of the parking area there is a marked trail that leads into a wooded area. Probably most striking about the setting of the ONM is the longhouse (see fig. 13), about ten feet wide by sixteen feet long, just in front of the main entrance. The longhouse replica, made of a wood frame and wood shingles, has occupied different places on the museum site throughout the years. In its current placement, visitors to the ONM cannot help but pass by the longhouse.

The longhouse replica (*Kanúses nékaʔikʌ*) immediately marks the space as Oneida. It conveys a multifaceted meaning of both place and a belief system. The Wisconsin Oneidas are a distinct people and consider themselves a nation. However, they also participate in a shared cultural system that is based on the teachings of the Peacemaker and Handsome Lake, and they recognize a spiritual kinship with other Haudenosaunee people (also known as the Iroquois Confederacy, or Six Nations). The ceremonies of the longhouse are the outward and public expression of a living spirituality. The longhouse permeates every aspect of life, proscribes ethics, and helps one deal with hardships; it has been called, "the highest form of political consciousness."[2] Longhouse spirituality reinforces the social life of the community and distinguishes its participants from others. While the replica outside the ONM is not used for ceremonies, it is still associated with the belief system and is used by ONM staff and the community for a variety of functions. The longhouse and the ONM represent tsiʔniyukwalihoʔtʌ or "the ways" of the people for Oneida and Haudenosaunee people. It is part of kaʔnikuli·yó ("the Good Mind"), which has been described as a process toward balance, harmony, and peace. Kaʔnikuli·yó is not a state of being or the ultimate goal, but a discipline toward peace.[3] It requires continual reflection and work. The kaʔnikuli·yó provides a way in which to mediate dissension in a framework of cultural resilience and nation building. When the Wisconsin Oneidas refer to the longhouse, they mean not only the physical structure but also a way of life and much of what encompasses tsiʔniyukwalihoʔtʌ. Additionally, it is shorthand that refers to the people who take part in the ceremonies.

Inside the ONM there is also a smaller structure that is meant to resem-

13. The longhouse (Kanúses nékaʔikʌ) located just outside the Oneida Nation Museum. Photo courtesy Linda Torres.

ble the longhouse, in the hands-on area, where visitors are encouraged to view and handle items such as lacrosse sticks, pottery, clothing, and rattles.

The longhouse connotes security — it is a shelter, after all. If the replica outside the ONM seems exposed to the elements, it also gives the impression of having protection from them. It seems simultaneously *of* the surroundings as well as existing separately from them. Inside the structure are low benches, fire pits, and smoke holes. It is a simulation, not nearly as large as the current community longhouse at Oneida, Wisconsin, but rather a model that is meant to evoke the sentiment of tsiʔniyukwalihoʔtʌ. Because it is necessary to rebuild the structure every seven years or so, it also seems a transitory yet enduring sign of Oneida culture and history.

It is important to view the longhouse replica in terms of the overall history of the Wisconsin Oneidas. Assimilation policies and removal from their Aboriginal territory resulted in the absence of a community longhouse in Wisconsin for nearly a century (though personal rituals and some smaller ceremonies remained). However, the longhouse outside the ONM does not signify a memorial to its absence from the community, nor is it a marker of the past. Instead, the longhouse replica testifies to an ongoing revitalization among the Wisconsin Oneidas. Given the weighted meaning of the longhouse way of life and government and its relationship to the Wisconsin Oneidas, it is evidence of how the ONM constructs a historical narrative that is represented to both tribal members and non-Oneidas. This study discusses the mediating of the space of the ONM and the relationship to the broader Haudenosaunee community that it represents. Overall, the ONM functions as a marker of identity that links the Oneidas to New York. It is a site that places the Oneidas both *in* and *of* Wisconsin.

This paper focuses on the meaning of the ONM as a cultural center for the Wisconsin Oneida community. It is informed by my tribal membership as a Wisconsin Oneida and internships in the mid-1990s working with the collections of the ONM. An important aspect of this analysis questions how a museum can be created by and intended for the community and subsequently how it is recognized as a medium for transmitting tribal knowledge. The space of the ONM is of authority; it is one of several community interpreters and upholders of Oneida ideals and beliefs. The ONM is a guardian of cultural values that helps make it possible for the Wisconsin Oneidas to connect with their past in New York and strengthen their relationship to other Haudenosaunee people. By giving a tribally sanctioned and official narrative coherence to their history and culture, the ONM operates as a touchstone through which tribal members can affirm their Haudenosaunee identity. It protects as well as keeps the past. Yet it is not a static monument to ancient times, for the ONM also shapes how people engage with their sense of self as contemporary Oneidas.

Removal: Oneidas of the Homeland to Oneidas in Wisconsin

Although the Oneidas were known from their first arrival in Wisconsin and until the middle of the twentieth century as the "New York Indians," they also became very much the historical product of their experiences in Wisconsin. They were viewed as somehow separate from other Oneidas. The distance was in both geography and philosophy. There are some who contend that the Wisconsin Oneidas are very much different from other Oneidas, that their settlement in Wisconsin after removal was a permanent and impermeable break with other Haudenosaunee. In this view, the Wisconsin Oneidas gave up any chance of returning as a community to their homeland. It is a Native nation, but its persistence as Haudenosaunee is questioned today by a few.[4] In order to understand how the ONM strenuously and effectively contests this interpretation of their relationship to the Haudenosaunee, it is necessary to examine the factors that led to their removal to Wisconsin.

The Oneidas, or Onʌyoteʔʌa·ká ("People of the Standing Stone"), are one of six nations that comprise the Haudenosaunee.[5] Eighteenth-century treaties recognized Oneida territory as a large swath of land that ran through what is now central New York State, some five million acres. Because a particularly desired transportation route known as the Oneida Carrying Place was in this territory, non-Natives began to settle there immediately. The pressure for Oneida removal was intense, particularly between 1785 and 1815.[6] Land speculators, increased settlement due to the rising population of New York State, the influence of Christian missionaries, and differences within the Oneida Nation all contributed to Oneida removal.[7]

Today, there are three main Oneida communities: in New York (2,000 members); near Southwold, Ontario (5,000 members of the Thames Oneidas); and in Wisconsin (15,000 members). In addition there are Oneidas in other territories, including Grand River (a Six Nations territory in Canada), as well as reservations in Oklahoma. The majority of Oneidas have a long history of alienation from their Aboriginal land base. The first formal removals to Wisconsin took place in a series of events between 1820 and 1838. Shortly afterward, more Oneidas removed to a settlement near Southwold, Ontario, between 1839 and 1845. In addition, because non-Native settlers refused to allow them to remain, many of the Oneidas who stayed in New York State after 1845 moved a short distance from Oneida territory to live as guests at Onondaga, home to the Clan Mothers and the Chiefs Council of the Confederacy. The people in each of the Oneida communities formed deep attachments to their new places and in many ways became separate communities with their own histories and ways of being. However, continued Oneida mobility and travel between Oneida communities fostered feelings of kinship and a belief in a unified Oneida Nation, if not in the present circumstances or in the near future, at least as a narrative of the past that each shared and believed in.

Travel has often been viewed as a displacement of Indigenous cultural identity and values, as it seemingly threatens a place-bound vision of Native people that depicts them as being part of the landscape. In contrast to this view, travel is an intrinsic part of most Oneidas' identities, both individually and as a common way of understanding themselves as a group. Travel has decisively informed a historical narrative that stresses the ways in which mobility was a part of many Oneidas' lives before the diaspora. This belief was sustained after removal as many Oneidas traveled and lived interchangeably at the different Oneida communities as well as other Haudenosaunee territories. Mobility has not erased a feeling for the homeland for those Oneidas who live in settlements outside New York State, as travel among Wisconsin, Canada, and New York have strengthened connections to the homeland for all Oneidas. As evidence of a common idea of the homeland, all three Oneida communities have been active and in many ways have shared in a land claim for the Aboriginal land base in New York State for much of the twentieth century.

The Oneidas brought to their new homes many of their belief systems of community well-being and kinship relationships that had existed prior to removal, alongside cultural practices such as planting corn, beans, and squash. When they arrived in Wisconsin, their hereditary chiefs and political system were in flux. Once in Wisconsin they did not openly practice the cyclical ceremonies of the longhouse, though some continued to practice in secret. Political meetings continued to be held in the Oneida language well into the middle of the twentieth century, though it is clear that Oneida political beliefs and governing structures were in transition and that those changes further developed in their new environment in Wisconsin.[8] These transformations became further embedded in Wisconsin as the community became more the Oneidas *of* Wisconsin and many regarded their tenure there as more or less permanent. Much of this was a necessary component for nation building in Wisconsin, and the difficulties of removal had made that clear to anyone who thought of simply leaving and going to yet another place. Any further tribal discord thus needed to be worked out in Wisconsin, not an easy feat for a community under stress from removal and with differing views and responses to American colonialism.

Some community adaptations have contributed to a view of the Wisconsin Oneidas as being a community that is mired in conflict, with increasing assimilation as the result. In 1974 Campisi observed in his research that the Wisconsin "Oneida is a Christian society. There is no longhouse nor is any of the Iroquois ceremonial cycle practiced."[9] While this may be a question of access to Longhouse practitioners as opposed to a definitive statement on the belief systems of all Oneidas in Wisconsin, it sums up one accepted assessment of the Wisconsin Oneidas as Christian and assimilated. Others have emphasized the factionalism among the Oneidas and Haudenosaunee, particularly in the period prior to removal.[10] For much of the twentieth century, the open and public absence of longhouse ceremonies and hereditary chiefs and Clan Mothers leads many to assume that the Wisconsin Oneidas have had a substantive and absolute break with the Haudenosaunee, of which citizenship is in part based on participation in the longhouse.[11]

Transnational issues within the Confederacy have contributed to this image of the Wisconsin Oneidas. The Oneidas, as a whole, occupy a contested role in the Confederacy. Their assistance to the colonists during the Revolutionary War has been represented by the Wisconsin and New York Oneidas as something to be proud of and as indicative of their long-lasting relationship with the United States. Conversely, others have framed this support as a potential weakening of the Confederacy.[12] In addition, the Wisconsin and New York Oneidas' aggressive economic pursuits in casino gaming and their adaptive forms of government (the oxymoronic, "newly traditional" structure of the New York Oneidas and the elected Indian Reorganization Act form of government of the Wisconsin Oneidas) have made them an easy mark for those who feel that the actions by the Wisconsin and New York Oneida communities threaten Haudenosaunee sovereignty. The Wisconsin Oneidas have had to define their identities not only in the context of their own community, or to other Oneidas, but also in the larger Haudenosaunee world. As a community, they have largely objected to outside characterizations of them as assimilated and cut off from the Confederacy. Nowhere is this more evident than in the exhibits of the ONM.

The Oneida Nation Museum: Creating Separate Space in a Tribal Museum

The Wisconsin Oneidas have worked through this discussion of identity in the sphere of the ONM. They have tried to make their museum for tribal people and to accommodate and disseminate a narrative that says that the Wisconsin Oneidas remain Haudenosaunee. Challenging these attempts is the institutional nature of museums, a tool of American culture that has been hostile to Native people.

Western museums are a powerful colonizing force. Many have long placed Native Americans on one end of a continuum as being savage and the antithesis of Euro-American civility. Robert Berkhofer has argued, "Whether evaluated as noble or ignoble, whether seen as exotic or degraded, the Indian as an image was always alien to the White."[13] Western museum exhibits typically exoticize and distance the visitor from Indigenous people, placing the Native irrevocably in the past. In this view, the Indian was what the white man was not, the polar opposite of how white Americans defined themselves. U.S. museums added legitimacy to these cultural values even as they disseminated them, and are an important tool in upholding ideas about the exotic other.[14]

Scholars have viewed the Haudenosaunee and their nationalist expressions of sovereignty through this evolutionary lens, placing them on a linear historical timeline that was somewhat further in progress to other Indians, given the value the colonial powers placed on the political structure of the Confederacy; but the Iroquois were still viewed as well behind the white man. Some Haudenosaunee people actively sought to use and adapt this image. Wisconsin Oneida author Laura Cornelius Kellogg argued in 1920, in her book *Our Democracy and the American Indian*, that the concept of democracy had its roots in the Haudenosaunee, "who planted the first seed of civilization in the land—just as my fathers who first dreamed of democracy on this continent."[15]

Lewis Henry Morgan, whose 1851 *League of the Ho-dé-no-sau-nee, Iroquois* is often seen as the first modern ethnographic study, saw white men as the successors to the Iroquois. This idea of the vanishing Indian meant that Morgan felt free to take on attributes of the Haudenosaunee in a fraternal literary society, donning Native dress in what Deloria has called "playing Indian."[16] The idea of evolution necessitates a comparison, and Indigenous cultures invariably come up as lacking on the model used by early anthropologists and museum curators.

U.S. museums are critical in upholding certain ideas of the nation, for they are one tool by which a community from divergent backgrounds is able to "imagine" a shared past and future, to borrow from Benedict Anderson. They provide an avenue for building a nation-state with a coherent view of the past.[17] Exoticism and primativism subsequently manifest in the ways that museums exhibit people from other cultures, as this reinforces a view of the nation as one that is uncontested in its primacy and legitimacy. In most cases, this evolutionary view of cultures excuses conquest and colonialism, presenting such histories as being inevitable (if tragic). Manifest Destiny and perceptions of the frontier contribute to a shared national ignorance of the harm such belief systems have on Indigenous people, as they are translated into policies such as allotment, the reservation system, and boarding schools.[18]

Tribal museums are charged with the difficult task of challenging officially sanctioned views of history that most non-Natives unquestioningly believe; simultaneously, they try to create and maintain a place for their own people to learn about their stories of the past. They directly confront the nationalizing intentions of Western museums that treat Natives as savage and extinct, existing only as a footnote to a U.S. national story of exceptionalism.

In the late nineteenth and early twentieth century, concerned with physical survival and the continuance of their communities and ways of life, Native people often entrusted museums with items of significant cultural patrimony for fear they would end up in private collections. In these cases, Native people did not receive them back for many years, if at all.[19] People working on behalf of museums commissioned, bought, and outright stole from Indigenous communities in a frenzy of collecting from "vanishing" cultures at the end of the nineteenth century.[20] This has led to a great distrust of museums, which are rightfully seen as part of a larger imperial project, places exclusively for non-Natives. The image of the museum as a place that holds your ancestors' bodies and epitomizes the cultural theft of your people is not a place that you are likely to visit.

It has been very difficult to change this representation of Indigenous people in museums that are controlled by non-Natives, though in recent years museum theory and practice have incorporated a critique of exhibitions of Indigenous people. Museum practices may incorporate such new techniques as shared curatorial practices with Indigenous people.[21] Although the authority of museums has been contested as a result of this critique and shared practices, many tribes found that even if they had positive relationships with the non-Native staff of museums, they still were in an unequal power relationship that contributed to the continued dispossession of their people. Legislation and policies, particularly the Native American Graves Protection and Repatriation Act of 1990, have not solved this problem. For some museums, there is still a belief that Native people will not care for cultural items properly, which in Western terms is focused mainly on preservation. Some curators may no doubt cringe at the thought of repatriated items turning to dust on a remote mesa, unable to accept that those items are completing their life cycle. In this way, "the museum became an inescapable contact (conflict) zone."[22]

In contrast, tribal museums can provide the space for the representation of more authentic narratives about the past of Indigenous people and point the way toward the future. They provide an important voice for the tribe's stories, history, values, and beliefs. In his study of the Mashantucket

Pequot Museum and Research Center in Connecticut, which opened in 1998 and is today the largest of the tribal museums in the United States, Bodinger de Uriarte argues that "Pequots continue to develop a narrative of cultural continuity and belonging, both for a reinforced sense of community on the reservation and as a counter to critiques of their cultural legitimacy."[23]

Though the literature on the relationship of Indigenous people to non-Native museums is substantial, as is a critical analysis of the portrayal of Indigenous people in museums, research on tribally controlled and operated museums is comparatively smaller. One reason for limited (though growing) sources that focus on specific tribal museums may be that they are a relatively recent development, tied to a rise in the past few decades in tribal control over the way their history and culture is represented to the outside world. For many of these tribes, increased economic development from their tribally owned casinos has allowed them the opportunity to build museums and cultural centers that are focused on the community as well as on research and exhibition. These places are visited by tribal members and scholars interested in their resources, as well as by tourists and educational groups.

It was in the context of countering non-Native museums that the Wisconsin Oneidas decided to open their own tribal museum. The ONM was created under a Bicenntennial Grant in 1976 and opened its doors in 1979. It holds a significant collection of Oneida material (the Shako:wi Cultural Center of the Oneida Indian Nation of New York State is another museum devoted specifically to the Oneidas). The collection was started with community contributions as well as with the purchase of items from local artists. The ONM permanent holdings were later supplemented with a large purchase of Oneida materials from the now-defunct Turtle Museum in Niagara Falls, New York. The ONM's staff particularly prize a six-foot man made entirely of cornhusks by Oneida artist Irvin Chrisjohn, while the general collection includes some 1,500 material culture objects (including black ash baskets, Iroquois pottery, raised-beaded traditional clothing, water drums, and snowsnakes), 500 photographic materials, 50 audiotapes and 500 videotapes containing an ongoing oral history project with Oneida elders, and a papers archives.[24]

The ONM was among the first tribal museums. In 1989 there were only twenty-five tribally owned and operated museums. Today, museums and cultural centers, created and controlled by Native Americans, have experienced a period of expansion and construction—one source estimated there to be about 120 tribal museums in 2005 and many more in the planning stages.[25]

The Opening of the Oneida Nation Museum: Building a National Identity Linked to the Haudenosaunee

The Wisconsin Oneidas purposely called their new museum the Oneida *Nation* Museum. Doing so asked people to think of the Wisconsin Oneidas as a nation, and the ONM complicates that by expressing in their exhibit space and through sponsored events the idea that they are a nation linked to the Haudenosaunee. A great deal of attention has been paid to the ways in which people imagine and construct an ordered narrative that allows people to conceive of a shared past and identify things in common that they might not otherwise conceptualize. To define this as a social process is essential to understanding the ways in which Indigenous communities have defined themselves as nations. Too often Native Americans have been relegated to the periphery of the modern nation-state, either romanticized or had their assimilation sanitized by arguments that it was for their own good. A large part of American national identity has this myth as its bulwark. When an Indigenous nation is viewed as a cultural artifact—as opposed to solely a political, economic, or geographic one—the subsequent analysis allows for an inclusion of those who are excluded from this narrative through erasure, enforced invisibility (hiding in plain sight), or outright decimation.

Tribal museums stress a national identity by telling stories that are based on their unique cultures and histories. The Haudenosaunee have been active nationalists from their early dealings with outsiders—viewing themselves as individual nations that are linked politically and spiritually as a confederacy. The image of the Confederacy as a government, military power, culture, and spiritual authority defined the sovereignty of its member nations in their interactions with outside groups. In addition, a number of activists in the twentieth century claimed these nationalist ideals in grassroots political activism, and others continue to do so. One name by which they are known, Six Nations, stresses this nationalist emphasis. The Oneidas also sought to build a nation out of the extreme dislocation and diaspora that brought them to Wisconsin, balancing the life they had left with the one they would live in the new reservation.[26]

In many ways, the Oneida reservation at Duck Creek, Wisconsin, is both geographically and psychologically far from the homelands of New York State. Travel and mobility of the Oneida people keep both a connection to the Aboriginal territory and a Haudenosaunee identity possible for Wisconsin Oneida members. One way the Wisconsin Oneida government has sought to remain close to its Aboriginal territory is to sponsor what they call "Homeland Tours," first held in the mid-1980s. These tours take Oneida community members (usually from both the Wisconsin and Thames communities) by bus to sites in New York State to visit and experience places of historic significance to the Oneidas. In a video made in 1996 that documented the tour, these sites were recorded as powerful places that still remained so for the Wisconsin Oneidas. The hold of the homeland was palpable, evident in the tears and emotions that overtook many of the participants. For some people, it was surprising that they would be affected that viscerally by a place.[27] It is the same for members of the Thames Oneida community.[28] In 2007 ONM staff members accompanied the Homeland Tour, setting up a photo display and small exhibit for the participants to view while in New York.

Audra Simpson discusses how the meaning of nationalism is translated and transformed daily "on the ground" by those narratives in the community where boundaries and borders are understood to be linked to policy, culture, tradition, location, and a wide variety of affairs for the Kahnawake Mohawks.[29] The Wisconsin Oneidas are very similar. Many individuals on the Homeland Tours had not realized how connected they were to both the places in New York State and to other Oneidas from different communities until they traveled there as a group. Records from the Homeland Tours provide accounts of nationhood from the participants, which are explicitly informed by their relationships to other Oneidas and Haudenosaunee people.[30]

The interplay and stress between the local (Wisconsin Oneidas), national (the three Oneida communities), and transnational (Haudenosaunee) may be challenged and reconciled by community processes. Some of the characteristics appear to be immutable, while some ideas of identity are much more fluid. Some of this is directly related to the mobility of the community and its members, as travel affects the ways in which they view authenticity. Primarily, the interpretation of Haudenosaunee identity has thus far been composed of largely conservative values, intent on proper adherence to the teachings of Handsome Lake and the Peacemaker.

Challenges to the Oneida Nation Museum: Reconciling Competing Discourses

There is an ineffable quality to tsi?ʌ·niyukwaliho?tʌ, likely because of its multiple meanings. It is important to emphasize the sometimes impossible task of museums to present a coherent narrative out of what are always fragmented and at times conflicting stories. Tribal museums are no different in this respect, and the process by which the onm mediated these divisions and incorporated these stories was complicated at the outset.

One of the first exhibits of the onm was directly challenged by some of the Wisconsin Oneidas. At the center of the dispute was an exhibit of Haudenosaunee Medicine Masks, along with accompanying information that explained their healing roles in the Longhouse society. By virtue of providing the information to outsiders, the exhibit seemed to place the entities in the past, which was an affront to Wisconsin Oneidas who were active in establishing the longhouse in the community. In addition, the exhibition and explanation of the entities are forbidden, for Haudenosaunee Medicine Masks are viewed not as static objects but instead are imbued with a force that must be carefully used only by those who are trained to do so. Some people have called the entities "False Face" masks, though the Hatuwi and longhouse members consider this to be a derogatory term. They are instead known as the Grandfathers or the Ancient Ones and are used only by those individuals within that belief system. Any further knowledge of the medicine masks lies with its members, and boundaries on their interpretation and knowledge transfer are enforced strictly. To transgress these ideas is to violate Haudenosaunee beliefs and sovereignty.[31]

Members of the onm Advisory Board and staff responded to the community critique by arguing that these particular Medicine Masks were made for commercial purposes, not spiritual ones. They defended the exhibit as one of scholarly interest, one that was not meant to infringe on the belief systems of tribal members.[32] That they were exhibited was illustrative of significant differences and competing ideas in how the Wisconsin Oneidas would represent themselves and their history in the ONM. Since many Wisconsin Oneidas did not practice this belief system at the time of the ONM opening (though they have steadily grown in numbers since then), there may have been an assumption that it was acceptable to exhibit them. In this situation, neither intent nor Oneida control over the ONM mattered to longhouse community members, for they would have protested the exhibition in any case.

This was a serious dispute on acceptable knowledge transmission that needed to be reconciled before the ONM could be accepted by the community. If the Wisconsin Oneidas were to consider themselves Haudenosaunee, continuing the exhibit might be an obstacle, since most Haudenosaunee are in agreement on the prohibition of exhibiting masks. The Chiefs Council of the Confederacy, the traditional governing body of the Haudenosaunee, has clarified their stance on the display of medicine masks. It leaves no doubt that the exhibition is forbidden, as is the pursuit of knowledge about them by those who were not members of the longhouse medicine society, stating, "The exhibition of masks by museums does not serve to enlighten the public regarding the culture of the Haudenosaunee as such as exhibition violates the intended purpose of the mask and contributes to the desecration of the sacred image." In addition, knowledge is proscribed and "the non-Indian public does not have the right to examine, interpret, or present these beliefs, functions, and duties of the secret medicine societies of the Haudenosaunee."[33] Those who protested the exhibit also did so in terms that challenged the standard anthropological view that every part of a culture is open to the public, in part to provide the opportunity for community dialogue on the issue.[34]

The decision to display the masks (or, at a minimum, exhibit photographs or written descriptions of their use) is problematic, for scholars have already written about them extensively.[35] Non-Natives were not always excluded from ceremonies of the longhouse, particularly in the first half of the twentieth century, as they are generally today. Many of these studies were researched before the 1970s, and some seem concerned more with an ethnographic documentation of the form of the ceremonies and the Medicine Masks and less with their healing function and power in the longhouse. In many of these studies, there is virtually no self-reflexive examination of what the prohibition means or of what breaking the prohibition does to the belief system of the community. In the early days of the exhibit, there was an attempt to explain the motivations behind the exhibit by ONM staff, which at least demonstrated an understanding of the impact the public exhibition would have on the community.[36] Because some outside scholars are less accountable to the communities they research, they may have had the luxury to disregard the impact of this dissemination of knowledge in a way that the ONM, as a tribal museum controlled by the community, did not.

To separate the medicine masks from the community in which they function renders the practice and the belief system incomprehensible. In recent years, the Grandfathers have been repatriated back to Haudenosaunee nations from several major non-Native museums, although many more still remain outside the community, held in various museums, galleries, and private homes. In addition, there are still individuals who make them for commercial sale.[37]

There is a healthy level of respect for the Grandfathers, for to do otherwise is to disturb the balance and harmony for which a community strives. This is common in other Indigenous societies as well. For these reasons, Wisconsin Oneida members protested the opening of the exhibit at the ONM in 1979 and at various times afterward. Linda E. Oxendine, in her discussion of the ONM and the controversy surrounding the exhibit, relates how one Oneida community member attributed the exhibit to a de facto boycott of the ONM by many tribal members in the early years of the museum's operation. Tribal members did not want to enter into a place with such an exhibit. They were afraid.[38]

Tensions between those who understood the history of the medicine masks as something primarily outside of Wisconsin and therefore in the past and those who are reclaiming this belief system is still evident. Many tribal members do not wish to directly discuss the episode.[39]

Ideas of Authenticity Translated into the Exhibits of the Oneida Nation Museum

Shadowing this controversy, and indeed fueling it, was a parallel revitalization in the 1970s of the longhouse ceremonies, first openly held in 1983 after more than a century in Wisconsin without them.[40] The ceremonies imbue those practitioners with spiritual authority in issues related to the Longhouse and the relationship of the Wisconsin Oneidas with the rest of the Confederacy. Faced with intense outside pressures for change and mindful of the ongoing effects of colonialism, tribal members who participated in these early ceremonies were particularly conservative in upholding traditional ways of being. They maintained boundaries in order to more effectively implement the longhouse in the Wisconsin Oneida community. As such, they were strenuously against the exhibition of the Haudenosaunee medicine masks.

They succeeded in affecting change at the ONM. Responding to community complaints, a new board of directors at the ONM eventually took down the display, effectively ending much of the conflict; although, until 1993 a painting remained that presented stories about how the entities were brought to the people.[41] Today there is no overt discussion of the masks in the exhibits at the ONM, though mention of healing ceremonies is made in a painting in the small longhouse exhibit that houses the hands-on area of the ONM. To illustrate how completely the controversy was reconciled by the ONM, it is worth noting that some of those individuals who protested the initial exhibit later became employed by the ONM and the Oneida Cultural Heritage Department, which is the governmental division that houses the museum, language program, historical research, repatriation, the library, and the historic preservation program. The protesters were incorporated into the administration of those cultural institutions that preserve and shape the ways in which the Oneidas of Wisconsin view their history and move toward their future. For many, their values are essentially a merging of Wisconsin Oneida and Haudenosaunee traditions. In addition, some of those people who at first supported the exhibit came to cede authority to those who have more knowledge of such things, viewing it as a struggle they do not understand and therefore do not have the ability or the desire about which to make decisions. Though the discourse of the Haudenosaunee medicine masks was primarily within the tribal community, it was inextricably linked to outside factors.

The ONM eventually took to their responsibilities respectfully and diligently. During my brief tenure at the ONM, as a college student more than a decade ago, the medicine masks were being cared for in accordance with the wishes of the traditional community. In a period of transition, they were still technically accessible by museum staff but were subject to unique curatorial practices that took into account their status as animate beings who needed certain things: air, respect, corn. They were located very near me while I was working on an inventory of the ONM collection. However, I felt no need or desire to work with them, because even without a clear understanding at that time of their meaning and relevance, I felt wary of them.

Ultimately, the tribal dispute in this case was a positive social force. The outcome and mediation of the conflict was not guaranteed, but it is indicative of the ways that the Wisconsin Oneidas are able to reconcile conflict and incorporate dissent in the community. Some of the underlying opposition was not fully resolved, and it is unrealistic to assume that a diverse community will agree on everything. In this way, factionalism can be a seen as continual, if episodic, rather than as a solely negative force. Though some might view those people who initially supported the exhibit as having been assimilated and those who did not as somehow "more" Oneida, this study cannot support that claim. Acculturation and tradition are not fixed positions that can be assigned to certain groups of people; rather they are a fluid force through which people navigate in their understanding of "the what and the how" in being Oneida.

Indigenous people have had to struggle with living up to ideas of authenticity that have been imposed by non-Natives. Native people have well learned outsiders' expectations, even while simultaneously contesting them. Non-Natives have the power to hold Native Americans to unrealistic and damaging standards in determining what makes an "authentic Indian."[42] But Indigenous people have not been passive victims without agency. They effectively help to shape the discourse of what is authentic and what is not, able to shape outsiders' perceptions of them even as they are often on the losing side of vastly unequal power relationships.

There are certain community mechanisms that privilege a Haudenosaunee identity for the Wisconsin Oneidas. These locations serve to authenticate what are considered to be valid expressions of Haudenosaunee identity. The longhouse community, the ongoing land claim, and the ONM all play roles in the ongoing recognition that the history of the Wisconsin Oneidas encompasses more than just the geographic place of Wisconsin. Outside factors continue to change the ways in which the reclamation of tradition manifests in the community. To better understand the ways in which Indigenous people revitalize tradition, one might study the process of "the working through of a history among now radically dislocated and subordinated people, rather than the fortunate resurgence of a subdued essence."[43] In this way, Wisconsin Oneida ideas of tradition and authenticity are inextricably linked to and thus affected by colonialism and American imperialism.

This does not mean that there is anything less "real" about tradition and tsiʔniyukwalihoʔtʌ, but it does mean that an analysis of the forces that affect how tradition is viewed is important. In the longhouse belief system of contemporary Wisconsin Oneidas, there is still an emphasis on the proper interpretation of the original instructions that were given to the Oneidas at the time of creation and that focus on the relationship to the natural environment and connections to others.[44] This is uniquely interpreted based on the history of the Wisconsin Oneida community. Similarly, the community is the context that is necessary to understand the exhibits of the ONM. The site of the ONM is therefore critical to the understanding of the meanings of the longhouse replica.

Tsiʔniyukwalihoʔtʌ: Situated in a Sovereign "Safe" Space

Late June and early July is typically a busy time for the ONM. The Wisconsin Oneidas host a large, annual contest powwow that attracts hundreds of dancers. General Tribal Council meetings, a parade, tribal elections, and the annual Oneida Days are also held during this time. The ONM participates by hosting the Oneida Cultural Festival, a one-day event that typically has exhibits, artist demonstrations, Oneida hymn singers, and Longhouse smoke-dance competitions. In 2007 a Native country-and-western band ended the day. These events serve together to remind people that the Oneidas still exist as a culturally distinct people, adapting and maintaining their identity within the contemporary context.

The physical location of a museum is crucial to a discussion of the ways in which it is experienced.[45] The ONM is a scripted space that represents an Indigenous identity to Wisconsin Oneidas as well as non-Oneidas. This space encompasses the grounds of the ONM as well as the exhibits inside. When visitors walk outside, the longhouse replica is immediately in front of them. If they look just down the road, they can see both tribal housing and a tribally owned gas station and convenience store. Thus, one is confronted with the sovereign space of the Wisconsin Oneida reservation. How one perceives the longhouse replica is dependent upon the recognition of Oneida sovereignty.[46] In some cases, visitors cannot help but view the longhouse replica in the context of the living culture of the Wisconsin Oneidas. If visitors are lucky, at some times of the year they will go outside and see singers, dancers, artists, and food—part of the various community events that are sponsored by the ONM throughout the year, not only in the summer. There might be someone tending the garden or preparing to walk on a nature path that is designed to foster both traditional ecological knowledge as well as the materials for baskets or carvings. All of these activities that occur on ONM grounds emphasize the boundaries of the space in which a tribal museum is located. It is not a museum in Milwaukee or Chicago—instead, it is located in the sovereign space of Oneida, Wisconsin.

Tribal control over the ONM is paramount in any consideration of the history and culture represented—it changes the discourse and analysis substantially. The stories tribal museums tell and to what extent they challenge the dispossession and colonization of Indigenous people are ways of exercising cultural sovereignty.[47] Many tribal museums do so by emphasizing stories that demonstrate the continued existence of their people. This provides insight into how tribes may adapt the institution of the museum to more adequately represent "their ways." In discussing how tribal control of the Makah Cultural and Research Center privileges local knowledge, Janine Bowechop and Patricia Pierce Erikson identify how the Makah language became a way to organize the storage of excavated objects from the Ozette archaeological site, in contrast to established curatorial practices that would most likely take place in a non-Native museum. Instead of storing the objects by size or function, for example, the Makah names for the items were used to organize them linguistically. In some cases, the objects, though similarly named, did not necessarily fit with how someone might arrange them. Their relationship was only discovered when the translated names were compared. Through this process, the language and its underlying meanings and relationship to Makah ways of knowing was privileged and revitalized. At that point, the authors argue, the Makah Cultural and Research Center became particularly significant for the Makah people. "This adaptation of the museum—to expand the preservation goals beyond the preservation of artifacts to the preservation of a living culture—is an essential component of the Indigenization of the mainstream museum model."[48]

In a similar way, the ONM has moved from the purely visual aspect of museum exhibition, which relies on the passive reception of the viewer, to one that also includes language classes, workshops, cultural dances, and socials. Through the addition of such practices, it becomes a potential site for nation building and decolonization. Many non-Native museums have incorporated more experiential exhibits and ways to connect with the community, though it seems particularly appropriate for tribal museums to function also as community centers.

Further study is needed on how tribal museums represent their communities and histories in comparison to how they represent other Indigenous people. For example, how the ONM presents its exhibits and stories as opposed to how the Shako:wi Cultural Center of the Oneida Indian Nation of New York presents theirs would provide an interesting discussion on how the two historically and culturally related communities view nationalism and Haudenosaunee identity. There are major differences as well as connections between the two communities. Significantly, comparing two tribal museums will turn the lens from a Native versus non-Native emphasis to one that more fully encompasses the complicated and contested ways in which Native people are linked to one another.

There are characteristics of the Wisconsin Oneidas that differ from other Haudenosaunee nations: citizenship that recognizes the ancestry of both the mother and father; governing style; geography; and interest of community members. These are not insignificant considerations, and they deeply complicate and divide the membership of the Wisconsin Oneidas as they create and discuss the stories of the Oneida Nation. Somewhat countering these barriers are the institutions of the Wisconsin Oneidas, where people actively represent a Haudenosaunee identity. The ONM is not the only place where this affinity and link to other Oneidas and Haudenosaunee people can be experienced. An ongoing land claim, the Oneida Language Revitalization Program, and the Oneida tribal schools are only a few of the more obvious places that stress this relationship.

Current ONM staff members emphasize that they want to provide a safe space in which to learn about being Oneida and about the myriad ways that this information can be interpreted.[49] The stories people tell about themselves, their culture, and history are diverse and are often in conflict with one another; so the ways that the ONM can mediate these conversations without alienating a large proportion of the community require a delicate process of continual negotiation. This means that the ONM tries to provide opportunities to rethink and adjust their exhibits and events. Every January, for example, the ONM is closed to most visitors in order to undergo a period of reflection and renovation. New exhibits and ways to connect with the community have emerged from this time.[50] In this way, ONM staff members recognize the importance of the process of creating, as well as the exhibit content itself. Given that kaʔnikuli·yó ("the Good Mind") is a process rather than a state of being, the ONM's ongoing efforts to create a safe and meaningful space for Wisconsin Oneidas are particularly appropriate and further evidence of tsiʔniyukwalihoʔtʌ.

Oneidas who don't live in the area come to visit the ONM as one way to connect with the community; this happens especially in the summer around the time of the annual powwow, when a great many of them return home to visit family and stay in touch with who they are as Oneida people. The ONM, therefore, exists as a place for the nonlocal Oneidas to affiliate not only with the Wisconsin Oneida community but also with other Oneidas and Haudenosaunee people. Out of the 15,000 tribal members, nearly 6,000 live outside the state of Wisconsin, while over 6,000 tribal members live either on the reservation or in the surrounding two counties.[51] There is almost an equal number of those who can access the reservation community easily and those who cannot. This creates a delicate balance in how members understand themselves as Oneida. In 2007 it is much "safer" for Indigenous people to connect with their language and culture, relative to a century ago when assimilation policies limited the extent to which one could freely do so. It is a privilege to have spaces like the ONM, spaces that were fought for and that still remain because of the tireless efforts of people who valued these things. To maximize the benefits of these spaces, they cannot be used unreflexively. Indigenous people need to think about what it means to have these spaces if they are to be of the best use.

Reflection on the meanings of tsiʔniyukwalihoʔtʌ is evident in the exhibits of the ONM and the longhouse replica. The longhouse is used for functions that are geared toward both Oneidas and non-Oneidas. Visitors to the ONM typically engage with the longhouse. At the culmination of most tours, weather permitting, ONM staff members take visitors to the longhouse replica for storytelling. It has also been used for events that are limited to Oneida participants, as in a recent workshop on Haudenosaunee gender roles and responsibilities. Participants noted that being in the longhouse, "changed the tone of the meeting." In this workshop, a discussion of Haudenosaunee women's roles was transformed when they were in the longhouse replica. In the facilitator's view, the longhouse environment seemed to transport the participants to another place and open their minds to the words that were being spoken, allowing them to better experience the "how" of being Oneida.[52]

For the Wisconsin Oneidas, "our ways" are rooted in a connection with other Haudenosaunee. This kinship exists in much the same manner as does the longhouse replica in front of the ONM: it is an enduring reminder of a shared past, but one that must be continually rebuilt and shifted to accommodate the changing needs of the community.

Notes

Arlen Speights, Mario A. Caro, and Carol Cornelius helped bring clarity to the paper with their generous and thoughtful comments. It could not have been completed without the assistance of the staff of the Oneida Nation Museum and the Cultural Heritage Department in Oneida, Wisconsin. YawΛʔkó.

1. At its inception, the museum was named as the Oneida Nation Museum. In recent years, the Oneida Nation of Wisconsin has been consciously reclaiming the Oneida language, and most tribal operations now have Oneida names. Tsiʔniyukwalihoʔtʌ ("this is our way," or "our kinds of ways") is the Oneida name for the Oneida Nation Museum. However, while some tribal operations are known exclusively by their Oneida names, such as the *Kalihwisaks* ("She Looks for the News") newspaper and *Tsyunhehkwʌ* ("It Provides Life for Us"), a traditional and natural food and health products center, tribal members continue to call others, like the Oneida Nation Museum, by the names they were originally given. I refer to Tsiʔniyukwalihoʔtʌ as either "the ONM" or "the museum," since that is the way most Wisconsin Oneidas will recognize it. Because the focus is on nationalism, authenticity, and kinship to other Haudenosaunee, the concept of tsiʔniyukwalihoʔtʌ is also briefly explored.

2. *Akwesasne Notes*, ed., *Basic Call to Consciousness*, rev. ed. (1978; repr., Summertown TN: Native Voices, 2005), 85.

3. Frieda J. Jacques, "Discipline of the Good Mind" (unpublished paper in author's possession).

4. For an argument against tribal governments such as the Wisconsin Oneidas asserting jurisdiction in New York State, see Robert Odawi Porter and Carrie E. Garrow, "Legal and Policy Analysis Associated with Migrating Indigenous Peoples: Assessing the Impact on the Haudenosaunee within New York State," Working Paper Series No. 05-1 (Syracuse NY: Syracuse University College of Law, January 25, 2005).

5. The other nations are Cayuga, or Gayogoho:no ("People of the Great Sawmp"); Seneca, or Onödowága ("Keepers of the Western Door"); Onondaga, or Onoñdaʔgeháʔ ("People of the Hills"); Mohawk, or Kanien'kehaka ("People of the Flint"); and Tuscarora, or Sgarooreh' ("Shirt Wearing People").

6. Laurence M. Hauptman, *Conspiracy of Interests: Iroquois Dispossession and the Rise of New York State* (Syracuse NY: Syracuse University Press, 1999), 31.

7. Reginald Horsman, "The Origins of Oneida Removal to Wisconsin, 1815–1822," in *The Oneida Indian Journey from New York to Wisconsin, 1784–1860*, ed. Laurence M. Hauptman and L. Gordon McLester III (Madison: University of Wisconsin Press, 1999), 53.

8. Jack Campisi, "The Wisconsin Oneidas between Disasters," in Hauptman and McLester, *The Oneida Indian Journey*, 76–79. For an analysis on the continuity of the Oneida Chiefs Council and the continuation of Longhouse ceremonies, see Carol Cornelius, "Continuous Government of Oneidas in Wisconsin" (unpublished paper, Oneida Cultural Heritage Department, Oneida WI, 2004).

9. Jack Campisi, "Ethnic Identity and Boundary Maintenance in Three Oneida Communities" (PhD diss., State University of New York at Albany, 1974), 184.

10. See Barbara Graymont, *The Iroquois in the American Revolution* (Syracuse NY: Syracuse University Press, 1972).

11. For an intriguing discussion on the rights and responsibilities of Haudenosaunee people, see Robert Odawi Porter, "Haudenosaunee Citizenship" (paper presented at the 2007 International Citizenship Conference, Syracuse University, April 28, 2007), http://www.law.syr.edu/academics/centers/ilgc/iicc_agenda.asp.

12. Doug M. George-Kanentiio, *Iroquois on Fire: A Voice from the Mohawk Nation* (Westport CT: Praeger, 2006), 82–83.

13. Robert F. Berkhofer Jr., *The White Man's Indian: Images of the American Indian from Columbus to the Present* (New York: Vintage, 1978), xv.

14. For an examination of typical exhibition models of Native Americans, see James Nason, "'Our Indians': The Unidimensional Indian in the Disembodied Local Past," in *The Changing Presentation of the American Indian* (Washington DC: Smithsonian Institution, 2000), 34–39.

15. Laura Cornelius Kellogg, *Our Democracy and the American Indian* (Kansas City MO: Burton, 1920), 23.

16. Philip J. Deloria, *Playing Indian* (New Haven CT: Yale University Press, 1998), 77.

17. For an analysis of the ways in which specific conceptions of the nation are displayed in museums, see David Boswell and Jessica Evans, eds., *Representing the Nation: a Reader; Histories, Heritage and Museums* (London: Routledge, 1999). Also, for an examination of the disciplinary boundaries of art museums and the manner in which such places can be considered "ritual structures," see Carol Duncan, *Civilizing Rituals: Inside Public Art Museums* (London: Routledge, 1995).

18. Most Americans believe, or believed, in the "Vanishing Indian" image. For an examination of how this myth contributed to a view of the American West, see Patricia Nelson Limerick, *The Legacy of Conquest: The Unbroken Past of the American West* (1987: repr., New York: W. W. Norton, 2006).

19. Harold Faber, "NY State Will Return Wampum Belts to Onondagas," *New York Times*, August 13, 1989.

20. For a discussion of the rise of salvage anthropology and the rise of the anthropology museum between 1875 and 1905, see Douglas Cole, *Captured Heritage: The Scramble for Northwest Coast Artifacts* (Norman: University of Oklahoma Press, 1985), 286–88.

21. Christine F. Kreps, *Liberating Culture: Cross-Cultural Perspectives on Museums, Curation, and Heritage Preservation* (London: Routledge, 2003), 92–96.

22. James Clifford, *Routes: Travel and Translation in the Late Twentieth Century* (Cambridge MA: Harvard University Press, 1997), 207.

23. John Joseph Bodinger de Uriarte, "The Casino and the Museum: Imagining the Mashantucket Pequot Tribal Nation in Representational Space" (PhD diss., University of Texas at Austin, 2003), 64.

24. Rita Lara, personal communication with author, Oneida Nation Museum, Oneida WI, August 9, 2007.

25. Jack McNeel, "Museums of the Nations Blossom across the Country," *Indian Country Today*, August 9, 2005.

26. Laurence M. Hauptman and L. Gordon McLester III, *Chief Daniel Bread and the Oneida Nation of Indians of Wisconsin* (Norman: University of Oklahoma Press, 2002), 99.

27. *Oneida Homeland Tour Videos, 1995–96*, videocassette (Oneida WI: Oneida Land Claim Commission, 1996).

28. For a discussion of the Thames Oneidas on a similar trip, see Madelina Sunseri, "Theorizing Nationalisms: Intersections of Gender, Nation, Culture, and Colonialism in the Case of Oneida's Decolonizing Nationalist Movement" (PhD diss., York University, 2005), 274.

29. See Audra Simpson, "Paths toward a Mohawk Nation: Narratives of Citizenship

and Nationhood in Kahnawake," in *On Political Theory and the Rights of Indigenous People*, ed. Duncan Ivison, Paul Patton, and Will Sanders (Cambridge: Cambridge University Press, 2000), 113–36.

30. *Oneida Homeland Tour Videos, 1995–96.*

31. I am indebted to Tonya Shenandoah, July 10, 2007, and Bob Brown, August 6, 2007, for their thoughts.

32. Linda E. Oxendine, "Tribally Operated Museums: A Reinterpretation of Indigenous Collections" (PhD diss., University of Minnesota, 1992), 154.

33. "Haudenosaunee Sacred Masks/Sacred Objects Policy," *Akwesasne Notes* 1 (Spring 1995).

34. Carol Cornelius, personal communication with author, Oneida wi, September 13, 2007.

35. Many sources are by non-Haudenosaunee scholars, though their informants were typically Haudenosaunee, some of whom individually gave the researchers generous permission to write about the ceremonies. It is not my intention in this study to transgress contemporary prohibitions, so I discuss these sources generally only in terms of method and not for their specific content.

36. Oxendine, "Tribally Operated Museums," 153–54.

37. Richard Hill Sr., "Reflections of a Native Repatriator," in *Mending the Circle: A Native American Repatriation Guide*, ed. Barbara Meister (New York: American Indian Ritual Object Repatriation Foundation, 1997), 72.

38. Oxendine, "Tribally Operated Museums," 154.

39. This discourse can perhaps only be fully understood by those who are directly involved. I respectfully discuss the conflict here because it shows how it was mediated and reconciled within the onm. The resolution demonstrates that the onm is a place where representing a Haudenosaunee identity is important.

40. Oneida chiefs were "raised," or installed as leaders with the appropriate titles, in 1925 and again in 1933 but the legitimacy and authenticity of these events has been questioned. See Kristina Ackley, "Renewing Haudenosaunee Ties: Laura Cornelius Kellogg and the Idea of Unity in the Oneida Land Claim," *American Indian Culture and Research Journal* 32, no. 1 (2008) 57–58.

41. Oxendine, "Tribally Operated Museums," 154.

42. Paige Raibmon, *Authentic Indians: Episodes of Encounter from the Late Nineteenth-Century Northwest Coast* (Durham nc: Duke University Press, 2005), 39–40. Raibmon has an excellent and insightful discussion of the ways in which the Kwakwaka'wakw and Nuu-chah-nulth were active and showed agency in creating shared meanings of authenticity, which holds implications for other Indigenous people.

43. Stuart Hall, "Culture, Community, and Nation," in Boswell and Evans, *Representing the Nation*, 41.

44. See John C. Mohawk, *Creation Story: John Arthur Gibson and J. N. B. Hewitt's Myth of the Earth Grasper* (Buffalo ny: Mohawk, 2005).

45. For a discussion of the ways in which visitors engage with the National Museum of the American Indian, see Mario A. Caro, "You Are Here: the NMAI as a Site of Identification," in "Critical Engagements with the National Museum of the American Indian," ed. Amy Lonetree and Sonya Atalay, special issue, *American Indian Quarterly* 30, nos. 3–4 (2006): 543–57.

46. I am grateful to Mario Caro for sharing his research in Mario Caro, "Rethinking Dioramas: Sovereignty and the Production of Space" (unpublished paper in author's possession, 2007)

47. Amanda J. Cobb, "Understanding Tribal Sovereignty: Definitions, Conceptualizations, and Interpretations," *American Studies* 46, nos. 3–4 (2005): 127.

48. Janine Bowechop and Patricia Pierce Erickson, "Forging Indigenous Methodologies on Cape Flattery: the Makah Museum as a Center of Collaborative Research," *American Indian Quarterly* 29, nos. 1–2 (2005): 268.

49. Lara, personal communication, August 9, 2007.

50. Carol Cornelius, personal communication with author, Oneida WI, August 7, 2007.

51. Oneida Tribal Enrollment Department, *Oneida Tribe of Indians of Wisconsin Membership Information*, Unpublished Report, Oneida WI, June 2007.

52. Cornelius, personal communication, August 7, 2007.

10

Reimagining Tribal Sovereignty through Tribal History

*Museums, Libraries, and Archives
in the Klamath River Region*

BRIAN ISAAC DANIELS

There are a number of curious ironies in the burgeoning number of tribal museums, libraries, and archives among Indigenous communities across the United States. In the nineteenth century, nation-states employed museums and archives to preserve particular aspects of culture in order to inspire a sense of a common history for the nation. By demarcating what was official history and culture and by training citizens to treat the past and its representative objects as official and definitive, states encouraged the formation of a homogenous, ideological community that could become a governable entity. Museums, libraries, and archives were intended to instruct those who ventured within their walls. These institutions marked official history and culture; they trained people to view objects in particular ways; they taught a narrative of the past; and they offered ways with which to understand the present. As part of this effort, in the United States, museums preserved sacred Native American objects and lands in order to illustrate the "taming" of the wilderness and "triumph" of American civilization over its Indigenous peoples.

This nineteenth-century narrative has been rightly challenged through the advocacy of Native American activists and their academic allies since the civil rights era of the 1960s and 1970s. New museum exhibitions and cultural research programs are now undertaken after careful consultation and collaboration with Native people, who have insisted upon a voice in how they are represented and interpreted. Many Native American tribes have gone further to control their heritage. These communities, whose histories were once erased by nationalist institutions, have formed their own cultural heritage programs and created a new wave of tribal museums, libraries, and archives.

There are important questions that are worth asking about this phenomenon, pointed questions about mutations of national ideology. If institutions like museums, archives, and libraries were once part of an apparatus that institutionalized sovereignty at the level of the nation-state, what happens when similar institutions appear among local tribal communities? How might these institutions shape tribal conceptions of sovereignty? It would be good to examine how tribal museums, libraries, and archives reshape the conceptions of sovereignty within the tribe, and thereby recast the role of preserved information, culture, and history in community life. Cultural preservation, which parses "authentic" and "sacred" culture from its vernacular contexts, can enable novel forms of political debate, strategic organization, and rights-based legal claims. At the same time, it can transform the self-description and presentation of tribal communities and the identity of its members.

In this chapter, I consider the development of tribal museums, archives, and libraries in the Klamath River region, a remote corner of northwestern California. The Klamath River seems an unlikely place to begin a discussion of the complexities of tribal sovereignty and history with the rise of casino-funded tribal museums and the high-profile placement of the National Museum of the American Indian on the National Mall in Washington DC. However, this secluded river canyon is the site for two significant legal cases about the cultural rights of Native Americans. Tribal communities first asserted a right to cultural preservation under the American Indian Religious Freedom Act of 1978 for the Klamath River High Country. Furthermore, two tribal communities in this region have had a long-running feud about the rights they hold upon reservation lands. Here, I outline the historical circumstances of these legal battles and the consequences that they have wrought for tribal communities. In the aftermath, tribal communities worked to develop their own cultural heritage programs, citing an imminent need to document and to save the culture around them. How tribal archives, museums, and libraries have flourished in the Klamath River—and the different permutations that they have taken—speaks to the ways that documentation promises a cultural renaissance of a different kind than the nationalist museums, archives, and libraries of another historical era. Individually, the Hupa, Yurok, and Shasta tribal communities have employed cultural documentation for their own ends.[1] While these tribes live near each other in the Klamath River area, their different histories and political situations have engendered different strategic uses of their respective museums, libraries, and archives. Why these institutions take the differing forms that they do points to the variety of solutions to problems of Indigenous sovereignty that can be found in the control of information about culture and history.

Culture in Court

The importance of heritage institutions today cannot be understood without reference to the historical context from which they emerged. The tribal museums, libraries, and archives in the Klamath River region all developed during the last quarter of the twentieth century in tandem with the litigation of two court cases. *Jesse Short et al. v. The United States* and *Lyng v. Northwest Indian Cemetery Protective Association* together demonstrated the necessity and utility of the idea of culture as an organizing principle. These cases exposed local ideas about culture to American legal structures, and their outcomes are still debated among Native Americans in the Klamath River region. Moreover, they influenced the ways in which museums, libraries, and archives were structured by tribes throughout the area.

The first case has its origins in the formation of the Hoopa Valley Reservation. In 1864 the Indians now called the Hupas and the Yuroks were placed together upon a single, integrated reservation, in which all Indians were entitled to equal property rights. However, when the Hoopa Valley Tribe came into existence as a formal organization in 1950, only enrolled members of that tribe were eligible for income from timber profits. The Yurok were ineligible for these payments and resisted forming an organization similar to the Hoopa Valley Tribe because they claimed to be members of the Hoopa Valley Reservation. A legal suit filed in 1963 by sixteen aggrieved, self-described Yuroks demanded that timber sale proceeds benefit all the Indians on the reservation regardless of tribal affiliation. By 1967 *Jesse Short et al. v. The United States* included over 3,000 claimants and their descendants. Their suit was ultimately successful in 1972, when the U.S. Court of Claims ruled in the Yuroks' favor.

The court had a remedy in mind to correct for years of underpayment to Yuroks. It established a trust fund while enrollment criteria were developed in order to determine who, precisely, was a Yurok and who, precisely, was a member of the Hoopa Valley Tribe, in a reservation and a region where both tribes had long intermarried. Although the core decision survived successive challenges throughout the remainder of the 1970s and 1980s and the Bureau of Indian Affairs attempted to implement a series of plans to satisfy the decisions, a final settlement was reached by the 1988 Hoopa-Yurok Settlement Act. This act divided the reservation into two parts, split the trust fund, enjoined the Yuroks to form their own tribal government, and laid out the criteria of who would be eligible to be an Indian on either reservation.[2] "Yuroks" were now legally subject Yuroks; "Hupas" were now legally subject members of the Hoopa Valley Tribe. But there was a caveat. In many cases, self-described Hupas became legal Yuroks and vice versa. New legal subjectivities came with conferred rights from each respective tribal government. It became the task of each new sovereign Indian nation, over the overriding ethnic concerns, legal entanglements, problems of enrollment, and bureaucratic pitfalls, to foster a sense of national identity, imagine a new community, and form the instrumental technologies that are governmentality.[3] In sum, each nation had to forge Indian citizens with a vested pride in their specific heritage, despite the fact that Yuroks and Hupas share in many of the same religious practices and speak mostly English.

Unlike *Jesse Short et al.*, which addressed what rights can be derived from divisive ethnic-identity politics, the second lawsuit demonstrated the necessity and vulnerability of culture in the legal life of Indigenous communities. In the late 1960s the U. S. Forest Service conceived a plan to construct a seventy-five-mile road between the small towns of Gasquet and Orleans in an area slated for logging. Abbreviated to an optimistic euphemism, the GO-Road, as it came to be known, would have cut through the heartland of the High Country—the place where Native American doctors in the Klamath River region have long gone to learn their healing powers and to communicate with the spirit world. But before any construction could take place, the culture that might be destroyed had to be properly documented and recorded. The Forest Service commissioned a number of reports detailing the Native American use of the High Country, with varying results. One archaeologist authored a report asserting the land's spiritual sterility; other anthropologists argued for its continued vitality to local Native Americans. When the Forest Service finally overrode the recommendations of anthropologists not to build the road, citing a compelling national interest to fell timber in the region, a conglomeration of Indian activists organized under the banner of the Northwest Indian Cemetery Protective Association. They filed suit against the Forest Service, citing an avalanche of violations to the National Historic Preservation Act; the Federal Water Quality Control Act; the Wilderness Act; the Administrative Procedure Act; the National Forest Management Act of 1976; the Multiple Use, Sustained Use Act; and, perhaps most significantly, the First Amendment and the American Indian Religious Freedom Act, better known as AIRFA.

Signed into law in 1978, AIRFA made it the "policy of the United States to protect and preserve for American Indians their inherent right of freedom to believe, express, and exercise the traditional religions of the American Indian, Eskimo, Aleut, and Native Hawaiians, including but not limited to access to sites, use and possession of sacred objects, and the freedom to worship through ceremonials and traditional rites."[4] The GO-Road became the legal test case for the law; and the plaintiffs were successful in the initial circuit and appellate court decisions, with the help, so some Yuroks say, of some furious medicine making prior to key testimony. The GO-Road was finally stopped when the lands were designated by legislative fiat as wilderness; but the Forest Service, asserting its ability to override AIRFA, appealed its case to the U.S. Supreme Court in *Lyng v. Northwest Indian Cemetery Protective Association*. Here, the Indians lost their case. Writing for the majority on a split decision, Justice Sandra Day O'Connor opined, "The Free Exercise Clause [of the First Amendment] is written in terms of what the government cannot do to the individual, not in terms of what the individual can exact from the government. Even assuming that the Government's actions here will virtually destroy the Indians' ability to practice their religion, the Constitution simply does not provide a principle that could justify upholding respondents' legal claims."[5] In effect, the Court found that Indians' *beliefs* were protected, but not their *prac-*

tices; or, more bluntly and perhaps more realistically, Americans, Indian or otherwise, could believe whatever they might like but held no constitutional guarantee that they should be able to act upon their deeply held convictions. In practical terms, the decision was moot, and the GO-Road turned into what locals call the NO-GO Road. But *Lyng* nevertheless became a precedent for future legislation and litigation about matters concerning Native American religions and cultural preservation.[6]

Despite the setback of the *Lyng* decision, what became apparent to the tribes throughout the Klamath River area was the political power of cultural documentation. Culture could define communities; it could provide a legal framework for protecting sacred lands; it could offer a justification for the persevering and organizing politics. These legal decisions were followed by a cultural renaissance that witnessed the revival of tribal traditions, the repatriation of artifacts to the tribe, the resurgence of tribal language programs, and a renewed interest in tribal traditions. But in order for all of this to happen, culture had to be known. It was, of course, already known by the tribe's elders and ritual leaders. However, culture had to be *publicly* known, and it became the role of the political leaders to invest in cultural documentation. The rise of tribal museums, libraries, and archives in the Klamath River is linked to the needs of tribal communities to create and to control outward representations of their culture.

Displaying Culture

Among the Native American communities in the Klamath River area, the Hoopa Valley Tribe has developed the public display of its culture most fully. The Hoopa Tribal Museum came into existence in 1972, when the Economic Development Administration, under the U.S. Department of Commerce, funded the construction of a shopping complex in the center of Hoopa Valley. The complex is the locus of community life and includes the tribal court, the grocery store, the post office, the only hotel for miles around, and the museum itself. The museum is modest, approximately 1,500 square feet in size. Almost from its inception, there have been plans to enhance its size and stated mission. In the 1980s, at the time when the Hoopa-Yurok Settlement Act and *Lyng v. Northwest Indian Cemetery Protective Association* were pending, the tribe sought to update its museum by hiring a consultant to lay out a plan for a new cultural center. The costs, however, proved to be prohibitive, and the tribal council and the museum director have since worked to raise enough funds to expand the museum and promote its place in community life.[7] Nevertheless, it is the presence of the museum, and its material holdings in the heart of the reservation community, that elevates it to such importance.

The museum houses a collection of materials from the cultural life of the Hoopa Valley Tribe. There are elaborately woven baskets, stone tools, deerskin clothing, and ceremonial regalia on display in glass cases. The tribal communities in this region are renowned for their headdresses that are made from hundreds of flaming-red woodpecker scalps and their mounted albino deer hides, each of which is used, respectively, as part of the Jump Dance and White Deerskin Dance in the month of September. These spectacular objects enter the museum from a variety of sources. The museum owns approximately one-third of its collection, purchased primarily from non-Indian collectors and augmented in recent years by successful repatriations of dance regalia from the Peabody Museum at Harvard University. The remaining two-thirds of the collection is on long-term loan from families who live on the reservation, who perceive the museum as better protected against fire and theft than their homes, as able to provide expert care for sacred material, and as a place to proudly display family heritage.[8] This last factor is essential. Native Americans in the region explain that regalia "cry" to be danced, to be put into use, to be a part of daily life. Owning regalia has long been a marker of status within the community; it is a sign that the bearer is descended from one of the families that had a right to possess and to dance with it. There are some religiously prescribed occasions for display, like the Jump Dance and White Deerskin Dance days. Loaning family regalia to a museum is an opportunity to display regalia on a permanent, year-round basis and to thereby index a family's status within the community and their full embrace of their cultural heritage.

The Hoopa Tribal Museum describes itself as a living museum, a place where objects are preserved and stored until they leave the museum to be used in a cultural event. In this sense, it acts as a repository of objects and of knowledge rather like a safety deposit box. Its purpose is to safeguard heritage in order to make it accessible to people on the reservation and those few who come to visit. There is a spiritual element to the kind of care that the museum provides; curatorship entails responsibility because the objects are suffused with supernatural power and danger.[9] But by caring for objects and by gathering them together in an institution that is different than familial custody, the museum provides a unique venue for demonstrating the existence and permanence of the tribe's culture by labeling what constitutes the domain of culture itself. Like all museums, the Hoopa Tribal Museum must select what goes on display, what will be taught to the audience, and what interpretations it will provide. The issue of audience begs a fundamental question. For whom is this museum intended? Like many tribal museums on reservations that are far-flung from urban centers, the museum is not exactly on a main highway. Nestled in the mountain valley bottom where the Trinity River empties into the Klamath, the Hoopa Valley Reservation is 330 miles north of San Francisco, the last 60 miles of which are over winding mountain roads. The region has a rugged character that discourages all travel, and for this reason the idea of "public" display constitutes a remarkably small and particularly intent audience.

Most people come to the tribal museum because they have another reason to be at the tribal shopping complex where it is located. They might have business with the tribe, have shopping to do at the grocery store, desire a chance at Indian bingo, or visit their post office boxes. But when Native people do come to the museum, they have a chance to talk to each other in their own language, to reminisce about their traditional culture, and to teach the traditional ways to anyone in their tribe who is willing to learn.[10] While public school groups from Humboldt County occasionally come to visit, this living museum is nevertheless conceived as primarily sustaining the culture of the Hoopa Valley Tribe through the act of elevating what is unique about Hupa culture, distinct from the realm of ordinary experience. By acting as a repository for the material exemplars of cultural life and providing a space in which discussion about those exemplars can occur, the tribal museum demonstrates an ideal of what culture should be. The museum is therefore a site in Hoopa Valley in which Hupa culture becomes pronounced, fixed, and visible. It is a place where the Hupas tell a story about themselves to themselves, and to anyone else who is willing to listen.

Documenting Culture

Downriver from Hoopa Valley, the Yurok Indian Reservation runs the length of the Klamath River to the shores of the Pacific Ocean. For over a century, this stretch was known as the Extension, relative to the main Hoopa Valley Reservation. Less accessible and therefore less improved by roads and electric power, the Yurok government has worked since its 1988 split with the Hoopa Valley Tribe to develop and assert its own autonomy as a tribal authority. In a place where all development is conspicuous, the new tribal government's headquarters incorporates the design of a plank dwelling house, with the modern conveniences and decor of a corporate office. Yurok tribal leaders have been explicit in their desire to engage in an act of nation building so that the community can have a future as a sovereign tribal entity. Part of this task has involved drafting a governing constitution for the tribe, one that grants pride of place to Yurok culture. The Yurok have declared that it is their nation's task and purpose to "preserve and promote [Yurok] culture, language, and religious beliefs and practices, and pass them on to [their] children, [their] grandchildren, and to their children and grandchildren . . . forever."[11] As the Yurok have developed their tribal government, they have also assembled the infrastructure for their cultural-heritage programming. Rather than taking the form of a museum, as with the Hoopa Valley Tribe, the Yurok have instead turned to the language of neoliberal governance to control the flow of information about their culture.

Appreciating the bureaucratization of culture among the Yurok demands a familiarity with policies, agencies, and acronyms that have become the parlance of modern governmentality. In 1992 Congress amended the National Historic Preservation Act to allow federally recognized Indian tribes to participate in the governance and stewardship of historic sites and "cultural properties" on tribal lands. Once a tribe agrees to participate in the program, the Tribal Historic Preservation Officer, or THPO, is charged with identifying and maintaining inventories of culturally significant properties, nominating properties to national and tribal registers of historic places, conducting reviews of government agency projects on tribal lands, and developing educational programs. Significantly for questions of sovereignty in the American polity, these duties mirror the bureaucratic functions of a State Historic Preservation Office, or SHPO. In historic preservation, Native American tribes are on equal footing with state mandates. The Yurok received its THPO status in 1996. With five national forests, five national wilderness areas, one national park, and additional Bureau of Land Management properties in the Klamath River area, there are ample government properties over which the Yurok can make cultural claims for purposes of preservation. The Yurok THPO is also involved in the governance of its tribal heritage through the California Historical Resources Information System, or CHRIS. This state government agency is responsible for the Historical Resources Inventory, maintained at county-level information centers. The Yurok THPO, in its state-level bureaucratic role, is called the Northwest Coastal Information Center, and is responsible for maintaining the records of cultural and historical properties in California's Humboldt and Del Norte counties.

The Yurok THPO is located inside a former Forest Service building, a few miles north from the Yurok government's tribal offices. In its guise as the Northwest Coastal Information Center, it holds records for over 2,000 cultural resource sites, including cemeteries; villages; scatters of stone chips, flakes, and tools; and sacred sites immortalized in rock, stream, and mountainside. These sites are cultural and historical "properties" — lands that have been identified by professional anthropologists, archaeologists, and historians, and vetted by other government functionaries to meet a set of criteria for what constitutes the legally cultural and historical. In order for a site to be deemed significant, it must be included in, or eligible for, listing in the National Register of Historic Places. The National Register is a list of districts, sites, buildings, structures, and objects that are significant in American history, architecture, archaeology, and culture.[12] Fulfilling these demands requires legibility for governmental action. The map, the survey, and the census have long been employed as tools to entrench state power.[13] That is to say, state policies of any kind require a degree of prior bureaucratization and knowledge that draws citizens, their actions, and the landscape itself into the sphere of governmentality. By mapping the landscape and making visible specifically cultural and historical realms, these sites become targets for acts of governmental action. The records at the Yurok THPO are primarily site reports that give basic information about the cultural value of a place and provide a map to mark the cultural and historical from the ordinary and mundane. Indeed, these records parse what is sacred in contemporary American democracy from its profane opposite.

Despite the focus on documenting and preserving cultural heritage, it is not immediately apparent to whom all of this documentation is important or even relevant because it is primarily for regulatory and state-oriented projects. Yuroks assert the need for cultural preservation and point out that maps of cultural properties can be useful in building roads, resolving land-claims disputes, or identifying and preserving traditional sites. However, very few Yurok people need access to the documents that are held by the archive. What use, then, is the archive? The archive serves two functional purposes for the Yurok Tribe. It makes visible sites for the act of preservation through tribal, state, or federal governmental action. In so doing, it grants to the Yurok tribal government the ability to mark what is sacred and to fulfill its own constitutional mandate by ensuring that what is preserved as culture can be passed from children to grandchildren, forever. At the same time, the tribe, by holding the information on its own reservation, in its own archive, can enact a degree of control over the flow of information about their heritage, their history, and their culture. The bureaucratization of culture in the archive has continued apace with the development of the tribe's government itself. The promise of the tribal archive is its potential for knowledge that can be used for future action for the benefit of the tribe; there is a security in the ability to know what constitutes culture as much as there is security in knowing culture itself.

Demonstrating Culture

The Shasta Nation faces different issues regarding its sovereign status altogether. Unlike the Yurok and the Hupa, the Shasta Nation does not have a reservation. Its ancestral homelands are upriver from the Yurok, along the Klamath, near the famous, glacier-gouged volcano that bears the tribe's name. The community has an unusual political status because the Shasta Nation falls into the bureaucratic void of "unrecognized" tribes. Although its tribal members trace their descent back through several generations of Native American ancestors, kinship alone does not legitimate an Indian nation in a political sense. Rather, an Indian nation must be recognized according to law for it to be considered politically legitimate. Heritage plays a looming role in this determination.

The criteria for federal recognition of an Indian tribe were first issued in 1978 and took their current form in 1997. All Native American groups that are not already recognized from older political arrangements and desire "official" status must meet seven criteria that invite claims about culture. First, a community must demonstrate its continuous existence as a political entity since 1900. Second, the majority of members must constitute a distinct community. Third, the tribal leadership must exert influence on the community. Fourth, the tribe must have clear membership criteria. Fifth, the membership must be able to demonstrate its descent from a tribe that is historically identifiable. Sixth, all members of the community must belong solely to that community and not to any other tribe. Finally, the tribe must not have been legislatively terminated by Congress.[14]

There is a significant cultural dimension to each of these recognition criteria, a dimension that can only be shown through certain kinds of evidence about Indian identity. Identification as an Indian entity by anthropologists, historians, scholars, and in printed academic journals is one required way to demonstrate "continuous existence." But providing evidence of a distinct community requires a further explication of the substance of a community's culture. A petitioning group must demonstrate significant in-group marriage "as it may be culturally required," significant social relationships between members, cooperative labor between community members for shared economic interests, evidence of shared sacred or secular ritual activity, and, perhaps most significantly, "cultural patterns shared among a significant portion of the group that are different from those of the non-Indian populations with whom it interacts. These patterns must function as more than a symbolic identification as Indian. They may include, but are not limited to, language, kinship organization, or religious beliefs and practices."[15] The federal recognition criteria further specify that at least 50 percent of the petitioning community must retain such cultural patterns. In order to be an Indian nation, a community must demonstrate how it is different. In effect, culture, as set out by these legal criteria, becomes the practical means for advancing political claims about citizenship and its entitlement rights in the multicultural democracy of the United States.

The Shasta Nation has worked since 1982 to claim formal status as a recognized Native American tribe, a claim that is subject to evaluation by the Bureau of Acknowledgment and Recognition. Better known by the acronym "BAR," this division of the Department of the Interior has a double meaning for many self-described Shasta. It is recognized as the governmental branch from which rights are granted, but it is also the agency that will "bar" Indian people from achieving the recognition that they desire. For many Shasta, being Indian, and therefore their eligibility as a recognized tribe, hinges upon their historical experience as a discriminated minority group that shares an awareness of its collective past. Their identity as Shasta is bound with an understanding that they, as people, are survivors of a past in which massacres against them were common, racism was rampant, and bureaucratic decisions threatened to undercut their sense of belonging to an Indian community. Historical awareness, however, does not translate easily into the language of governmentality. The cultural requirements embedded in the seven BAR criteria demand proof through a verification of culture, a kind of certification that is made possible through the preservation and presentation of documentary artifacts that link the Shasta to their homelands and to their history. The Shasta needed and have, therefore, created an extensive archive about themselves. For whom is this archive important? It is not an archive of aggregate data, as among the Yurok, controlled by the tribal government and held primarily for outsiders. Nor is it a museum that reinforces what Hupa culture is for reservation residents. The onus is on the people who call themselves Shastas to gather historical artifacts in the hope that they will have, in their cumulative impact, the political effect of demonstrating that the tribal nation exists in a legal sense. History dangles the promise of future sovereignty.

As with all archives, the tangible remains of the past are carefully housed, preserved, and labeled in order for information to be properly amalgamated into historical or political arguments. The importance of this archive is best realized by considering its physical setting in relation to its carefully tended contents. Located miles away from the nearest highway over circuitous, unpaved, one-lane roads, the Shasta Nation's tribal archive is situated in a rustic, two-room, wooden building with a wood-fired stove. It includes many of the trappings of a well-equipped modern archive, with a photocopier, a microfilm reader, and a computer, all of which had to be brought a considerable distance and maintained. The archive is a labor of love for the few people involved with it. The creation of the archive is the brainchild of a woman deeply devoted to her tribe's history. For years she has amassed every newspaper, anthropological publication, and photocopy of archival microfilm that makes reference to her tribe. There are complete copies of Indian censuses and enrollment records, some being 100 years old or more, that are the bureaucratic detritus of another era, which are invaluable to proving descent, marriage, and tribal continuity. The archive houses contemporary scientific reports as well—the "gray literature" that is produced by expert consultants and pertains to Shasta archaeological sites on public lands and the "cultural resource inventories" that are prepared by government planners. All of this documentation sits in row upon row of filing cabinets, stuffed full of bound documents and file folders that hold the potential to someday, and somehow, defend the political aspirations of the Shasta Nation.

Culture and the Nation-State

We have thus far reviewed the heritage efforts of three Indigenous communities: the Hupa, Yurok, and Shasta. Two are recognized nations, one with a museum and the other with an archive, which demonstrate the communities' full possession of culture. The third is unrecognized and struggles to unearth every shred of evidence that can legitimate what its members already know is true: that it is an Indian nation that persists into the present day. The Hoopa Tribal Museum is concerned primarily with creating a space that demonstrates culture to the people of its own reservation. It is a public declaration of what it means to be Hupa. Conversely, the Yurok THPO has a minimal public dimension. It is meant for government use; its contents are technical, bureaucratic, and intended for specialists who generate further information about heritage. In contrast to the other two, the Shasta tribal archive gathers information with the aim of making a future legal claim. It is not a location that the public would visit, nor does it offer a public service. These institutions appear to have radically different orientations in their purpose and function. What can these three Indigenous heritage institutions tell us about the evolution of museums, libraries, and archives within nation-states?

In order to answer this question, we must first consider the role of museums, libraries, and archives in nation-states themselves. Among theorists of nationalism, Benedict Anderson has offered a compelling explanation for the impact of institutions like museums and archives in the process of state building. In assuming roles as guardians of tradition, nation-states linked together the image of an idealized homeland with scientific reports, popular books, and museum displays that were produced by experts in the social sciences. When coupled with nationalist desires, the past was mobilized to project an ideal of national unity and greatness. In this epistemological regime, any object — whether archaeological artifact or bureaucratic document — must be marked for special attention. The power of an object is that it is a token instance, a representative of a class of objects. Archaeological digs, the collection of paintings and sculpture, and the accumulation of books have all contributed to the formation of museums and archives. Collecting and preserving artifacts has alienated them from everyday life and, in an unusual way, sanctified them. They became what constituted the "sacred" within the secular state. National patrimony entails not only the assimilation of the past but also its metamorphosis into something of national value contained in the museum and archive. This kind of heritage is not true history, because the past is made malleable to fit the present needs of state power. It is an invented tradition of the past that is produced by and for the state to demonstrate and legitimize its ideological hegemony over an imagined nation.[16]

Key to this transformation is how a community is imagined, or, more specifically, the ends to which a community is imagined. Nationalism demands the formation of a novel, homogeneous nation over other possibly prior ethnic, class, and religious considerations. The nation encompasses a community that is too large, by definition, for every individual to know one another. Nevertheless, a national community is defined by what it holds in common. There are two important points here. First, nationalism transformed heterogeneous populations into homogeneous communities that understood themselves as nations. A number of factors contributed to this historical phenomenon. As we have seen, museums objectified national treasures, and archives preserved the documents that were relevant to state power. Other developments shaped nationalism as well: the use of the census and maps to define a body politic; vernacular languages and newspapers to spread common reading material; and a uniform conception of time and history. Taken together, these phenomena encourage an imagined sense of connectedness with those who are sharing these experiences within the same social polity. Nations demand the formation of a community's culture. To be sure, nations are never culturally uniform and orthodox, despite the persistent efforts of the state. There is, however, one crucial area that unites a community: the recognition of the state's ultimate sovereignty.

We now turn to a second factor that defines nationalism. Nation-states have sovereign laws that prescribe the political boundaries of the community and the physical borders of the homeland. The state's sovereign power is active within that space, and this power hinges upon the ability of the state to construct the notion of the homeland and the community by policing its borders. The sovereignty of the state is paramount and, in the United States, grounded upon liberal theory that asserts the priority of rights through the sovereign individual. But individuals are not the only constituencies within a nation-state. In order to create the culturally uniform nation, the state must survey, define, and make legible the heterogeneous mutations to the ideal homogenous state. By so doing, the state defines the identity groups that challenge the totalizing nation-state. It also sets the terms of their participation. In present-day multicultural democracies, ethnic-identity groups like the Indigenous tribes studied here coalesce in their contemporary forms *through* their interactions with nation-states. Native American groups aspire to a primordial status—that they existed as sovereign nations prior to their historical experience with nationalism. While it is true that Indigenous groups existed before modern-day nations, it is equally true that their experience with nationalism and the laws and sovereignties that have been created by nation-states has reshaped those same communities. We must understand Indigenous polities—as well as the museums, libraries, and archives that they create—through the lens of nationalism that now focuses the authorship of new histories.

Culture and Indigenous Sovereignty

Museums, libraries, and archives, whether located in a national capital or on a remote reservation, share a similar aim. They aspire to the dream of total knowledge about a particular domain of social experience. These institutions collect everything that is known about a culture, heritage, and a people. Complete representation requires documentation, token instances of powerful objects, and enough information to permit reconstruction. National museums bring together the objects that unite a people. National archives and libraries collect the documentation of government, of a nation's people, and of national treasures. The state is the object of representation. Similarly, tribal museums display the objects that unite a people. Tribal archives and libraries contain the documentation of culture that the community holds so very dear. In these institutions, the tribe is the object of representation. States and tribes share the aim of using the process of representing and preserving their culture as a way to mark their heritage as an exemplar for the people whom they count as members. Yet, there are differences that we must consider between tribal and statist heritage institutions.

Indigenous museums, archives, and libraries are now emerging with different assumptions about sovereignty than the centuries-old nationalist museums and archives that defended the nation-state. Statist institutions intended to cultivate a viewing disposition—an attitude toward the past—that would enhance the prestige and demonstrate the national community's homogenous unity. At first glance, there appears to be an aspect of this phenomenon found in tribal heritage institutions. An important task for the Native American tribes reviewed in this chapter has been the very formation of their respective communities. The Hoopa Valley Tribe and the Yurok Tribe needed to define membership and citizenship for their respective polities, in order to assert the sovereignty of their tribes. The Shasta Nation struggles to accomplish the same task. Heritage institutions are an asset in this task for Indigenous communities, in the same way that they proved to be useful for nation-states. For this reason, it appears that the Hoopa Tribal Museum, the Yurok THPO, and the Shasta Nation's tribal archive are engaged in an incipient ethnonationalism. By seeking to transform their communities into what they want them to be, these tribes specify the boundaries of their polity, the content of their own cultures, and the grounds of their future sovereignty claims.

However, to view Indigenous polities as merely engaged in the act of imagining their communities would miss the historical nuances of the present-day milieu in which tribal museums, libraries, and archives are developing. Indigenous communities are not simply repeating the same nationalist process. Instead, Indigenous polities are situating their communities within the prior, entrenched sovereignty of nation-states. For this reason, the cases of the Hoopa Valley Tribe, the Yurok Nation, and the Shasta Nation are instructive. These three tribes developed their respective heritage institutions after their own sovereignty claims were tested and contested at the level of the nation-state. They are not "imagined communities" in the sense that students of nationalism have contended. That idea describes an older kind of nationalism, one that does not account for contemporary Indigenous politics. Rather, Indigenous polities are well-justified communities — well justified by the impulse of modern democracies to be all-inclusive, well justified by the documentation that demonstrates their existence within nation-states, and well justified by their assertion of legal rights with historical facts to support their claims of priority against the nation-state.

This process is reinforced by the bureaucratic heritage institutions that are found among contemporary Indigenous polities. Tribal museums, archives, and libraries confirm difference by providing cultural knowledge, mapping difference, separating cultural property rights from one tribe to the next, and asserting that a specific tribe is the rightful bearer of a specific cultural legacy. These facts make Indigenous museums, archives, and libraries different from their nationalist counterparts. No longer do these institutions serve the sole purpose of aiding in the imagining of community. Rather, Indigenous museums, libraries, and archives imagine difference within a multicultural nation-state. Whereas the nation-state's heritage institutions have been concerned with demonstrating the homogeneity of the state, these new institutions place a premium upon the production of difference and emphasize the heterogeneity within the nation-state as well as their own autonomy. Indigenous polities like the Hoopa Valley Tribe, Yurok Tribe, and Shasta Nation must position themselves within a framework of American sovereign power — a problem illustrated by the 1988 Hoopa-Yurok Settlement Act and the *Lyng v. Northwest Indian Cemetery Protective Association* decision. While the sovereign state encourages the forms taken by these claims, it cannot control the historical justifications that ethnic identity groups now employ.

Herein is the final irony. The apparatus that sustained the nation-state—its museums, libraries, and archives; its professional historians, archaeologists, and conservators; its legalities that couple rights to histories—are all very easily appropriated. The homogenous narratives required by nation-states are upended by Indigenous heritage institutions that use the same means of collection and documentation as their nationalist predecessors. In this way, the nationalist enterprise is being complicated by the very ways that were originally devised to sustain it.

Notes

1. The similar terms *Hupa* and *Hoopa* are used throughout this chapter, although they each mean something different. The term *Hupa* is used to refer to culture or ethnicity. *Hoopa* refers to a physical location or political organization in northern California. To illustrate the relationship: the Hoopa Valley Tribe is the legal name for a group of self-described Hupa.
2. The administrative problems of the Hoopa Valley Reservation and the Yurok Extension are best known from the Bureau of Indian Affairs' policy review statement, which the Yurok Nation distributes to outsiders who want to learn something about the situation. See Lynn Huntsinger and others, *A Yurok Forest History* (Sacramento CA: Bureau of Indian Affairs, 1994).
3. By "governmentality," I refer to the system of governing techniques, methods, and practices by which a sovereign power produces citizens. The political theory of governmentality has been expounded upon by Michel Foucault, see Michel Foucault, "Governmentality," in *The Foucault Effect: Studies in Governmentality*, ed. Graham Burchell, Colin Gordon, and Peter Miller, trans. Rosi Braidotti (Chicago: University of Chicago Press, 1991), 87–104.
4. The *American Indian Religious Freedom Act* became law on August 11, 1978. Public Law 95-341, codified as U.S. Code 42 (1996).
5. *Lyng v. Northwest Indian Cemetery Protection Association*, 485 U.S. 439 (1988).
6. Thomas Buckley, *Standing Ground: Yurok Indian Spirituality, 1850–1990* (Berkeley: University of California Press, 2003), 170–210.
7. Doris Farris Howell, "Developing an Appropriate Fundraising Plan for the Hoopa Tribal Museum" (Master's Thesis, San Francisco State University, 2000), 22.
8. Lee Davis, "Locating the Live Museum," *Museum Anthropology* 14, no. 2 (1990): 17.
9. Davis, "Locating the Live Museum," 18.
10. Davis, "Locating the Live Museum," 18.
11. Yurok Tribe Const. (Klamath CA: Yurok Tribe, 1993), 5.

12. Section 101 of the National Historic Preservation Act directs the Secretary of the Interior to expand and maintain a National Register of Historic Places to include cultural resources of state and local as well as national significance in order to ensure that future generations have an opportunity to appreciate and enjoy the nation's heritage. National Register listings must meet the criteria found in National Parks Service, Dept. of the Interior, *Code of Federal Regulations*, title 36, chap. 1, sec. 60.4.

13. James C. Scott, *Seeing Like a State: How Certain Schemes to Improve the Human Condition Have Failed* (New Haven CT: Yale University Press, 1998).

14. On the difficulties faced by unrecognized tribes, see Les W. Field, "Complicities and Collaborations: Anthropologists and the 'Unacknowledged Tribes' of California," *Current Anthropology* 40, no. 2 (1999): 193–209; Bruce G. Miller, *Invisible Indigenes: The Politics of Nonrecognition* (Lincoln: University of Nebraska Press, 2003); and Mark E. Miller, *Forgotten Tribes: Unrecognized Indians and the Federal Acknowledgment Process* (Lincoln: University of Nebraska Press, 2004).

15. This passage is found in Bureau of Indian Affairs, *Code of Federal Regulations*, title 25, chap. 1, sec. 83.7.

16. My discussion of nationalism is influenced by Benedict Anderson, *Imagined Communities: Reflections on the Origin and Spread of Nationalism*, rev. ed. (1983: repr., London: Verso, 1991). The sanctification of objects in museums as a part of nationalism is an area that is only beginning to receive the theoretical attention that it requires. My commentary is based upon David Lowenthal, *The Heritage Crusade and the Spoils of History* (Cambridge: Cambridge University Press, 1998); Krzysztof Pomian, *Des Saintes Reliques à l'Art Modern: Venise-Chicago, XIIIe–XXe Siècle* (Paris: Gallimard, 2003); and Dominique Poulot, *Patrimoinie et Musées: L'Institution de la Culture* (Paris: Hachette, 2001).

11

Responsibilities toward Knowledge

The Zuni Museum and the Reconciling of Different Knowledge Systems

GWYNEIRA ISAAC

The A:shiwi A:wan Museum and Heritage Center in Zuni, New Mexico, was established in 1991 as an institution dedicated to engaging younger generations in significant aspects of their cultural heritage. The guardianship of knowledge in Zuni is partitioned among clans and religious societies and is taught on a need-to-know basis in order to ensure the transfer of associated responsibilities. As a corollary, Zuni expectations privilege the transfer of knowledge through oral tradition and initiation into these esoteric societies. During the development of the Zuni museum, however, tensions surfaced between the Anglo-American and Zuni approaches to the treatment of knowledge. As a result, the museum faced the challenge of defining its role within the complex Zuni hierarchy for the maintenance of knowledge.

This inquiry examines how conflicts have arisen between Zunis and Anglo-Americans over the ways in which responsibility is assigned to the reproduction of knowledge. To understand these conflicts more fully, I look at the history of the duplication of knowledge, firstly from Zuni perspectives and secondly from Anglo-American viewpoints, reflecting on areas where these histories engage and values are shared or disputed. I also examine cultural ideas about the reproduction of knowledge, such as taboos on duplication, the control of associated technology, and the concept of embodied knowledge. To pursue this inquiry I ask, what are the different cultural values that are ascribed to the reproduction of knowledge? In order to understand the contexts in which Zunis experience these conflicts between Zuni and Anglo-American knowledge systems, I focus on the A:shiwi A:wan Museum as the institution through which these histories and values are negotiated.

A Case History in Duplicates

A recurring theme in my research is the cultural value that is attributed to the process of the duplication of knowledge. It should come as no surprise, therefore, that my introduction to Zuni was through a series of photographs of the Pueblo that were created by Bureau of American Ethnology (BAE) anthropologist, Matilda Coxe Stevenson, and which were taken during the years 1879–1911. These images now form part of the collections of the National Anthropological Archives at the Smithsonian Institution; and a duplicate set now exists that was created for the Zuni museum in 1991 to form their founding collection. The curation of this duplicate collection, however, is not entirely straightforward. On arrival at Zuni, the images were assimilated into the Zuni system for the treatment of knowledge; and the collection was divided into two parts with images revealing ritual knowledge being moved to the Zuni Heritage and Historic Preservation Office, where access is only granted to the initiated members of the religious societies.[1] The subsequent history of these images provides insight into Zuni concerns about the mechanical reproductions of knowledge. From the contemporary contexts and treatments of these photographs, we are also given a unique opportunity to look at an identical series of objects in two different cultural contexts and under two distinct knowledge systems.

The process of reproduction lies at the heart of how knowledge is transmitted, practiced, and circulated; yet the act of duplication has not been evaluated within theoretical frameworks for the study of knowledge systems. My aim is to develop a framework that explores how value is assigned to duplications, both in their original context and as they traverse different cultural situations. Two concepts that are relevant to this framework emerge: first, that knowledge is comprehended through the process of reproduction and, second, that knowledge is embodied both by the practitioner and by the objects that are produced through the practitioner's knowledge.

The terms used within this inquiry—*copy*, *duplicate*, and *reproduction*—

are defined here according to this specific framework. *Copy* and *duplicate* refer to something that is made, in appearance, exactly like its original. In this context these may be produced in large quantities without embodying the knowledge that was required in their original production. For example, photocopying an Auden poem requires having the knowledge for operating a photocopy machine, not the knowledge used by Auden to create the poem. The term *reproduction* is used here explicitly for the processes involved in the duplication of knowledge. In addition, I use the phrase *reproductive technology*, which is commonly associated with biological reproduction; however, I introduce it here to refer to the mechanical reproduction of knowledge, such as photographs and film. This is not designed to conflate two seemingly separate concepts but rather to forge new ways for us to perceive the efficacy that is assigned to mechanical reproductions in reproducing cultural values and possibly culture itself.

The responsibilities toward the treatment of knowledge are best understood as the means that people adopt to ensure the effective transmission and maintenance of knowledge. It also implies that there is a need for accountability for the consequences resulting from how knowledge is used and circulated. In other words, knowledge is ascribed a specific cultural value according to its varied functions as a process for socializing people.

Thus far, I have introduced a distinct relationship between the processes that are used to reproduce knowledge, such as photography, and the system of knowledge within which it is used. To comprehend the localized relationships between knowledge and context of use, I choose not to focus solely on judicial or theocratic areas of power but to emphasize what I have termed the vernacular approaches to the treatment of knowledge.[2] The term *vernacular* is useful in this context as it connotes language that is communicated orally rather than through text. The vernacular is key to understanding some of the tensions between the Zuni and Anglo-American systems. Museums are also recognized as institutions that bridge formal and informal approaches to education; the concept of vernacular approaches to knowledge is therefore apposite to this inquiry. Similarly, it can be viewed as a regional way of doing things that allows for the mediation of expectations about how a knowledge system should operate and how people actually experience it. Once incorporated into a framework that allows for the cross-cultural examination of the reproduction of knowledge, vernacular approaches permit a fluid interpretation of both tangible reproductions, such as photographs, and intangible forms, such as oral traditions.

Hierarchies of Responsibility:
Zuni Approaches to Knowledge

The Zuni system of knowledge is best understood via theoretical perspectives that take into account the ways in which power is derived from ritual knowledge. Hierarchies of authority in the Pueblos have often been misinterpreted by anthropologists, who perceived political power as largely being drawn from governmental rather than religious offices. Peter Whitely opposes this view in his study of Hopi politics, pointing out that "the reason for differing and confusing views of Hopi ethnography lies in the radical disjunction of Western and conceptual domains (primarily 'politics' and 'religion'), which tend to underpin anthropological thought."[3] In effect, Anglo-Americans view power as being divided between the religious and political. Yet in Hopi, "power derives from various sorts of esoteric knowledge, which carry a high social value."[4]

In Zuni, through the use of ritual knowledge, priests have the ability to affect the well-being of the community, such as peoples' health, the weather, and the fertility of crops. While Anglo-Americans may locate power in governmental offices, Zunis attribute greater power to the priesthood. As Whitely points out, "in a society where it is collectively believed that individuals can control the causes of sickness, death, famine, and so forth, through supernatural means, the boundaries drawn between 'supernatural' and 'political' power dissolve into irrelevance."[5] Anthropologists had also incorrectly interpreted the Pueblos as being egalitarian because there was no noticeable difference in the distribution of material wealth. This misreading stems from an inability to understand how status is in fact drawn from access to ritual knowledge. As Elizabeth Brandt suggests, the control of material wealth is not the way in which power in the Pueblos is determined or measured.[6] Ultimately, it is the differential rights to knowledge that structures the social hierarchy.

Since ritual knowledge is esoteric, it follows that the specific uses of and approaches toward secrecy are important factors in understanding how knowledge can or cannot be transmitted in Zuni. Many historians of the Southwestern Pueblos had assumed that secrecy was only practiced against outsiders. Anthropologists had also made correlations between the development of secret knowledge and economic and political power. For example, according to Hugh Urban, "secrecy is a more easily defined 'ownership' of knowledge because it is controlled for economic gain."[7] In Zuni, however, secrecy is practiced against both insiders and outsiders and is valued more highly as a pedagogical device than as an economic one. Within the intellectual architecture that determines the treatment of knowledge, something is secret because it is powerful, rather than the customary view that it is powerful because it is secret. For knowledge to maintain its power requires responsibility in using it appropriately. As a result, secrecy becomes a vital tool in the pedagogical process and a means to monitor how knowledge is transmitted and used.

Another essential principle in the Zuni system of knowledge is the view that knowledge—and in particular, ritual knowledge—is valuable to the group only if it is used responsibly by the individual. The social hierarchy in Zuni is not only established according to the *possession* of ritual knowledge and therefore the associated power but also in relation to the level of *responsibility* that is related to that knowledge. Zunis refer to membership and priesthood in the religious societies as immense responsibilities rather than as high-ranking social positions. For example, the Zuni religious societies consist of four levels, stretching from the individual to the cosmos itself. The initial layer is made up of the Dikya:we ("Medicine Orders"), who are responsible for the supervision of medicine and healing. In the next level, the A:biła:Shiwani ("Bow Priests") are in charge of the laws that maintain civil obedience within Zuni, including the protection of Zunis from external forces and invaders. The subsequent level of leadership is reserved for the Kodikyanne ("Kachina Leaders"), who are responsible for maintaining connections with the ancestral spirits and therefore the welfare of Zunis by overseeing ritual observances. The highest level, the Shiwani ("Rain Priests") are accountable for the "welfare of the total Zuni world," thus being capable of and responsible for influencing not only the people of Zuni but also the elements of the universe, such as rain, wind, and all life forms.[8] From this schema, we can see how responsibility increases; and, at the level of the Shiwani, the priests are accountable for the entire cosmos. Zunis, however, rarely discuss the hierarchy of power, but rather the burden of responsibilities taken on by these individuals for the well-being of the community.

Oral tradition is utilized by Zunis as an effective tool to ensure that associated responsibilities are transmitted alongside traditional and ritual knowledge. In this process, instructors can control the context in which knowledge is transmitted as well as observe and comment on students' use of this knowledge. It is also viewed as crucial for students to learn the nature of the instructive frameworks in which the oral tradition is performed, as this is the structure within which knowledge is embedded and given meaning. In effect, traditional narratives are not merely about the content of the stories and prayers—they also perform at a metaphorical level, in which the instructive framework conveys social protocols and responsibilities portrayed in the stories.

In Zuni today, however, there is apprehension that youngsters may not be getting the opportunity to learn about and use as much of their traditional culture and history as earlier generations had done. This is credited to the fact that wage-earning jobs and schools have widened the gaps between generations. The demographics of Zuni also reveal that there are proportionally fewer people represented in the older generations, so the numbers of extended family who are living in the same house have diminished. While the younger generations have voiced that they want the knowledge, elders are worried the youth will not take on the responsibilities that are associated with its care. They recount how some young men attempted to record prayers using tape recorders, with the hopes that this will make them easier to learn. As a result, according to the elders, they have attempted to assume the knowledge of their teachers without absorbing the associated protocols that are developed through the mentoring relationship. In speaking about the burden of the responsibility assigned within religious societies, one member of the community commented that "a lot of [people] within their lineage don't really want to participate because it's a big, big requirement."[9] These responsibilities include fasting, separation from family, and extended time spent in the kivas, or religious societies, many of which may prevent people from maintaining full-time wage-earning jobs.

Zunis also worry that the broad circulation and dissemination of esoteric knowledge by anthropologists and other non-Zunis has threatened the structure that has been designed to maintain responsibility toward the transmission and use of knowledge. Once knowledge leaves the contextualizing or socializing process of oral tradition, there is fear that it will be used for individual gain rather than for the well-being of society.

Mechanical Reproductions and Anglo-American Ways of Knowing

Aristotle, "who was the first man to collect books, and who taught the kings of Egypt to set up libraries," founded one of the earliest institutions established within European society for the organization of knowledge.[10] It is from Aristotle's original collection that the term *museum* is derived. Significantly, these early collections were based on texts—a practice that has subsequently dominated the West's approach to the duplication and circulation of knowledge. Jack Goody and Ian Watt also noted how the maintenance of these texts increased people's ability to notice the changes that were taking place to society. As a consequence of this assumed stability of certain media, museums became accountable not only for the collection of knowledge but also for its preservation. As a result, the individual's responsibility for maintaining knowledge gradually shifted into the institutionalized maintenance of knowledge.

By the nineteenth century, the European and American scientific communities were wholly engaged with new technologies that allowed them to explore Enlightenment philosophies through empirical methods. The invention of new recording techniques such as photography, cartography, and eventually film were embraced for their technical ability to provide accurate facsimiles of the world. The overarching schema driving these endeavors was the belief that all knowledge could eventually be organized into a coherent whole. "Comprehensive knowledge" was the idea that "knowledge was singular and not plural, complete and not partial, global and not local, that all knowledge would ultimately turn out to be concordant in one great system of knowledge."[11] As a result, technologies that provided the scientific replication of the world were transported into the field to produce data that could be easily collected and ordered within central repositories and reproduced at will.

Throughout the eighteenth and nineteenth centuries, models and replicas were seen as valuable ways for their creators to embody scientific explorations and the mastering of technological knowledge. Replicas were also used by anthropologists to experiment with how things were made and to demonstrate these processes to interested audiences, assuring that the knowledge circulated widely. Accordingly, anthropologists who were working in the American Southwest not only emphasized the collection of artifacts but also found ways to duplicate as much knowledge as possible, fearing it was to be lost because of the imagined assimilation of Zunis into Western society.

Frank Hamilton Cushing is not only recognized as one of the first anthropologists to work in Zuni Pueblo; he may also be credited as one of the primary ethnologists to experiment with the process of learning archaic knowledge by reproducing artifacts. In the 1860s in both Britain and America, there was a growing interest among prehistorians in exploring the technologies that were used by ancient peoples in their creation of stone tools. Cushing appears to have been the initial prehistorian in the United States to experiment with flint knapping. As early as 1879 he gave demonstrations on the methods that were used to create arrowheads. In a presentation organized for the American Anthropological Society for Washington, in Washington DC, Cushing discussed "the knapping methods he had seen American Indians use and . . . gave a demonstration of point-making."[12] As a young boy, Cushing devoted time to making replicas of Native American artifacts. His interests were not only in creating such items but, through that creation, in obtaining an intimate knowledge of their construction and use. In an 1895 article, he writes openly about this pursuit of experiential knowledge: "If I were to study any old, lost art . . . I must make myself the artisan of it—must, by examining its products, learn both to see and to feel as much as may be the conditions under which they were produced and the needs they supplied or satisfied; then rigidly adhering to those conditions and constrained by their resources alone, as ignorantly and anxiously strive with my own hands to reproduce, not to imitate, these things as ever strove primitive man to produce them."[13]

According to Jesse Green, Cushing also experimented with "pottery, basket weaving and the construction of birch-bark and log canoes"[14] John Wesley Powell, director of the BAE, accredited Cushing as the pioneer in a "new method of research by experimental reproduction."[15] Later in life, Cushing viewed experiential knowledge as underpinning all of his ethnographic methods, writing in an autobiographical note that the method he had "initiated of ethnologic and archaeologic study by means of actual experience and experimentation" encouraged him to place himself in the position of the makers, "not only physically but intellectually and morally as well, [to] gain insight into their inner life and institutions."[16]

Cushing arrived in the Pueblo of Zuni as part of the first ethnographic expedition that was organized under the aegis of the newly founded BAE. Following a decision by Powell, Cushing stayed behind in Zuni to continue to collect information on the history, religious practices, and language of the Zuni people. In particular, in his desire to reveal the secrets of the ancient storehouses of knowledge, he eventually sought initiation into a religious society, the Priesthood of the Bow, using this position to obtain knowledge of the "inner life" of Zunis that he had so ardently sought. In a well-documented example of the duplication of Zuni paraphernalia, he recreated a facsimile of an Ahayu:da, or Zuni War God, and restored it with a series of associated offerings as a gift for the eminent British anthropologist Edward Burnett Tylor, the curator of the Pitt Rivers Museum at Oxford University.[17] The Ahayu:da was, according to Cushing, such a faithful replica that it could be considered as a scientific specimen. Coincidentally, it held political powers for Cushing, as it was given in order to cement his professional relationship with the influential Tylor, and demonstrated his intimate knowledge of the religious societies of Zuni.

The adoption of photography by anthropologists provides a further example of the influential role that was played by reproductions in the development of scientific methods. From its introduction to the world in 1839, photography was employed as an effective tool for the collection of data, and it was rapidly taken up by archaeologists and ethnologists to transport accurate visual information back from the field.[18] This is apparent in the dedicated manner in which Matilda Coxe Stevenson implemented the camera as part of her fieldwork in Zuni. During the early years of BAE research, Stevenson pioneered the use of the camera as an anthropological tool for observation, eventually taking over 3,000 images of rituals and daily life in the pueblos. Her correspondence to the bureau demonstrates her belief that the camera allowed her to capture dance movements and complex processes that previously had been difficult to document.[19] She actively experimented with the camera as an instrument that could provide her with the most accurate visual reproduction of Zuni practices as well as the means to distribute this research to others.

Cushing's overt and Stevenson's subtle methods for reproducing Zuni knowledge illuminate Anglo-American beliefs about the collection of knowledge from other cultures. Stevenson met and befriended a Zuni known as We'wha, who has since received much attention as an example of a man-woman, or berdache.[20] Following a productive research relationship in Zuni, Stevenson invited We'wha to live with her in Washington DC to continue to compile an ethnography of Zuni culture and religion. According to one of the curators at the U.S. National Museum, Otis Mason, "for six months this woman [We'wha] has taught her patroness the language, myths, and arts of the Zunis—now explaining some intricate ceremony, at another time weaving belt or blanket under the eye of the camera."[21] Images of We'wha's visit to Washington show him demonstrating each step of the weaving process for the camera, demonstrating how Stevenson relocated We'wha to Washington DC as the body of Zuni knowledge.

There has been an ongoing antagonistic relationship between Zunis, who do not want knowledge circulated outside of its context of responsibility, and anthropologists, whose responsibilities and expectations depend on its broad circulation. For example, when We'wha became aware that Stevenson was planning to use photographs of sacred objects and rites for her book, he became "much shocked, for the Zunis . . . do not think it right to make pictures of such things."[22] This should have come as no surprise to Stevenson, as her interest in photographing religious ceremonies had previously been met with grave disapproval in Zuni. In her 1904 ethnography of Zuni she writes, "The populace were so opposed to having their masks and rituals 'carried away on paper', that it was deemed prudent to make but few ceremonial pictures with the camera, and the altars and masks were sketched in color by the writer without the knowledge of the people."[23] Similarly, Cushing was met with zealous attempts to prevent the sketching of dances: "When I took my station on a housetop, sketch books and colors in hand, I was surprised to see frowns and hear explosive, angry expostulations in every direction. As the day wore on this indignation increased, until at last an old, bush-headed hag approached me, and scowling into my face made a grab at my book and . . . tore it to pieces."[24]

This history has revealed how Anglo-Americans attributed value to the duplication and inscription of knowledge, seeing it as an efficient technique for students and researchers to prove their close understanding of a particular area, ensuring its preservation and future circulation. As demonstrated, Zunis see reproduction as proof of knowledge and therefore dangerous if it is enabling knowledge or its embodiments to be removed from its proper context of responsibility. As a legacy of this history, the Zuni museum must explore these tensions as it negotiates its position within the pueblo's hierarchy of responsibility toward knowledge.

Mediating Responsibilities:
A Museum for the Zuni People

The idea for a museum in Zuni was first envisioned in the 1960s by the tribal council and members of the Zuni Archaeology Program (ZAP).[25] These groups set out to establish a space that would help them in their endeavor to preserve the archaeological history of Zuni within the pueblo itself, rather than have artifacts housed in museums outside of the community. By the 1970s the community-based Museum Study Committee shifted this goal by examining the museum concept and discussing how the conventional Anglo-American museum model posed problems to Zuni philosophy. In particular, tensions surfaced between external expectations about the display of material culture and internal concerns about the removal of knowledge from its original context. A number of national museums had already taken an interest in the development of a museum in Zuni as a possible place for the relocation of items of a religious nature, which were to be repatriated to the tribe. The Museum Study Committee, however, determined that "the care and maintenance of religious and sacred objects was the responsibility of the religious leaders" and that "such artifacts did not belong in any museum, especially a tribal museum at Zuni."[26] In effect, ritual knowledge was determined to be outside of the museum's area of responsibility.

The history of the A:shiwi A:wan Museum illustrates how Anglo-American and Zuni approaches to the transfer of knowledge needed careful negotiation. Since the idea of the museum was first introduced as a means for conserving archaeological sites and artifacts, the museum has experienced two important transitions. First, the institution shifted away from conventional Anglo-American concerns for displaying artifacts and moved toward representing Zuni interests in exploring living traditions; second, the present museum director, Jim Enote, began emphasizing apprenticeships as an effective way to transmit knowledge.[27]

As part of the first transition, moving away from the Anglo-American museum model, the museum board chose to adopt the ecomuseum concept, which had been developed by the museologist George Rivière.[28] This provided an opportunity to develop an institution that would be more reliant on local expertise. It also allowed Zunis to explore the traditional methods that are used to convey or transmit knowledge. Subsequently, community members, who are responsible for the care of objects of cultural importance, were recognized as the caretakers of the knowledge about the significance and history of these items. The identification of the people of Zuni as repositories of knowledge inspired new issues. As much of Zuni history and living performances of this history are maintained within ritual societies, the museum would have the problem of finding ways to educate the youth about their heritage without upsetting the hierarchy for the responsibility toward knowledge. Similarly, the museum was faced with the challenge of providing knowledge in a manner that would be appropriate to Zuni pedagogical values, which privilege oral transmission. In the following section, I provide examples that illustrate the ways in which the museum mediated between Anglo-American and Zuni perspectives on the treatment of knowledge. Significantly, all four examples involve the negotiation of Anglo-American values that are introduced with reproductive technology.

As mentioned previously, in the early 1990s a collection of 3,000 photographs of the pueblo held at the National Anthropological Archives was duplicated and transferred to the Zuni museum. Although many of the images had been accessible to the U.S. public, Zuni religious leaders were unacquainted with the extent of photographs portraying religious events. Once members of the community were exposed to these images, elemental issues surfaced about the role of the museum as a purveyor of esoteric knowledge. In response, a program was developed by the museum in which religious leaders from the newly created Zuni Cultural Resources Advisory Team screened these images and separated photographs that contained esoteric objects, ceremonies, or landmarks. These images were transferred to the Zuni Heritage and Historic Preservation Office; and, subsequently, only initiated members of the religious societies were given access to the photographs.[29] Although dividing the photographic collection applied restrictions that were contrary to national guidelines guaranteeing equal access, the then director, Nigel Holman, defended the decision. He argued that it mirrored basic principles of behavior that were a part of daily life in the pueblo. He contended that acquiring knowledge in Zuni and, specifically, acquiring religious knowledge came with exacting responsibilities about its maintenance.[30] In effect, unless it followed local protocols for the treatment of knowledge, the museum would not be accepted by the community.

The second example comes from conflicts that surfaced in the museum over the use of computers. The purpose of Anglo-American museums has traditionally been viewed as collecting, interpreting, and distributing knowledge. Reproductive technologies, such as computers and videos, are now inextricably linked with the drive to increase access, as seen in the increasing number of museum Web sites and computerized databases. In the context of the Zuni museum, however, these modes of reproductive technology further challenged the Zuni oral transmission of knowledge, acting as catalysts that pushed staff members to determine how to maintain knowledge within a public institution.

Following the installation of a computer terminal that would be used to teach the elements of the Zuni language to younger generations, teenagers approached staff members with requests to learn particular prayers. Staff members were comfortable with teaching these prayers; but when it was suggested that a computer program be developed to provide the prayers, the staff discussed the various problems that would be presented by this approach. In particular they would need to assess exactly which prayer would be appropriate for the context a youth had described and then explain the responsibilities that accompanied the prayer. This would not be possible where a youth would only interact with the computer. Within the Zuni community, those who rely on the oral transmission of knowledge hold the view that oral traditions are not merely about the content of the stories and prayers. Oral traditions perform at a metaphorical level, in which the instructive framework conveys social protocols that are rendered by the stories. Some members of the community fear that recording oral history with tape recorders allows the uninitiated to listen without interacting with the authoritative source of this knowledge. As a result, the museum staff members have chosen not to develop the computer as a central device for the dissemination of knowledge.

In a more recent example, Robin Boast, from the Museum of Archaeology and Anthropology at Cambridge University, initiated a project involving collections from Kechiba:wa, an ancestral village located outside of the Pueblo of Zuni.[31] The primary objective was to develop a database using contemporary Zuni views on the collections. Jim Enote, the Zuni museum director, argued that it was not apposite for Zunis to add knowledge to a database that would be housed outside of Zuni. Instead, he contended, the database could be designed according to Zuni protocols and housed in the pueblo. While Anglo-American practices view reproductive technology as a means to broaden access to knowledge, a database, from a Zuni perspective, often represents the potentially dangerous removal of knowledge from the system of responsibility. In response, Boast agreed to these conditions, citing that research that acknowledged the Zuni knowledge system should be prioritized, as opposed to applying incompatible methodology that only emphasized the content rather than the context of the databases.[32]

A fourth example illustrates how the museum staff developed inventive mechanisms for reconciling Anglo-American and Zuni approaches to recording and reproducing knowledge. In 1997 the museum prepared a mural to illustrate the origins of Zuni clans. Community members who visited the museum discussed the five mural panels, and it became practice that the stories were told alongside the tour of the mural. The paintings now function as iconographic aids to Zuni storytelling. As knowledgeable Zunis or the artists converse with younger generations about the symbolism of the designs, the mural promotes the use of oral tradition. In addition, a knowledgeable practitioner can guide someone through the mural; therefore he or she can control the amount and the context in which the information is transmitted and thus the associated responsibilities. As a result, the museum project involves younger generations in the Zuni pedagogical system, combining Zuni viewpoints on and expectations about storytelling together with the museum's desire to facilitate the education of the younger generation.[33]

Conclusions

During repatriation negotiations between the Zuni Tribe and a number of U.S. and European museums, debates arose over facsimiles of Zuni artifacts that had been made by anthropologists and hobbyists. Many curators viewed these as "replicas" or "fakes," yet Zuni asserted that these were faithful reproductions of ritual knowledge. The best example of this is presented by the Ahayu:da that Cushing created for Tylor. Cushing himself wrote in a draft of a letter to Tylor, "I carved a facsimile of it. . . . I restored as completely as possible the paraphernalia of the God that this fetich [*sic*] might be presented to you just as it is usually to the populace of Zuni by the Priesthood of the Bow. To me this task was easy as each year since my initiation into that order it has been my elected province to make one of another of these same things."[34]

Not unexpectedly, Zunis saw the Ahayu:da as a demonstration of Cushing's embodiment of the knowledge that he had learned from the priesthood. The Zuni religious leaders requested for the item to be repatriated, implying that, if it was a faithful replica complete with paraphernalia, it was animated by this knowledge and no different from Ahayu:da created by Zuni priests. A similar request was made to the Museum of New Mexico, which housed a series of replica masks. T. J. Ferguson, Roger Anyon, and Edmund Ladd, who were consultants within the repatriation process at Zuni, suggested, "The Zuni's criteria of what is 'real' and what is a 'replica' or 'model' differs from that of non-Indians. The Zuni religious leaders consider all 'replicas' to be sensitive artifacts that should be repatriated. . . . The 'replicas' were made either by Zuni people with access to esoteric information or by other people using masks made by Zuni priests as their model. In either event, the masks embody knowledge and power that many Zunis consider to be proprietary to Zuni religious organizations."[35]

Since Zunis have presented this particular conception of replicas, reactions from museums and curators have been more varied. Following explanations by Zunis concerning their expectations about the treatment of replicas, some of these items have been given to the tribe; yet a number of museums are concerned that this would set a precedent that will change the value of "replicas" as understood in Anglo-American terms. In effect, the fear is that this shift in the meaning and control of the process of duplications would restrict the openness that is expected within scientific exploration. The inability of some museums to resolve these requests from Zuni also implies that we need to explore more fully how these different knowledge systems engage and where interests conflict and overlap.

It is appropriate at this juncture to ask how effective has this framework been in explaining different approaches to the reproduction of knowledge? I started by questioning the different cultural values that are ascribed to the reproduction and dissemination of knowledge. I demonstrated how nineteenth-century anthropologists working at Zuni subscribed to the idea of comprehensive knowledge, pursuing technologies such as photography that aided this endeavor. In this Western cultural context, the accurate duplication of knowledge allows for wider and more immediate circulation of knowledge to broad audiences — a factor seen as appropriate for scientists who are working on behalf of the general public. In contrast, Zunis see the maintenance of knowledge as the responsibility of particular individuals who look after it for the group, so as to protect them from both the burdens of its maintenance and its potentially dangerous powers. While differences occur concerning how knowledge is maintained and circulated, both societies see the process of reproducing knowledge (as opposed to simply copying it) as being analogous to experiencing and embodying it. Once knowledge is reproduced, however, its treatment differs according to Zuni and Anglo-American protocol. In Zuni, the duplicate falls under a restricted system of access, while in Anglo-American contexts, duplicates are purposely circulated to increase access to knowledge. We must be careful, however, not to oversimplify the divide between Anglo-American and Zuni approaches to knowledge or the technology associated with its reproduction. For example, photography should be seen not only as simply an Anglo-American way of knowing but also as a technology used by Zunis, often as a means to negotiate between Anglo-American and Zuni knowledges. For example, when Zunis discovered the amateur Indian hobbyist group the Smokis of Prescott, Arizona, were imitating esoteric religious dances, their first action was to travel to the annual show and videotape performances to be used as evidence of this inappropriate use of esoteric knowledge.

The negotiations that are taking place in the A:shiwi A:wan Museum also reveal how reproductive technologies, such as photographs and databases, carry with them complex social values originating from each cultural context. I have shown how the museum found innovative ways to explore and privilege Zuni pedagogical values. Recent projects that have been designed at the museum by the director, Jim Enote, provide further examples of conscious decisions to address conflicts between Anglo-American and Zuni approaches to reproducing knowledge. In a new museum project, Zuni artists and experienced elders have been invited to create drawings of Zuni places of significance.[36]

Like the museum mural, these cultural "maps" are designed to be interpreted orally by knowledgeable practitioners. What is striking is that these maps now represent the active building of a repository of mnemonics within the museum, which is wholly reliant on people for their transmission of traditional knowledge. In a similar vein, Enote has also devised apprenticeship programs for Zuni youth to learn from elder farmers, emphasizing the importance of the relationships through which the appropriate treatment of knowledge is transmitted.[37]

Locating the process of reproduction at the center of an analytical framework provides an apt entryway into understanding not only how people control knowledge but how they assign responsibility to its production, reproduction, and circulation. A basic analytical principle also underlies this inquiry: responsibility is assigned to determine the social role of knowledge. I have focused here on a specific relationship between Anglo-American and Zuni knowledge systems and on a specific contemporary institution, the A:shiwi A:wan Museum. Through this inquiry, however, I hope to have demonstrated a framework that provides a closer understanding not only of the ways in which different values are ascribed to duplicates but also of how these are negotiated and reconciled within museums, therefore reconciling these values within a context particular to the cross-cultural engagement of knowledges.

Notes

1. Nigel Holman, "Curating and Controlling Zuni Photographic Images," *Curator: The Museum Journal* 39, no. 2 (1996): 108–22.

2. Gwyneira Isaac, *Mediating Knowledges: Origins of a Zuni Tribal Museum* (Tucson: University of Arizona Press, 2007).

3. Peter Whitely, "The Interpretation of Politics: A Hopi Conundrum," *Man* 22, no. 4 (1987): 696.

4. Whitely, "Interpretation of Politics," 700.

5. Whitely, "Interpretation of Politics," 706.

6. Elizabeth Brandt, "Internal Stratification in Pueblo Communities" (paper presented at the meetings of the American Anthropological Association, Washington DC, December 4–5, 1985).

7. Hugh Urban, "The Torment of Secrecy: Ethical and Epistemological Problems in the Study of Esoteric Traditions," *History of Religions* 37, no. 3 (1998): 220.

8. Wilfred Eriacho, "Zuni Government" (preliminary study for a Zuni High School history course, Zuni Tribal Archives and Records Program [ZTARP], Pueblo of Zuni, n.d.).

9. A:shiwi A:wan Museum and Heritage Center board member, personal interview with the author, Pueblo of Zuni, January 15, 1997.

10. Jack Goody and Ian Watt, "The Consequences of Literacy," *Comparative Studies in Society and History* 5, no. 3 (1963): 332.

11. Thomas Richards, *The Imperial Archive: Knowledge and the Fantasy of Empire* (London: Verso, 1993), 7.

12. Lewis Johnson, "A History of Flint-Knapping Experimentation, 1838–1976 [and Comments and Reply]," *Current Anthropology* 19, no 2. (1978): 338.

13. Frank Hamilton Cushing, quoted in Johnson, "History of Flint-Knapping Experimentation," 340.

14. Jesse Green, ed., *Zuni: Selected Writings of Frank Hamilton Cushing* (Lincoln: University of Nebraska Press, 1979), 7.

15. John Wesley Powell, "Remarks" in "In Memoriam: Frank Hamilton Cushing," ed. Frederick Webb Hodge, special issue, *American Anthropologist* 2, no. 2 (1900): 361.

16. Frank Hamilton Cushing, quoted in Green, *Zuni*, 6.

17. William Merrill and Edmund Ladd, with T. J. Ferguson, "Lessons for Repatriation from Zuni Pueblo and the Smithsonian Institution," *Current Anthropology* 34, no. 5 (1993): 523–67.

18. Elizabeth Edwards, ed., *Anthropology and Photography: 1860–1920* (New Haven CT: Yale University Press; London: Royal Anthropological Institute, 1992).

19. Gwyneira Isaac, "Re-Observation and the Recognition of Change: The Photographs of Matilda Coxe Stevenson," *Journal of the Southwest*, September 22, 2005: 411–55.

20. Will Roscoe, *The Zuni Man-Woman* (Albuquerque: University of New Mexico Press, 1991).

21. Otis Mason, "The Planting and Exhuming of a Prayer," *Science* 8, 179 (1986): 24–25.

22. *National Tribune*, May 20, 1886.

23. Stevenson, Matilda Coxe, "The Zuni Indians: Their Mythology, Esoteric Fraternities and Religious Ceremonies," in *Twenty-Third Annual Report of the Bureau of American Ethnology for 1901–1902* (Washington DC: U.S. Government Printing Office, 1904), 17.

24. Frank Hamilton Cushing, *Zuni: Selected Writings of Frank Hamilton Cushing*, ed. Jesse Green (Lincoln: University of Nebraska Press, 1979), 60–61.

25. Roger Anyon and T. J. Ferguson, "Cultural Resource Management by the Pueblo of Zuni, New Mexico, USA," *Antiquity* 69, (1995): 913–30.

26. Museum Study Committee, minutes, Zuni Tribal Archives, Pueblo of Zuni, quoted in Isaac, *Mediating Knowledges*, 91.

27. Jim Enote, personal communication with author, Pueblo of Zuni, August 2006.

28. George Henri Rivière, "The Ecomuseum — An Evolutive Definition," *Museum* 148 (1985): 182–83.

29. Nigel Holman and Andrew Othole, "Historic Photographs, Museums and Contemporary Life in Zuni," (paper presented at Objects of Myth and Memory Exhibition, Second Culin Symposium, Heard Museum, Phoenix, Arizona, January 30, 1993).

30. Holman, "Curating and Controlling Zuni Photographic Images."

31. Robin Boast, personal communication with author, October 2006.

32. Boast, personal communication, October 2006.

33. Isaac, *Mediating Knowledges*.

34. Frank Hamilton Cushing draft of letter to Edward Burnett Tylor, entry 330, Cushing Papers, Southwest Museum, Los Angeles, California.

35. T. J. Ferguson, Roger Anyon, and Edmund Ladd, "Repatriation at the Pueblo of Zuni: Diverse Solutions to Complex Problems," in "Repatriation: An Interdisciplinary Dialogue," special issue, *American Indian Quarterly* 20, no. 2 (1996): 263.

36. Enote, personal communication, August 2006.

37. Enote, personal communication, August 2006.

12

Museums as Sites of Decolonization

Truth Telling in National and Tribal Museums

AMY LONETREE

Beginnings

The beginnings of this project are rooted in my previous work on the Smithsonian's National Museum of the American Indian (NMAI) and its presentation of Indigenous history and memory in their exhibitions. In May 2007 I completed a coedited volume on the NMAI with Amanda J. Cobb entitled *The National Museum of the American Indian: Critical Conversations*. While working on this volume, I also had the pleasure of presenting my scholarship on the NMAI to a range of audiences at scholarly and museum-related conferences, which afforded opportunities for me to wrestle with my ideas regarding the NMAI's significance to the changing historical relationship between Indigenous peoples and museums. In my scholarship on the NMAI, I have asserted that, while the museum advances an important collaborative methodology in their exhibitions, their historical exhibits fail to present a clear and coherent understanding of colonialism and its ongoing effects. My critiques focus mostly on the institution's presentation of Native American history in the gallery Our Peoples: Giving Voice to Our Histories, which I argue conflates Indigenous understanding of history with a postmodernist presentation of history and, secondly, fails to tell the hard truths of colonization and the genocidal acts that have been committed against Indigenous people.[1] I focus on the second of these two issues in the discussion that follows. Given the silences around the subject of colonialism and its ongoing effects. I argue that the museum fails to serve as a site of truth telling and remembering and that it remains very much an institution of the nation-state. Thus, I caution against referring to this site as a "tribal museum writ large" or, even more problematically, as a "decolonizing museum," which both scholars and NMAI staff members have done.

My desire to complicate the discourse on the NMAI stems from my concerns about the co-optation of the language of decolonization by scholars who assert that this institution is a decolonizing museum. In an article published shortly after the museum's opening, Australian archaeologist Claire Smith argues, "As a National Museum charting new territory, the NMAI is leading a nation down a path of understanding and reconciliation. . . . A cultural and spiritual emblem on the National Mall of Washington DC, the Smithsonian's National Museum of the American Indian exemplifies decolonization in practice. Through being consciously shaped by the classification systems, worldviews, and philosophies of its Indigenous constituency, this new national museum is claiming moral territory for Indigenous peoples, in the process reversing the impact of colonialism and asserting the unique place of Native peoples in the past, present, and future of the Americas."[2]

The assertion by Claire Smith that the NMAI is a "decolonizing museum . . . reversing the impact of colonialism" ignores the absence of a clear and consistent discussion of colonization throughout their museum. This type of discussion is critical, for, as Waziyatawin Angela Wilson and Michael Yellow Bird argue, "The first step toward decolonization then is to question the legitimacy of colonization."[3] The silence around the history of colonialism throughout the Americas at the NMAI fails to challenge the public's steadfast refusal to face this nation's genocidal policies that had, and continue to have, a devastating impact on Indigenous people. Nor does this silence assist Native communities in recognizing how colonialism has affected all areas of their lives, including how to embark on the necessary changes to move toward decolonization and community healing.

Another point of concern is Smith embracing the idea that the NMAI is "leading a nation down a path of understanding and reconciliation." This seems presumptive given that the U.S. government has never formally apologized to Indigenous people nor is there a reparations process in place. Canadian scholar Pauline Wakeham in her article, "Performing Reconciliation at the NMAI: Postcolonial Rapprochement and the Politics of Historical Closure," highlights the process by which the NMAI, through its opening ceremonies, "bypasses any performance of apology for colonial injustices and moves straight to a joyous, de-politicized celebration of reconciliation."[4] Even though her emphasis in this argument was on the opening ceremonies of the museum, I would argue that this desire to move to a "joyous, de-politicized celebration of reconciliation" permeates the entire institution and is certainly reflected in its exhibitions. The exhibits in all three of the permanent galleries at the NMAI fail to explicitly address the hard truths of colonization and imply that this is a closed chapter in our history.

I want to make it clear that I am not discounting the role that Native American knowledge systems played in influencing aspects of the development of the NMAI, nor am I dismissing the museum's important collaborative methodology with Indigenous communities throughout the Western Hemisphere. But this alone is not decolonization.

The NMAI represents the most ambitious collaborative project to date, and collaboration and the inclusion of Native voice in all aspects of museum practice reflects the most important new direction in the last thirty-plus years of our relationships to mainstream museums. Instead, my goal is to raise awareness of the complicated identity of the NMAI, which reflects a still-evolving relationship between Indigenous peoples and museums, and to caution against referring to the NMAI as a decolonizing museum or as a form of "museological reconciliation" achieved that can problematically "lend itself to complicity with and co-optation by the state for the purposes of staging postcolonial rapprochement via the cultural milieu of museums," as Pauline Wakeham argues.[5]

Decolonizing Representations: Truth Telling in Exhibitions

While attempting to complicate the discourse on the NMAI, I have been faced with several questions regarding how to effectively present Indigenous history within exhibition spaces. In essence, if there are problems with this particular national museum's presentation of Native American history, how does one effectively represent the complicated and challenging history that both addresses the hard truths of colonization and also honors Indigenous understandings of history? Furthermore, if I caution against referring to the NMAI as an example of a decolonizing museum, what would a "decolonizing museum" look like?

During my research at both national and tribal museums over the last ten years, I have been greatly influenced by the work of those Indigenous intellectuals who have been working in the area of decolonization, and I have been thinking critically about how museums can serve as sites of decolonization. Indigenous scholars Waziyatawin Angela Wilson and Michael Yellow Bird recently assembled a collection of essays focusing on decolonization strategies for Native communities, which has greatly informed my analysis. In this volume, *For Indigenous Eyes Only: A Decolonization Handbook*, nine intellectuals from a range of tribal and disciplinary backgrounds provide insights into the work that needs to take place in Indian Country to bring about decolonization and healing for our communities. The purpose of this volume is to encourage critical thinking skills so as to "mobilize a massive decolonization movement in North America."[6] The contributors powerfully and persuasively illustrate the "importance of understanding how colonization has taken root in our lives" and explore how to counteract the devastating impact of colonialism by encouraging critical thinking on Indigenous governance, education, citizenship, diet, language, repatriation, and stereotypes and images.

In *For Indigenous Eyes Only*, a compelling final essay by Waziyatawin Angela Wilson emphasizes the importance of truth telling and calls for a truth commission in the United States, similar to truth commissions that took place in South Africa and other parts of the world, to address the ongoing and systematic attacks on Indigenous bodies, land, sovereignty, and lifeways that have continued to occur throughout the Western Hemisphere. She states that this is necessary to bring about the healing of our communities and to empower future generations of Indigenous people. Additionally, the only way for Native people to heal from the historical trauma that we have experienced—genocidal warfare, land theft, ethnic cleansing, disease, and the attempted destruction of our religious and ceremonial life at the hands of the government and Christian churches—is for us to speak the truth about what has happened, document the suffering, and name the perpetrators of the violence in our history. Wilson argues that, given the steadfast denial of Americans to face this history, truth telling becomes a crucial part of the decolonization process.[7]

Furthermore, in speaking the truth about the violence in our history, we are also ensuring that future generations can never claim ignorance of this history. As Archbishop Desmond Tutu states, regarding the South African Truth and Reconciliation Commission, "No one in South Africa could ever again be able to say, 'I didn't know,' and hoped to be believed."[8]

This call for truth telling as a decolonizing strategy is critical, and our museums should serve as sites where the hard truths are told honestly and specifically. We need to make sure that our museums include the difficult stories that serve to challenge deeply embedded stereotypes—not just the ones of Native disappearance that museum presentations of the past have reinforced in the nation's consciousness, but the willed ignorance of this nation to face its colonialist past and present. In my years studying exhibits that have been related to Native Americans, I have found that most contemporary museums are successful in producing exhibits that challenge the vanishing-Indian stereotype by emphasizing contemporary survival and sustained presence; but they have had limited success in presenting a hard-hitting analysis of colonization. I believe it is time for a more careful and critical discussion of how the hard truths of Native American history are presented in our museums of the twenty-first century. Truth telling is a critical aspect to decolonization, and our museums need to assist in these efforts. As Taiaiake Alfred states,

Decolonization . . . is a process of discovering the truth in a world created out of lies. It is thinking through what we think we know to what is actually true but is obscured by knowledge derived from our experiences as colonized peoples. The truth is the main struggle, and the struggle is manifest mainly inside our own heads. From there, it goes to our families and our communities and reverberates outward into the larger society, beginning to shape our relationship with it. In a colonized reality, our struggle is with all existing forms of political power, and to this fight, we bring our only real weapon: the power of truth.[9]

It is the absence of the hard truths of the specifics of Native-white relations at the NMAI that have led me to view this site as a missed opportunity to educate and assist tribal communities in efforts toward decolonization and healing. I am left then with the question of how museum exhibitions can effectively disrupt colonial constructions of Native history and culture, engage in truth telling, and also honor Indigenous understandings of history and contemporary survival. I believe that I have found a place that is very successful in achieving these complex goals and that reflects a decolonizing museum practice in a tribal museum.

The Ziibiwing Center: Indigenizing Museum Practice

I first visited the Saginaw Chippewa's Ziibiwing Center for Anishinabe Culture and Lifeways in May 2006 while attending a tribal museum development symposium on their reservation. I have since returned for numerous research visits. What became immediately apparent during my first visit is how this community center embodies a decolonizing museum practice and creates an engaging learning experience for visitors. The 32,000-square-foot facility includes a state-of-the-art research center, a gift shop and café, and a 9,000-square-foot exhibition space that features the history, philosophy, and culture of the Saginaw Chippewa community as told from their perspective. This cultural center, though unique in content, grows out of an emerging movement of large-scale, tribal-museum development of the last twenty years that includes places such as the Museum at Warm Springs (Warm Springs, Oregon), the Tamástslikt Cultural Institute (Pendleton, Oregon), the Mille Lacs Indian Museum (Onamia, Minnesota), and the Mashantucket Pequot Museum and Research Center (Mashantucket, Connecticut).[10]

The Ziibiwing Center reflects some of the most current and innovative exhibition strategies, including exhibitions that are more thematic than object centered; film presentations and multimedia that are state of the art; more storytelling and first-person voice; and, most significantly, emphasis on twentieth-century survival within the context of what Native people survived in the first place.[11] The museum provides an engaging and in-depth presentation of Saginaw Chippewa history and culture in the permanent exhibition Diba Jimooyung: Telling Our Story, which opened in 2004. A range of topics are covered in the gallery, including precontact Anishinabe history and seasonal living; tribal creation stories and the oral tradition; first contact with Europeans; the lasting legacies of colonization; and contemporary issues such as language revitalization efforts, protection of tribal sovereignty, gaming, repatriation efforts, and reclaiming and revitalizing Saginaw Chippewa culture and identity today.

What I will highlight here is the Ziibiwing Center's treatment of two themes that I believe represent the best interpretative strategies and reflect a decolonizing agenda: (1) their representation of history that reflects more closely an Indigenous understanding of history (as opposed to a postmodern sense of history) through a presentation of the oral tradition and (2) their ability to speak the hard truths of colonization in their exhibitions.

As Indigenous peoples, we have long established that we have a different way of understanding history than non-Native people, the most important differentiation being our adherence to the oral tradition. As Wilson states, "We have our own theories about history, as well as our own interpretations and sense of history, in which our stories play a central role."[12] The privileging of the oral tradition is what happens on the exhibition floor at the Ziibiwing Center and provides the overarching framework for the visitor to engage with Anishinabe history and culture. Through their presentation of the oral tradition within the exhibits, this museum engages with the best emerging scholarship in Native American history, which seeks to "position oral traditions as vehicles to create histories that better reflect Native people's perspectives on the past."[13]

The exhibitions highlight the "Seven Prophecies/Seven Fires" of the Anishinabe people, which are part of their oral tradition. The museum is organized around the prophecies, and this is a very effective and intimate manner in which to narrate their history. As visitors travel through their 9,000-square-foot exhibition, each of these prophecies is introduced on text panels; and visitors then hear the prophecy—spoken first in Anishinabe, followed by an English translation. The prophecies are the narrative thread that connects the contents of the museum and provides an understanding of their tribal philosophies and spirituality.[14]

By representing historical events within the context of the prophecies instead of through a rigid adherence to the specifics of U.S.-Indian relations, the museum is engaging in an important decolonizing strategy that privileges the oral tradition and Indigenous conceptions of history. The historical material is in there, but it is presented in a tribally based framework of understanding history that illustrates the themes of the prophecies. A case in point is their treatment of history within the fifth prophecy, their time of separation and struggle during the nineteenth century, which I will elaborate upon in a moment.

Another important point about their desire to have the prophecies be the overarching narrative structure is that the museum, while honoring tribal understanding of history, also provided a well-organized structure in which the visitor can engage with the material. There is organization in this museum — and it is definitely clear and coherent while introducing new knowledge to the visitor.

The uniqueness of the Ziibiwing approach, having oral tradition be the guiding narrative structure for the museum, builds and expands upon other previous efforts at sites that I have visited and studied. In my research on the Mille Lacs Indian Museum in Onamia, Minnesota (a collaborative project with the Minnesota Historical Society and the Mille Lacs Band of Ojibwe), the museum's exhibition narrative — while informed by oral histories of past and present band members, several of whom are quoted throughout the museum — is not organized to follow the oral tradition as an overarching framework.

I offer this recollection not to disrespect the choices of the Mille Lacs Band advisory board but to contextualize the significance of the Ziibiwing Center's staff decision to have the prophecies be the organizing structure of the museum. I have witnessed changes in tribal-museum development over the last fourteen years, and it is important to acknowledge these changes. In the case of the Mille Lacs Band, the decisions of the advisory board were based on their own unique identities and circumstances as a collaborative project with the Minnesota Historical Society at a particular moment in time, which served their interests and the needs of their intended audience. But in the case of the Ziibiwing Center, the staff members felt it was appropriate to share their oral tradition and spirituality, and as one staff member recognized, "We tried something that we felt was very daring and unusual, but made sense to us."[15]

Narrating the Hard Truths of Colonization

The second point I would like to make regarding the effectiveness of the narrative strategy at the Ziibiwing Center relates to their presentation of colonization. The community's desire to build this museum had everything to do with wanting it to be a site of "knowledge making and re-membering" for their community and also a place where the difficult stories could be told.[16] As one staff member stated, "We felt by building this facility and acknowledging our past, it would allow us to begin a heal-ing process for our community and the communities that surround us. Years of generational trauma, experienced as a result of years of oppres-sion and alienation, have left our community with many blanks in their communal history."[17]

By narrating their history in this museum, the community did not shy away from speaking the hard truths of colonization and the lasting legacies in their community. A significant amount of floor space at the museum is devoted to emphasizing their survival within a colonial con-text—a direct challenge to stereotypical displays that were produced in the past that emphasized Native disappearance in the wake of westward expansion. However, the museum does not avoid telling the difficult sto-ries of land theft, disease, poverty, violence, and forced conversion at the hands of Christian missionaries. The context of what makes their sur-vival so amazing and worthy of celebration is their treatment of coloni-zation in the preceding sections. And they devote a considerable amount of floor space in the museum to address important contemporary issues and Saginaw Chippewa survivance. However, there are no silences about the forces that sought to destroy them. For example, we can look at the following text panel that occurs in the section of their museum focusing on the effects of colonization. Additionally, notice their use of the active voice:

Gichi Ogimaa Do Naakonigewinan
The Laws/Rules Made by the Government

The United States government implemented many policies that were destructive to our way of life.

Government policies included ruthless efforts to remove the Anishin-abek from their lands. Genocide, smallpox, and forced removal were ways to secure the highly valuable and fertile grounds of the Michigan Territory. For the Anishinabek who would not move, the government brought an era of cruel acculturation through the establishment of gov-ernment and missionary schools.[18]

They also do not shy away from speaking about the devastating impact of alcoholism, which they describe as a "weapon of exploitation":

Waawiindimaagewinan Gii Zhichigaadek
When the Promises Were Made

This is how a treaty signing may have looked.
An interpreter, hired by the government, "translated" the negotiations between the two nations. Many gifts were brought to the treaty table as "gestures" of goodwill, including alcohol. Alcohol was a foreign substance to the Anishinabek and we had no context for its use. It was intentionally used as a weapon of exploitation.[19]

In this section of their museum, where the hard truths are spoken in the Effects of Colonization Gallery, the exhibits focus on the tragic period in their history that includes "loss of land, life, and language." The design elements in this section illustrate this sense of intense pressure — it is here that the walls literally begin to narrow, thus giving a sense that the world is closing in on them. This gallery relays a painful story, which is done so effectively by layering information and including voiceovers and images that provide a visual break to the painful stories visitors are reading. The maps, text panels, images of their ancestors, and treaties, all provide an important context on this devastating period of the fifth prophecy, which "foretold that the Anishinabek would encounter separation and struggle for many generations."[20]

The use of audio in this section is very effective. In one area, visitors hear voices of individuals who are reading some of the documents featured on nearby text panels. The words of Ojibwe leaders and government officials such as Lewis Cass and John Hudson are all heard as you walk through this space. Listening to the venomous language of the colonizers is very difficult, and the exhibit strategically makes sure that no one misses hearing these words. It is easy to pass by and not read a text panel, but it is another thing entirely to miss these words as they are repeated over and over again overhead as you move through this space. Listening to the deep-seated hatred of someone that Lewis Cass and others had for the Ojibwe people is an emotional experience, and the exhibit makes it almost impossible to avoid this.

Another important point about the impact of this section is that it touches upon the intergenerational trauma that was experienced during this period and connects the social problems of today to what happened in the past. The community is also not afraid to acknowledge that there are problems they still must confront as a result of the effects of colonization, and I greatly respect their willingness to speak of what we as Indigenous people know but are somewhat reluctant to talk about within a museum context. All too often our concern of coming across as if we are subscribing to the language of victimization, or perhaps the more legitimate concern that this information could potentially reinforce stereotypes, prevents us from speaking the hard truths about our present social problems and connecting those issues to the colonization process. In an effort to "acknowledge our past . . . and begin a healing process for our communities and the communities that surround us," the curators at the Ziibiwing Center bravely state,

Gichi Aakoziwin Miinawaa Nibowin
Great Illness and Death

Government policies resulted in profound health problems for the Anishinabek.
The Anishinabek fell into poverty and despair from our loss of land and livelihood. The settlers brought diseases for which the Anishinabek had no immunity or cure. Many villages were completely wiped out by these new sicknesses. Tuberculosis and mass burials were common. The Anishinabek suffered greatly and we still suffer the effects of this era today. Due to the poverty that we have endured, health problems such as diabetes, tuberculosis, heart disease, and alcoholism still plague us.[21]

During the planning process, audience evaluations were conducted with community members and museum professionals to assess the effectiveness of particular sections, and feedback on the Effects of Colonization Gallery indicated that this "was a very painful and emotional era for people to visit, see, and hear."[22] In light of this information, the curators decided to provide a place where people could collect their thoughts and have a moment of reflection after witnessing these painful truths. In an attempt to provide a healing space so as to "not leave . . . open wounds in the hearts of our people,"[23] the exhibition team developed a gallery entitled Blood Memory. This unique exhibit is very effective, engaging, and profoundly moving.

As you are standing in the latter part of the Effects gallery, audio is used effectively to draw you toward the Blood Memory space, which has a curvilinear, almost womb-like design and the healing smell of cedar.[24] You begin to hear a heartbeat and a beautiful song that three women from the community are singing. The singing helps pull you forward from the difficult space in colonization to this healing space. The following text panel introduces this concept:

Mindjimendamowin
Blood Memory

Blood memory is an inherent connection we have to our spirituality, ancestors, and all of Creation.

Blood memory can be described as the emotions we feel when we hear the drum or our language for the first time. The Creator gives these emotions to us at birth. We use these emotions or blood memories to understand our heritage and our connection to our ancestors. Blood memory makes these connections for us.

Today, many Anishinabek use their blood memory to relearn our language. Our beautiful and descriptive language is deeply rooted in the land and our connections to it. As more and more Anishinabek recall their blood memory, our language and our spirituality will be spoken for the next Seven Generations.[25]

Included in the Blood Memory space is a display with beautiful objects that have been made by tribal individuals, objects that are meant to convey this important "take home message": even through the darkest and most painful period in their modern history the Saginaw Chippewa ancestors managed to create works of great beauty. The display case Creating Beautiful Things in Difficult Times features beautiful beadwork items including bandolier bags, vests, belts, and leggings with labels identifying specific objects.

The idea that these objects embody the strength of their ancestors reflects an important point made by Ruth Phillips: "Historical objects are witnesses, things that were there, then. They bear their makers' marks in their weaves, textures, and shapes, and have a compelling agency to cause people living in the present to enunciate their relationships to the past."[26] The relationship to the past embodied in the Ziibiwing Center objects connects contemporary tribal members to their ancestors and artistic traditions, and it conveys an important message of tribal strength, which is a part of their identity as Saginaw Chippewa.

By presenting examples of their rich artistic tradition in this manner, the museum is providing a unique perspective on early twentieth-century material culture. While I have seen many museums present these types of objects in a manner that challenge age-old art versus ethnographic categories or that demonstrates cultural continuance by placing contemporary objects nearby, this is the first place I have seen an effort to explicitly have these objects illuminate survival during the "crying time." Their presence reminds tribal members of their ancestor's strength and endurance.

The Effects of Colonization Gallery along with the Blood Memory Gallery, in my mind, represent one of the most effective methods that a tribal museum can use to assist community members in the truth telling and healing processes. The Ziibiwing Center did not shy away from telling the difficult stories. But alongside those stories they also provided a healing place where tribal members could gain strength from understanding and reclaiming their rich cultural inheritance and identity.

Museums, as we know, are as much about the present and future as they are about the past. As we look to the future, I believe it is critical that museums support Indigenous communities in our efforts toward decolonization, through privileging Indigenous voice and perspective, through challenging stereotypical representations of Native people that were produced in the past, and by serving as educational forums for our own communities and the general public. Furthermore, the hard truths of our history need to be conveyed, both for the good of our communities and the general public, to a nation that has willfully sought to silence our versions of the past. We need to tell these hard truths of colonization — explicitly and specifically — in our twenty-first-century museums. As Apache historian Myla Vicenti Carpio argues, "It is vital that Indigenous communities freely discuss (and even debate) the history and impacts of colonization to begin healing and move toward the decolonization of Indigenous peoples."[27]

My current research on the Ziibiwing Center of Anishinabe Culture and Lifeways builds upon my previous work on the NMAI and on my concern over the labeling of the NMAI as a "decolonizing museum." While I fully support the NMAI's collaborative methodology of working with tribal communities from throughout the hemisphere, my concern is over the absence of a clear, coherent, and hard-hitting analysis of colonialism and its ongoing effects. And without that context, the museum falls short in moving us forward in our efforts toward decolonization.

As one of the newest tribally owned and operated museums, the Ziibiwing Center exemplifies a decolonizing museum practice through privileging oral tradition and through speaking of the hard truths of colonization to promote healing and understanding for their community. The complex story of this tribal nation is presented powerfully and beautifully and embodies the best new representational strategies; it is heavily informed by important scholarship in the Native American studies field. It is no surprise that visitors have responded very favorably to the museum's exhibitions, as conversations with staff members have indicated. Tribal and non-tribal members have referred to their engagement with the permanent exhibit Diba Jimooyung: Telling Our Story as "a spiritual experience."[28] This museum provides an important forum for Saginaw Chippewa members to gain understanding of their unique history and culture and is designed to empower current and future generations. Founding director Bonnie Ekdahl suggested that the "healing of our own community" is the primary goal for this museum; and by honoring the oral tradition and engaging in truth telling, they are taking important steps forward in that direction.[29]

Notes

Portions of this essay appeared in a shorter exhibition review in the *Journal of American History* 95, no. 1 (2008): 158–62. Copyright © Organization of American Historians. All rights reserved. Excerpted with permission.

1. Amy Lonetree, "Continuing Dialogues: Evolving Views of the National Museum of the American Indian" in *The Public Historian*, Invited Roundtable on the National Museum of the American Indian, 28, no. 2 (2006): 57–61; and Amy Lone-

tree, "Missed Opportunities: Reflections on the National Museum of the American Indian," in "Critical Engagements with the National Museum of the American Indian," ed. Amy Lonetree and Sonya Atalay, special issue, *American Indian Quarterly* 30, nos. 3–4 (2006): 632–45. Revised and expanded form of the essay as Amy Lonetree, "'Acknowledging the Truth of History': Missed Opportunities at the National Museum of the American Indian," in *The National Museum of the American Indian: Critical Conversations*, ed. Amy Lonetree and Amanda J. Cobb (Lincoln: University of Nebraska Press, 2008), 305–27.

2. Claire Smith, "Decolonising the Museum: The National Museum of the American Indian in Washington DC," *Antiquity* 79, no. 304 (2005): 437.

3. Waziyatawin Angela Wilson and Michael Yellow Bird, "Beginning Decolonization," in *For Indigenous Eyes Only: A Decolonization Handbook*, ed. Waziyatawin Angela Wilson and Michael Yellowbird (Santa Fe NM: School of American Research Press, 2005), 2.

4. Pauline Wakeham, "Performing Reconciliation at the NMAI: Postcolonial Rapprochement and the Politics of Historical Closure" in Lonetree and Cobb, *National Museum of the American Indian*, 354.

5. Wakeham, "Performing Reconciliation," 355.

6. Wilson and Yellow Bird, "Beginning Decolonization," 3.

7. Wilson and Yellow Bird, "Beginning Decolonization," 7.

8. Desmond Tutu, quoted in Waziyatawin Angela Wilson and Michael Yellow Bird, "Relieving Our Suffering: "Indigenous Decolonization and a United States Truth Commission," in Wilson and Yellowbird, *For Indigenous Eyes Only*, 204.

9. Taiaiake Alfred, *Wasáse: Indigenous Pathways of Action and Freedom* (Peterborough ON: Broadview Press, 2005), 280.

10. For a recent analysis of the Mashantucket Pequot Museum, see John J. Bodinger de Uriarte, *Casino and Museum: Representing Mashantucket Pequot Identity* (Tucson: University of Arizona Press, 2007). Other important monographs focusing on tribal museum development include Gwyneira Isaac, *Mediating Knowledges: Origins of a Zuni Tribal Museum* (Tucson: University of Arizona Press, 2007); and Patricia Pierce Erikson, *Voices of a Thousand People: The Makah Cultural and Research Center* with Helma Ward and Kirk Wachendorf (Lincoln: University of Nebraska Press, 2002).

11. I do not want to diminish in any way the importance of objects in exhibitions. What I am referring to here is the recent move to allow themes, rather than objects, to drive exhibit content. In newer types of exhibitions, objects are still very important but are used as illustrations of certain themes.

12. Waziyatawin Angela Wilson, *Remember This: Dakota Decolonization and the Eli Taylor Narratives* (Lincoln: University of Nebraska Press, 2005), 50.

13. Jennifer Nez Denetdale, *Reclaiming Dine History: The Legacies of Chief Manuelito and Juanita* (Tucson: University of Arizona Press, 2007), 7.

14. The Fall 2006 issue of *Museum Design* magazine featured an interview with Bianca Message—president of Andre & Associates, the center's exhibit-design firm—describing the uniqueness of the center's approach to present their tribal philosophies. "A Conversation with Bianca Message," *Museum Design*, Fall 2006, 1–16.

15. "Narrative: History of the Diba Jimooyung Permanent Exhibit/Two Voices; The Ziibiwing Cultural Society and the Exhibit Designer," Exhibit Curator Files, Ziibiwing Center for Anishinabe Culture and Lifeways, Mt. Pleasant, Michigan.

16. Erikson, *Voices of a Thousand People*, 30.

17. "Narrative: History of the Diba Jimooyung Permanent Exhibit/Two Voices," p. 2.

18. This quotation was taken from a text panel in the Effects of Colonization exhibit (Area 7) at the Ziibiwing Center for Anishinabe Culture and Lifeways.

19. Effects of Colonization exhibition text panel.

20. Effects of Colonization exhibition text panel.

21. Effects of Colonization exhibition text panel.

22. "Narrative: History of the Diba Jimooyung Permanent Exhibit/Two Voices," p. 7.

23. "Narrative: History of the Diba Jimooyung Permanent Exhibit/Two Voices," p. 7.

24. "A Conversation with Bianca Message," 24.

25. This quotation was taken from a text panel in the Blood Memory exhibit (Area 9) at the Ziibiwing Center for Anishinabe Culture and Lifeways.

26. Ruth B. Phillips, "Re-placing Objects: Historical Practices for the Second Museum Age," *Canadian Historian Review* 86, no. 1 (2005): 108.

27. Myla Vicenti Carpio, "(Un)disturbing Exhibitions: Indigenous Historical Memory at the NMAI," in "Critical Engagements with the National Museum of the American Indian," ed. Amy Lonetree and Sonya Atalay, special issue, *American Indian Quarterly* 30, nos. 3–4 (2006): 631.

28. "Narrative: History of the Diba Jimooyung Permanent Exhibit/Two Voices," p. 3.

29. Founding director Bonnie Ekdahl as quoted in, "A Conversation with Bianca Message," 16. Ekdahl also shared this view during a panel presentation at Embracing a Community: A 21st Century Tribal Museum Model Symposium, at the Ziibiwing Center of Anishinabe Culture and Lifeways, Mt. Pleasant, Michigan, May 2006.

Contributors

Kristina Ackley (Oneida Bad River Ojibwe) is a member of the faculty in Native American Studies at Evergreen State College. She received her MA in American Indian Studies from the University of Arizona and her PhD in American Studies from the State University of New York at Buffalo. She is currently working on a comparative analysis of Oneida nationalism and expressions of sovereignty.

Miranda J. Brady's research addresses issues of representation, identity, and power in the use of public media. She examines how technologies of mediation and cultural policies are employed by institutions to shape the terms of American Indian involvement in public and political life. In 2007 Brady was awarded a short-term fellowship from the Newberry Library's D'Arcy McNickle Center for American Indian History. Her recent work is concerned with the use of digital media in public spaces, discourse, and political economy. Brady's dissertation examined the intersection of cultural policy, power, nationalism, and digital technology in the National Museum of the American Indian. She is an assistant professor of Journalism and Communication at Carleton University, Ottawa, Canada.

M. Teresa Carlson is originally from Vancouver Island on British Columbia's west coast. She has a BA and postgraduate diplomas in cultural resource management from the University of Victoria. She has worked in museums and cultural centers for almost twenty years. She found the years she spent at Stó:lō Nation creating a cultural center and archaeological repository to be the most rewarding, as she was able to engage in collaborative research, including various topics in Aboriginal self-governance, culture and heritage, rights and title, education, and exhibits and programming. In 2001 she moved to Saskatoon with her husband, Keith, and their two children. She is currently the acting director of the Diefenbaker Canada Centre at the University of Saskatchewan, the only Prime Ministerial museum, archives, and research center in Canada. The Diefenbaker Centre hosts a wide variety of exhibits and associated educational programming.

Brenda J. Child (Red Lake Ojibwe) is an associate professor of American studies at the University of Minnesota, Twin Cities. Her book *Boarding School Seasons: Ameri-*

can Indian Families, 1900–1940 won the North American Indian Prose Award. She is a member of the executive council of the Minnesota Historical Society and the Indian advisory committee to the Eiteljorg Museum.

Brian Isaac Daniels is a doctoral student in history and anthropology at the University of Pennsylvania. His research focuses upon how cultural heritage laws and cultural institutions engender historical awareness. Daniels has an extended ethnographic commitment to western North America, where he has worked with Native communities on issues surrounding heritage rights, repatriation, and recognition. As a joint-degree student he is currently at work writing two dissertations: one about the political uses of heritage laws by Indigenous communities and the other about museums, preservation laws, and the production of history in the United States. His research has been underwritten by fellowships from the Woodrow Wilson Foundation, the Wenner-Gren Foundation, and the Smithsonian Institution.

Gwyneira Isaac obtained her PhD from Oxford University in 2002; she is an assistant professor and director of the Museum of Anthropology at the School of Human Evolution and Social Change at Arizona State University. Her research focuses on the relationships people develop with their past through material culture, leading her to explore the history of anthropology and photography as well as the development of tribal museums in the Southwest. Bridging these different topics has resulted in her interest in developing theories that integrate anthropology, art, and history to form interdisciplinary and cross-cultural approaches to the study of society. She has conducted fieldwork at the A:shiwi A:wan Museum and Heritage Center in Zuni, New Mexico, and at the Smithsonian Institution in Washington DC. Her book, *Mediating Knowledges: Origins of a Zuni Tribal Museum*, has recently been published by the University of Arizona Press.

Hal Langfur teaches the history of Brazil, colonial Latin America, and the Atlantic world as well as ethnohistory at the State University of New York at Buffalo. He is the author of *The Forbidden Lands: Colonial Identity, Frontier Violence, and the Persistence of Brazil's Eastern Indians, 1750–1830* and editor of the forthcoming *Native Brazil: Beyond the Cannibal and the Convert, 1500–1889*. His articles have appeared in various U.S. and Brazilian academic journals, including the *Journal of Social History*, the *Hispanic American Historical Review*, the *Americas*, *Ethnohistory*, *Revista da História*, and *Tempo*. He is currently working on a book-length study entitled "Adrift on an Inland Sea: The Projection of Colonial Power in the Brazilian Wilderness."

Paul Liffman is a research professor in the Center for Anthropological Studies at the Colegio de Michoacán; he previously worked as a consultant and translator for the Wixarika (Huichol) exhibit at the National Museum of the American Indian. His dissertation, "Huichol Territoriality: Land and Cultural Claims in Western Mexico," is based on six years of fieldwork with Huichols, primarily in San Andrés Cohamiata, as well as with AJAGI, the nongovernmental organization that most strongly backed Huichol demands for land restitution. This fieldwork was supported by Fulbright and Wenner-Gren Foundation grants and by CIESAS–Occidente. The thesis deals with the relationship between ceremonial place-making and with the construction of territory and its representation in legal and cultural claims in the courts, political venues, Indigenous schools, and the press.

Amy Lonetree is an enrolled citizen of the Ho-Chunk Nation of Wisconsin. In 2002 she earned a PhD in ethnic studies from the University of California, Berkeley, where she specialized in Native American history and museum studies. Her scholarly work focuses on the representation of Indigenous people in both national and tribal museums; she has conducted research on this topic at the Smithsonian Institution's National Museum of the American Indian, the Minnesota Historical Society, the Mille Lacs Indian Museum, the Ziibiwing Center of Anishinabe Culture and Lifeways, and the British Museum. She has published articles based on this research in *American Indian Quarterly* and *Public Historian* and has recently edited a collection, with Amanda J. Cobb, on the Smithsonian Institution's National Museum of the American Indian (University of Nebraska Press, 2008). She is currently assistant professor of American Studies at the University of California, Santa Cruz.

Brenda Macdougall is an assistant professor in the Department of Native Studies at the University of Saskatchewan. Having recently completed her dissertation and PhD at the University of Saskatchewan, Macdougall has begun work on several research projects, including developing a digital archive capturing sources related to Western Canadian First Nations and Metis history in the twentieth century, examining the history of the Round Prairie Metis, and collaborating with researchers from the universities of Alberta and Saskatchewan as well as from the Northwest Saskatchewan Metis Council to produce an atlas of the Metis experience in northwestern Saskatchewan. She is currently teaching in the Department of Native Studies at the University of Saskatchewan.

Zine Magubane is an associate professor of sociology and African diaspora studies at Boston College. She is the author of *Bringing the Empire Home: Race, Class, and Gender in Britain and Colonial South Africa*; editor of *Postmodernism, Postcoloniality, and African Studies*; and coeditor of *Hear Our Voices: Black South African Women in the Academy*. Magubane has published in *Gender and Society*, *Cultural Studies*, and *Africa Today*. She is currently working on a book called *Brand the Beloved Country: Africa in Celebrity Culture*, which looks at the role of celebrity philanthropy in Africa.

Ann McMullen holds a PhD in anthropology from Brown University and, since 2000, has been a curator at the Smithsonian Institution's National Museum of the American Indian. Beyond work on the NMAI's 2004 inaugural exhibitions, her research and publications have focused on Native people of northeastern North America, especially material cultures, traditions, innovation, and commercialization; the intersection of ethnography and ethnohistory; Native historiography and invented traditions; and the nature and transformation of Native communities and community networks.

Jacki Thompson Rand is an associate professor of history at the University of Iowa. She received a PhD from the Department of History at the University of Oklahoma in 1998. Her book, *Kiowa Humanity and the Invasion of the State*, is a study of Kiowa relations with the state during the last quarter of the nineteenth century; the book centers on the lives of ordinary Kiowa women and young men during the establishment of the Kiowa, Comanche, and Apache reservation in 1867 through the post-allotment period to 1910. Through the tracking of material objects associated with Kiowa women and young men she has created a study of reservation and postreservation society and economy, of actions taken by the state at the federal and agency level that shaped the context of Kiowa lives, and of the persistence of Kiowa humanity shaped by tribalism in the face of inhumane treatment and conditions. Rand has recently completed a fellowship at the Newberry Library, where she embarked on her next project, an examination of twentieth-century Indian-State relations in a transnationalist framework.

Ciraj Rassool is an associate professor of history and chairperson of the History Department at the University of the Western Cape in South Africa, where he also directs the African Program in Museum and Heritage Studies. He has written widely on public history, visual history, and resistance historiography. Rassool is a trustee of the District Six Museum and the South African History Archive. He is also a councilor of Iziko Museums of Cape Town and the National Heritage Council. He is coauthor of *Skeletons in the Cupboard: South African Museums and the Trade in Human Remains 1907–1917*; and coeditor of *Recalling Community in Cape Town: Creating and Curating the District Six Museum* and *Museum Frictions: Public Cultures/Global Transformations*.

Jennifer Shannon is currently a postdoctoral teaching fellow in the Department of Anthropology at The University of British Columbia. Her research interests include Indigenous rights and representation, focusing more recently on Indigenous self-representation, collaborative practice, and the anthropology of museums. Prior to her work at Cornell, from 1999 to 2002 she worked as a researcher in the curatorial department at the Smithsonian Institution's National Museum of the American Indian, contributing to two ongoing galleries: Our Peoples: Giving Voice to Our Histories and Our Lives: Contemporary Life and Identities. Based on two years of fieldwork from 2004 to 2006 at the National Museum of the American Indian and in Native communities featured in its exhibitions, Shannon's dissertation documents the collaborative relationships and exhibit-making processes involved in the making of the Our Lives gallery about contemporary Native life.

Ray Silverman is a professor of history of art and Afroamerican and African Studies and serves as director of the Museum Studies Program at the University of Michigan. From 1988 to 2002 he was a member of the Michigan State University faculty. In addition to teaching courses dealing with the visual cultures of Africa, he has curated a number of exhibitions dealing with African visual culture at the MSU Museum and Kresge Art Museum and at the UCLA Fowler Museum. Silverman's research and writing has examined the interaction between West Africa and the cultures of the Middle East and Europe, the history of metal technologies in Ethiopia and Ghana, the social values associated with creativity in Ethiopia, the visual culture of religion in twentieth-century Ethiopia, and the commodification of art in Ethiopia and Ghana. Most recently he has been exploring museum culture in Africa, specifically how local knowledge is translated in national and community-based cultural institutions.

Susan Sleeper-Smith is the author of *Indian Women: Rethinking Cultural Encounter in the Western Great Lakes* and coeditor of the collection *New Faces of the Fur Trade*. She has published in *Ethnohistory, AHR, JAH, Reviews in American History*, the *William & Mary Quarterly*, and *Recherches amérindiennes*. Her work focuses on metissage as a site of inquiry, an exploration that opens new pathways for examining encounter as well as the construction of national histories. She is a member of the Indian Studies faculty at Michigan State University and serves as the director of the CIC–American Indian Studies Consortium. A Mortar Board recipient for outstanding teaching, she counts her students and her teaching as her most important credentials.

Index

archaeology, 76, 77, 117, 169, 275, 296, 311
archives, 18, 28. *See also* tribal archives
Aristotle, 309
Army Medical Museum. *See* U.S. Army
    Medical Museum (AMM)
artifacts, 1–2, 84–85, 169–70, 265, 299,
    336n11; All Roads Are Good exhibit,
    224–25, 226; AMM and, 138; authen-
    ticity, 243n14; captured weapons as,
    88; climate control and, 145; cocura-
    tors and, 223; collectors' attachment
    to, 67–68; Creation's Journey exhibit,
    225; Hupa, 254, 289–90; Huichol,
    211; labeling, 98n56, 144; lack of
    documentation, 104n84; NMAI
    and, 11–12, 92n28, 244n30; Metis,
    173; Ojibwe, 333–34; Oneida, 259,
    266; personal talismans, 166–67; as
    primary texts, 69, 78, 89n16, 103n78,
    144; repatriation of, 83, 93n34, 136,
    288, 313, 317; representative of a class,
    297; reproduction of, 310; "rubbish
    theory" and, 105n89; "salvage" and,
    11; situated in cultural context, 224;
    as "speaking subjects," 221; theft,
    94n40; Zuni, 313, 314, 317. *See also*
    dance regalia; funerary and sacred
    objects; preservation; replicas
art museums, 69, 89n14, 280n17
art, Native. *See* Native art
A:shiwi A:wan Museum and Heritage
    Center, 253–54, 303–4, 313–14
Asociación Jalisciense de Apoyo a los
    Grupos Indígenas, 216n24
assimilation, 262, 267, 273, 277
Atlanta Braves, 147
audience. *See* museum audience
audio in museums, 331, 333
Australia, 247n68
authenticity, 242n11, 243n14, 244n33,
    269, 273, 284; community museums

and, 120; dioramas and, 108; ethnographic showcases and, 50; Kwakwa
ka'wakw and, 281n42; NMAI and, 218,
219, 221, 224, 227, 228, 231, 239; South
Africa, 60, 108, 112; tribal museums
and, 265; West Side Stories, and, 177
Autshumato, 113
Aztecs, 197

Baartman, Saartjie, 53–54, 57, 58
BAE. *See* Bureau of American Ethnology
    (BAE)
Bancos de San Hipólito, Durango, 207
baptism, 187n11
BAR. *See* Bureau of Acknowledgement
    and Recognition
Bartolomé, Miguel, 204
Batoche National Historic Site, 168, 176
Battle of Seven Oaks, 159, 185n4, 185n6
Batwa, 58
Baudrillard, Jean, 67
Baumann, Richard, 200
beadwork, *174*, *182*, 333; in art, *175*, *177*,
    183
Beauval, Saskatchewan, 182
Belcourt, Christi, 175, 177
Benga, Ota, 58, 62
Bennett, Tony, 82
berdaches, 312
Berkhofer, Robert, 263
Bernstein, Bruce, 90n18, 238
Bird, Junius, 90n23
Bird, S. Elizabeth, 146
Black Body (Mohanram), 61
blended languages. *See* languages,
    blended
Bleek, Wilhelm, 112
blood, 199, 202, 204
"blood memory," 333
Blood Red Gringo. *See* Red Gringo
Blue Mestizo, 198

Chipewyan people. *See* Dene people

Chippewa people. *See* Ojibwe people

choirs, South African, 60, 114

CHRIS. *See* California Historical Resources Information System (CHRIS)

Chrisjohn, Irvin, 266

Christianity, 15, 325; Indianized, 200; Oneidas and, 262

Christian missionaries, 50–51, 52, 59, 161, 187n10

Circa 1925 at the Museum of the American Indian (exhibit), 224

Civilian Conservation Corps (CCC), 251

claims, 193. *See also* land claims; sovereignty claims

class. *See* social class

Clifford, James, 67, 194, 207

climate control, 145

Cobb, Amanda J., 81, 322

cocurators. *See* community curators and curating

coevalness, denial of, 56–57, 104n85

coins, 201, 202

collaboration, 146, 156, 167, 218, 240, 252, 253

collection exchanges. *See* museum collection exchanges

collectors, 65–68, 70–80, 94nn40–41, 98n57; as "stewards," 221

colonialism, 12–13, 264; collecting and, 67, 68; Metis and, 185m5; museums and, 69, 81, 166, 167, 323, 326; Oneidas and, 262, 274; South Africa, 107, 108, 113, 114, 116; tribal museums and, 251, 255

colonization, 3, 4, 81, 83, 335; "colonized Indians," 34; ethnography and, 9, 28; NMAI and, 141; Portuguese, 15, 18; Ziibiwing Center and, 329–30, 332. *See also* decolonization

Columbus, Christopher, 1

communications technology in museums, 140–42, 143–44, 229

community centers, 255, 276, 327–35

community curators and curating, 206, 216n24, 218–19, 222–23, 228, 229, 232–37, 239, 246n61, 247n68; dioramas and, 145–46

community museums, 119–22, 210

Community University Research Alliance (CURA), 156, 158, 164, 165

compromise, 147, 239

computer use, Zunis and, 315, 316

Congress 2007, 171

Conn, Steven, 76

constituencies, museum. *See* museum constituencies

Constitution Act, 1982 (Canada), 162

constitutional amendments, Mexico, 207–8

consultants, 288, 317; anthropological, 197, 216n24; museum, 145, 167, 200, 245n49

content control of exhibitions, Native. *See* Native content control of exhibitions

copying. *See* duplication

corporate partnerships, 147

Cosmorama (London), 55, 56

Costner, Kevin, 146

Council of Traditional Leaders, 115

court cases, 285–88

Court of King's Bench, 54

crania. *See* skulls

craniology, 143

craniometrists, 48

Cree, 161, 162, 163, 186n9. *See also* Bungi; Michif

crisis, 241n10

Cuba, 100n65

cultural interpreters, 140

cultural preservation, right to, 284

"governmentality" (word), 301n3
Grant, Cuthbert, 159, 185n6
graphic design, 177, 180
grave robbing, 117, 118
"gray literature," 296
Great Britain, ethnographic showcases
    in, 45–52, 54–61, 62
Great Lakes Research Alliance for the
    Study of Aboriginal Arts and Cul-
    tures, 104n82
Green, Jesse, 310
Green Lake, Saskatchewan, 161
Grey Nuns, 181, 187n10
Griqua, 114, 115

Haakanson, Sven, 227
Haak'u Museum, 252–53
Hadebe, Fidel, 111
Hales, Henry, 95n44
Half-Breed Claims Commission, 171,
    190n23
"half-breed" (term), 184n3
Hamilton, Carolyn, 109
Harjo, Suzan Shown, 80, 99n60, 152n24
Harper, Stephen, 181
Haudenosaunee people, 255, 257–64,
    267–73, 276, 277, 278. See also
    Oneidas
HBC. See Hudson's Bay Company (HBC)
headdresses, 289
Hearst, William Randolph, 74
The Heye and the Mighty (Force), 72
Heye, Carl, 70
Heye, George Gustav, 11, 65–67, 70–80,
    81, 85–86, 94n40, 139; hiring of non-
    academics, 96n47; "Native" identity
    of collection, 146; New York City
    and, 97n48; potsherds and, 105n88
Hihndorf, Shari, 84
Hilden, Patricia Penn, 84
Hill, Rick, 145
historic sites, 291–92; Canada, 168

historiography, 142, 324–25, 328–29
Hobsbawm, Eric, 66
Hollywood films, 146–47, 153n34
"Homeland Tours" (Oneida), 268
hooks, bell, 61
Hoopa people. See Hupa people
Hoopa Tribal Museum, 254, 288–90,
    296, 299
Hoopa Valley Reservation, 285
Hoopa Valley Tribe, 285, 286, 288–90,
    299
Hoopa-Yurok Settlement Act, 286, 288,
    300
Hopi politics, 306
Horniman, Frederick John, 75, 95n43
"Hottentot Venus." See Baartman,
    Saartjie
Howe, Greg, 235
Hudson, John, 331
Hudson's Bay Company (HBC), 159, 160,
    161, 185n6, 191n27
Huichol people, 129–30, 192–217
human exhibitions. See ethnographic
    showcases
human remains, 147, 166, 167; AMM
    and, 138, 139, 151n19; repatriation, 13,
    100n65, 106, 118, 119, 134; South Af-
    rica, 117–18, 119, 126n40; and, 152n24.
    See also American Indian remains;
    skeletons; skulls
hunting, 163, 164, 192, 194, 195, 208, 209;
    Ojibwe, 256; sacrificial, 211
humans' smell. See smell of humans
Huntington, Archer, 75, 76, 97n48
Hupa people, 285, 286, 296

identity, 116, 259, 268–69, 273, 286;
    federal recognition and, 294; Hupa,
    286, 296; Yurok, 286
Igloolik, Nunavut, 222, 226, 228, 230,
    237–38

sonian, 65, 72, 79, 86, 133; mission statement, 149n4; NMAI exhibit on, 224; repatriation and, 93n34; stated purpose, 98n52

Museum of the Cherokee, 251

museums, community. See community museums

museums' entertainment function. See entertainment function of museums

museums, digital. See digital museums

museums of art. See art museums

museums, public. See public museums

Museums, the Public, and Anthropology (Ames), 221

museums, tribal. See tribal museums

museums' vernacular approaches. See vernacular approaches of museums

"museum" (word), 309

Museu Nacional (Brazil), 35

NAFTA. See North American Free Trade Agreement

NAGPRA. See Native American Graves Protection and Repatriation Act

Nakawe, 211

Nama, 114, 115

Nanook of the North, 143

narratives. See stories

Natal, 55

National Air and Space Museum, 231

National Anthropological Archives, 304, 314

National Council of Indigenous People (proposed), 115

National Forest Service. See U.S. Forest Service

National Griqua Forum, 115

National Historic Preservation Act, 291, 302n12

nationalism, 78–80, 84, 134, 148, 205, 264, 297–98, 300; AMM and, 138; Haudenosaunee, 258, 264, 267–68,

276; Indigenous, 200; Mohawk, 268; Oneida, 262; South Africa, 114; United States, 267, 283–84; Yurok, 291

National Khoisan Heritage Route, 114, 115

National Khoisan Legacy Project, 106, 107, 113, 119

National Museum (Brazil). See Museu Nacional (Brazil)

National Museum of African American History and Culture, 81, 147

National Museum of African Art, 92n29

National Museum of Anthropology (Mexico). See Museo Nacional de Antropología

National Museum of Natural History (NMNH), 98n56, 133, 139, 149n1; Inuit exhibit, 227, 228

National Museum of the American Indian (NMAI), 3, 11–12, 65–105, 129–31, 133–55, 218–47, 255, 322–37; American Indian employees, 255; architecture, 140, 144–45, 230–31, 231, 245n49; audience, 136–37, 143; birth, 78; climate control, 144–45; collection provenance, 70–71; communications technology, 140–41; constituency, 137, 143, 234; corporate partnerships, 147, 148; Cultural Resources Center, 72–73, 143, 213, 228; Curatorial Department, 234–37; Exhibition Master Plan, 226; "Fourth Museum," 143; funding, 146–47m, 154n64, 210; George Gustav Heye Center, 72, 78–79, 147; grand opening, 232, 324; Huichols and, 196, 200, 205–6, 210, 211, 212, 213, 216n24; image protection of, 93nn33–34; Listening to Our Ancestors, 232, 238–39; Mall Museum, 73, 130–31, 136–37, 140, 143, 147, 154n64, 218, 230–31, 232,

nudity, 45
nuns, 181, 187n10

object and subject. *See* subject and object
objects. *See* artifacts
Oblates. *See* Order of Mary Immaculate
O'Connor, Sandra Day, 287
oil lamps, 224
Ojibwe language, 333
Ojibwe people, 47, 59, 255; Lewis Cass and, 331; Mille Lacs, Minnesota, 251, 256; Michigan, 327–35
Oneida Carrying Place, 260
Oneida Cultural Festival, 274
Oneida Cultural Heritage Department, 272
Oneida language, 262, 276
Oneida Nation Museum, 254–55, 257–82
Oneidas, New York, 259, 260, 261, 263, 266; Ontario, 261; Wisconsin, 257–64, 266–82
online museums. *See* digital museums
Onondaga NY, 261
oral tradition, 303, 314, 315–16, 328, 329
Order of Mary Immaculate, 161, 187n10
organization of knowledge. *See* knowledge organization
origin stories, 197, 200–203
Orion Pictures, 146
Osage Tribal Museum, 251
other, 45, 52, 61, 167, 263; collectors as, 68
"Otipimsuak" project, 156, 158, 184n2
Otis, George, 138
Our Democracy and the American Indian (Kellogg), 264
Our Lives. *See* National Museum of the American Indian, Our Lives gallery
Our Peoples. *See* National Museum of

the American Indian, Our Peoples gallery
Our Universes. *See* National Museum of the American Indian, Our Universes gallery
Oxendine, Linda E., 271
Ozette archaeological site, 275

paintings, *175, 177,* 272, 316
Peabody Museum of Archaeology and Ethnology, 76, 289
Pearce, Susan, 67, 68
pedagogy, Zuni, 307, 314, 317
Pedro Páramo (Rulfo), 205
Pemmican Wars, 185n4
Penn Museum. *See* University of Pennsylvania Museum
Pepper, George, 70, 77, 89n16, 95n44, 97n51
Pequots, 266
Peringuey, Louis, 117
Perot, H. Ross, 79
pest control, 144–45
Peterson, Jacqueline, 184n4
peyote, 194, 199, 200, 203, 204
Philadelphia Centennial Exhibition (1876), 138, 151n22
Philippines, 88n11
Phillips, Ruth, 85, 218, 334
photographers, 108, 198; Native, 103n80
photographs, 108, 190n25, 270, 314–15
photography, 309; Zunis and, 253, 304, 311–12, 314–15, 318
phrenology, 47
Pierce, Charles Sanders, 206
pilgrimages. *See* treks, ceremonial
Pitt Rivers, Augustus Henry Lane Fox, 75, 95n43
Pitt Rivers Museum, 98n56
poaching, 163
Podruchny, Carolyn, 187

Poolaw, Linda, 81
Portugal, war on Botocudo, 15, 17, 21–27, 30, 31–33, 35, 36
Portuguese, 29, 31, 37
postmodernism, 227, 239, 322, 328
potsherds, 105n88
Powell, John Wesley, 151n21, 310–11
PowerPoint, 173
power (social relations), 61, 167; Zunis and, 306, 308
powwows, 223, 274, 277
Prates, Manoel Rodrigues, 19, 20
Pratt, Mary Louise, 194
preservation, 276, 284, 291–93; museum collections and, 144, 145, 265, 289, 309. *See also* cultural preservation
priests, 161, 187n10; Zuni, 306, 307–8, 317
"primitive" (word), 9, 10, 167
Primrose–Cold Lake Air Weapons Range, 163
Prince João. *See* João VI
problematization, 133–55
processions. *See* treks
progress, 2
prophecies, 328–29
provinces, Canada. *See* Canada, provinces
pseudoscience, 48–49
public museums, 2, 83, 97n51
Pueblos, 306, 307. *See also* Acoma Pueblo; Zuni Pueblo
Punch, 55–56
Puri, 17, 28, 29, 30

quinquilharias. See trinkets

Raath, Mike, 118
racialism, 48, 121
racism, 49, 61, 295. *See also* apartheid
Rand, Jackie Thompson, 82
Rau, Reinhold, 110

reality, 53
reburial of human remains, 118, 119
Red Gringo, 197–98
Reflections of a Cultural Broker (Kurin), 221
religion, 325; Zuni, 314, 319. *See also* Christianity
religious freedom, 287–88
reparations, 163–64, 188n15, 323
repatriation, 137, 167; of artifacts, 83, 93n34, 99n60, 136; of dance regalia, 289; of human remains, 13, 99n60, 100n65, 106, 118, 119; legislation, 189n18. *See also* National Museum of the American Indian Act
replicas, 154n51, 177, *178*, *179*, 243n14, 245n46; Frank Cushing and, 310–11; history of, 309–10; longhouses, 257, *258*, 259, 274, 275, 278; Zunis and, 317, 318
reproduction of knowledge. *See* knowledge reproduction
resistance, 18, 19, 25, 61–62, 83; Khoisan, 113; silence as a form of, 58–59, 62
responsibility, Zuni and, 307, 308, 313–17, 318, 319
restitution, 101n72, 208
rhetoric, 2, 32, 66, 79, 232; "crisis rhetoric," 241n10
Riel, Louis, 159, 180, 181, 185n6, 191n26
Riles, Annelise, 229
Riviére, George, 314
roads, 286–88, 293
Robinson, Edna, 191n26
Roman Catholic Church. *See* Catholic Church
Roosevelt, Anna, 72
Rosen, Herbert R., 142
Royal Museum (Brazil). *See* Museu Nacional (Brazil)
"rubbish theory," 105n89

Rulfo, Juan, 205
runaway slaves, 19, 29
Rupertsland, 188n12

sacred objects. *See* funerary and sacred objects
sacred places, 194–95, 203
sacrificial hunting, 211
sacrificial offerings, 194, 195, 199
Saginaw Chippewa Indian Tribe, 327–35
Sainte-Hilaire, August de, 28–29, 30, 35
St. George's Gallery, Knightsbridge, 46, 47, 58
St. Laurent Metis, 238
St. Lawrence River, 187
St. Louis World's Fair (1904), 58
Salinas de Gortari, Carlos, 207
salvage anthropology, 11, 69, 280n20
salvage ethnography, 76
SAM. *See* South African Museum (SAM)
SAMA. *See* South African Museums Association (SAMA)
San, 46, 48–49, 50, 52, 54, 57, 110, 111, 112, 115
San Andrés Cohamiata, 196, 199, 200, 203, 212, 216n24
San Cultural Heritage Committee, 111
Santiago, 200, 201–2, 203, 205
Saskatchewan, 156–91; First Nations population, 188n13
Saskatchewan Native Theatre Company, 177
Saville, Marshall, 70, 75, 95n44, 96n47
schools, 60. *See also* boarding schools
scrip, 162, 164, 172, 182, 190n23
script editors and editing, 235, 236
secrecy, 306–7
Seneca-Iroquois National Museum, 252
serpents, on currency, 197; on flag, 214n6
Shakaland Zulu Cultural Village, 109

Shako:wi Cultural Center, 266, 276
shamans, Huichol, 192, 193, 194, 197, 198, 212
Shasta Nation, 254, 293, 295–96, 299
Shaw, Margaret, 112
Shelton, Anthony, 67
shrines, Franciscan, 201; Marian, 165, 172, 177, *178*
Shxwt'a:selhawtxw, 169, 170, 189n20
Sierra Madre, 192, 196
silence, as a form of resistance, 58–59, 62
silver mines, 200
Silverstein, Michael, 228, 231–32
Simpson, Audra, 268
Singer, Beverly, 141
singers, South African, 60
Six Nations. *See* Haudenosaunee people
"Six Nations" (name), 267–68
skeletons, collecting of, 117, 118–19, 126n40
Skeletons in the Cupboard (Legassick and Rassool), 118, 119
skulls, 138. *See also* craniology; craniometrists
Skotnes, Pippa, 112
Sky City Cultural Center, 252–53
slavery, 26, 37, 54. *See also* runaway slaves
Small, Lawrence, 73, 139, 155n67
smell of humans, 28
Smith, Claire, 323
Smith, James, 72
Smith, Paul Chaat, 80, 101n72, 142, 149n3
Smithsonian Institution, 76, 81, 92n29; mission, 224; NMAI and, 12, 65, 73, 79, 99n63, 136; Philadelphia Centennial Exhibition (1876) and, 151n22; Public Affairs office memos, 151n19; publications, 221; scientific legitimacy and, 151n21. *See also* National

Smithsonian Institution (*continued*)
Anthropological Archives; National
Museum of the American Indian
(NMAI)
Smokis, 319
snakes. *See* serpents
social class, 51. *See also* middle classes,
upper classes
social power. *See* power (social relations)
Social Sciences and Humanities Research Council (SSHRC), 156, 158
social status. *See* status
Soto Soria, Alfonso, 211
sound in museums. *See* audio in museums
South Africa, 13, 46–47, 49, 51–52, 55, 59,
60, 106–26
South African Cultural History Museum, 112
South African Museum (SAM), 106,
112–13, 116–17, 119
South African Museums Association
(SAMA), 106, 118
Southeast Alaska Indian Cultural Center, 251–52
souvenirs, military. *See* military souvenirs
sovereignty, 253, 284; Haudenosaunee,
263, 264; Huichol, 195, 208–9, 211;
Ojibwe, 256; Shasta, 295. *See also* cultural sovereignty; state sovereignty
sovereignty claims, 195
Spain, 197, 199, 200, 203
Spanish-American War, 88n11
Stanley, George, 185n5
state, 292, 297, 298; Huichols and, 204–5;
museums and, 264. *See also* "unrecognized" tribes
state sovereignty, 298
status, 306
stereotypes, 1, 2, 11, 108, 153n34, 219, 326,

332; in film, 146; Inuit, 227; masculinity and, 181
Stevenson, Matilda Coxe, 304, 311–12
sticks, 85
Stocking, George, 67
Stó:lō, 168–69, 170, 173, 189n19
stories, 207, 326; authentic, 265; Huichol, 206, 208; Metis, 158, 164, 170,
171, 172, 182–83; nationalism and,
267; NMAI exhibits and, 226; tribal
museums and, 252, 275, 277; Zuni,
308, 316. *See also* origin stories
Strother, Z. S., 52
subject and object, 51, 52–53, 61, 219,
224, 231
sugar plantations, 15
suicide, 62
sun, 199–200, 201, 202
Supreme Court cases, 256, 287–88
surveillance. *See* looking
"survivance" (word), 150n9

Taíno people, 100n65
Tanana, 199–200, 202
tape recorders, 308, 316
Tayau, 199–200, 205
technology and knowledge transmission, 303
television, 146, 149n3
temples, Mexico, 209
temporal distancing, 69
Teters, Charlene, 147
text in museum exhibits, 212, 217n35,
222, 232–33, 236, 239; community
curating and, 218, 223; ethnographic,
219, 224; Native-authored, 226;
transcripts and, 225, 229; West Side
Stories, 158, 173, 176–77, 183, 190n22
Thackeray, Francis, 118
Thames Oneidas, 261, 268

theatrical display of humans. *See* ethnographic showcases
theft, 94n40, 167
Thompson, Michael, 105n89
timber sales, 285
Tlingit, 252
tour guides, Native. *See* Native tour guides
tourism, 107, 109, 112, 115, 123, 207, 217n33. *See also* cultural tourism; "Homeland Tours" (Oneida)
traditional land-use interviews, 164
tradition, Native people and, 82, 83
transcripts of interviews. *See* interview transcripts
transmission of knowledge. *See* knowledge transmission
travel, 261, 268, 269. *See also* tourism; treks
travel accounts, 35, 52, 69; bibliography, 42n41
treaties, 162, 163, 182; court cases, 256
treks, ceremonial, 197, 198, 199, 200, 203, 208
tribal archives, 292–93, 295–96, 299
Tribal Historic Preservation Officers, 291; Yurok, 292
tribal museums, 3–4, 137, 168, 169, 170, 251–52; Alaska, 251–52; California, 252, 288–89; Michigan, 255, 327–35; Minnesota, 251, 329; New Mexico, 252–54, 303–4, 313–14; Oklahoma, 251; Washington, 252, 275–76; Wisconsin, 254–55, 257–82
Tricameral Constitution (South Africa), 124n12
tricksters, 198
trinkets, 21, 22, 24
truth commissions, 325, 326
tukite, 209
Turner, Ted, 147

Turtle Museum (Niagara Falls, New York), 266
Tutu, Desmond, 326
Tylor, Edward Burnett, 311

ugliness, 50
United Kingdom. *See* Great Britain
United Nations, 115
University of Pennsylvania Museum, 70, 76, 96n45
University of Saskatchewan, 166, 168
"unrecognized" tribes, 293–96
upper classes, 51
Urban, Greg, 228, 231–32
Urban, Hugh, 307
urban Indians, Chicago, 238
U.S. Army Medical Museum (AMM), 133, 137–39, 148, 151n19
U.S. Customs House, New York City, 72, 79, 147
U.S. Department of the Interior, Indian Affairs. *See* Bureau of Indian Affairs
U.S. Forest Service, 286–87
U.S. Supreme Court cases. *See* Supreme Court cases

Vallo, Brian, 252–53
Vanishing Cultures in South Africa (Magubane), 108, 123n8
Vasconcelos, Diogo Ribeiro, 23–24
"vernacular" (word), 305
vernacular approaches in museums, 305–6
videos in museums, 142, 218, 229, 230, 266, 315
villages, Brazil, 18, 20, 24, 33–34, 42n38. *See also* cultural villages
Virgin Mary, 165, 172, 177, *178*
virtual kiosks. *See* digital kiosks
virtual museums. *See* digital museums
Volkert, Jim, 225

Breinigsville, PA USA
02 September 2010
244719BV00003B/1/P